Folke Gernert
Divination on stage

Folke Gernert

Divination on stage

Prophetic body signs in early modern theatre in Spain and Europe

DE GRUYTER

Publication funded by the German Research Foundation (DFG)

Funded by
DFG Deutsche
Forschungsgemeinschaft
German Research Foundation

ISBN 978-3-11-069574-8
e-ISBN (PDF) 978-3-11-069575-5
e-ISBN (EPUB) 978-3-11-073480-5
DOI https://doi.org/10.1515/9783110695755

This work is licensed under the Creative Commons Attribution-NonCommercial-NoDerivatives 4.0 International License. For details go to http://creativecommons.org/licenses/by-nc-nd/4.0/.

Library of Congress Control Number: 2020950024

Bibliographic information published by the Deutsche Nationalbibliothek
The Deutsche Nationalbibliothek lists this publication in the Deutsche Nationalbibliografie; detailed bibliographic data are available on the Internet at http://dnb.dnb.de.

© 2021 Folke Gernert, published by Walter de Gruyter GmbH, Berlin/Boston
The book is published open access at www.degruyter.com.

Cover image: Georges de La Tour (ca. 1630), "The Fortune Teller", Metropolitan Museum of Art. Wikimedia Commons: File:Georges de La Tour 016.jpg.
Typesetting: Integra Software Services Pvt. Ltd.
Printing and binding: CPI books GmbH, Leck

www.degruyter.com

Acknowledgements

The present book is mainly an English translation of the chapters about theatre of my monograph on the textualization of physiognomic lore in Spanish Golden Age literature together with an article about birthmarks in Calderón:

> Gernert, Folke. *Lecturas del cuerpo. Fisiognomía y literatura en la España áurea.* Salamanca: Universidad, 2018.

> Gernert, Folke. "*La devoción de la Cruz* desde la fisiognomía. La violencia de Eusebio entre predeterminación y libre albedrío." *La violencia en Calderón.* Ed. Gero Arnscheidt and Manfred Tietz. Vigo: Academia del Hispanismo, 2014. 229–250.

The first chapter of this book is a considerably shortened and revised version of the corresponding chapters (chapter 0 and chapter I) of *Lecturas del cuerpo*. Chapters 2 and 3 and sub-chapters 2 to 4 of Chapter 4 largely correspond to Chapter III.3 of the Spanish book while sub-chapters 1 of Chapter 4 is an English Translation of "*La devoción de la Cruz* desde la fisiognomía. La violencia de Eusebio entre predeterminación y libre albedrío." Since the article on Calderón appeared some years ago, I have decided to use editions of the dramas under discussion that have appeared in the meantime and to update the bibliography. Chapter 5 is an elaborated version of Chapter II.2.3 of *Lecturas del cuerpo*.

I would like to thank the publishers, Ediciones de la Universidad de Salamanca and Academia del Hispanismo, for the kind permission to reprint this material here. Furthermore, I would like to thank Werner Schäfer very much for the translation of the text into English and the stimulating exchange about the subtleties of the English version.

Contents

Acknowledgements —— V

Introduction —— 1

Chapter 1
Divination and the human body —— 5
1 Body signs in context —— 5
2 History of physiognomy —— 8
2.1 Physiognomy in print —— 12
3 The interpretation of the hand —— 22
3.1 Palmistry marginalised: the gipsies —— 28

Chapter 2
Dramatic readings of the hand and the body in the theatre of the 16th century —— 31
1 The Italian model —— 31
2 The *Égloga interlocutoria* by Diego Guillén de Ávila —— 42
3 The palm-reading gipsies in Gil Vicente and other playwrights —— 47
4 Palmistry and physiognomy in Lope de Rueda —— 62

Chapter 3
17th century theatre and occultism —— 69
1 Palmistry in the theatre of Cervantes —— 69
2 The occult knowledge of Lope de Vega —— 76
2.1 *Servir a señor discreto* (1614–1615) —— 100
2.2 Body readings between mockery and truth —— 104
3 Tirso de Molina and physiognomy —— 120
4 Body signs in Rojas Zorrilla —— 126
5 Occult knowledge in Juan Ruiz de Alarcón —— 129
5.1 *La cueva de Salamanca* (1617–1620) —— 132
6 Agustín Moreto and Lope's model of hand reading —— 137

Chapter 4
Calderón and the condemnation of the divinatory arts on the stage —— 143
1 Body signs in Calderón's early work: *La devoción de la Cruz* (1622–1623) —— 144
1.1 Birth marks and analogical thinking —— 149
1.2 Calderón and the signatures: Julia's and Eusebio's birthmarks —— 152

1.3 *La devoción de la Cruz*: a prodigious history? —— **157**
2 Predetermination and free will —— **162**
2.1 *La vida es sueño* (1635) —— **162**
2.2 *Apolo y Climene* (1661) and *El tesoro escondido* (1679) —— **166**
3 Women as bearers of occult knowledge in Calderón —— **170**
3.1 *El mayor encanto, amor* (1635) —— **170**
3.2 *Los encantos de la culpa* (1645) —— **174**
3.3 *Los tres mayores prodigios* (1636) —— **178**
3.4 *El jardín de Falerina* (1649) —— **180**
4 Calderón and physiognomy —— **184**

Chapter 5
Divination and marginalised women on stage —— 187
1 Female diviners in 17th century France: The *affaire des poisons* —— **188**
2 La Voisin – a real soothsayer on the scene in *La Devineresse* (1679) —— **192**

Epilogue —— 197

Bibliography —— 199
Primary sources —— **199**
Secondary sources —— **206**

Name index —— 243

Introduction

Your face, my thane, is a book where men May read strange matters (Macbeth)[1]

Theatre and, especially, comedy, which aims at *imitationem vitae* and *speculum consuetudinis* according to the definition Donato puts into Cicero's mouth,[2] is the literary genre which best reflects contemporary attitudes towards the occult arts and science.[3] As a matter of fact, sorcerers, necromancer and astrologers are regular characters in the European and Spanish theatre of the Golden Age.[4] Italy's *commedia erudita*, which provides a new theatrical model in the 16th century, introduces in Ariosto's *Il negromante* the prototype of the cheating magician which was to become highly successful.[5] Whereas much scholarly attention has been paid to magic[6] and astrology[7] in the theatre, less attention has been paid to the reading of body signs, moles and lines on the forehead and hand.

---

1 Shakespeare, *Macbeth* I, 5, vv. 60–61, ed. Braunmuller (1997, 127).
2 "Comoediam esse Cicero ait imitationem uitae, speculum consuetudinis, imaginem ueritatis" (Donatus, "De comoedia", ed. Weßner, 1902, 22) [Comedy is as Cicero says imitation of life, mirror of customs and the image of truth]. On this aspect, see Vega Ramos (1996) and (2004) as well as Chalkomatas, who observes: "Die Definition der Komödie als derjenigen Gattung, die sich am meisten auf die Darstellung des weltimmanenten Lebens konzentriert, musste also dem Konzept der Mimesis eine zentrales Rolle zuerkennen. Dafür sprechen alle aus der Antike erhaltenen Definitionen der Gattung, darunter auch diejenige, die angeblich von Cicero selber stammt" (2007, 138–139). [The definition of comedy as the genre which most focuses on the representation of everyday life must concede a central role to mimesis. All definitions of this genre preserved from Antiquity, including the one which allegedly goes back to Cicero himself, support this].
3 As Dahan-Gaida rightly observes, literature is "un formidable résonateur des savoirs irriguant la culture, savoirs qu'elle absorbe et met en scène dans une sorte de mise en abyme du champ de la connaissance" (2006, 17) [a formidable resonator of the knowledge irrigating the culture, knowledge that it absorbs and stages in a kind of *mise en abyme* of the field of knowledge]. For science on the Spanish stage see García Santo-Tomás (2019). Physiognomics is not represented among the various disciplines dealt with in the collection.
4 On magic in French literature see Courtès (2004), and, with special attention to theatre, Friedrich (1908). On French theatre of the 17th century see Gutierrez-Laffond (1998) and for a comparison between *Il Negromante* and Corneille's *Illusion comique* Dickhaut (2016).
5 The comedy was translated into Latin as *Necromanticus* by Juan Pérez Petreyo, into French as *Le Négromant* (1573) by Jean de La Taille. On the Latin translation see Gago Saldaña (2001) and on the French see Benedettini (2010).
6 On magic and occultism in the Spanish theatre of the Golden Age see Pavia (1959), Diago (1992) and Arellano (1996). On the character of the necromancer see Alonso Asenjo (1991) and the dissertation project by Anne Bermann.
7 On 16th century theatre see Vélez Sainz (2014) and the studies by Halstead (1939) and (1941), Lorenz (1961), Armas (1980), (1983), (1993), (2001), (2006) and (2017), Hurtado Torres (1983)

Most of modern studies on the textualization of physiognomic theories in fiction deal with the narrative literature of the 18th, 19th and 20th centuries, with particular emphasis on the impact of Lavater. It was above all nineteenth-century realism and its link with approaches from the natural sciences that made researchers interested in the role of physiognomy in the construction of literary characters. The most obvious and most studied case is that of Balzac, Lavater's reader, who repeatedly used these theories, especially when describing the physiognomy of marginalised and criminal individuals. Pérez Galdós' interest in physiognomic studies is similar to that of the author of the *Comédie humaine* in Spain. The most studied medieval author with a view to the fictionalization of physiognomy is perhaps Geoffrey Chaucer,[8] followed by the Archpriest of Hita.[9] Regarding the Catalan Middle Ages, we have a well-documented study by Carré (2010) that disproves the claims of some researchers concerning the minor importance of physiognomy in medieval narrative. On the other hand, there are very few works dedicated to lyric poetry[10] which, due to its own unoriginal nature, lends itself – as Rodler (2000, 9–10) argues – less to the textualization of physiognomic theories.

With the exception of some isolated allusions to Rabelais[11] and Montaigne,[12] the fictionalization of physiognomy 16th and 17th century literature has not yet received due attention. As far as Spanish literature is concerned, some studies on physiognomy in *Celestina*[13] or authors such as Cervantes,[14] Quevedo[15] and Gracián[16] have been published since Caro Baroja's seminal study.

---

and (1984), Thiengo de Moraes (2003) and Vicente García (2009) with reference to various dramatic writers of the 17th century. Gandolfi (2018, 273) proposes "a voyage through the history of theatrical astrologers / astronomers tracing the evolution of the complex relationship between stars and stage and at the same time analysing the ascent of the contemporary science-play format where the dramaturgy either inflates becoming verbose, philosophical and sometimes ironical or tends to dissolve in a multisensory experience of cosmos, history and society called Postdramatic Theatre".
8 See among others Hanson (1970), Friedman (1981), Brasswell-Means (1991) and Wurtele (1999).
9 Gernert (2018, 239–260).
10 See the works of Vigh (2014) on Italian baroque poetry.
11 See Jordan (1911, 713).
12 See La Charité (1989).
13 See Walde Moheno (2007), who places particular emphasis on the procuress' ugliness and medical explanations for female hirsutism.
14 See Madera (1992) and Hiergeist (2016).
15 See Vega Rodríguez (1996).
16 See Laplana Gil (1997, 106).

As far as theatre is concerned, studies on the textualization of physiognomy and chiromancy are rather rare notwithstanding the performative potential of physiognomics which Baumbach insightfully speaks of:

> Not only can physiognomic reading be performed, but a specific physiognomy can arise from performance: the 'true' face can be 'masked' by fake expressions, which subvert the natural correspondence between the outer form and inner being. With a heightened awareness of its performative and manipulative aspects, physiognomy moves from the *liber mundi* to the *theatrum mundi*, which makes it accessible to a broader spectrum of disciplines, such as ethics, communication, linguistics, and philosophy, and allows its successful re-entry into the sciences. (2012a, 102)[17]

The most widely researched author regarding the theatricalization of physiognomic theory and practice is undoubtedly William Shakespeare.[18] Despite the many explicit allusions to physiognomy and chiromancy in Molière's theatre (*Le mariage forcé*,[19] *L'amour médecin*[20] or *L'Avare*[21]), scholars have paid relatively

---

17 See Mur (2017) for physiognomic discourse and European theatre in the 18th and the beginning 19th centuries.
18 See Camden (1941), Wilson (1965), Torrey (2000) and Baumbach (2007) and (2012b). In his book about *Character and the Individual Personality in English Renaissance* Curran (2014) deals only marginally with physiognomy. In her study on occult knowledge on the Shakespearean Stage Floyd-Wilson (2013) deals with palmistry in the anonymous play *A Warning for Fair Women*.
19 Sganarelle, who would like to marry, tries to be clear in advance about the outcome of his plan, as Panurge once did. As in Rabelais' novel, the future groom seeks help from a character who is characterised by an absurd variety of different forms of knowledge, among them "Onirocritique [. . .] Cosmimométrie, Géométrie, [. . .] Spéculoire et Spéculatoire [. . .] Médicine, Astronomie, Astrologie, Physionomie, Métoposcopie, Chiromancie, Geomancie, etc.", Molière, *Le mariage forcé*, ed. Forestier (2010, I, 970). [Onirocritics . . . Cosmometry, Geometry . . . Speculatory, and Speculatatory . . . Physic, Astronomy, Astrology, Phisiognomy, Metoposcopy, Chiromancy, geomancy, etc., English translation 1732, 43]. As the plot progresses, two gipsy women predict Sganarelle's imminent marriage, but do not answer his question about the fidelity of his future wife. What deserves particular attention is their reference to the outer appearance of Sganarelle: "Première Égytienne. Tu as une bonne physionomie, mon bon Monsieur, une bonne physionomie. Deuxième Égyptienne. Oui, bonne physionomie. Physionomie d'un Homme qui sera un jour quelque chose." Molière, *Le mariage forcé*, ed. Forestier (2010, I, 953). [1. Gipsy. Thou hast a good Physiognomy, my good Master, a good Physiognomy. 2. Gipsy. Ay, a good Physiognomy. The Physiognomy of a Man that one Day will be something. English translation 1732, 43].
20 In *L'amour médecin*, it is the servant Lisette who explains to the worried father Clitandre's physical closeness to Lucinde through a supposed physiognomic examination: "C'est qu'il observe sa physionomie, et tous les traits de son visage", Molière, *L'amour médecin*, ed. Forestier (2010, I, 629). [It is that he observes his physiognomy and all the features of his face].
21 In *L'avare* it is the bawd Frosine who pretends to read his future from Harpagon's face and hands: "Frosine. Assurément. Vous en avez toutes les marques. Tenez-vous un peu. Ô que voilà bien là entre vos deux yeux un signe de longue vie! / Harpagon. Tu te connais à cela?

little attention to this subject in the work of the French playwright.[22] As far as Spanish theatre is concerned, little research has been done on the subject.[23] This book intends to fill this void. It is focused on the analysis of the different forms of interpretation of the human body on the Spanish stage in the Romanic context of the 16th and 17th centuries.

To be able to analyse the reading of body signs in Spanish theatre, it is essential to find out what physiognomic and chiromantic studies were circulating in Spain and were, therefore, available to Spanish playwrights. This entails reviewing the history of physiognomy from the perspective of the history of the (scientific) book and of reading and studying both the different translations of each physiognomist[24] and the dissemination of the manuals in print. It is obvious that texts written in Spanish or translated into Spanish were read in Spain and the number of editions allows us to assess the degree of diffusion they may have had. In the case of manuals in Greek, Latin, French and Italian, printed outside Spain, the panorama of their diffusion is less evident. In the first chapter I will give an overview of the history of physiognomy and chiromancy in order to contextualise the analysis of the plays and their (pseudo)scientific underpinnings historically.

/ FROSINE. Sans doute. Montrez-moi votre main. Ah mon Dieu! quelle ligne de vie! / HARPAGON. Comment? / FROSINE. Ne voyez-vous pas jusqu'où va cette ligne-là? / HARPAGON. Hé bien, qu'est-ce que cela veut dire? / FROSINE. Par ma foi, je disais cent ans, mais vous passerez les six-vingts. Molière, *L'avare*, ed. Forestier (2010, II, 29). [FRO. Decidedly. You have all the appearance of it. Hold yourself up a little. Ah! what a sign of long life is that line there straight between your two eyes! / HAR. You know all about that, do you? / FRO. I should think I do. Show me your hand. Dear me, what a line of life there is there! / HAR. Where? / FRO. Don't you see how far this line goes? / HAR. Well, and what does it mean? / FRO. What does it mean? There . . . I said a hundred years; but no, it is one hundred and twenty I ought to have said. English translation Wall 1894, without pagination].

22 See Jordan (1911, 715–716) and Powell (1987). For the theatricalization of scientific knowledge in Molière see Brunel (2014).

23 An exception is Lanuza-Navarro who dedicates a section of his study on astrological medicine in Spain and in the Spanish golden theatre to "Physiognomics: representing a knowledge shared by physicians and astrologers" (2014, 207–210). In his article "Fisiognómica, pintura y teatro" Moreno Mendoza (2006) is devoted more to sculpture than to theatre.

24 See for the importance of translations for scientific exchange in the 16th and 17th centuries Pantin who insists on the fact that "changing the language often provided an opportunity for altering the text" (2007, 167).

Chapter 1
Divination and the human body

1 Body signs in context

'Physiognomy is the prejudice coagulated in book form'[1] says Hans Blumenberg in *The Legibility of the World* with reference to Lichtenberg's physiognomy criticism, which is inspired by Lavater's interpretative optimism and ironically sketches a frightening scenario:

> Wenn die Physiognomik das wird, was Lavater von ihr erwartet, so wird man die Kinder aufhängen, ehe sie die Taten getan haben, die den Galgen verdienen, es wird also eine neue Art von Firmelung jedes Jahr vorgenommen werden. Ein physiognomisches Auto da Fe. (Lichtenberg 1983, F 517)
>
> [If physiognomy becomes what Lavater expects it to be, children will be hung before they have done the deeds that deserve the gallows, so a new type of confirmation will be made every year. A physiognomic Auto-da-Fé.]

In early modern times, the problem horizon against which physiognomics is to be considered was a slightly different one: The doctrine of the reading of body signs, especially when it projected its thirst for knowledge into the future, came into conflict with the concept of human freedom of will, a concept which was controversially discussed ever since the polemical dispute between Luther and Erasmus and which had acquired a dogmatic character for Catholic Spain since the Tridentinum. The determinism inherent in physiognomics and related disciplines thus had to be reconciled with the prevailing theological discourse, which endowed man with a *liberum arbitrium*. One way of coping with predestination which is inherent in the nature of these disciplines was to interpret the physiological dispositions as *inclinatio*, an inclination which could be countered by virtuous action. The legitimacy of physiognomic interpretation, which is repeatedly negotiated in the prologues of the relevant tracts, was established in very different ways. Particularly instructive in this context is the *Commentarius de praecipuis generibus divinationem*, published in 1553 in Wittenberg by Caspar Peucer. The German reformer answers the question "Quod sint aliqua divinationum genera non impia, nec superstitiosa, et Christianis concessa" (1553, 1r) [Which are the forms of divination neither impious nor superstitious and permitted for Christians] for such different fields of knowledge as physiognomy, chiromancy

---

[1] "Physiognomik ist das in Buchform geronnene Vorurteil", Blumenberg (1981, 201).

Open Access. © 2021 Folke Gernert, published by De Gruyter. This work is licensed under the Creative Commons Attribution-NonCommercial-NoDerivatives 4.0 International License.
https://doi.org/10.1515/9783110695755-002

and astrology by saying that in all cases signs, with God's permission, can be interpreted by men.

Conceptually, physiognomy works like other semiotic practices that interpret different body signs, especially chiromancy and metoposcopy, but also the reading of moles or birthmarks. Unlike chiromancy and perhaps metoposcopy, physiognomy is not, in the first place, one of the *artes manticae*,[2] although the reading of body signs since classical antiquity[3] has also been used to know the future.[4]

> La physiognomonie n'entre dans le champ de la divination que dans la mesure où elle prétend prédire la destinée de l'homme d'après les traits de son visage et l'aspect général

---

2 See about divination Aphek & Tobin (1989), Bloch (1991), Burnett (1996), Minois (1996), Boudet (2006) and Tuczay (2012) and Annus (2010) for divination practices in the ancient world. On divination and forecasting of the future there is also a whole series of collective volumes with highly specialised contributions; see the publications edited by Hogrebe (2005), Bergdolt and Ludwig (2005), Sturlese (2011), Fidora (2013) and Boudet, Ostorero & Paravicini Bagliani (2017).

3 According to Dasen ancient physiognomy "could also have a predictive dimension" (2014, 155). The researcher refers to the treatise of the Latin anonymous, in which "one reads that 'Polemon and Loxus advance this discipline to such an extent that they affirm it can predict some things in the future'" (Dasen 2014, 155). For other practices that read the future from the human body, see Dasen (2008), Chandezon, Dasen & Wilgaux (2013) who observe: "Dans le monde grec antique, tout, dans le corps humain, peut devenir signe et faire l'objet d'une interprétation. De l'art médical à la physiognomonie, en passant par la mantique, de nombreuses *technai* ont développé une sémiologie du corps qui relèvent d'une façon commune de penser le corps et de chercher à le déchiffrer, mais avec des finalités différentes [. . .] Ces *technai* ont progressivement affirmé leur autonomie tout en s'intéressant aux mêmes signes corporels, et les indices de la porosité de leurs frontières abondent. Comme la mantique, la physiognomonie peut ainsi accorder aux mouvements du corps une valeur de présage, tandis que l'art médical utilise l'observation de signes pour établir un pronostic et anticiper l'évolution de la maladie." (111). [In the ancient Greek world, everything in the human body can become a sign and be interpreted. From medical art to physiognomy, through mantic art, many *technai* developed a semiology of the body which is based on a common way of thinking about the body and trying to decipher it, but with different purposes . . . These *technai* have gradually asserted their autonomy while being interested in the same body signs, and clues to the porosity of their boundaries abound. Like divination, physiognomy can thus give body movements an omen value, while medical art uses the observation of signs to establish a prognosis and anticipate the evolution of the disease].

4 See Bordes (2003, 308): "La adivinación es el instrumento de trabajo común en el análisis del fisiognomista, pero algunos autores interpretan los signos externos del cuerpo no para establecer una correspondencia con el carácter, sino para realizar unas suposiciones sobre el pasado o futuro individual." [Divination is the common working tool in the analysis of the physiognomist, but some authors interpret the external signs of the body not to establish a correspondence with the character, but to make some assumptions about the individual past or future].

de son corps. Mais plus généralement, elle vise à connaître les mœurs et les passions d'un individu par l'examen de ses caractères physiques. (Boudet 2006, 114)

[Physiognomy enters the field of divination only insofar as it claims to predict man's destiny according to the features of his face and the general appearance of his body. But more generally, it aims to know the morals and passions of an individual by examining his physical characteristics.]

It is precisely the divinatory dimension that influences the legitimacy of these practices and which is the reason why physiognomy is often considered – unlike chiromancy and metoposcopy – as a licit practice. The reading of body signs as a technique to know the future is often associated with the world of magic. In fact, some specialised studies on magic and witchcraft include chapters on physiognomy, chiromancy and other divinatory practices.[5] However, as Rapisarda rightly observes, "magia e divinazione sono due pratiche in realtà 'epistemologicamente' assai differenti" (2005, 233) [magic and divination are two practices that are actually 'epistemologically' very different]. The former "mira a modificare con procedure 'costrittive' la realtà esterna all'individuo" [aims to modify the reality outside of the individual with 'coercive' procedures] while the latter is dedicated to the "prescienza del futuro" (2005, 233) [foreknowledge of the future]. As the aforementioned Italian researcher explains, the confusion is already present in Isidore of Seville and is particularly palpable in the case of necromancy, which lost its etymological meaning ('divination through the dead') and came to designate 'black magic'.

It is with natural magic that physiognomy and related semiotic practices share a conceptual basis. The planetary influence that is supposed to be represented in the mountains of the hand or in the lines of the forehead can be considered, as well as the external corporal signs, indicative of the inner and invisible virtues of a person, a sort of *qualitas occulta* comparable to the force that the stone magnet exerts on the metals or the healing effect of a talisman.[6] As Foucault says, "dans une *épistémè* où signes et similitudes s'enroulaient

---

[5] See Boudet (2006), Tuczay (2012) and recently Zamora Calvo (2016), who devotes short chapters of her study of the *Artes maleficorum* to metoposcopy (99), physiognomy (101) and chiromancy (107).
[6] See for the difference between manifest and occult qualities in the Middle Ages Weill-Parot (2010). Since Thorndike's (1923–1958) monumental history of magic and experimental science, occultism has been the subject of many scientific studies. See for the *qualitates occultae* Hutchinson (1982), Blum (1992) and Meinel (1992) as well as for Renaissance occultism Shumaker (1972), a collective volume edited by Vickers (1984), Vickers (1988), a collective volume edited by Buck (1992), Weill-Parot (2013), Saif (2015) and a collective volume edited by Classen (2017). For occultism from classical antiquity to the 20th century see Partridge (2014).

réciproquement selon une volute qui n'avait pas de terme, il fallait bien qu'on pensât dans le rapport du microcosme au macrocosme la garantie de ce savoir et le terme de son épanchement" (1966, 47) [in an *episteme* where signs and similarities rolled up in a volute that had no ending, it was necessary to perceive in the relationship of the microcosm to the macrocosm the guarantee of this knowledge and the end of its effusion]. Speaking of the 'relationship between magic and erudition' in early modern times, the French philosopher observes:

> Le monde est couvert de signes qu'il faut déchiffrer, et ces signes, qui révèlent des ressemblances et des affinités, ne sont eux-mêmes que des formes de la similitude. Connaître sera don interpréter: aller de la marque visible à ce qui se dit à travers elle, et demeurerait, sans elle, parole muette, ensommeillée dans les choses. (Foucault 1966, 47)

> [The world is covered with signs that need to be deciphered, and these signs, which reveal similarities and affinities, are themselves only forms of similarity. To know will be to interpret: to go from the visible mark to what is said through it, and without it would remain a mute word, asleep in things.]

From this perspective, the human body is susceptible to being read like a book by those who know the alphabet of physiognomy.

2 History of physiognomy

The Pseudo-Aristotelian *Physiognomonica* (3rd century BC) is the oldest systematic monograph on body reading.[7] Based on this treatise, physiognomy combines three methodological approaches:[8] the emotional method, the ethnological method and the zoological method.[9] We have news of later physiognomic work from the third pre-Christian century, by the doctor Loxus, which is lost.[10] The next text that has survived is the physiognomic work of Antonius Polemon (ca. 88–145),[11]

---

7 See the edition of the text in the anthology of Förster (1893, I, 69–71) and the translations into English (Barnes 1984), Italian (Raina 1993 and Ferrini 2007), German (Vogt 1999) and Spanish (Calvo Delcán & Martínez Manzano 1999).
8 See Armstrong (1958) and Zucker (2006, 4).
9 For the bestiary of the ancient physiognomists see Zucker (2006) and for zoomorphic comparisons in physiognomy from antiquity to the 19th century Baltrusaitis (1957, 8–46).
10 See the anthology by Förster (1893, I, 1–91) and Misener (1923), Evans (1969), Boys-Stones (2007, 58–64) and Junkerjürgen (2009, 54).
11 See the edition by Hoyland (2007) and the collection of articles about this author published by Swain (2007) and particularly Swain himself (2007, 176): "The *Physiognomy* survives in a Greek version by Adamantius, which is undoubtedly fourth-century, and an Arabic translation

which has come down to us in an Arabic translation from 1379,[12] in an abbreviated Greek paraphrase, thanks to Adamantius[13] and also thanks to the so-called Latin Anonymous.[14] Also preserved in a medieval manuscript was the Pseudo-Aristotelian *Secretum secretorum*,[15] apparently a long letter by the Greek philosopher addressed to his disciple Alexander the Great, which is actually a text from the 10th century, the *Sirr al-asrar*, compiled in Syria. It is a kind of mirror of princes that brings together all kinds of knowledge, including a treatise on physiognomy.[16] All these physiognomic books and their Arab continuations reached the West in the course the Middle Ages.[17]

(the Leiden) which exists in a single manuscript. We have also the fairly reworking of the Anonymus Latinus (including much material from Loxus and Ps.-Aristotle), which can be useful in determining Polemon's meaning in case of difficulty, and in addition the parallel Arabic versions (the Istanbul recension; hereafter TK) which are heavily reworked from the original, lost Arabic translation, but from time to time offer obvious corrections of the Leiden manuscript".

12 See Evans (1941, 97) and Barton (1994, 102–131); for the examples used by Polemon see Mesk (1932).

13 The *De Physiognomonica* of Adamantius, written around 325, is – as Repath (2007, 487) notes – "essentially an abridgement of Polemon's treatise".

14 See Laurand (2005) and Repath (2007, 549–635), who comments, edits and translates the text and proposes "a date certainly beyond the middle of the third century AD and more probably somewhere near the end of the fourth" (550).

15 See Paschetto (1985, 98): "[. . .] il *Secretum* non era solo un trattato di fisiognomica ma, dopo aver parlato dell'arte di governare e di questioni mediche, dedicava ampio spazio alla magia, all'astrologia ed alle scienze occulte, ivi comprese l'onomatomanzia e gli incantesimi." [The *Secretum* was not only a treatise on physiognomy but, after talking about the art of governing and medical matters, it devoted a great deal of space to magic, astrology and the occult sciences, including onomatomancy and spells]. For the *Secretum secretorum* see also the studies collected in Ryan & Schmitt (1982) and Williams (2003), as well as the study of the Arabic and German versions of Forster (2006).

16 Williams deals with the Aristotelian *spuria* in the Middle Ages and questions the alleged naivety of medieval scholars with regard to works such as the *Secretum*: "It is easy to laugh at the schoolmen's acceptance of such patently spurious works as the widely read *Secretum secretorum*, the extended missive supposedly sent by the Stagirite to his former pupil Alexander the Great. In this book Aristotle gives Alexander advice on all sorts of useful occult lore, like how to fashion a powerful amulet to afflict one's enemies with fear and trembling, where to find a floating red stone that will provoke horses to neigh (thus discomfiting an opposing army), and what special ingredients to use in preparing a panacea that might have been invented by Adam himself. How could even the newly licensed arts teacher, let alone the seasoned philosopher-theologian, actually take such silliness as coming from Aristotle's pen?" (1995, 30); see also the section on the attribution of the *Secretum* (1995, 45–46).

17 See for physiognomy in the Arab World Mourad (1939), Viguera Molins (1977), Autuori (1984), Ghersetti (1994), (1995) and (1999) and Akasoy (2008), who studies physiognomy as a bridge between medicine and astrology. For translations from Arabic and the debt of European

In the 12th century, physiognomy was still absent from such compendia of knowledge as the *Didascalion* by Hugh of Saint Victor (1096–1141);[18] even in the *De divisione philosophiae* (ca. 1145) by Dominicus Gundissalinus (ca. 1115–post 1190) only chiromancy is mentioned.[19] Physiognomics was reborn in the West in the 13th century thanks to the (re)discovery of Latin, Greek and Arabic texts. Already at the beginning of the 12th century, more precisely around 1100/1120, the work of the Latin Anonymous was discovered and began to circulate widely in the following century.[20] The translation of the *Liber ad Almansorem* by Mohammed Rhasis (865–925)[21] by Gerardo da Cremona,[22] whose second book is dedicated to physiognomy, dates from the end of the 12th century, around 1175. Likewise, the Pseudo-Aristotelian writings with a physiognomic content are translated at that time from Arabic into Latin. There are two Latin translations of the *Secretum Secretorum*.[23] At the beginning of the 12th century, John of Seville made a partial translation with the title *Epistola ad Alexandrum de dieta servanda* (also known as *Epistula Aristotelis ad Alexandrum de regimine sanitatis*)[24] and at the beginning of the next one, probably before 1230, a certain Philippus Tripolitanus[25] presented a more extensive Latin text which was the

---

occultism to Islam see Vernet (1999, 264–269) and Herbers about the translation activity in Toledo: "Magische Künste wurden auch – zumindest in einigen philosophischen Schriften etwa seit dem 13. Jahrhunderts – aufgrund der Rezeption arabischer Schriften in den Kanon der Wissenschaften integriert" (1999, 246–247) [Magical arts were also integrated into the canon of sciences – at least in some philosophical writings since the 13th century – due to the reception of Arabic texts].
18 See the bilingual edition of the *Didascalicon* of Muñoz Gamero & Arribas Hernáez (2011) and Agrimi (2002, 5).
19 See the edition of *De divisione philosophiae* by Fidora (2007, 228).
20 The treaty was published under the title of *De Physiognomonia liber* by Rose (1864–1870, 105–139), in the anthology of Förster (1893, II, 3–145) and more recently in an Italian translation by Raina together with his edition of the Pseudo-Aristotelian *Physiognomonica* (1993) and by André (2003) in a bilingual French-Latin edition; see for the Latin Anonymous Rose (1864–1870, 61–102), Evans (1941, 103), Agrimi (2002, 5) and the introduction by André.
21 See for Muhammad Ibn-Zakariyā ar-Rāzī or simply Rasi, Rhazes or Rhasis Escobar Gómez (1995) and for the reception of Rhasis by Andreas Vesalius Compier (2012).
22 This translation was published under the title of *Abubecri Rasis ad regem Mansorem de re medicina liber II* in the anthology by Förster (1893, II, 161–180); see Autuori (1984) and Agrimi (2002, 5). There are two recent editions of a 14th century Italian *volgarizzamento* by Piro (2011) and Salem Elsheikh (2016).
23 See for the section on physiognomy of the *Secretum secretorum* Cardoner (1971, 82–85).
24 See William (2003, 31–59). Bizzarri (2010, 15–16) suspects in his edition that it was translated 'perhaps between the years 1109 and 1130, at the request of a Queen Doña Teresa, who could not be identified'. See also Pensado Figueiras (2015).
25 See Möller (1963, LVIX), William (2003, 60–108) and the edition by Bizzarri (2010, 16).

most popular version throughout the Middle Ages.²⁶ There were several Spanish translations in the Middle Ages:²⁷ *Poridat de las poridades*, of John of Seville's version, and *Secreto de los secretos*, on the basis of the text by Tripolitanus,²⁸ are followed by the Aragonese translation by Juan Fernández de Heredia (1308?–1396).²⁹ The second treatise, erroneously attributed to the Stagirite, the *Physiognomonica*, was translated in the middle of the same century by Bartolomeo da Messina from Arabic into Latin.³⁰ Sections on physiognomy, inspired by the Greek and Arabic texts cited, would appear from now on in encyclopaedias, such as the *Speculum maius* (ca. 1256) by the Dominican Vincent of Beauvais (1184/1194–1264),³¹ and in scientific books such as *De animalibus* (1262–1268) by Albert the Great (1200–1280).³² Two original physiognomic treatises from the Middle Ages deserve separate mention: The Scottish scholar Michael Scott (ca. 1175–ca. 1235) wrote his *Liber phisonomie* (*post* 1228), which combines

---

26 See Thorndike (1923–1958, II, 267–278) and Eamon (1994, 45–46). Three Latin versions of the *Secretum Secretorum* are published in the Förster anthology (1893, II, 181–222). See recently the volume on the trajectory of the text in Europe by Tilliette, Bridges & Gaullier-Bougassas (2015).
27 See for the French translations Monfrin (1964), Hunt (2000), Zamuner (2005, 50–57 and 57–60 for the Provençal), Gaullier-Bougassas (2015), Lorée (2015); for the Portuguese and Catalan Zamuner (2005, 64–66 and 2005, 66–91) and for the Italian versions Cecioni (1889), Morel Fatio (1897), Franzese (1994), Zinelli (2000), Perrone (2001), Rapisarda (2001), Milani (2001), (2014) and (2015b with the edition of the physiognomic section in one of the testimonies 308–314), Zamuner (2005, 92–109) and Campopiano (2015). As for the chapters on physiognomy, Burnett notes: "Curiosamente, aunque aparecen en árabe, los apartados sobre fisiognomía y onomancia están ausentes de todas las versiones europeas del *Secreto de los secretos*, a excepción de la castellana y de las derivadas de ella" (2002, 133) [Curiously, although they appear in Arabic, the sections on physiognomy and onomance are absent from all European versions of the *Secret of Secrets*, with the exception of the Spanish and those derived from it]. Nonetheless, some versions discovered later include this section, such as the French version of the 15ᵗʰ century, studied by Lorée (2015).
28 See for its circulation in Castile Bizzarri (1996). The Argentinian scholar suspects that the translation of the *Secret* is contemporary with the *Siete partidas* and that the *Poridat* may be earlier (Bizzarri 2010, 19). See for the *Secreto* also the edition by Jones (1995) and Bizzarri (2015) as well as for *Poridat*'s illustrations Cacho Blecua (2016).
29 See Val Naval (2002).
30 See the text in the anthology by Förster (1893, I, 4–92) and in the recent critical edition by Devriese (2019).
31 Since there is no modern edition of this medieval encyclopaedia, we must go to the incunabulum editions as *Speculum Naturale*, Venice, Hermann Liechtenstein, 1494, available online http://daten.digitale-sammlungen.de/~db/0005/bsb00056560/images/ (visited on 29.5.2020).
32 See Agrimi (2002, 8).

physiognomics with the theory of complexions at the court of Frederick II.[33] Peter of Abano (ca. 1250–1316),[34] a Paduan doctor based in Paris, studies body signs in relation to astrology in his *Compilatio Physionomie* (1295).[35]

2.1 Physiognomy in print

The ancient and medieval physiognomies were given new life in print: the first physiognomic study to be printed was the *Liber compilationis phisonomie* by Peter of Abano in 1474. The Scottish scholar's *Liber phisonomiae* was published repeatedly from the princeps edition (Venice, Jacopo da Fivizzano, 1477). The first vernacular translation of this treatise is to Spanish; it appeared without mentioning Scott's name in the *Compendio de la salud humana* (1494 and 1495).[36] That this compendium was almost a bestseller can be gathered from the fact that, well into the 16th century, the book was republished by the Cromberger, who used to have a nose for sales. In addition to the presence of annotated copies in current Spanish libraries and in the inventories of wills of the time, the continued interest in Michael Scott is reflected in the rewriting of his physiognomic theories in other publications such as, for example, the *Libro de phisonomia natural y varios secretos de naturaleza* (1598) by Jerónimo Cortés.

The physiognomic studies of classical antiquity and, first of all, those works still attributed to the Stagirite were of great interest to humanists and, above all, to physicians with Hellenistic training who tried to produce reliable editions from the Greek originals, much to the detriment of the Arab tradition, considered to be corrupt. Actually, some editions tell us eloquently how these Pseudo-Aristotelian works were read and studied in early modern times. The printed diffusion of the work of the Peripatetic is closely linked to the Aristotelianism of the Renaissance universities and particularly to the so-called school of Padua.

---

33 There is a modern edition of the Latin text with an Italian translation by Porsia (2009) and a Latin edition by Voskoboynikov (2019); see for Scott's *Liber phisonomiae* Damiani (1974), Jacquart (1994), Agrimi (2002, 5 and 22–29) and Ziegler (2008). As for Michael's sources see Burnett (1994, 109).
34 There is no modern edition of the *Compilatio Physionomie*; see for Peter of Abano's physiognomy Paschetto (1984, 139–150) and (1985) and Jacquart (1993) and (2013).
35 See in this regard Paschetto (1985, 106), Federici Vescovini (1991, 45) and Porter (2005, 73).
36 The Spanish version was edited by Sánchez González de Herrero & Vázquez de Benito (2009).

From 1482 the *Physiognomonica* was included, in Bartolomeo da Messina's translation, in some Latin editions of the complete works of the Stagirite, while – as Schmitt observes– the *Secretum* "never appeared in a Latin edition of the *Opera*" (1982, 125). Between 1495 and 1498 Aldo Manuzio published a major folio edition of Aristotle in Greek, which includes, in the third of its five volumes, the *Physiognomonica*. The existence of the Greek original allows the philological recovery of the text. The *Secretum secretorum*, on the other hand, belongs to the second of the two categories of *spuria* established by Schmitt: he distinguishes "those coming from a Greek original and those for which there was never a Greek text" (1982, 124). Although these texts were of little interest to humanist philologists, the *Secretum Secretorum* had an enormous diffusion printed from the *editio princeps* (Cologne, Arnold ter Hoernen around 1475) in the translation of Philippus Tripolitanus. As Kraye observes, "[t]he *Secret of Secrets* was published together with a number of different texts – plague tracts, medieval preaching aids, astrological and magical treatises concerned with medicine [. . .] – but it did not appear in the company of any genuine Aristotelian work" (1995, 208–209). One of these books was no other than Michael Scott's *Physiognomy* in the 1484 edition, which came out of Johann Veldener's presses in Leuven. Two Latin editions of the *Secret of Secrets* are currently published in Spain, but neither of the medieval Castilian versions (*Poridat de las poridades* or *Secreto de los secretos*) sees the light of day in print. However, the text circulates in printed form in Italian, German, English and especially in French. As Kraye remarks, incunabula editions – in Latin and French – do not usually disseminate the full text and often combine abridged versions with other works of various kinds. Silvi rightly remarks that "ce qui parait caractériser ce traité, c'est une sorte d'instabilité chronique, une mouvance qui se vérifie tant au niveau du texte que du paratexte qui l'entoure et des autres textes auxquels il se trouve, parfois, associé" (2015, 158) [what seems to characterise this treatise is a kind of chronic instability, a movement that is evident both in the text and in the paratext that accompanies it and in the other texts with which it is sometimes associated]. According to the aforementioned French researcher, the printing press divulges the *Secret of Secrets* as "ouvrage d'édification politique et moral" (2015, 174) [work of political and moral edification]. Williams, who underlines the use of the treatise as *speculum principis*, remembers that "the *Secretum* continued to be offered to rulers into the Early Modern era: to Henry VIII and Edward VI of England in the 16th century; to Philip IV of Spain in the 17th century" (2004, 141).

The new translations of the Pseudo-Aristotelian *Physiognomonica* published in the 1530s are in turn part of the trend of medical humanism that applies philological tools to scientific literature in the Greek language. It is striking that a few years after Andrés Laguna's translation, another physician dedicated himself to the recovery of the same text, the German Jodocus Willich (1501–1552), a friend of Melanchthon, who, in 1538, published the Latin *Physiognomonica Aristotelis* (Wittenberg, Nickel Schirlentz). While the *Physiognomonica* continues to be published, in Bartolomeo da Messina's translation, and remains a subject of study even in the 17th century, the *Secreta Secretorum* was last published in Latin in 1555 along with a whole series of other texts.

Polemon's work[37] was first published in the original Greek together with those of Adamantius and other divinatory texts as an appendix to the *Various Histories* of Aelianus in 1545. The first Latin translation of Polemon, by Nicholas Petreius (1486–1568), a native of Corfu, was issued in 1552 accompanied by other unpublished Greek texts on the human body like Melampus' *De neuis corporis*. The first translation of Polemon into a vernacular language is a Spanish one printed at the end of the 16th century in Milan, followed by an Italian version of 1612 made by the sixteen-year-old Francesco Montecuccoli, whose brother Carlo had submitted a new Latin translation the same year.

The story of Adamantius' print transmission is much more complex.[38] The Greek original was published on its own prior to Polemon's work in France in 1540 and four years later in a bilingual Latin-Greek edition by the German Hellenist physician Janus Cornarius (1500–1558) along with other texts. Another Latin translation was provided by Pomponio Gaurico (*ca.* 1484–1530) in 1551.[39] Later on, well into the 17th century, a French translation was published, made by another precocious young man: the twelve-year-old Henry de Boyvin du Vauroüy dedicated his *La physionomie* of 1635 to none other than Richelieu.

The physiognomic theories of Polemon and Adamantius, as well as those of Aristotle and the lost work of Loxus, are also disseminated through the treatise of the so-called Anonymous Latin. This physiognomic work, *De Physiognomonia liber*, was published under the title of *De diversa hominum natura*, (Lyon, Jean de Tournes, 1549) by Antoine Du Moulin (ca. 1520–1580).

In the dedication of his French translation of Artemidorus, the humanist Charles Fontaine observes: "Aussi de ce temps heureux du Roy Françoys [. . .] nous avons l'art de Phisionomie, Chiromance, Astrologie mieulx et plus correctement imprimé, que depuis cinq cent ans. Et par son autorité et commandement

---

37 See the collection of articles on this author published by Swain (2007) along with editions and translations of his physiognomic works. For occurences of the name in a corrupted way in the Italian translation of the *Secretum secretorum* see Milani (2015a).
38 Consult for this author and the transmission of his work Förster (1897, 298–299) and Repath (2007, 487–548).
39 See for Gaurico as physiognomist Vigh (2014, 171–202).

nous voyons toutes sciences se resjouyr, et renouveller"[40] [From the fortunate times of king Francis I . . . we have the art of physiognomics, palm reading and astrology better and more properly printed than in the 500 years before. And because of his authority and command we see all sciences flourish and revive].

The 15th and 16th centuries saw the appearance of new manuals and treatises specialising in physiognomy and related subjects, such as metoposcopy or chiromancy, which are in part commentaries on the classical texts or re-editions of. As Porter points out, these publications attracted the interest of a large number of readers from all strata of society:

> They were published in all formats, from cheap, ephemeral single-sheet pamphlets to the most lavishly illustrated, hand-painted vellum or leather bound folios, and distributed across Europe and later to America, far beyond the main printing centres of Europe's urban growths, to a reading and listening audience made up of a wide range of ages, sexes, occupations, and incomes. (2005, vii)

At the beginning of the 16th century, Alessandro Achillini's *De Chyromantiae principiis et physionomiae* (Giovanni Antonio de Benedictis, 1503) was published in Bologna.[41] The Bolognese professor had conceived this text, which is significantly presented as a *quaestio*, as an introduction to the physiognomic and chiromantic work of his student Bartolomeo della Rocca,[42] known by the nickname of "Cocles" (*Chyromantie ac physionomie anastasis cum approbatione Alexandri de Achilinis*, Bologna, Giovanni Antonio Benedetti, 1504). His intention was to claim the scientific status of this semiotic practice. We know very little about the aforementioned Cocles.[43] He seems to have been a kind of itinerant fortune teller who was regularly expelled from the small courts of the Romagna for predicting some kind of infamous death to the powerful; having

---

40 Fontaine, *Dédicace à quelque personnage d'authorité* (1546, 6).
41 See Zambelli (1978, 59–86), Matsen (1974 and 1975, 437–451) and Porter (2005, 20 and 53).
42 For the relationship between Achillini and Cocles see Porter (2005, 154–155).
43 The few known data from Cocles' biography are extracted by Zambelli (1978, 79–81) from the works of Girolamo Cardano, Luca Gaurico and a certain Orazio Bicarti; also see Zaccaria (1989). González Manjarrés (2015, 169) argues: "Su biografía es un caso prototípico: consideraba que el dominio de la fisiognomía y la quiromancia servía para conocer de verdad a los demás, para prever su conducta e incluso para adivinar los acontecimientos futuros, y así llegó a tener un gran prestigio y una importante clientela por su habilidad de fisiognomista y quiromántico, hasta que murió asesinado unos días después de la publicación de su obra" [His biography is a prototypical case: he considered that the mastery of physiognomy and chiromancy served to really know others, to foresee their behaviour and even to guess future events, and thus he came to have great prestige and an important clientele for his ability as a physiognomist and chiromancer, until he was murdered a few days after the publication of his work].

done so with Ermete Bentivoglio cost him his own life on September 24, 1504 at the hands of a hired assassin paid by the heir to the lordship of Bologna.[44] Cocles' work seems to have been an important sales success, judging by the number of publications circulating today under his name, although they may have nothing to do with him. In 1510, the printer Johann Schönsperger published his first book in Augsburg under the title of *In disem biechlin wirt erfunden von Complexion der Menschen zu erlernen leiblich und menschlich natur ir sitten, geberden und naiglichait zu erkennen und urtaylen*. Although Cocles' name does not appear on the cover, nor in the prologue or in the colophon, the work is usually attributed to him.[45] As Duntze (2007, 134) rightly notes, this *Complexionsbüchlein* is not an extract of the *Chyromantie ac physionomie anastasis* but a compilation of the physiognomic theories of *Secretum secretorum* and those of Michael Scott, which were enormously successful in Germany. In 1530, the printer Christian Egenolf changed the title of the booklet and explicitly attributed it to Cocles: *Phisonomei. Eins jeden Menschen Art, Natur und Complexion aus Formierung und Gestalt des Angesichts, Glieder und allen geberden zu erlernen. Bartholomeus Coclitus von Bononien*. This publicity stunt explains the attribution of the text and has misled its readers until today. When Johann Albrecht, a printer in Strasbourg, translated the text from German into Latin, along with Egenolf's new foreword, it was a good idea to attribute the work to a doctor and philosopher to give it an air of seriousness. It also adds 15 engravings that illustrate the physiognomic part and that follow the same scheme as those used in the book by Ioannes ab Indagine.

Johann Albrecht's compilation was translated into French and published in 1546 with the same illustrations and under the title of *Le compendion et brief enseignement de physiognomie & chiromancie* (Paris, Pierre Drouard). The text was republished by the same printer only three years later, in 1550 and 1560, as well as on several other occasions in the 16th and 17th centuries.

A very different diffusion was to have the text that in 1521 the printer Johann Schott published in Strasbourg, the *Introductiones apotelesmaticae elegantes in chiromantiam, physionomiam, astrologiam naturalem* by Ioannes ab Indagine, reedited in 1522, 1531, 1534 and in 1541 with a larger number of engravings and, already in 1523, in a German translation with the same graphic material. The Latin text continued to be republished in the 16th century in Germany and also, and above all, in France. It was translated into French by Antoine de Moulin, editor and translator of Adamantius, in 1549. The illustrations in the Lyon edition were made by

---

44 Porter (2005, 155).
45 See Reißer (1997, 56–61), Reske (2007, 32).

the engraver of Jean de Tournes, Bernard Salomon (ca. 1508–ca. 1561), who was inspired – according to Sharratt (2005, 78) – by the Cocles editions. The first reprint of Indagine's publications in the 17th century was published in 1603 in Germany, in Oberursel to be precise, by the Lutheran printer Cornelius Sutor, together with the texts of two other problematic authors, Guglielmo Gratarolo and Pomponio Gaurico. Indagine's work was prohibited by the Spanish indexes of 1559 and 1583.[46] In the *Index Expurgatorius Hispanus* (1707) of Sarmiento y Valladares, Indagine is still listed as a first-class author.[47]

In the middle of the century some original, less known treatises on the meaning of the human body were also printed: *De cognitione hominis per aspectum* (Rome, Antonio Blado, 1544) by the physician Michelangelo Biondo, editor of Peter of Abano,[48] as well as a dialogue on *I Segni de la natura ne l'huomo* (Venice, Giovanni de Farri et fratelli, 1545)[49] by the physician Antonio Pellegrini, author of the Italian translation of the *Encomium Moriae* (Venice, Giovanni della Chiesa, 1539).,[50] A long chapter on physiognomy is also found in the onomantic

---

[46] Bujanda (1984, V, 394). The Index of 1583 prohibits all works by the German author, see Bujanda (1993, VI, 404); see for banning in the 17th and 18th centuries Bujanda & Richter (2016, 675).

[47] In the indexes of banned books, first-class authors, also called of *damnatae memoria*, are authors whose complete works are banned a priori. In the case of authors of scientific works this condemnation may be due to other publications of theirs, especially theological ones, see Pardo Tomás (1991, 118).

[48] There is a modern bilingual Latin-Italian edition by Rodler (1995). As the editor notes in her "Introduzione", Biondo's work was distinguished by a "costante volontà di riduzione divulgativa" (1995, 13) [constant desire for a reduction for the purpose of popularisation]. According to Wilson, Biondo's work is "a reflection on the social value of physiognomy and the moral questions that accompany external appearances" (2011, 181).

[49] See the concise summary in Wilson (2011, 181), who underscores that the text "brings together the dialogue format of courtesy books with the indexing of facial features, types, and emotions that characterises physiognomy treatises. On the first day, Alessandro Dolce encounters the English ambassador and the Spanish consul at Murano where they talk about affects and inclinations based on the body's disposition. They reconvene the second day at Dolce's house, when they are joined by other Venetians – a doctor, a philosopher, and a theologian – with whom they debate the signs of human nature. As Pellegrini explains at the beginning of the tract, the delight men take in learning about the differences between each other enables men to understand themselves".

[50] See Bennett, who notes regarding the relationship between the translation of Moria and the physiognomic study: "In *I Segni de la Natura* Pellegrini attempts to understand man before all other creatures because self-knowledge was recommended by the ancients [. . .] This study of physical and psychological features is not a surprising sequel to Pellegrini's translation of the *Moria* where he is most interested in the nature of man as fool" (1984, 41). Likewise, Seidel Menchi relates the dedication to occultism with Erasmism: "L'attaccamento ai libri di Erasmo

study by the Veronese doctor Annibale Raimondo (1505–1591). After the middle of the century, the Belgian musician, astrologer and mathematician Jean Taisnier (1508–1562) in 1562 published an extensive physiognomic and chiromantic work in Cologne, titled *Opus mathematicum octo libros complectens: innumeris propemodum figuris idealibus manuum et physiognomiae*. Several copies of the first edition of 1562 are preserved in Spain, two in the National Library of Madrid and another in the Marqués de Valdecilla Historical Library of the Complutense University (BH FLL 14738). This copy was expurgated by Friar Hieronymus Lucas de Alaejos, the senior librarian of the El Escorial Library, who was in charge of selling the duplicate books from the library of Philip II.[51] In spite of this evident censorial intervention in the book, Taisnier was not sanctioned in the Spanish indexes nor in the expurgatory of 1707. However, it was a dangerous book for its owners. In 1583, a certain Pedro Suárez de Mayorga, a supporter of chiromancy, was denounced in New Spain for his possession of the *Taisnerio*.[52]

The pre-Lavarian physiognomist par excellence[53] is the Neapolitan natural philosopher Giovanni Battista Della Porta (1535–1615),[54] renowned throughout Europe.[55] He is the author of several physiognomic studies, published in Latin and Italian, although his best known book is *Magia naturalis* (1558),[56] which is his only

---

si associa [. . .] alla lettura di opere di filosofia occulta, particolarmente al trattato *De occulta philosophia* di Agrippa di Nettesheim. Da questo punto di vista le vicende che illustreremo sono solo un campione di una casistica più vasta, nella quale rientrano per esempio il caso di Paolo Cataldi o la parabola di Antonio Pellegrini, traduttore dell'*Encomium moriae*, che proseguì la sua attività letteraria con un'opera di fisiognomica." (1987, 291) [The attachment to the books of Erasmus is associated . . . with the reading of works of occult philosophy, particularly the treatise *De occulta philosophia* by Agrippa of Nettesheim. From this point of view, the events we will illustrate are only a sample of a larger case history, which includes for example the case of Paolo Cataldi or the parable of Antonio Pellegrini, translator of the *Encomium moriae*, who continued his literary activity with a work of physiognomy.] For the translation of Erasmus in the European context see Ledo & Boer in their edition of the Spanish translation (2014, 11).

51 See Gernert (2014b) and (2018a).
52 See Jiménez Rueda (1946, 220–221) and Caro Baroja (1990, II, 300, footnote 21).
53 See Macdonald (2005, 397–414).
54 Regarding the influence of the scientific and cultural environment of Naples on Giovanni Battista and his brother, see Badaloni (1960).
55 Simon, who studies the methodology of the Neapolitan, characterises him as "ami de Giordano Bruno, inspirateur de Kepler en optique, lu par Descartes" (1980, 96) [friend of Giordano Bruno, Kepler's inspiration in optics, read by Descartes].
56 There are translations into Italian (1560), French (1565), Dutch (1566) and later also into German (1612) and English (1658); Balbiani (2001) and the collective volume edited by Zeller (2008). For the reception of the book in Spain see Rojo Vega (2008, 283).

publication sanctioned in Spain and included in the 1583 Quiroga index[57] as well as in the expurgatory of Valladares and Sarmiento (1707). In his own country, the Neapolitan philosopher had serious problems with the Inquisition. In the case of *De humana physiognomonia*[58] the desired imprimatur takes three years to arrive. When he finally published the book, in 1586, he added a paratext in which he defended himself against accusations of determinism. When Della Porta wanted to publish the Italian translation of the new version of *De humana physiognomia*, he had to turn to the influential Roman nobleman Federico Cesi, who got him permission from the Roman Inquisition in 1610.[59] This treatise, which gathers much of the previous physiognomic knowledge,[60] highlights in the text and illustrations the comparisons between human beings and animals.[61] Della Porta's method is

---

[57] In addition to the classic work of Reusch (1883–1885), the most recent publication of the Indexes by Bujanda is fundamental, particularly the volumes dedicated to the Spanish Inquisition (1984, V) and (1993, VI, 393–394 and 456). In spite of these condemnations we have evidence of the presence of the work in Spain.

[58] There is a critical edition of Paolella (2011) and (2013) that summarises in its introduction the complicated history of the publication of the Latin and Italian texts (XI–XXIV); see also the study by Verardi (2011a) and for the presence of classical poets in this work González Manjarrés (2010).

[59] See Piccari (2007, 43–44); for Della Porta's relations with Cesi, a founding member of the Accademia dei Lincei, see Gabrieli (1927).

[60] See Bouchet (1957, 20–21) and González Manjarrés (2016, 71); Basile (2016, 58) rightly speaks of the 'encyclopedic completeness' of the work.

[61] "La pretensión de Della Porta era confeccionar, con intención pedagógica, una suerte de manual que al tiempo sistematizase y sintetizase todos los conocimientos y métodos fisiognómicos que han ido acumulándose a lo largo de los siglos. Su lectura recuerda a un almanaque o collage compuesto de numerosos grabados y citas fisiognómicas, médicas, filosóficas, literarias y biográficas articuladas según un plan preciso and ordenadas bajo su criterio." (Lozano Pascual 2009, 209) [Della Porta's aim was to produce, with a pedagogical intention, a kind of manual that would systematise and synthesise all the knowledge and physiognomic methods that had been accumulated over the centuries. Its reading is reminiscent of an almanac or collage composed of numerous physiognomic, medical, philosophical, literary and biographical engravings and quotations articulated according to a precise plan and ordered according to his criteria]. See for the Pseudo-Aristotelian background of animal parallels Muratori (2017). González Manjarrés (2016) studies the 'critical notes' of Della Porta to the Pseudo-Aristotle while Vigh devotes himself to the "impostazione morale prevalentemente aristotelica nella descrizione dei vizi, delle virtù e dei comportamenti" (2016, 113) [predominantly Aristotelian moral approach in the description of vices, virtues and behaviour]. For authorship and sources of the illustrations see Paolella (2016) and for repeated use of the engravings Schmidt (2007, 286–287).

not based exclusively on bookish knowledge but makes use of empirical data and observation.[62] The merit of the Neapolitan consists in having separated physiognomy from astrology.[63] Despite problems of censorship, Della Porta's books were read throughout Europe in a large number of reprints until the second half of the 17th century.

It was possibly the success of the physiognomic work and the research by Giovanni Battista Della Porta which spurred the emergence of studies of bodily signs of various kinds that were published in the 80s and 90s of the 16th century, even after the bull *Coeli et Terrae Creator*, in which, in 1586, Pope Sixtus V prohibited the exercise of judicial astrology and other forms of divination.

The spread of physiognomic knowledge in the Iberian Peninsula was due, from the end of the 16th century until well into the 19th century, to one man of whom we know very little. I am referring to Jerónimo Cortés, author of a *Libro de phisonomia natural y varios secretos de naturaleza* (Valencia, Garriz, 1599).[64] This is the first physiognomic manual written directly in Spanish, although a large part of its materials come from Michael Scott; together with him, they are cited as sources in the prologue "Tisnerio [. . .] y Pedro de Ribas".

---

[62] See in this regard the study of the structure of the physiognomic sign in Della Porta of Caputo, who concludes: "In conclusione si può dire che la cultura, l'umanesimo, il neoplatonismo di Giovambattista Della Porta vengono filtrati tramite una *competenza* logica aristotelica che costituisce il sostrato del suo pensiero. Egli non è un logico ma uno scienziato la cui attività scientifica à consona alle nuove esigenze sociali, antiaccademica, antiaristocratica, antidogmatica per scoprire quale sia il fondamento naturale dei fenomeni osservati e raccontati" (1982, 102) [In conclusion, it can be said that Giovambattista Della Porta's culture, humanism and Neoplatonism are filtered through an Aristotelian logical *competence* that constitutes the substratum of his thought. He is not a logician but a scientist whose scientific activity is consonant with the new social, anti-academic, anti-aristocratic, anti-dogmatic needs in order to discover the natural foundation of the observed and narrated phenomena].

[63] Trabucco (2002, 47). Verardi (2008, 83) explains this decision with the Papal Bulls against divinatory practices: "Contribuiscono, poi, alla trasformazione della disciplina fisiognomica anche alcuni eventi storici, ultimo fra tutti la presa di distanza di Sisto V dalle pratiche astrologiche, che spinsero il più grande fisionomo del Rinascimento, Giovanni Battista Della Porta, a liberare la proprio filosofia da qualsiasi residuo astrologico." [Some historical events also contributed to the transformation of the discipline of physiognomy, the most recent of which was the distancing of Sixtus V from astrological practices, which pushed the greatest Renaissance physiognomist, Giovanni Battista Della Porta, to free his philosophy from any astrological residue].

[64] ee the electronic edition curated by Saguar, which provides readers with a database of all the editions and the copies preserved in each of them: http://hispanistik.uni-trier.de/v-machine/JeronimoCortes/FisonomiaNatural.xml (visited on 14.6.2020).

In Spain there is also evidence of a *Historia de animales y phisiognomia* by a certain Luis Fernández, a physician from Carrión de los Condes, dedicated to the Marquise of Frómista. This 16th century text, still unpublished, obtained the license to be printed in 1591.[65]

In the first half of the 17th century, a large number of reprints of previous physiognomic studies appeared, mainly by Jerónimo Cortés, but also, although to a lesser extent, by Girolamo Manfredi (1600, 1607, 1629), Johannes ab Indagine (in Latin and French translation 1603, 1604, 1621, 1622, 1638) and Giovanni Battista Della Porta, together with those of lesser-known authors such as Antonio Pellegrini (1622). But in addition to the reprints, which testify to the great interest in the subject, new texts continue to appear, which in many cases are presented, from the very title, as continuations of Aristotelian principles. While in Italy, France and Germany a multitude of very different texts are printed, in Spain, after Cortés, only one other treatise, *El sol solo y para todos sol de la Filosofía sagaz y anatomía de ingenios* by Esteban Pujasol was published.[66] We have little news about this Aragonese priest, a native of Fraga, who was attracted by the subject in spite of its delicate nature for the ecclesiastical authorities. Pujasol's physiognomic work, which researchers often relate to the *Examen de ingenios* of Huarte de San Juan,[67] is in part a reduction of Della Porta as Cardoner (1971, 90) has shown.

After the 1660s, no new physiognomic studies were published, but the works of Cocles (1679, 1698, 1700), Indagine (1662, 1663, 1672, 1682), Della Porta (1668, 1677) and Cortés (1662, 1664, 1675, 1680, 1681, 1689, 1695, 1701)[68] were still being reprinted, in addition to the reissues of the texts from the first half of the century. Courtine insists on the continuity of the physiognomic treatises of the first half of the 17th century with the previous tradition:

> Jusqu'aux années 1660 environ se multiplient les traités qui reprennent imperturbablement les mêmes leçons antiques, accompagnés de nombreuses 'métoposcopies', ces traités de divination astrologique qui vont offrir aux lecteurs de l'âge classique des interprétations des marques gravées par les planètes sur le front des humains. C'est dire que la tradition physiognomonique est dominée dans les deux premiers tiers du XVIIe

---

[65] The manuscript is preserved in the Library of Menéndez Pelayo (sign M. 243) Riandière La Roche (1990), who provides a detailed description of the content, promising an edition of the text, which, however, has not yet been published.

[66] There is a modern edition (1980) with a brief introduction and another facsimile edition (2000) without paratext.

[67] See Ibarz (1991) and Ricarte Bescós (2008, 58–60).

[68] For a complete list of the editions of Cortés' book, see the electronic edition of Saguar: http://hispanistik.uni-trier.de/v-machine/JeronimoCortes/FisonomiaNatural.xml (visited on 14.6.2020).

siècle par une pensée et une perception analogique du corps humain, conforme aux théories des signatures héritées des philosophies de la nature du moyen âge et de la renaissance. (1995, 50)

[Until about the 1660s, treaties multiplied, which invariably repeated the same ancient lessons, accompanied by numerous 'metoposcopies', those astrological divination treatises that would offer readers of the classical age interpretations of the marks engraved by the planets on the foreheads of humans. In other words, the physiognomic tradition was dominated in the first two thirds of the 17th century by an analogical thought and perception of the human body, in line with the signature theories inherited from the nature philosophies of the Middle Ages and the Renaissance.]

According to Porter, physiognomy ceased to be a form of knowledge at this time and became more and more "simply a laughable, if amusing, game" (2005, 18). For Wilson this "ludic turn might be understood as a symptom of anxiety wrought by the double bind of the politics of faciality, of the need for faces to conform on the one hand, and their failure, on the other, to be meaningful any longer" (2011, 187).

3 The interpretation of the hand

Chiromancy and metoposcopy are disciplines closely linked to physiognomy and therefore there are many treatises dealing with both disciplines.[69] It is therefore not surprising that, in printed transmission, physiognomy shared spaces and readers with palmistry, metoposcopy and other divinatory arts such as judicial astrology, geomancy or onirocriticism, among many others. Since Alessandro Achillini (*De Chyromantiae principiis et physionomiae*, 1503) and Bartolomeo della Rocca, "Cocles" (*Chyromantie ac physionomie anastasis*) the convergence of both semiotic practices is highlighted in the title of the publications as is the case in the texts of Ioannes ab Indagine (*Introductiones apotelesmaticae elegantes in chiromantiam, physionomiam, astrologiam naturalem*, 1521) and Jean Taisnier (*Opus mathematicum octo libros complectens: innumeris propemodum figuris idealibus manuum et physiognomiae*, 1562) in the 16th century. In the following century, Christian Moldenarius, Jean Belot (*Instruction familière et très facile pour apprendre les sciences de chiromance & phisiognomie*, 1619) and Sieur de Peruchio (*La chiromance, la physiognomie et la geomance*, 1657) continued along this path; other authors, however, preferred to keep them separate, as for example Cureau de la

---

[69] See Poma (2010, 118).

Chambre, who published two single treatises containing chiromantic (*Discours sur les principes de la chiromance*, 1653) and physiognomic (*L'Art de connoistre les hommes*, 1659) reflections.

Palmreading, like physiognomy, had been known since classical antiquity,[70] although it does not seem to have been very widespread and important.[71] An observation by Aristotle in his *Historia animalium* I.12.493b32 about the meaning of the lines of the hand "added a certain respectability to the subject" (Burnett 1987, 192).[72] Although no classical treatise has survived, early medieval palmistry relies on the authority of the Stagirite.

> In Latin the earliest separate treatment of chiromancy as a distinct subject, art or science, appears to have been in translation from the Arabic – albeit somewhat dubiously – ascribed to Adelard of Bath and John of Seville of the twelfth century. In both cases Aristotle is sometimes named as the original author. (Thorndike 1965, 674)[73]

The oldest recorded text is found in the so-called Eadwine Psalter of the 12th century;[74] around that same time we find the first references to palmistry[75] in the *De*

---

[70] Burnett (1987, 192) mentions references in Artemidorus, Pollux and Suidas. Rapisarda notes, conversely, in the "Introduzione" in Rapisarda & Piccione (2005, 20): "Non c'è alcuna prova che la cultura classica abbia praticato, almeno in forma sistematica, questa tecnica divinatoria e nessuna menzione se ne ritrova, nell'Occidente latino, in testi che siano anteriori al 1150. È nella cultura tardo-greca, imperiale e bizantina, che se ne cominciano a trovare occasionali citazioni, come in Artemidoro, in Polluce (II secolo d. C.) e nel lessico Suda (X secolo d. C.), insieme a qualche frammento papiraceo di testo scritto" [There is no evidence that classical culture has practised, at least in a systematic way, this divinatory technique and no mention of it can be found, in the Latin West, in texts dating back to before 1150. It is in the late Greek, imperial and Byzantine culture that occasional references to it are beginning to be found, as in Artemidorus, Pollux (2nd century A.D.) and in the lexicographer Suidas (10th century A.D.), together with a few papyrus fragments of written text]. See also Tuczay (2012, 101) and Castelli (2006, 495–496).

[71] Palmistry is not listed among the practices that Cicero refutes in *De divinatione*, see the Latin edition with German translation by Schäublin (1991) and the Spanish edition by Escobar (1999) with the respective paratexts.

[72] See Rapisarda in the "Introduzione" in Rapisarda & Piccione (2005, 15).

[73] See for the authorship of medieval chiromancy and the attributions to Aristotle Pack (1969, 189), Schmitt & Knox (1985, 21–24) and Rapisarda in the "Introduzione" in Rapisarda & Piccione (2005, 23–24) as well as Fürbeth's (2003, 103) observations. See also Sabattini's (1946) catalogue of chiromantic works.

[74] The text was published by Burnett (1987) and with an Italian translation by Rapisarda & Piccione (2005, 61–76); see Rapisarda in the "Introduzione" in Rapisarda & Piccione (2005, 22–23) and the studies on this psalter published by Gibson, Heslop & Pfaff (1992).

[75] Fürbeth (2003, 101).

divisione philosophiae (ca. 1145) by Dominicus Gundissalinus (ca. 1115–post 1190)[76] and in the *Policraticus* (ca. 1159) by John of Salisbury (1115–1180), which defines palmists as those who by a reading of the lines of the hand predict unknown events. Even Thomas of Canterbury (1118–1170) could not escape temptation and was probably one of the first famous clients of these soothsayers.[77]

In the Middle Ages there was a whole series of treatises on the art of interpreting the lines of the hand that have been published in our time by Rapisardi and Piccione (2005).[78] As is usual in all disciplines at the beginning of the modern world, the knowledge previously written in manuscript was transmitted by the printing press; as a matter of fact, some of the medieval chiromantic manuals were already published in the period of incunabula in Germany and Italy, with engravings that show the different lines and mountains of the hand. The most successful 15th century chiromantic manual outside its country of origin was that of Andrea Corvo de Mirandola. Its spread at the beginning of the 16th century is documented by very early translations into French, German, Italian and Spanish.[79] On occasion, Corvo's handbook on palm reading was printed together with the chiromantic and physiognomic texts attributed to Bartolomeo della Rocca. The work of Cocles, which combined in print the studies on physiognomy and palmistry for the first time were commented by Patrizio Tricasso Cerasari in a treatise that was published almost simultaneously in Latin and Italian (*Super Chyromantiam Coclytis dillucidationes* and *Expositione del Tricasso Mantuano sopra il Cocle*, both Venice, Elisabetta Rusconi, 1525). Tricasso had previously gained a reputation as a palmist with a treatise that was still sold in French translation still in the 17th century. The presence of Patrizio Tricasso da Cerasari in Spain and the problematic status of the author is documented thanks to the spectacular discovery of the hidden books in Barcarrota;[80] in the walled-in hideout two of his chiromantic publications were found, one in Latin and the other in Italian,[81] which must have been considered by their owner to be just as

---

76 See the chapter *De astronomia*, in which Dominicus Gundissalinus speaks of various divinatory arts, *De divisione philosophiae*, ed. Fidora (2007, 228), studied by Agrimi (2002, 5 and nota 8); see regarding Gundissalinus and science Fidora (2003, Spanish translation 2009, 108 for palm reading), (2011) and (2013).
77 See Rapisarda in the "Introduzione" in Rapisarda & Piccione (2005, 11), Boudet (2006, 100–101) and Castelli (2006, 496).
78 See Pack (1969), (1972), Pack & Hamilton (1971) and Burnett (1987).
79 The Spanish text was edited by de Páiz Hernández (2006).
80 See Gernert (2014b, 105–106) and, on the question of whether the owner of the library was a converted Jewish bookseller or physician, Rico (2000) and Serrano Mangas (2004) and (2007).
81 See Lama (2007), Sánchez Salor (1999 and 2007), Gernert (2014b) and the edition of the text by Sánchez Salor & Ruiz García (2000).

compromising as the work of Erasmus or the obscene *Cazzaria*. However, the Spanish indexes did not explicitly forbid Tricasso's chiromantic studies, which were, nevertheless, condemned by the Roman indices of 1559 and 1596.[82]

Another specialist in chiromancy and divinatory arts of the 15th century was Antioco Tiberto. The author, a practising palmist, was executed by Pandolfo Malatesta because he had predicted him exile and poverty.[83] His only known book is the *Chiromantia* (Bologna, Benedetto Faelli, 1494) which was republished twice by Johannes Dryander (i.e. Juan Enzinas) with dedications to the jurist Johannes Furderer von Richtenfels and the archbishop of Mainz Albrecht von Brandenburg (1490–1545), one of Luther's most popular antagonists.

In Italy we also find the physician and philosopher Galeotto Marzio da Narni (ca. 1425–ca. 1494),[84] author of a *Chiromantia perfecta*, written around 1490. In this treatise, he tries to invalidate the criticism of St Thomas' chiromancy by arguing that the art of reading in the lines of the hand is part of physiognomy.[85] Moreover, he bases palmistry conceptually on a theory reminiscent of the Paracelsus concept of signatures that allows one to deduce the value of things from their external appearance.[86] This interesting small publication, which was possibly only the beginning of a larger project,[87] was not printed until the 20th century and went rather unnoticed despite Marzio da Narni's considerable reputation as a physiognomist.[88]

Giovanni Battista Della Porta, the most emblematic author of physiognomic studies, also devoted himself to metoposcopy and chiromancy, but both studies were published only posthumously, in 1677, both in a loose edition and as an appendix to *Magia naturalis*. Poma (2010, 118–119) dates the drafting of the chiromantic treatise between 1603 and 1608. Thanks to the correspondence with Federico Cesi, we know that between 1608 and 1610, Della Porta had put a lot of effort, although without success, into seeing his short book published.[89] However, the founder of the Accademia dei Lincei was careful to preserve the unpublished

---

[82] Bujanda (1996, X, 387).
[83] In fact, the lord of Rimini died in exile in Rome after being thrown out of his signoria in 1503 by Cesare Borgia according to Paolo Giovio in his *Elogia* (1972, 79–80).
[84] See Briggs (1974, 75), Vasoli (1977), *Galeotto Marzio e l'umanesimo italiano ed europeo* (1983), Porter (2005, 13), Miggiano (2008), Federici Vescovini (2011, 97–98).
[85] See Castelli (2006, 502–503).
[86] See D'Alessandro (1994, 168).
[87] See D'Alessandro (1994, 166).
[88] See Frezza (1951, LIII–LIV) in his edition of Marzio da Narni's *Chiromanzia*.
[89] See for details the introduction to the edition of Trabucco (2003, XI–XIII) and Verardi (2011b, 51).

manuscripts of his friend with the intention of publishing them as soon as possible. Another *linceo*, Francesco Stelluti, promised in the prologue of his synoptic edition of *Della fisionomia di tutto il corpo umano di Signor Giovanni Battista Della Porta ora brevemente in tavole sinottiche ridotta* (Roma, Vitale Mascardi, 1637) a reprint of this book, with more illustrations, which would be accompanied by "un curioso trattato della mano dell'uomo paragonata alli piedi d'alcuni animali quadrupedi, e di uccelli" (1637, without pagination) [a curious treatise of the hand of man compared to the feet of some quadruped animals, and birds]. It was finally Pompeo Sarnelli, the publisher of *Magia naturale* in Italian, who – within the framework of "un nuovo programma di recupero dell'opera del filosofo napoletano" (Trabucco in his introduction to Della Porta 2003, XIX) [a new program to salvage the work of the Neapolitan philosopher] – published the treatise on palmistry. Sarnelli also wrote a *Proemio* in which he insisted on the scientific status of palmistry and its legality, relying on the authority of Martin del Rio.[90] Della Porta himself complained in his prologue about the circulation of "scritti d'ignoranti ciurmatori, come di Tricassio et Andrea Corvo, che erano impostori e saltimbanca"[91] [The writings of ignorant charlatans, as of Tricassio and Andrea Corvo, who were impostors and tricksters]. In his own work, the Neapolitan scholar tries to guarantee the validity of palm reading by subordinating it to the theoretical principles of physiognomy.[92] Della Porta himself describes his empirical methodology in his *Proemio* with all the gruesome details:

> Et acciò che havessi abbondanza degli huomini sopra accennati, convenni col boia napolitano, ch'era all'hora un certo, nominato Antonello Cocozza, che quando egli deponeva dalle forche gli appiccati, e gli portava al Ponte Ricciardo [. . .] mi avisasse l'hora di quella trasportatione. Et io, andando a quel luogo, osservava le dispositioni delle mani e de' piedi, e quelle disegnava con uno stilo nelle carte a ciò destinate, oppure con il gesso ne formava i lor cavi, acciò che buttandovi doppo la cera ne havessi in casa i lineamenti, e da ciò havessi campo di studiarvi la notte in casa e di conferirli con gl'altri; e conferiti

---

90 See the "Proemio di Pompeo Sarnelli", in Della Porta, ed. Trabucco (2003, 83): "Ella è la chiromantia una scienza, la quale, per mezzo delle linee della mano, dà chiarissimo inditio del temperamento e complessione di ciascheduno, e da questo si viene ad indagare con qualche probabilità la lunghezza o brevità della vita, e le inchinationi dell'anima." [Chiromancy is a science, which, by means of the lines of the hand, gives a very clear indication of the temperament and complexion of any one, and from this comes to induce with some probability the length or shortness of life, and the inclinations of the soul].
91 "Proemio dell'autore", Della Porta, ed. Trabucco (2003, 90). See also Poma (2010, 119).
92 See Poma (2010, 118)
   See Trabucco (1995, 283–284) and Verardi (2011b, 55).

insieme i segni ne cavassi la verità, facendo sempre l'istesso, fin a tanto, che trovassi tutti i segni, che dinotano tal'uno dover essere sospeso; e così sodisfacessi a me stesso. [93]

[And so that I might have an abundance of the men mentioned above, I agreed with the executioner of Naples, who was then a certain Antonello Cocozza, who, when he took the bodies down from the gallows, and brought them to Ponte Ricciardo [. . .] gave me the time of that transport. And I, going to that place, observed the dispositions of their hands and feet, and drew them with a stylus on the papers intended for that purpose, or I formed with plaster their shape, so that by throwing them in the wax afterwards I could have their features at home, and from that I could study them at night and compare them with others; and, putting all the signs together, I could find out the truth, and doing the same till I could find all the signs, that show that someone is to be hanged; and so I satisfied myself.]

This description recalls the activities of the women of Celestina's lineage and shows that certain scientific practices were still relegated to a marginalised world, as was the case in Fernando de Rojas' time with anatomical studies.

The Italian philosopher and poet Tommaso Campanella (1568–1639) wrote, during his Parisian exile, a chiromantic treatise at the behest of none other than Cardinal Richelieu. As Ernst remarked, in France, "Campanella was appreciated in court circles for his astrological knowledge and understanding of the occult" (2010, 261),[94] although his *Chiroscopia* is an unoriginal work, inspired in part by the *Anastasis chiromantica* of Cocles.[95] Later, in the chapter "De signis" of his *Dialectica*, one of the five parts of the *Philosophia rationalis*, written between 1613–1619 and published in 1638, Campanella develops a semiotic theory that distinguishes between natural and artificial signs. According to Delumeau "il était persuadé que certains signes 'naturels' dans les astres, sur terres ou dans l'homme permettent en quelque façon de présager l'avenir" (2008, 259–260) [he was convinced that certain "natural" signs in the stars, on the earth or in man are in some way a harbinger of the future]. Likewise, in his *Metaphysica* (1623) the author of *La città del sole* (1602) dedicates articles II–VI of chapter XI of book XVI to the divinatory arts and defends the legality and veracity of palmistry and physiognomy, citing Aristotle and Della Porta.[96]

---

93 "Proemio dell'autore", Della Porta, ed. Trabucco (2003, 91–92). See about this anecdote Ernst (1995, 89) and Muratori (2017, 2).
94 Campanella went into exile in France in 1634 after several problems with the Roman Inquisition. See for his stay in the French capital Ernst (1995) and (2010, 243–266).
95 See Ernst (1995, 89).
96 Campanella, *Dalla metaphysica*, ed. Ernst (2007, 37); see also the editor's introduction (XV–XVIII). Also in the *Del senso delle cose e della magica* Campanella cites the Pseudo-Aristotelian physiognomic manual, ed. Bruers (1925, 158).

In France, two short chiromantic books were published in the 1660s: *La science curieuse ou traité de la chyromance* (Paris, François Clousier, 1665, 1667 and 1675), an anonymous text that is partly a translation of the Latin work of Jean Taisnier, and partly of an obscure character called Adrien Sicler, who styles himself "médecin spagyrique" [spagyric doctor].

Throughout the 15th, 16th and 17th centuries, palmistry was a scientific practice to which renowned scholars devoted themselves. We do not only know of humanists who wrote about palm reading, but we even know that they put it into practice. The German humanist Joachim Camerarius (1500–1574) relates an episode about a palm reader who had seen in the hand of a young, healthy girl that she would die within eight days. The prognosis would have been verified after one week as he had been told by no lesser man than another humanist, Willibald Pirckheimer (1470–1530).[97]

3.1 Palmistry marginalised: the gipsies

Although palmistry is considered a scientific practice, worthy of the dedication of scholars, it is usually associated with the marginalised world of the gipsies since this people arrived in Europe at the beginning of the 15th century, supposedly from Egypt.[98] The *Journal d'un bourgeois de Paris* provides detailed information on the arrival of the gipsies in France in 1427:

> Brief, ce estoient les plus povres creatures que on vit oncques venir en France de aage de homme. Et neantmoins leur povreté, en la compaignie avoit sorcieres qui regardoient es mains des gens et disoient ce que advenu leur estoit ou à advenir, et mirent contans en plusieurs mariaiges, car elles disoient (au mari): *Ta femme (ta femme t'a fait) coux*, ou à la femme: *ton mari t'a fait coulpe*. Et qui pis estoit, en parlant aux creatures, par art magique, ou autrement, ou par l'ennemy d'enfer, ou par entregent d'abilité faisoient vuyder les bourses aux gens, et le mettoient en leur bourse, comme on disoit.[99]

> In short, they were the poorest creatures that have been seen coming to France since time immemorial. And despite their poverty, there were witches in the group who read in the hands of the people and told them what had happened in the past and what would happen in the future. And they stirred up strife among several married couples: for they said (to the husband), *Thy wife hath made thee a cuckold*, and to the wife, *Thy husband hath*

---

97 See Gernert (2013c, 46).
98 See for the history of the gipsies and their arrival in Europe Leblon (1985), Gómez Vozmediano (2005), Aguirre Felipe (2008) and Rheinheimer (2009, 159–167) and for the magical practices of the gipsies Leland (1962).
99 Tuetey (1881, 220).

deceived thee. And what was worse, talking to those creatures, by magic art, or otherwise, or with help of the enemy of hell, or by skill, they made people have their purses emptied, and put it in their purses, as they say.

The anonymous chronicler also reports on the reaction of the church authorities to these divinatory practices carried out by the bohemians and the sanctions against their clients.[100] The German physician Johann Hartlieb (ca. 1400–1468) associates in chapter 103 ("Von den zygeinern, wie sy die ainvaltigen laichen" [About the gipsies aand how they betray the simpletons]) of his anti-superstitious treatise *Das puch aller verpoten kunst* ("The book of all forbidden arts") chiromancy with the gipsies.[101] Throughout the 16th and 17th centuries there is a lot of documentation about the gipsies[102] and especially the palmreading gipsy women.[103] Tomaso Garzoni observes in his *Piazza universale* (1585):

> E oggidì è tanto avilita quest'arte ch'i cingari soli [. . .] attendono a quella, dando, con spasso e trastullo del mondo, buona ventura a tutti, guardando su la mano, e dicendo mille novelle alle paparote massimamente, non con minor falsità che gioco, essendo da tutti stimata una professione ridicola ed erronea da dovero.[104]

> [And today this art is so humbled that only the gipsies are practising it, awarding, to the joy and amusement of the world, good fortune to all, looking up one's hand, and saying a thousand novelties to the utmost stupid, with no less falsehood than play, being esteemed by all as a ridiculous and erroneous profession in truth.]

Anti-superstitious writers such as Martín del Río or Juan de Horozco y Covarrubias condemn chiromancy as a deceitful art, invented by the gipsies. In Spain, during the first half of the 17th century, treaties against the gipsies were

---

100 "Et vrayement, je and fu III ou IIII foys pour parler à eulx, mais oncques ne m'aperceu d'ung denier de perte, ne les vy regarder en main, mais ainsi le disoit le peuple partout, tant que la nouvelle en vint à l'evesque de Paris, lequel and alla et mena avecques lui ung frere meneur, nommé le Petit Jacobin, lequel par le commandement de l'evesque fist là une belle predicacion en excommuniant tous ceulx et celles qui se faisoient et qui avoient creu et monstré leurs mains", Tuetey (1881, 220–221) [And truly, I went there three or four times to speak to them, but I did not lose a penny, nor did I see them looking at people's hands, but thus said the people everywhere. When the news came to the bishop of Paris, he went there and took with him a Friar Minor, called Petit Jacobin, who by the bishop's command made a beautiful sermon there, excommunicating all those who have shown their hands and believed what they were told].
101 Hartlieb, *Das Buch der verbotenen Künste*, ed. Eisermann & Graf (1998, 170).
102 See in this regard Caro Baroja (1993, 17), Solms (2008, 51–62) and Tuczay (2012, 80–82).
103 See Predari (1841, 102), Gutiérrez Nieto (1993, 997), Aguirre Felipe (2009, 86–87), and Castelli (2006, 506–510).
104 Garzoni, *La piazza universale di tutte le professioni del mondo*, ed. Cherchi and Collina (1996, 676).

published, such as the discourse entitled *Expulsión de los gitanos* (1619) by Sancho de Moncada or the *Discurso contra los gitanos* (1631) by Juan de Quiñones, which reiterated the censure of predicting good fortune.

Chiromancy as a divinatory art practised by gipsies is a well-established literary motif. One of the most famous readers of the lines of the hand in Spanish literature is perhaps the protagonist of Cervantes' exemplary novel *La Gitanilla*.

Chapter 2
Dramatic readings of the hand and the body in the theatre of the 16th century

1 The Italian model

Amongst the various occult arts, palmistry lends itself particularly well to be put on stage. One should remember that Ludovico Ariosto opens one of his first plays, *I suppositi* (1509), with a scene in which Pasifilio, a scrounger, pretends to be a palmist in order to be invited for dinner[1] by the ancient Cleandro:

PASIFILO. [. . .] Lasciami vedere la mano.

CLEANDRO. Sei tu chiromante?

PASIFILO. Chi ne fa maggior professione di me? Mostramela di grazia. O bella e netta linea, non ne vidi un'altra mai così lunga: tu camperai più che Melchisedech.

CLEANDRO. Tu vuoi dir Matusalem.

PASIFILO. Io credevo che fussi tutto uno.

CLEANDRO. Tu sei poco dotto ne la Bibia.

PASIFILO. Anzi dottissimo, ma in quella che sta ne la botte. Oh, come è buono questo monte di Venere! Ma non siamo in loco commodo: vogliotela vedere un'altra matina ad agio, e ti farò intendere cose che ti piaceranno.

CLEANDRO. Tu mi farai cosa gratissima.[2]

[PASIFILIO: Let me see your hand.

CLEANDRO: Are you a palmist?

PASIFILIO: Who should make a better job of it than me? Be so good as to show it to me. Oh, what a beautiful and straight line! I've never seen one as long as this. You will live longer than Melchizedek.

CLEANDRO: You mean Methuselah.

PASIFILIO: I thought it was all the same.

---

1 On this aspect, also see Paques (1971, 75)
2 *I suppositi in prosa*, I, 2, ed. Gareffi (2007, 287).

CLEANDRO: You aren't very learned in Biblical matters.

PASIFILO: Quite learned, but in that Bible which comes out of the barrel. Oh, how beautiful this Venus mount is! But we are not in a very pleasant place. I want to show it to you at your leisure some other day, and I will make you see things which you will relish.

CLEANDRO: That will be very agreeable.]

Ariosto maintains this scene in the versified form of the comedy which he wrote between 1528 and 1531.[3] Other dramatic authors like the physician Agostino Ricci (1512–1564) were inspired by Ariosto. In his comedy *I tre tiranni* (1530)[4] it is not the bawdy procuress Artemona who reads the hand of the old Girifalco but, again, a scrounger, Listagiro, who does so at the instigation of this friend Pilastrino.

PILASTRINO. [. . .] E, perché veda
ora qualcosa, mostrali la mano.
Guarda, maestro Abraham.

LISTAGIRO. Per contentarvi.

---

3 *I suppositi in versi*, I, 2 ed. Gareffi (2007, 357–358, vv. 192–206): "PASIFILO: [. . .] Mostratemi la man. CLEANDRO: Sei tu, Pasifilo, / Buon chiromante? PASIFILO: Io ci ho pur qualche pratica. / Deh, lasciatemi un po' vedervela. CLEANDRO: Eccola. / PASIFILO: O che bella, che lunga e netta linea! / Non vidi mai la miglior. Oltra il termine / Vi veggo di Melchisedech aggiungere. / CLEANDRO: Matusalem vuoi dir? PASIFILO: Non è un medesimo? / CLEANDRO: O come sei mal dotto nella Bibia! / PASIFILO: Anzi dotto ci son, ma ne la bibia / Ch'esce fuor della botte. Ve' bellissimi / Segni ch'avete nel monte di Venere! / Ma questo luogo non è molto comodo: / Io voglio un'altra mattina vedervela / Ad agio, e farvi alcune cose intendere / Che non vi spiaceran. CLEANDRO: L'avrò gratissimo". [PASIFILO: . . . Show me your hand. CLEANDRO: Are you a good palmist, Pasifilo? PASIFILO: I've got some practice at it. Oh, just let me look at her a little bit. CLEANDRO: Here she is. / PASIFILO: Oh, what a beautiful and straight line! I've never seen a better one. Beyond the term, I see you reach Melchizedek. / CLEANDRO: You mean Methuselah. PASIFILO: I thought it was all the same. / CLEANDRO: You aren't very learned in Biblical matters. PASIFILO: On the contrary, I am quite learned, / but in that Bible which comes out of the barrel. How beautiful are the signs You have in Venus mount! / But we are not in a very pleasant place. I want to to look at her / at your leisure some other morning, and I will make you see things / which you will relish. CLEANDRO: I'll be very grateful.]

4 The comedy "fu rappresentata in Bologna il 4 marzo 1530, ottavo giorno dall'incoronazione dell'imperatore che, per celebrare quella giornata, assunse il ruolo di generoso anfitrione e si pose di nuovo al centro di una esteriorità spettacolare" (Gallo in the introduction to his edition of *I tre tiranne* 1998, xxi) [was put on stage in Bologna on the 4th of March 1530, on the eighth day of the coronation of the new emperor, who, in order to celebrate that day, took on the role of the generous host and put himself once again at the centre of an ostentatious spectacle]; on this aspect, also see Ferrer Valls (1991, 60) and the introduction by Cortijo Ocaña in his edition of the Latin translation of the *Suppositi* by Juan Pérez (2001, 28)

GIRIFALCO. Ecco. Guarda, maestro, se a' tuoi giorni
vedesti man sí bella e dilicata,
colorita e ben fatta.

LISTAGIRO. Bella, bella,
se Dio mi guardi. Tu non debbi molto
curarla con saponi ed acqua fresca,
per ordinario. [. . .]

LISTAGIRO. Ho veduto a la prima.
Oh bella vita! oh bei monti! oh begli anguli!
oh che bei segni! oh! gran particolari
v'è da vedere! Io, per me, mai non vidi
la più felice man. Guarda, messere.
Non voglio far come che sogliono certi
che dicon mille cose, poi fra tutte
non si ricoglie un vero. Io sempre dico
qualche particolar che sia notabile
e lascio le lunghezze [. . .]

PILASTRINO. Orsú! Incomincia.

LISTAGIRO. Prima, per quello che si può vedere,
hai una vita lunga più che n'abbi
altra visto già mai. Viverai tanto
che, per vecchiezza, debbi andar carpone
per terra con le mani e verrai sordo,
orbo ed attratto: ma v'è tempo ancora
più d'ottant'anni. [. . .]
Ancor non penso
ch'abbi figliuoli; ma, in fra poco tempo,
ti se n'aspetta (per quello che mostrano
quelle linee che vedi in fra quei monti
che fan duo stelle) duo maschi a la fila,
perché si fa la congiunzion di Giove
ne la casa di Venus.[5]

---

5 Ricchi, *I tre tiranni* II, 3, ed. Gallo (1998, 47–49, vv. 212–280). On this aspect, also see Paques (1971, 76) and Gallo in the introduction to his edition of *I tre tiranni* (1998, XXXVIII): "Un'ampia estensione è occupata dalla scena in cui agiscono Pilastrino, Girifalco e Listagiro [. . .] questi, che peraltro è un parassita qualunque, sostiene il ruolo del chiromante, per sottoporre Girifalco a una caricata derisione: Girifalco è in apparenza elogiato e apprezzato per i suoi pregi e per la sua felice futura sorte fino all'assurdo più incredibile, di modo che le frasi, che suonano in senso positivo alle orecchie del vecchio per la sua dabbenaggine, assumono un significato per lui pesantemente sfavorevole dinanzi al pubblico". [An ample extension involved in the scene in which Pilastrino, Girifalco e Listagiro are on stage . . ., the latter, who is no more than a common scrounger, sustains his role of palmist by making Girifalco the butt of a derisive

[PILASTRINO: . . . And, for you to see something now, show them your hand. Look, master Abraham.

LISTAGIRO: To satisfy you.

GIRIFALCO: Here. Look, master, have you in your days seen such a fine and delicate, such a colourful and well-designed hand?

LISTAGIRO: Fine, fine indeed, by God / in the name of God. You probably don't usually wash them with soap and water.

LISTAGIRO: . . . I saw it at once. Oh, precious life! Oh, precious mountains! Oh, precious angles! Oh, precious signs! Great particularities can be seen here! I, for one, have not yet seen a more fortunate man's hand. Look, master! I do not want to act like others who say thousands of things, and not one of them is true in the end. I always speak of one notable thing, of one special thing, and spare myself lengthy explanations. . . .

PILASTRINO: Come now, begin!

LISTAGIRO: To begin with, a long life is ahead of you, longer than has yet been heard of. You will live so long that you, for old age, will have to crawl along the ground with your hands, and you will go deaf and blind and wrinkled; but there's still 80 years to go . . . It seems to me you have no offspring yet but in due time (as those lines show which you can see there amongst these mountains in the form of two stars) you will have two male offspring in a row because we will see the conjugation of Jupiter in the house of Venus.]

As compared to Ariosto, Ricci makes much more use of the comic possibilities the reading of the hand on stage offers. With Ariosto, a scenic model is established – the impostor who pretends to be a palmist in order to fool a guileless old man[6] – which was to have continuity in Spanish theatre.[7]

---

caricature: Girifalco is seemingly praised and appreciated, up to an absurd degree, so that the phrases which, thanks to his gullibility, sound favourable to the old man's ears, assume a heavily unfavourable meaning for the audience].
6 Speaking of a woman in love, the necromancer Ruffo says: "e la causa, perché essa dell'opera mia mi richiede, è perché, buttando de figure e punti e avendo pure ben la chiromanzia, tra le donne, che credule sono, ho fama d'essere un nobil negromante" (Dovizi di Bibbiena: *La Calandria* II, 3, ed. Téoli, 1974, 25) [and the reason why she demands my labour is because, drafting the shapes and the points and mastering palmistry well, I am, amongst women, who are credulous, renowned to be a noble necromancer].
7 On the influence of Ariosto's theatre in Spain see Portnoy (1932, 129–212) and the introduction by Cortijo Ocaña to his edition of the Latin translation of the *Suppositi* by Juan Pérez (2001, 14).

I suppositi is put on stage in Valladolid in 1548 on the occasion of the wedding of Archduke Maximilian of Austria with the infant María, a sister of Philip II. The chronicler Juan Cristóbal Calvete de Estrella gives this account of the event:

> El día siguiente a la mañana, el Cardenal dixo la missa y los veló con la solemnidad que convenía; y a cabo de tres o quatro días que fueron casados, se representó en palacio una comedia de Ludovico Ariosto, poeta excelentíssimo, con todo aquel aparato de teatro y scenas que los romanos solían representar, que fue cosa muy real y sumptuosa.[8]

> [On the following morning, the Cardinal celebrated mass and veiled them with suitable solemnity; and after three or four days, when they were wedded, a comedy by Ludovico Ariosto, this outstanding poet, was performed in the palace, with all the apparatus and scenes the Romans used to have, making it a befittingly royal and sumptuous occasion.]

The play was translated into Latin by the Toledan humanist Juan Pérez Petreyo (1512–1545) in about 1540.[9]

The revered Italian model and the typical palmistry scene that it proposes has a certain transcendence in the neo-Latin Spanish theatre. The Valentian humanist Juan Lorenzo Palmireno (1524–1579) was likewise the author of a series of comedies in Latin which were designed to teach his pupils Latin. In the comedy *Octavia* (1564),[10] which has come down to us in fragments, the Valentian playwright dramatises a familiar conflict, that between the old man Chremylus, his wife Marcelina and his son Rapitius, who is in love with Octavia.[11] When the father realises that his son is in gaol, he, at the instigation of his friend Solinus, consults a Portuguese astrologer, who reads the gullible old man's hand after some *verborea jactanciosa*, 'boastful verbosity'.[12]

---

8 Calvete de Estrella, *El felicíssimo viaje del muy alto y muy poderoso príncipe don Phelippe*, ed. Gonzalo Sánchez-Molero & Cuenca Muñoz (2001, 27). Also see the introduction by Cortijo Ocaña to his edition of the Latin translation of the *Suppositi* by Juan Pérez (2001, 27 and footnote 27), containing a reference to the *Relación muy verdadera de las grandes fiestas que la serenísima reina doña María ha hecho al príncipe nuestro señor en Flandes en un lugar que se dize Uince, desde xxii. de agosto hasta el postrero dia del mes* (Medina del Campo, Juan Rodríguez, 1549 with a copy preserved in the Escorial) by Juan Cristóbal Calvete de Estrella. Cortijo Ocaña mentions an Antwerp edition of 1552.
9 As Arróniz (1969, 54) gathered, Petreyo also translated the *Nigromante* and *Lena* into Latin. In the Latin text of the *Suppositi*, the scene with the reading of the hand is maintained, beginning with Cleander's question "Nunquid nosti chyromantiam?", Pérez, *Suppositi*, ed. Cortijo Ocaña (2001, 48–49) [Do you know chiromancy?].
10 For the date, see Gil Fernández (2002, 135).
11 See Gil Fernández (2002, 135–136) for a detailed summary.
12 This is how Alonso Asenjo (1992, 10) puts it in an article on magic in the theatre of Palmireno.

CHREMYLVS: Amice, inspice, quæso, incisuras manuum, ut possis quæ expecto prædicere.

ASTROLOGUS: Si nihil attuleris, ibis, Homere, foras.

CHREMYLVS: En præbeo tibi drachmam.

ASTROLOGUS: *Ora Dio ti la mandi bona*! Crede autem, quæcumque dixero futura uerissima, si Deus uoluerit. Ego multa admiranda ciuibus meis passim ostendo et superioribus annis uenientem à Mauritania pestem prædixi. Dimisique circa urbes discipulos, qui insinuanti se malo occurrerent. Apud Alonem onustam nauem solus traxi quo uolui, cùm homines permulti ne mouere quidem suo possent loco. *Sí, bota Deus! Sí, bota Deus*! Et audacter polliceor me, si alterum totius terræ globum adipisci possem, utrumque alteri applicaturum. Est etiam mihi domi lignea columba, à me certa ratione compacta, et quæ aerem semel sortita perpetuò uolatu per ipsum inane spiritus intus incluso agitur, nisi solidum aliquod corpus offendat. *Sí, bota Deus! Sí, bota Deus!*

SOLINUS: *¡Ñáfete! ¡Seboso!*

ASTROLOGUS: *¿Qué falláys?*

CHREMYLVS: Nihil prorsus. Eia, manum inspice; ista prætermitte.

ASTROLOGUS: Habeo etiam canem dialecticum.

SOLINUS: Hic, cùm insisteret uestigijs leporis, qui nusquam uidebatur, et perquirens uenisset ad fossam, dubitabat utrum dextrum, an sinistrum iter insequendum leporem susciperet. Vt ueró primum sibi uisus est, tamquam disserendi peritus, satis rem perpendisse, e uestigio fossam, recta iter faciens, transiliuit. Hic, ut uideo, dialectico more perpendens omnia, iter absoluebat. Argute enim secum reputauerat. Vel hac, uel isthàc, uel illàc lepus in fugam se coniecit. Deinde syllogismum nectebat: Non profecto hàc, nec isthàc, ergo illàc fugit. Neque fallacibus conclusiunculis mihi errare uidebatur. Nam non perceptis citra fossam ad hoc uel illud latas uestigijs, relinquebatur leporem fossam transisse. Recte igitur canis fossam transiuit. *Sí, bota Deus!*

CHREMYLVS: Aut me prorsus eneca, aut quod peto, breuiter absolue.

ASTROLOGUS: Hæc linea mensalis usque ad montem Mercurij producta indicat te in mensa mercatores multos tuo splendido conuiuio exhilaraturum intra dies quatuor. Et hæc linea uitæ inter alias cæca monet ut hic maneas, donec cæcus quidam occurrat. Da operam, ut cæcum illum uel inuitum ad ædes tuas recipi cogas. Plura scire tibi non datum est. Vale. Etc. *[Fragmentorum finis.]*[13]

[CHREMYLUS: Friend, please examine the lines of my hand and tell me what awaits me in the future.

ASTROLOGUE: If Homer came withour money, he would be driven out.

---

13 Palmireno, *Octavia*, ed. Alonso Asenjo (2003, without pagination).

CHREMYLUS: Here's a coin.

ASTROLOGUS: *God give you good luck!* But be assured that everything I say will eventually happen, God willing. I spend the day showing incredible things to the men of my city, and a few years ago I predicted that plague that came from Mauritania, and I even sent some of my disciples to the neighbouring cities to inform me of any setback. In Alona, I single-handedly dragged a loaded ship at will, when a hundred men couldn't even move it. *Yes, I swear it by God! Yes, I swear it by God!* And sure enough, if I had another world at my charge, I might as well take care of them both. I also have a wooden pigeon at home, a work of myself, which with a single breath of air remains in flight as long as it does not impact another body. *Yes, I swear it by God! Yes, I swear it by God!*

SOLINUS: ¡Neophyte! ¡Dearest!

ASTROLOGUE: ¿What are you saying?

CHREMYLUS: That's enough. Come on, read my hand and stop with the stories.

ASTROLOGUS: I also have a dialectic dog.

SOLINO: This dog was following the trail of a rabbit that had lost sight of him, and here he came across a ditch and did not know which way the rabbit would have gone, the one to the right or the one to the left. Although he was very quick to think, he took a moment to reflect; when he had finished, he jumped across the pit and went straight on, ignoring the tracks. In faith, he was able to go ahead thanks to an exact dialectic reasoning. First of all he posed the question correctly: the rabbit must have thrown itself in some direction, either this one, or that one, or the other. Then he formulated a syllogism: it did not run this way, nor that way, and then it must have run that way. And I don't think he was wrong in his conclusions. In fact, if there were no footprints around the pit, the only thing left was that the rabbit would have gone through it. Then the dog was right to cross the pit. *Yes, I swear it by God!*

CHREMYLUS: Either you finish me off, or you do what I ask you to do.

ASTROLOGUS: This line of the heart, which reaches the mount of Mercury, tells me that you are going to offer a splendid banquet with many merchants within four days, and that you will enjoy it very much. And this line of life, the least marked of all, tells you to wait here for a blind man to appear. Be sure to give the blind man shelter, even if he doesn't want to. And I can't tell you any more. Goodbye. Etc.
End of the fragments]

It is an entertaining scene which reveals certain knowledge of the practice of palmistry. Since the rest of the play has not been preserved, we do not know if this mock prophesy acquires further protagonism in the course of the play.

In *Lo Ipocrito* (1542), a comedy by Pietro Aretino, a pedantic and, at the same time, ingenuous character appears on stage, that of a physician, a certain

Messer Biondello,[14] a caricature of a well-known historical physiognomist and friend of the author's, Michelangelo Biondello. He makes his appearance in III, ii introducing himself thus to a servant, Porfiria:

> BIONDELLO. È studio molto dilettevole e pulcro quel de la fisionomia, e però ho fatto uno opuscolo *De cognitione hominum per aspectum* secondo Aristotile, Scoto, Cocle, Indagine, e la eccellenzia di me filosofo moderno, peroché *frons magna et cuperata est inditium potatoris, nasus aquilinus testis est majestatis imperatorim, et facies rugosa testimonium senectutis.*[15]

> [BIONDELLO: It is a very delightful and clean study of physiognomy, and yet I have made a pamphlet, *De cognitione hominum per aspectum* according to Aristotile, Scott, Cocles, Indagine, and according myself the Excellence of a modern philosopher, although *a large and furrowed forehead is the sign of a drunkard, an eagle's nose is the mark of imperial dignity and a wrinkled face is evidence of age.*]

We have not only come up with an interesting document on the dissemination of physiognomic knowledge among playwrights. It is remarkable that Aretino should mention a study by Biondo published in 1544 and which, therefore, is of a later date than the comedy. Thus, the author most probably read it before his medical friend turned it in for publication in Rome.[16] As a matter of fact, the pedant mentions authorities also cited in *De cognitione hominum per aspectum*, Michael Scott, Cocles and Johannes ab Indagine besides Aristotle. The inkhorn terms used by Messer Biondello are parodies of the language found in manuals on physiognomy[17] in the manner of Rabelais' *Pantagrueline prognostication*, which predicted

---

14 Also see Romano (2008, 217, note 2) and Boccia in the *Nota introduttiva* to the edition of *Lo ipocrito*, ed. Rabitti, Garavelli & Boccia (2010, 160).
15 Aretino, *Lo ipocrito* III, 6, ed. Rabitti, Garavelli & Boccia (2010, 218). On this aspect, also see Paques (1971, 77).
16 This is Stabile's (1968) explanation as well as Boccia's in the *Nota introduttiva* (2010, 160) to his edition.
17 Boccia, in the *Nota introduttiva* to the edition of *Lo ipocrito* (ed. Rabitti, Garavelli & Boccia, 2010, 160–161), observes: "Sono riprese volutamente e comprensibilmente manipolate per essere adattate ad un testo-contesto comico, ma che attingono senza dubbio al trattato – a cominciare dagli *auctores* (Aristotele, Scoto, Cocle, Indagine), ampiamente utilizzati dal Biondo–, al formulario (*inditium / testis est*), per finire alla corrispondenza instaurata tra aspetto esteriore e comportamento. In quest'ultimo caso Aretino ritaglia un maggiore spazio alla propria libertà inventiva. *Frons magna et cuperata* costituiscono termini rinvenibili nella sezione *De fronte* [. . .] con la precisazione che il secondo aggettivo è deformazione dell'originale *caperata* [. . .] ma nell'economia del testo diventano *inditium potatoris*; lo stesso dicasi per *nasus aquilinus* e *facies rugosa*, rispettivamente trattati nelle sezioni *De naso* e *De vultu* [. . .] mentre del tutto aretiniane sono le definizioni corrispondenti" [They are taken deliberately and understandably manipulated to be adapted to a comic text and context, but they undoubtedly draw on the treatise – beginning with the *auctores* (Aristotle, Scotus, Cocle, Indagine) widely used by Biondo, and the

that "old age will be incurable this year because of the past years".[18] Although this is no more than an indirect allusion to Michelangelo Biondo, a kind of private joke amongst friends, this example from *Lo ipocrito* is indicative of the potential of physiognomic discourse being integrated into a theatre play.

In Giordano Bruno's (1548–1600) *Candelaio* (1582),[19] it is a magician who presents himself as the bearer of occult knowledge in front of Bonifacio in order to dupe the gallant and ingenuous husband:[20]

SCARAMURÉ. Ben trovato, messer Bonifacio.

BONIFACIO. Siate il molto ben ben venuto, signor Scaramuré, speranza della mia vita appassionata.

SCARAMURÉ. *Signum affecti animi.*

BONIFACIO. Si vostra Signoria non rimedia il mio male, io son morto.

SCARAMURÉ. Sì come io vedo, voi sete inamorato.

BONIFACIO. Cossì è: non bisogna ch'io vi dica più.

SCARAMURÉ. Come mi fa conoscere la vostra fisionomia, il computo di vostro nome, di vostri parenti o progenitori, la signora della vostra natività fu *Venus retrogada in signo masculino; et hoc fortasse in Geminibus vigesimo septimo gradu*: che significa certa mutazione e conversione nell'età di 46 anni nella quale al presente vi ritrovate.

BONIFACIO. A punto, io non mi ricordo quando nacqui: ma per quello che da altri ho udito dire, mi trovo da 45 anni in circa.

SCARAMURÉ. Gli mesi, giorni ed ore computarò ben io più distintamente, quando col compasso arò presa la proporzione della latitudine dell'unghia maggiore alla linea vitale, e

---

form (*inditium / testis est*), down to the correspondence established between external appearance and behaviour. In this latter case, Aretino carves out a bigger space for his own freedom of invention. *Frons magna et cuperata* constitute terms found in the section *De fronte* . . . with the clarification that the second adjective is a deformation of the original *caperata* . . . but in the economy of the text they become *inditium potatoris*; the same is true for *nasus aquilinus* and *facies rugosa*, dealt with in the sections *De naso* and *De vultu* . . . respectively, while the corresponding definitions are entirely Aretino's].

18 Rabelais, *Pantagrueline prognostication*, ed. Screech (1974, 11).

19 "The extremely long and complicated play, which was perhaps sketched out in Naples before 1576 and then completed in Paris just before 1582, never did get performed in Bruno's lifetime. And it never did meet with theatrical success over the next centuries [. . .]" Biow (2010, 326). The play was translated into French as *Boniface et le pendant*.

20 For a criticism of human stupidity in Bruno's comedy see Barr, who observes with regard to the three protagonists: "Their unrestrained desires, which become obsessive, make fools and dupes of them. It is thus that the insipid, the stupid, and the sordid converge" (1971, 354).

distanza dalla summità dell'annulare a quel termine del centro della mano, ove è designato il spacio di Marte; ma basta per ora aver fatto giudicio cossì universale *et in communi*.²¹

[SCARAMURÉ: Well descried, Messer Boniface.

BONIFACIO: You are very welcome, Signor Scaramuré, hope of my passionate life.

SCARAMURÉ: *Signum affecti anime.*

BONIFACIO: If your lordship does not mend my state, I am dead.

SCARAMURÉ: Yes, as I see it, you are in love.

BONIFACIO: That's the way it is. I don't have to tell you more.

SCARAMURÉ: As I know your physiognomy, the calculation of your name, your relatives and ancestors, *Venus retrogada in signo masculino*; *et hoc fortasse in Geminibus vigesimo septimo gradu*: which means certain mutation and conversion at the age of 46, in which you find yourself today.

BONIFACIO: For sure, I do not remember when I was born: but for what I have heard others say, I must be in my forties.

SCARAMURÉ: The months, days, and hours I will count more distinctly, when I with a compass will take the proportion of the latitude of the large nail to the vital line, and the distance from the top of the ring finger to that end of the middle of the hand, where the space of Mars is designated; but it suffices now to have made so universal *et in communi*.]

The character of the fraudster pretends to be the bearer of all kinds of occult knowledge²² in an address sprinkled with inkhorn terms in order to deceive the stingy dirty old miser. The knowledge of the magician, Scaramuré, that of palmistry

---

21 Bruno, *Candelaio* I, 10, ed. Bárberi Squarotti (2002, 296–297); also see the ed. Guerrini Angrisani (1976, 166–167). The editor comments on the horoscope proposed by Scaramuré: "nuova allusione al trapasso dall'amore sodomitico a quello naturale che Bonifacio, il cui oroscopo, secondo Scaramuré, presenta la congiunzione di Venere con una costellazione maschile (è da vedere in qui retrograda un'ennesima allusione ironica), nell'attuale età di quarantasei anni, dovrebbe compiere. Scaramuré, però, schernisce Bonifacio da ignorante qual è, ripete male i segni e fa errori grossolani ('*Geminibus*' per '*Geminis*')" (1976, 167, footnote 116) [new allusion to the transition from sodomite love to natural love that Boniface, whose horoscope, according to Scaramuré, presents the conjunction of Venus with a male constellation (with the wisdom of hindsight to be seen as the umpteenth ironic allusion to it), at his present age of forty-six years, should be accomplishing. Scaramuré, however, scoffs at Boniface for being ignorant, repeating the signs poorly and making gross errors (*Geminibus*' for '*Geminis*)].
22 On Bruno and hermeticism see Yates (1983), on Bruno and Renaissance science see Gatti (2001).

amongst them, is openly ridiculed. As Preda aptly observes, the point of the different jibes is to question all absolute truth.

> En effet, la *beffa*, le mauvais tour que les trois victimes de la pièce subissent sur différents niveaux, se réalise sur la scène du *Candelaio* à travers un jeu de travestissement frénétique qui dénonce la fausse stabilité du réel ainsi que toute vérité faussement totalisante. (2002, 159–160)

> [Indeed, the *beffa*, the bad trick that the three victims of the play suffer on different levels, is realised on the stage of the *Candelaio* through a frenetic game of disguise that denounces the false stability of reality as well as any false totalizing truth.]

Il Candelaio, which, after all, is the dramatic work of a philosopher,[23] is characterised, according to Arnaudo, by "una forma di libera osmosi tra i modi della commedia e quelli del dialogo filosofico" (2007, 693) [a kind of free osmosis of the features of the comedy and those of a philosophical dialogue].[24] Johnson, who studies Bruno's comedy from the point of view of Walter Benjamin, observes:

> The *Candelaio*, then, is the theatrical laboratory where Bruno first toys with solutions to the ancient conundrum. Despite appearances, Bruno's farce creates a theatrical space where ideas and their consequences can be played out; it creates what Benjamin calls [. . .] a *Denkraum* (i.e. a thought-space). (2010, 330).

This idea of the drama as a space for thinking has a certain heuristic value for the analysis of the textualization of the occult arts in Spanish theatre.

---

23 On the relationship between theatre and philosophical thinking in Bruno also see Trionfo (1982, 100), Cavallo (1992), Buono Hodgart (1999), Arnaudo (2007), Puliafito Bleuel (2007, 105–135), Bartolomé Luises (2009) and Kodera (2010).
24 On this point also see Ordine in his introduction to the first volume of Bruno's *Opere italiane*: "Bruno, in contrasto con le prescrizioni dell'aristotelismo cinquecentesco, finisce per fondere gli schemi della commedia e del dialogo 'rappresentativo' o mimetico, trasferendo elementi dialogici nel teatro e elementi teatrali nel dialogo. Il *Candelaio* si presenta così come una commedia filosofica, mentre i dialoghi mettono in scena qua e là una filosofia in commedia. In entrambi i casi, il Nolano fa deflagrare gli elementi costitutivi del genere. Nella sua unica opera teatrale, in fondo, a struttura drammatica viene ridotta al minimo" (2002, 28–29) [Bruno, in contrast to the prescriptions of 16th century Aristotelianism, ends up merging the schemes of comedy and 'representational' or mimetic dialogue, transferring dialogical elements into theatre and theatrical elements into dialogue. – *Il Candelaio* thus presents itself as a philosophical comedy, while the dialogues here and there put philosophy on stage. In both cases, Nolano bursts the constitutive elements of the genre. In his only play, when all is said and done, the dramatic structure is reduced to a minimum]; also see Ordine (2008).

2 The *Égloga interlocutoria* by Diego Guillén de Ávila

In the first classical Spanish theatre I have not been able to trace down many references to physiognomy and none as striking as that of Aretino and Giordano Bruno.[25] A very early example is the *Égloga interlocutoria* (prior to 1511)[26] by Diego Guillén de Ávila, which not only contains comic descriptions of the outward appearance of a shepherdess, apt to be understood from the point of view of physiognomy, but also contains spells[27] and a palm-reading gipsy.[28] In order to contextualise these references, it is necessary, for a start, to remember a few data about the author. Thanks to the work of Roca Barea, we have "some minimal biographical coordinates" (2006, 374) of Diego Guillén de Ávila.[29] His father, Pero Guillén de Segovia, was at the service of Alonso Carrillo de Acuña (1410–1482), Archbishop of Toledo, from 1463 on. Diego grew up as a boy in this highly cultured atmosphere.[30] As Roca Barea observes, "la vida intelectual de Diego Guillén aparece ligada a la de su padre de distintos modos, y es en parte consecuencia de los vínculos personales y políticos de Pero Guillén en el círculo de Alonso Carrillo" (2006, 391) [the intellectual life of Diego Guillén seems to be linked to that of his father in a number of ways and is partly the consequence of the personal and political ties of Pedro

---

25 According to Espantoso-Foley (1972, 26–32), the occult arts are only very occasionally staged in Spanish 16th century theatre. The researcher quotes an unpublished doctoral dissertation, which I have not been able to consult: Linton Lomas Barrett, *The supernatural in the Spanish comedia of the Golden Age*, Chapel Hill, University of North Carolina, 1938.
26 For the question of dating see Kohler in his edition of the text (1911, 168).
27 The spells in this eclogue and in Juan del Encina have recently been analysed by García-Bermejo Giner (2016a).
28 "Yendo el domingo tomar caridad / Topé con una de aquestas d'Ejito, / Llegábase a mí su poco a poquito / Diciendo que había de haber buenos hados, / mía fe, yo dile cuatro cornados; / Y díjome cosas, que es infinito. // Tanto me dijo, qu'estaba pasmado; / y aún más te diré. Catóme la mano, / Y entonces me dijo que aqueste verano / Sin duda ninguna sería desposado. / D'allí quedé yo tan engallinado / Oyéndole aquellas tales cosetas; / Hurtóme la yesca y dos agujetas, / Mas todo lo dó por bien empleado" Guillén de Ávila, *Égloga ynterlocutoria*, ed. Kohler (1911, 247, vv. 347–360) [On my way to charity of a Sunday / I came upon one of those from Ejito / She little by little came towards me, / Saying that there were good omens, / My faith, I gave her four coins; / And she told me things, no end of them. // She told me so much, that I was confounded; / And I will say more. She took my hand, / And then he told me that this summer / Without a doubt, I would be married; / And there I was, so delighted, / Hearing those things; / That she stole my tinder and two needles, / But I deem them well used]. See García-Bermejo Giner (2017) on this particular point.
29 Roca Barea (2006, 385–386) revalidates Kohler's hypothesis that the son of Pero Guillén de Segovia and the author of the *Égloga interlocutoria* are the same person.
30 Later, Diego Guillén was to write a *Panegírico* to Alonso Carrillo at the request of his nephew of the same name, the Bishop of Pamplona.

Guillén with the circle around Alonso Carrillo]. I am particularly interested in these ties because – as I pointed out in Gernert (2017b) – there is a handwritten note in the copy of the *Epílogo en medicina y cirugía conveniente a la salud* of the Biblioteca Nacional in Madrid (INC/1335) which connects the owner of the book with the circle around the Archbishop of Toledo. This note confirms that in the circles in which Diego Guillén de Ávila moved a book was circulated which spread the physiognomic theories of Michael Scott. It should be mentioned as well that Diego de Ávila translated the occult writings of Hermes Trismegistus for Gómez Manrique, giving it the title *Libro de la potencia y sapiencia de Dios* (1487).[31] These notes permit reading the description of the outward appearance of the character of the *Écgloga interlocutoria* in a physiognomic key. This is what the shepherd Hontaya[32] says about Teresa Turpina, the woman proposed as his son Turpino's future wife by the matchmaker, Benito:

> Es que muy poco me agrada Turpina
> Tiene mal ojo; y no estó contento.
> Nunca me ha entrado en el majinamiento,
> Por ser la mozuela un poco risueña,
> Y junto con esto presume de dueña:
> Por donde abernuncio el tal casamiento.
> Dígote más; que yo no m'agrado
> De moza que trae las cuentas bermejas,
> Y aún diz que trasquila sobacos y cejas
> Más de tres veces detrás dell arado.[33]

---

[31] In addition to the above-mentioned study by Roca Barea (2006, 389–390), see Gómez Moreno (1994, 77–79) and Alvar (2010, 148–149): "La tradición hermética, que continúa en tiempos de D. Enrique de Villena, se reforzará al final de la Edad Media con la traducción de los *Libros teosóficos* atribuidos a Hermes Trismegisto (o *Libros de la potencia y sapiencia de Dios*) que hizo el canónigo Diego Guillén de Ávila, concluida en febrero de 1485, aunque la copia manuscrita sea de 1491. El traductor utilizó la versión latina de Marsilio Ficino (de abril de 1474) [. . .] El neoplatonismo empieza a hacer una tímida aparición en Castilla". [The hermetic tradition, which continues in the time of D. Enrique de Villena, comes to be strengthened at the end of the Middle Ages with the translation of the *Libros teosóficos* attributed to Hermes Trismegistus (or *Libros de la potencia y sapiencia de Dios*), written by Diego Guillen de Avila, concluded in February 1485, although the handwritten copy is from 1491. The translator used the Latin version by Marsilio Ficino (April 1474) . . . Neoplatonism is beginning to make a timid appearance in Castile].

[32] As García-Bermejo Giner notes, this is a telling name and "la intención del autor es convertirla en epítome de dos de los sentidos del término *torpe*" (2017, 104, footnote 14). [the intention of the author is to make it the epitome of two of the meanings of the word *torpe*, 'clumsy'].

[33] Guillén de Ávila, *Égloga ynterlocutoria*, ed. Kohler (1911, 242, vv. 163–172). See the different interpretations of Hermenegildo's (1989, 281–282) and García-Bermejo Giner's (2017, 106–107) "cuentas bermejas".

> [Turpina is not to my liking
> She has the evil eye; and I am not happy with this.
> She has never attracted me
> Because she is not given to smiling,
> and besides she boasts of being a lady:
> Therefore I renounce such a marriage,
> and I will say it frankly: I do not like
> maidens with auburn beads,
> And it must be said: she shears her
> armpits and eyebrows more than
> three times behind the plough.]

The father's address ends with a reference to the hair removal, which suggests that Teresa has abundant body hair, a very unfavourable bodily sign in women and one that she shares with the *serrana* Alda of the *Libro de buen amor*.[34] In spite of the father's reservations, Benito insists on his wedding plan in a dialogue with Tenorio. In this festive conversation, further physical characteristics of the future bride are discussed.

> TENORIO. Asina la quiero sin más quillotrar:
> Anque parece qu'está muy delgada.
>
> BENITO. ¡Calla ruin! que no sabes nada;
> Que nunca tú l' has llegado á tentar.
> Ves, anque tiene la cara flaquilla,
> No pienses qu' es toda de aquella natura;
> Qu'estos dos dedos y más de gordura
> Entiendo que tiene en cada costilla.
> ¡O hí de puta, y qué rabadilla
> Debe tener la hí de vellaca!
> Una espaldaza mayor que una vaca,
> Y tetas tan grandes, qu'es maravilla.
>
> TENORIO. Aqueso me hace, Benito, saber;
> Que no es menester que más me la alabes,
> Aqueso que dices ¿cómo lo sabes?
> Que par Dios que no te lo puedo creer.[35]
>
> [TENORIO: I like her thus, without further ado.
> Although she is a bit slender.

---

34 Bermejo Giner (2017, 107) quotes Michael Scott on the negative evaluation of abundant body hair. Stern (1977, 64) describes the portrait of Turpina as "a grotesque caricature in the spirit of Juan Ruiz".
35 Guillén de Ávila, *Égloga ynterlocutoria*, ed. Kohler (1911, 249–250, vv. 429–444).

BENITO: Shut up, you fool! You don't understand.
For you have never tempted her.
Look, although her face is slender,
don't you think the rest is.
Look at those two fingers,
and there is more fatness, as I see it,
around her ribs. Heavens,
what a backbone the wretch must have!
A shoulder broader than a cow's,
and breasts so big that it is a wonder.

TENORIO: This opens my eyes, Benito.
You need not praise her any more.
How do you know what you say?
I cannot believe you more.]

Slenderness need not be an unfavourable sign from the point of view of physiognomy,[36] in contrast to excessive slenderness, as becomes obvious from the Spanish translation of Scott's manual:

> La persona muy luenga y flaca y delgada significa hombre indiscreto, vano, mintroso, de gruesso nudrimento, importuno para lo que dessea y que cree de ligero, flaco en lo que ha de fazer, perezoso y mucho de su cabeça.[37]
>
> [A tall and thin person indicates an indiscreet vain, untruthful person, of gross eating habits, wayward and gullible, weak in what she must do, weary and headstrong.]

The matchmaker's attempt to assuage the poor impression which Teresa's leanness can cause only makes things worse, the full hips he makes reference to being a sign of simple-mindedness.[38] Besides, non-canonical references to hips and the back end in the description of a woman must by themselves provoke hilarity in the audience. The large breasts have a special significance in the works of Michael Scott: Amongst the "signa mulieris frigidae naturae: et qua non

---

36 "El cuerpo ligero y delgado en el andar significa buena complexión" *Tratado de fisonomía* II, ed. Sánchez González de Herrero & María Vázquez de Benito (2009, without pagination) [A lithe and agile stride signifies a good complexion].
37 *Tratado de fisonomía* LXV ("De la estatura" [On the stature]), ed. Sánchez González de Herrero & María Vázquez de Benito (2009, without pagination). It is chapter CC of Scott, *Liber Phisionomiae*, ed. Porsia (2009, 244).
38 "Las costillas gordas y llenas de carne significan hombre rezio, tardío y muy simple" *Tratado de fisonomía* LII ("De las costillas" [On the ribs]), ed. Sánchez González de Herrero & María Vázquez de Benito (2009, without pagination) [Plump and fleshy ribs signify a hardy man, slow and very simple]. It is chapter LXXXVII of Scott, *Liber Phisionomiae*, ed. Porsia (2009, 236).

libenter coit" [sign of a women of cold nature who do not enjoy coitus], chapter 5 explicitly mentions "mammae grandes et proprie moles" [big and particularly opulent breasts].³⁹ The back part 'bigger than a cow's' are automatically associated with a mannish woman. According to Michael Scott, "espaldas anchas y gruessas significan hombre rezio, avaro, leal, de gruesso ingenio y nudrimiento, simple, de mucho trabajo, que come asaz y que está de buena gana en paz"⁴⁰ [broad and heavy shoulders indicate a hardy, stingy, loyal character, of gross understanding and eating habits, simple, hard-working, with an enormous appetite and one who wants to be left alone]. What is remarkable in this context is the characterization of people with a large back as heavy eaters, because Teresa's alleged frugality is the object of a comic dispute between Benito and Tenorio:

> TENORIO. [. . .] Bien me parece la moza chapada.
> Mas ¿quies que te diga, Alonso Benito?
> Entiendo que debe comer muy poquito:
> Que me semeja qu' está trasijada.
>
> BENITO. ¿Y dejas decirte aquesa porrada?
> Á buena fé qu' eres terrible persona.
> Tiene un papo mayor que una mona,
> Y estásme diciendo que no come nada.⁴¹
>
> [TENORIO: . . . This pretty woman is to my liking.
> But, do you know what I say, Alonso Benito?
> It seems to me she is rather skinny.
>
> BENITO: Will you stop saying such gibberish?
> In faith, you are a terrible person.
> She has a gullet as big as an ape's,
> And you're telling me she does not eat.]

As García-Bermejo Giner argues, the bulge under her chin which disfigures poor Teresa Turpino⁴² is "una de las manifestaciones del déficit de yodo que

---

39 Scott, *Liber Phisionomiae*, ed. The *Compendio de la salud humana* includes only a translation of the second part of the *Liber phisionomiae*, which is the physiognomic manual itself, starting from chapter XXII of the Latin original and omitting the chapters which deal with the signs of the woman of a hot and of a cold disposition.
40 *Tratado de fisonomía* XLV ("De las espaldas" [On the shoulders]), ed. Sánchez González de Herrero & María Vázquez de Benito (2009, without pagination). It is chapter LXXX of Scott, *Liber Phisionomiae*, ed. Porsia (2009, 230).
41 Guillén de Ávila, *Égloga ynterlocutoria*, ed. Kohler (1911, 254, vv. 593–600).
42 When Teresa accepts Tenorio as her husband, she does so emphasizing his and her own outward appearance: "Que digo que sí, aunqu'es lagañoso; / Pues con mi papo me quiso él

produce una llamativa inflamación de la glándula tiroides en la parte anterior del cuello, una forma extrema de hipotiroidismo que produce la apariencia de inmadurez [. . .] y, además de otros síntomas, en casos extremos, cretinismo" (2017, 109) [one of the manifestations of the lack of iodine, which produces a conspicuous inflammation of the thyroid glands in the area around the throat, an extreme form of hypothyroidism, producing the impression of immaturity . . . and, in extreme cases, cretinism]. Diego de Ávila shows his expertise at medical and physiological theories and instrumentalises them adeptly when it comes to creating his dramatic characters.

3 The palm-reading gipsies in Gil Vicente and other playwrights

The gipsies and their magic skills have, from the beginning, exerted a major influence on the imagination of artists[43] and writers.[44] We have previously referred to a palm-reading gipsy in the *Égloga interlocutoria*; in the *Celestina*, it is Pármeno who mentions the thefts of "los de Egipto cuando el signo nos catan en la mano"[45] [those from Egypt when they read our hands]. From the 1520s onwards, we come across plays which entirely revolve around one or two palm-reading gipsies,[46] the

---

á mí", Guillén de Ávila, *Égloga y Interlocutoria*, ed. Kohler (1911, 258, vv. 727–728) [I say yes, even though he has the rheum; / And despite my crop he loves me]. Hontoya had earlier described his son in these terms: "Mira las lagañas y negra melena" Guillén de Ávila, *Égloga ynterlocutoria*, ed. Kohler (1911, 248, v. 391) [Look at the rheum and the black hair].
43 See the documentation of the pictorial work which I have included in Gernert (2016).
44 On gipsies in Spanish literature of the Spanish Golden Age, see Leblon (1982) and Rodríguez de Lera (2002).
45 *Celestina* XI, ed. Rico et. al. (2000, 235), on this point also see Gutiérrez Nieto (1993, 1009). On different images of the palm-reading gipsy in the Spanish theatre of the 16th and 17th centuries with regard to the laws in force at the time concerning this ethnic group see: Vaiopoulos (2011).
46 Cf. Aguirre Felipe (2009, 251–251): "En Italia, desde el segundo decenio del siglo XVI, con un esquema métrico particular ya existente, aparece la forma de poesía dramática llamada 'zingaresche' que tiene como personaje principal a una 'zíngara'. Nacieron como chirigotas para el carnaval, y antes de 1518 se conoce ya una. El plurilingüismo era un fenómeno que conocía la comedia italiana entonces y la manipulación fonética empleada servía para caracterizar étnicamente a los personajes: el francés habla en *e* o en *sce*, el paleto umbro ('norcino') habla en *u*, el judío habla en *i*, el véneto habla en *ze*, etc.". [In Italy, from the second decade of the 16th century onwards, a metrical pattern being in force, the dramatic form known as "zingaresche" makes its appearance. They emerged as Carnival jokes, and before 1518 the first is already known. Multilingualism is a phenomenon which was known to Italian comedy and the way the sounds were handled helped mark the characters ethnically: the French characters

earliest such text probably being *Contentione di un villano e di una zingana* by Bastiano di Francesco or Bastiano Linaiuolo,[47] first published in 1520.[48] While the gipsy is reading a lady's hand, the peasant who has trouble understanding her makes despicable and funny comments:

> *Hora viene una Zingana et dice:*
> Diu vi cunteti tutte
> Le mie paparutte
> Una puca di caritate
> Le belle innamurate
> Tua ventura ti vu dire.
>
> VILLANO. O, sta un poco a udire.
>
> ZINGANA. Semu nate nellu Egittu
>
> Nostro corpu habbieno afllitti
> Nelli stenti e nelli affani
> Consumandu e mesi et gl'anni
> Alla neve, all'acqua, a' venti,
> Giurnu et notte in tanti stenti,
> Nustra casa è una grutta.
>
> VILLANO. Che cicala questa scotta?
> Non ho anco inteso straccio
> [. . .]
>
> ZINGANA. Deh, madunna, in curtesia
> Alla puvera meschina
> Duna, duna una quattrina,
> Bella, pulita figliuola.
>
> VILLANO. La parla alla spagnuola.

---

using *e* or in *sce* in their speech, the clodhopper from Umbria ("norcino") using *u*, the Jew using *i*, the character from the Vento using *ze*, etc.].

47 On this comedy writer of the pre-Rozzi see De Blasi (1970).

48 The first edition was published with the title of *Strambotti rusticali, e contentione di un villano e di una zingana. Da ricitare in uno convito di donne. Operetta piacevole & da ridere composta per Bastiano di Francesco da Siena* (Siena, per Michelangelo de' Libri ad instantia di Giovanni Landi, 1520); one copy is preserved in the Bodleian Library of Oxford with the catalogue number Douce E 26 (1). For the text, see Mazzi (1882, II, 190–191), Lovarini (1891, 93–94), who includes the later editions of 1533, 1562, 1564, 1568, 1577 and from the beginning of the 17th century (without giving the year), as well as Lohse (2015, 451–452), who dates it 1536.

ZINGANA. Diu ti guarda tu maritu
Bellu, frescu et pulitu
Che ti vuol tantu bene.

VILLANO. Sta un poco a udirmene.
Non t'ho inteso parola,
Che incanti la gragnuola
O pur hai bestemmiato?[49]

[*Now comes a gipsy and says:*
God be gracious to you all
my young geese.
A little bit of charity,
fair ladies in love,
Your good fortune I will tell you.

VILLANO: Oh, just listen for a while.

ZINGANA: We were born in Egypt
Our bodies have grieved
In the hardships and in the afflictions
Consuming months and years
In the snow, the water and the wind
Day and night in so many hardships,
Our home is a cave.

VILLANO: What a cicada, this gossip?
I still haven't understood a word.
. . .

ZINGANA: Oh, milady, as a courtesy
To the poor petty
[Give me] a *quattrino*,
Beautiful and proper girl.

VILLANO: She speaks like Spaniards.

ZINGANA: May God take care of your husband
Handsome, fresh and proper
Who loves you so much.

VILLANO: Listen to me for a moment.
I haven't understood a word,

---

49 I transcribe from a copy of a small anonymous work with the title of *Comedia di un villano et d'una zingana che da la ventura* (Firenze, no date or year provided), which is preserved in the university library of Bologna (A.5.Tab. 1.N.3.266.31, fols. 123r–126v).

> Did you enchant the hail
> Or did you blaspheme?]

The play's wit is grounded in the insults and misunderstandings caused by the gipsy's language, she replacing *o* by u^{50} and using words of Sicilian origin like *paparutte*.[51]

It is not very likely for Gil Vicente to have known this Italian play,[52] in spite of certain parallels with the palm-reading scene of the Portuguese author in *Auto de las Gitanas*, put on stage in Evora[53] in 1525 in the presence of João III. It is a short comedy revolving around the art of palm-reading.[54] As Calderón observes in the prologue to his edition of the Portuguese author's Spanish theatre, the "sencillez y la economía de recursos de este teatro se asientan [. . .] en las técnicas de variación, combinación y repetición tanto de temas y motivos como

---

50 Cf. Aguirre Felipe (2009, 252): "Los varios tipos de *zingaresche* entran desde el comienzo completamente en esta amplia producción plurilingüística; la 'zíngara' habla en *u*, y en 1520 Bastiano Linajuolo difunde ya un tipismo de 'zíngara' de difusión internacional". [The different types of *zingaresche* from the beginning fully become part of the ample multilingual production; the *zingara* uses *u*, and in 1520 Bastiano Linajuolo spreads a type of *zingara* which reaches international circulation].

51 See Lovarini (1891, 86); according to Mazzi (1882, II, 190), the gipsy speaks a Romanesque dialect. On the gipsies of Italy see Viaggio (1997) and Castelli (2006, 506–510).

52 Aguirre Felipe (2009, 252) assumes that the Portuguese author knew the Italian texts but adduces no documents regarding their circulation: "Y considerando que las formas y los temas del teatro circulan con tránsito fácil es lógico asociar el influjo de los comediógrafos italianos sobre los ibéricos en Gil Vicente cuando al habla típica de la 'zíngara' divulgada desde Italia que prevé la transformación /o/ > /u/ como ocurría en los textos italianos añade la variación local ibérica al poner en boca de sus "ciganas" el ceceo con el que los gitanos quisieron caracterizar un exotismo conocido en la Península Ibérica empleando ese rasgo meridional al expresarse en castellano". [And, considering that the forms and themes of theatre circulate easily, it stands to reason to assume that the Italian authors exerted some influence on those of the Iberian peninsular, including Gil Vicente, when, on top of the characteristics of the Italian plays like the replacement of /o/ by /u/, he includes typical Iberian characteristics like the *ceceo* with which the gipsies meant to express a form of exoticism well known in the Iberian peninsular by including a southern feature in their Castilian speech].

53 On the date of the first performance see Calderón in the prologue to his edition of the Spanish theatre of Gil Vicente (1996, XLVIII) as well as the additional footnote 263.a (1996, 505). The play was posthumously printed in *Copilaçam de todas las obras de Gil Vicente* in 1562.

54 According to Sales, this courteous play is to be read as encoded: "Todo o auto pode ter sido uma espécie de baile para debutantes onde grande parte da jovem nobreza, incluindo a princesa real, esta comprometida" (1988, 16). [The whole *auto* could have been a kind of dance for newcomers, amongst them a large number of young members of the nobility, including the royal princess].

de fuentes, personajes, lenguas y registros lingüísticos" (1996, XXXII) [simplicity and the economical use of resources of this theatre are based on . . . the variation, the combination and the repetition of themes and motifs as well as of sources, characters, language and linguistic register]. In the play under discussion, the humorous mimicry of the gipsies' language with their excessive *ceceo*[55] is intertwined with the fortune telling as a *leitmotiv*. No sooner have they entered the stage than Lucrécia, one of the four gipsies, invites the noble audience to foretell their future. "Diremuz el ciño, la buenaventura"[56] [We will tell the signs, the good fortune]. After the short apparition of four male gipsies, the gipsies Martina, Casandra, Lucrécia and Giralda regain their protagonism, reading a bright future into the hands of fourteen noble ladies.[57] First of all, it is Casandra's turn:

> Mustra la mano, ceñura,
> ho hayaz ningún recelo.
> ¡Bendígate Diuz del cielo!
> Tú tienez buena ventura,
> muy buena ventura tienez.
> Muchuz bienez, muchuz bienez:
> un hombre te quiere mucho,
> otros te hablan d'amurez;
> tú, señura, no te curez
> de dar a muchos ezcuto.[58]

[Show me your hand,
milady, trust me
May God bless you!
You have good fortune,
very good fortune you have.

---

55 On the language of the gipsies in Gil Vicente see Teyssier (1959, trad. 2005, 309–310 y 307–316); also see Sales (1988, 4–5) and Calderón's prologue to his edition of the Spanish theatre of Gil Vicente (1996, XLVIII) and the additional footnote 263.a (1996, 505). According to Ferrer-Lightner, the "jerga gitana se impone sobre la lengua oficial" (2006, without pagination) [gipsy jargon prevails over the official language].
56 Vicente, *Auto de las Gitanas*, ed. Calderón (1996, 264, v. 19); on the Portuguese text see the edition *As obras de Gil Vicente* by Camões (2002, II, 319–326).
57 Cf. Ferrer-Lightner (2006, without pagination): "En un recuento general entre todas las intervenciones se puede adivinar la presencia individual de catorce mujeres nobles. Las gitanas se dirigen individualmente a ellas". [In a general overview of all the interventions, we can identify a totality of fourteen noblewomen. The gipsies turn to them one by one]. For the good relationship between the Castilian nobility and the gipsies see the additional footnote 263c in the edition of the Spanish theatre of Gil Vicente, ed. Calderón (1996, 506).
58 Vicente, *Auto de las Gitanas*, ed. Calderón (1996, 267–268, v. 81–90).

Many goods, many goods:
a man is in love with you,
Others will speak of love to you;
Do not, milady, pay heed
to what others may say.]

This same pattern is repeated until they disappear dancing[59] when they realise that they will not be rewarded:

> CASANDRA. Ceñuras, com bendición
> oz quedad, pues no dais nada.
>
> LUCRÉCIA. No vi gente tan honrada
> dar tan poco galardón.[60]
>
> [CASANDRA: Ladies, you will
> but a blessing receive, you don't give.
>
> LUCRÉCIA: I have never seen such
> noble people give so little.]

As Ferrer-Lightner rightly observes, "la simplicidad del argumento no quita que haya gran riqueza de elementos dramáticos" (2006, without pagination) [the simplicity of the argument does not mean that there is a dearth of dramatic elements]. In his study of the scenic space of this *auto*, the American scholar insists that:

> el espacio de ficción dramática se funde con el espacio real en algunas de las obras de Gil Vicente, observamos aquí como las gitanas -actrices de ficción- conversan con un público real que actuará en relación a lo que es y representa en su realidad. Este es un público cortesano y aristocrático que busca distracción e impacto, pero que está acostumbrado a ser parte del espectáculo también. (2006, without pagination)[61]
>
> [the space of dramatic fiction melts with the space of reality in some of Gil Vicente's plays. The gipsies – fictional actors – address a real audience, which acts in accordance with what it is and represents in its reality. This is a courteous and aristocratic audience seeking distraction and connection but which is equally used to being part of the spectacle.]

---

59 On dance and music in the theatre of Gil Vicente see Calderón & Lloret Cantero (1993, 315) y López Castro (1997).
60 Vicente, *Auto de las Gitanas*, ed. Calderón (1996, 273, v. 219–222).
61 On the particularities of the scenic space in Gil Vicente see San Miguel (1991) and Camôes (1995).

The device of the palm-reading allows a particularly narrow interaction between the audience and the actors, which must have included some physical contact during the very act of palm-reading. What Camôes calls the "coincidencia entre espacio de representación y espacio representado" (1995, 157) [coincidence of the space of representation and the represented space] in Gil Vicente's theatre permits to criticise in a particularly efficient way the credulity of the people to whom Zimic refers:

> Además de esta sátira fundamental de la superstición, implícita en toda la acción de la obra, Gil Vicente formuló la actuación y los parlamentos de las actrices (que presentaría al público como genuinas gitanas) a base de ese íntimo conocimiento que tuvo de las cortesanas, con la intención muy traviesa de provocar la otra parte del diálogo, es decir, las reacciones muy variadas de aquéllas. (1983, 8)
>
> [Besides this fundamental satire of superstition, implicit in the whole plot of the play, Gil Vicente builds up the performance and the dialogues of the actresses (which he would present to the audience as real gipsies) on the basis of his intimate knowledge of the courtesans, with the mischievous intention of provoking the other part of the dialogue, that is to say, the very different reactions of the courtesans themselves.]

Given the moralizing intention which underlies Gil Vicente's dramatic technique,[62] it is legitimate to read *Auto de las Gitanas* as a lucid critique of superstition of great scenic effectiveness.

The only play in which palm-reading has a protagonism similar that it attains in Gil Vicente's *auto* is to be found in German 15th century theatre. The gipsy – not the gipsy woman – makes his appearance in a short play, *Die Rockenstuben* (i.e. *The Spinning Mill*) of 1536 by the German playwright Hans Sachs (1494–1576). Here, under the guise of palm-reading, the gipsy, speaking to a peasant, his wife and his servants[63] says all kinds of atrocities. Although both plays are in no obvious way related in their genesis, the parallel proves how much palm-reading gipsies were part of the cultural imagination of the time, so much so that authors from different theatrical worlds perceived their dramatic potential.

In the Castilian theatre of the 15th century, there are further examples of scenes in which palm-reading is linked to the gipsies. In the *Aucto de finamiento de Jacob*, datable – according to Márquez Villanueva (1985, 744, annotation 5) –

---

62 Cf. Cardoso Bernardes (2010, without pagination): "Aunque se trata de un lugar común, es necesario no olvidar que toda la obra de Gil Vicente se centra en la idea de *servicio moral*, prestado al rey y al reino". [Although this is a commonplace statement, it is worth remembering that Gil Vicente's work centres on the idea of a *servicio moral* paid to the king and the kingdom].
63 See the edition by Pannier (1898) and, on this particular aspect, Solms (2008, 53–55) and Tuczay (2012, 106).

in the third quarter of the 16th century, the character of a simpleton in introduced in a story of the Bible. A gipsy woman asks him for a donation and makes fun of him with this prediction:

GITANA. Dame una limozna, hermano
y dezirte e la ventura
mueztra daca, aca eza mano.

BOBO. Que soy contento des'arte.

GITANA. Dezcargate, ponle aqui.

BOBO. Mejor esta par de mi.

GITANA. Pienzas que quiero burlarte?

BOBO. No, mas creo yo que si.

GITANA. No te engañara el diablo,
porque erez honbre avizado
y un poquito enamorado,
y mira lo que te hablo,
que heres bienquisto y amado [. . .]
Bien mueztra esta rraya aqui
que herez un poco rrufian,
y ezta rraya tan cunplida
que llega azt'aca atraz
ez, Juan Gordo, que zabraz
que tienes tan larga vida
que en tuz diaz moriraz.
Tanbien, porque herez velludo,
zeraz dichoso y honrrado;
zeraz trez vezez cazado
y de todaz trez cornudo,
manzo y bienaventurado.[64]

[GITANA: Give me a little charity,
brother, and I will tell thy fortune.
Show me that hand, that hand of thine.

BOBO: This art pleases me.

GITANA: Let loose, put it here.

BOBO: This is better for me.

---

[64] *Aucto de finamiento de Jacob*, ed. Rouanet (1901, I, 207–208, vv. 213–245).

GITANA: Thou thinkst I will mock thee?

BOBO: No, but I think yes.

GITANA: Not the devil can cheat on thee,
because thou art a nimble man
and a little in love,
hark what I say,
thou art fair and beloved . . .
This here line well showeth
that thou art a ruffian,
and this here so ample
which reacheth till there behind
is, Juan Gordo, so that thou knowest
that thou will have a long life that thou wilt die when time is due.
Also, because thou art full of hairs,
thou wilt you will be fortunate and honoured;
thou wilt marry three times
and be cuckold also three times,
meek and full of fortune.]

This humorous episode, inserted in the serious context, uses, as Gil Vicente did, a gipsy literary dialect characterised by a pronounced *ceceo* as a means of provoking hilarity in the audience. As opposed to Gil Vicente but similar to Hans Sachs, the gipsy in the *Aucto de finamiento de Jacob* unabashedly pulls her client's leg.

The other play stemming probably from this period, *Aucto de la huida de Egipto*,[65] also intersperses an entertaining scene, with an old man and his half-witted son as protagonists. They accompany the Holy Family and a group of four gipsies,[66] who tell the fortune to the Virgin Mary and her child, Jesus:

GITANA 4ª. Catemozle la ventura
que a de tener adelante.

---

[65] García-Bermejo Giner recollects it in his *Catálogo* with the number 25.52 and refers to the staging of an *auto* of the same name in 1579 (1996, 181–182). On the dating of the *Códice de autos viejos* and the plays assembled there, see Herrán Alonso (2010, 627–628).

[66] Cf. Herrán Alonso (2010, 629): "La incorporación de otras figuras que no aparecen en el relato evangélico, ni en los apócrifos, obedece en el caso de los gitanos a otra tradición popular creada en torno a la estancia de la Sagrada Familia en Egipto." [The inclusion of other characters, characters who appear neither in the gospels nor in the apocryphal texts, is due, in the case of the gipsies, to another popular tradition created around the stay of the Holy Family in Egypt]. The play is mentioned in passing by Diago (1992, 62) in the context of the palm-reading scene.

GITANA 2ª. Zin zimiente de varon
herez tu madre garrida
dezte bonito garçon,
y virgen sin corruçion
herez dezpuez de parida.
Y quando virgen parizte
muy grande fue tu ventura,
que ningun dolor zentizte;
maz tu zeraz la maz trizte
que jamas se vio criatura.

GITANA 4ª. Puez, yo le quiero catar
la ventura maz zettera
dezte niño singular.

[BOBO] Yo creo andaiz por hurtar
qualque mantilla o quequiera. [. . .]

GITANA 4ª. Zegun que por dizcreçion
alcanzo dezte donzel,
hallo zer zu encarnaçión
cauza de rrezureçion
de muchoz en Yzrrael.
Y zera tan dichozito
y de tan grazioza zuerte
que, aunque le vedez chiquito,
lo que alli puez fue ezcripto
acabara con zu muerte.

GITANA 2ª. Zola una cruz e hallado
que tiene aqui por zeñal,
de dond'ez concetuado
que zera crucificado
por rremcdio univerzal.
Maz encima de la cruz
ay corona, ez de notar,
que aquezte niño Jezuz
luego en la tercera luz
tornara a rrezuzitar.[67]

---

[67] *Aucto de la huida en Egipto*, ed. Rouanet (1901, II, 384–385, vv. 303–344). As Rodríguez-Puértolas (1970, 107 and note 32) observes, the same situation is reduplicated in *La vuelta de Egipto* by Lope de Vega, which we will analyse *infra*.

[Gitana 4ª: Let's look at the fortune
which is awaiting her.

Gitana 2ª: Without the seeds of a man
art thou the comely mother
of this handsome youth,
and a virgin without a taint
art thou after giving birth.
And when thou gavest birth as a virgin
so great was thine fortune
that thou felt no pain;
and still, thou wilt be the saddest
creature there ever was.

Gitana 4ª: Well, I do not want to look
at the assured fortune
of this singular child.
[Bobo] Methinks you want to steal
a mantilla or something . . .

Gitana 4ª: By what I have gathered by
some discretion about this squire,
I find in his incarnation
the cause of resurrection
for many in Israel.
And he will be so lucky
and of such graceful fortune
that, though you see him a little child,
it was written that his life
will end in death.

Gitana 2ª: Only a cross have I found
which serves as a sign here,
which is deemed to say
that he will be crucified
as a universal remedy.
But up on the cross
there is a crown, and so it is known
that this Jesus child
with the third light of day
will resurrect again.]

The device of introducing the fortune-telling gipsies allows for a curious *variatio* of the Biblical account and a display of the mystery of Mary's virginity in words pronounced with their *ceceo* by the gipsies. Herrán contrasts the particularities of this *auto* with the bent of the religious theatre of the time:

> La pieza del *Códice de Autos Viejos* es representativa de un teatro religioso y, en gran medida, oficial e institucionalizado, en tanto que promovido por la autoridad civil y eclesiástica, pero que para los decenios posteriores a 1550 ejecutaban ya las compañías de actores profesionales. [. . .] este *Auto de la huida a Egipto* obedece, en primera instancia, a la configuración de una suerte de drama único que recorre la historia de la salvación desde la creación y caída del hombre hasta su redención por la Encarnación de Cristo y el misterio de la Eucaristía. Pero, además, este todo teológico y dramático propio del antiguo teatro conventual ha evolucionado de acuerdo a las exigencias de un nuevo público y de acuerdo a la moda del momento: sin que por ello se reduzca la carga doctrinal, la pieza ya no sigue de cerca la tradición exegética e introduce personajes graciosos como el bobo o tipo con peculiaridades de dicción como los gitanos. (2010, 630)

> [This play from the *Códice de Autos Viejos* is representative of a religious and, in large measure, official and institutionalised theatre, in so far as it is promoted by the civil and ecclesiastical authorities, but was, in the decades following 1550, put on stage by professional actors. . . . This *Auto de la huida a Egipto* complies, first and foremost, with the set up of a kind of single drama which follows the history of salvation from the creation and the fall of man to his redemption through the incarnation of Christ and the mystery of the Eucharist. But, at the same time, this theological and dramatic entity typical of the ancient conventual theatre has developed in accordance with the demands of a new audience and in accordance with the fashion of the time. Without minimizing its doctrinal charge, the play no longer closely follows the exegetical tradition and introduces comical characters like the simpleton or language peculiarities like those of the gipsies.]

In my view, the introduction of palm-reading gipsies also allows the demonstration of the Virgin Mary's humanity on stage, showing her as a mother deeply concerned with her child's future misfortunes.[68]

In order to return to the profane theatre, we will now attend to one last 15th century comedy with a palm-reading gipsy in it. It is Juan Timoneda's *Aurelia*,[69] probably the model for Lope de Rueda's *Eufemia*, which we will deal with later

---

[68] "O hijo, y por quantas vias / traspasas mi coraçon! / Rreglas de philosophias, / prefacios y profecias / profetican tu pasion; / y el cuchillo que a de dar / fin a tus penas estrañas, / bien se yo que a de cortar / tus carnes, y traspasar / mi anima y mis entrañas", *Aucto de la huida en Egipto*, ed. Rouanet (1901, II, 385, vv. 345–354) [Oh, my son, by how many paths / do you enter my heart! / Rules of philosophy, / prefaces and prophecies / attest to your passion; / and the knife which is to end / your rare pains, / must, as I know well, cut through / your flesh, and run through / my soul and my body].

[69] This comedy was included in the *Turiana* collection (Valencia 1564 and 1565), analysed by Juliá Martínez in the introduction to her edition of the literary works of Timoneda (1948, III, vii–xx).

on.⁷⁰ Both plays dramatise the story of Aurelia and her brother Salucio, who goes on a journey in search of the other half of a magic ring which has the capacity to make visible a tower, in which his father, the necromancer, has hidden all his treasures. In the fourth scene, a group of gipsies shows up in the house of Aurelia, worried because of the prolonged absence of the brother. The gipsies ask for a donation and offer to read her fortune. The distrustful maiden⁷¹ puts the gipsy to the test with a tricky question:

> AURELIA. ¿Seré otra vez casada?
>
> GITANA. Cazada ni despozada
> no erez, maz sello haz:
> mucho tristezica estaz,
> cara de flores. [. . .]
>
> AURELIA. Caéys en tantos errores,
> que 'n verdad
> nos quitáys la voluntad
> en ver vuestros entrevalos.⁷²

---

70 This theory, put forward by Diago (1984, 99), is backed up by Granja (1989, 156, footnote 17). On the theatrical art of Timoneda also see Diago (1981).

71 "GITANA. Ea, daca y dezirte han / la ventura. / AURELIA. Desdicha tengo segura; / ¡que más me haréys saber?", Timoneda, *"Comedia llamada Aurelia"*, ed. Juliá Martínez (1901, 193). [GIPSY: Come here, for your fortune / will be told. / AURELIA: Misfortune will sure be mine; / what else will you have me know?]. Diago (1992, 61): "[. . .] en la jornada cuarta de esta comedia hace su aparición un grupo de gitanos, una mujer, dos hombres y una 'criaturica', que responde exactamente a la convención del tipo marcada por Gil Vicente en su *Auto de las gitanas*. Es decir, cecean al hablar, emplean un lenguaje zalamero, presumen de cristianos, piden limosna y se ofrecen a leer la buena ventura en las rayas de las manos". [. . . in the fourth act of this comedy, a group of gipsies, a woman, two men and a "criaturica" appear on stage. This arrangement perfectly corresponds to the convention of the type established by Gil Vicente in his *Auto de las gitanas*. That is to say, they *cecean* when they speak [i.e. use the sound of <z> to represent <s>], they use flattery and they pretend to be Christians, they ask for a donation and offer to read fortune from the lines of their hands].

72 Timoneda, *"Comedia llamada Aurelia"*, ed. Juliá Martínez (1901, 193–194). Cf. Diago (1992, 62): "En esta comedia, a pesar de que la joven trata de confundirla preguntándole si volverá a casarse, la gitana sabe perfectamente que nunca ha estado casada, aunque lo estará pronto; como también sabe que la persona por la que Aurelia siente inquietud no es otro que su hermano". [In this comedy, although the young man tries to confuse her by asking her if she wants to marry again, the gipsy knows perfectly well that she has never been married, although she soon will. She knows as well that the person because of whom Aurelia feels restless is none other than her brother].

[AURELIA: Will I marry again?

GITANA: Married or betrothed
thou art not, but thou wilt be:
much sadness thou wilt feel,
thou flowery face . . .

AURELIA: Thou makest so many errors,
that in truth I no longer willingly
will hear thy interventions.]

When she is convinced of the gipsy's trustworthiness, she badgers her with her craving to learn about her future:

AURELIA. Dezime ya alguna cosa.

GITANA. Dichoza seraz, dichoza;
danoz, que no noz daz nada,
un dinerico, agraciada.
Por aquí,
veraz que sabraz de mí.

AURELIA. Toma.

GITANA. Azeña acá la mano.
Repozo ternaz temprano.

AURELIA. Plegue a Dios que sea ansí;
mi ventura me dezí
dónde está.

GITANA. Calla, Dioz te la dará;
un poquillo erez bravita;
luego luego ze te quita.

AURELIA. ¿Jesús, acertado ha!

GITANA. En tu caza, mirá acá,
no dezdenez:
tienez gran thezoro y bienez,
maz tú no lo puedez ver.
¡Calla, tuyoz han de ser,
no te penez, no te penez!
Lexoz, lexoz d'aquí tienez
tu enamorado;
por ti tiene gran cuydado.

AURELIA. ¿Es mi marido, o mi padre?

GITANA. Amboz oz parió una madre.[73]

[AURELIA: Tell me more.

GITANA: Fortunate thou wilt be, fortunate;
give us, thou hast not given anything yet,
give us a little money, thank you.
Thus thou wilt hear
what I have to tell thee.

AURELIA: Here.

GITANA: Show me your hand.
Settled thou wilt be soon.

AURELIA: Pray to God it may be like this.
Tell me where my fortune
will lie.

GITANA: Peace, God will grant it to thee.
Thou wilt be a little wild for a time,
but that will soon fade.

AURELIA: Gracious, she is right!

GITANA: Your house, look,
do not disdain it:
thou hast here great treasures and many goods
but you cannot see them.
But, woman, thine they will be!
Do not thou pine, do not pine!
Far, far from here, thou hast
a lover;
he careth so much for thee.

AURELIA: Is that my husband or my father?

GITANA: A mother gave birth to both of you.]

The audience realises that she is a true seer because she is familiar with the story of the invisible tower. Just like Aurelia herself,[74] the audience has no

---

73 Timoneda, "*Comedia llamada Aurelia*", ed. Juliá Martínez (1901, 194–195).
74 "AURELIA. ¡Jesús y assombrado m'ha, / por vida mía!; / yo por burla lo tenía, / mas ¿qué diré? ¿Qué acertado? / ¿Que todo cuanto han hablado / debe ser hechicería!" Timoneda, "*Comedia llamada Aurelia*", ed. Juliá Martínez (1901, 195) [AURELIA: By my troth / you have

reason to doubt the predicted happy ending. It becomes reality in Act V with Salucio's return with the magic ring and a groom for Aurelia. For all this, Juan Timoneda does not exploit in *Aurelia* all the dramatic potential the device of the palm-reading afforded. It is narrowed down to a picturesque note.

4 Palmistry and physiognomy in Lope de Rueda

Lope de Rueda (1510–1566) gives evidence of his great versatility as a playwright by the highly efficient use of the textualization of physiognomy and palmistry in his *pasos* and comedies.

In the *Comedia llamada Eufemia* (about 1542–1544 or 1554),[75] just as in *Égloga interlocutoria*, a mole is mentioned,[76] which, contrary to that of the play by Diego de Ávila, has a certain protagonism in the plot. Let me briefly remind the reader that in this comedy, which deals with an amorous mix-up possibly in the Boccaccio tradition,[77] Leonardo attempts to marry his sister Eufemia to a nobleman, Valiano. These plans are thwarted through the action of Paulo, a traitor who dishonours Eufemia making up an erotic involvement of the young woman. In order to support his lie, he shows his master a kind of trophy:

> En fin, que ella me dio para que me pusiesse en el sombrero o en la gorra un pedaço de un cabello que le nasce del hombro izquierdo en un lunar grande. Y por ser señales que el señor su hermano Leonardo, y tu muy privado, no puede negar, acordé de traello. Veslo aquí.[78]
>
> [In short, she has given me a piece of hair which grows from a big mole in her left shoulder, for me to wear it in my hat or in my cap. This being a sign which the Lord Leonardo, her brother nor you can ignore, I agreed to bring it. Here it is.]

The mole as a sign of identity is a highly popular motif, which likewise appears in the ninth *novella* of the second day of the *Decameron*,[79] just like the details

---

taken me by surprise! / For an antic I took it, / but what shall I say? That it is the truth? / That all they have said / must be witchcraft!].

75 On he question of dating see Ruggieri (2013, without pagination).
76 "Que tú de tornarte habías medio loco / D' estalle mirando aquel lunarito", Guillén de Ávila, *Égloga ynterlocutoria*, ed. Kohler (1911, 259, vv. 751–752) [For you had gone half crazy / by looking at that little birthmark].
77 On the current state of the debate concerning the influence of the *Novena Novella* of the second day of the *Decameron* see Ruggieri (2013). For Johnson (1968), the crucial difference is the supposed presentation of Leonardo as a convert.
78 Lope de Rueda, *Eufemia*, ed. Hermenegildo (1985, 102).
79 In this *novella*, Ginevra, the woman accused of infidelity, has "sotto la sinistra poppa un neo ben grandicello, dintorno al quale son forse sei peluzzi biondi come oro", *Decameron* II, 9,

about the hair. A comic touch, possibly involuntary, is the size of the hair which grows in Eufemia's mole and which makes its appearance on stage. Paulo shows it to his master, materializing it with a deictic "Here". Given that, unlike Boccaccio's traitor Ambrogiuolo, Paulo cannot plausibly have had occasion of having seen Eufemia naked, he turns to Cristina, the maid, who, ingenuous rather than malicious, provides the ominous hair of the mole. Not only through the construction of the plot, but also through the subtle characterisation of the maid Lope de Rueda shows great dramatic skill. A case in point is the introduction of the gipsy, a character not contained in the episode of the *Decameron*, who reads Eufemia's hand, as she is worried about the prolonged absence of her brother.[80] This long scene fulfils a number of different functions within the play which call for a more detailed analysis. Speaking to Cristina and Eufemia, the gipsy presents herself behaving according to the stereotype and with the well-known *ceceo*, though less pronounced than in other plays:

> GITANA. Calla, calla, garrida, garrida. Dame limosna por Dioz y diréte la buenaventura que tienes de haber tú y la señora.
>
> EUFEMIA. ¿Yo? ¡Ay cuitada! ¿Qué ventura podrá tener que sea próspera la que del vientre de su madre nasció sin ella?
>
> GITANA. Calla, calla, señora honrada. Pon un dinerico aquí. Sabrás maravillas.
>
> EUFEMIA. ¿Qué tiene de saber la que contino estuvo tan falta de consuelo cuanto colmada de çoçobras, miserias y afanes?
>
> CRISTINA. ¡Ay, señora! ¡Por vida suya que le dé alguna cosa, y oigamos los desatinos que aquestas, por la mayor parte, suelen dezir!
>
> GITANA. Escucha, escucha, pico de urraca, que más sabemos cuando queremos que nadie piensa.
>
> EUFEMIA. Acabemos. Toma y dale aquesso y vaya con Dios.
>
> CRISTINA. A buena fe, que antes que se vaya nos ha de catar el signo.[81]
>
> [GITANA: Peace, peace, fair lady. Give me a little offering, bless thee, and I will tell thee thy fate and that of thy lady.

---

ed. Branca (1951, I, 284) [beneath the left stern a very old mole, around which are perhaps six hairs as blond as gold]. On the popular motif see Thompson (1932) and, with reference to Lope de Rueda's comedy, the examples collected by Ruggieri (2013).
80 On the motif of the fortune-telling cf. *Eufemia* by Márquez Villanueva (1985, 744, footnote 5).
81 Lope de Rueda, *Eufemia*, ed. Hermenegildo (1985, 102).

EUFEMIA: What, mine? My little timid something? What prosperous fortune could one have who was torn from her mother's womb without her?

GITANA: Peace, peace, honourable lady. Put a little money here. You will hear wonders.

EUFEMIA: What may one want to know who has been so bereft of comfort and so full of worries, miseries and eagerness?

CRISTINA: Alas, good lady! By my troth, thou wilt live up to something, and let us hear what blunders those may tell.

GITANA: Hear me, thou magpie, we know most when we want no one to think.

EUFEMIA: Let's end this. Take this and go with God.

CRISTINA: By my faith, before she goes she must make us taste her sign.]

Eufemia and Cristina reveal two different forms of reacting towards the possibility to know the future. Eufemia's deep pessimism makes her quite uninterested in knowing what her future misfortunes may be. Hence, she does not even ask herself if this is possible or permissible. The maid, however, is portrayed as indiscreet. She wants to hear the gipsy's prophesy in order to divert herself and have a good time, showing, at the same time, a healthy scepticism regarding the veracity of the prediction. Besides, she is the one who sets the action in motion. On the one hand, it is her curiosity which makes Eufemia refrain from dismissing the gipsy as she had intended, on the other hand, she seeks to take revenge of the gipsy by branding her as a trickster.

EUFEMIA. Déxala, váyase con Dios, que no estoy agora d'essas gracias.

GITANA. Sossiega, sossiega, señora gentil, ni tomes fatiga antes de su tiempo, que harta te está aparejada.

EUFEMIA. Yo lo creo. Agora sí habéis acertado.

CRISTINA. No se entristezca, señora, que todo es burla y mentiras cuanto estas echan por la boca.

GITANA. ¿Y la esportilla de los afeites que tienes escondida en el almariete de las alcominías, ¿es burla?

CRISTINA. ¡Ay, señora, y habla por la boca del que arriedro vaya! Ansí haya buen siglo la madre que me parió que dize la mayor verdad del mundo.

EUFEMIA. ¿Hay tal cosa? ¿Qu'es posible aquesso?

CRISTINA. Como estamos aquí. Dezí más, hermana.

GITANA. No querría que te corriesses por estar tu señora delante.

CRISTINA. No haré por vida de mi ánima. ¿Qué puedes tú dezir que sea cosa que perjudique mi honra?

GITANA. ¿Dasme licencia que lo diga?

CRISTINA. Digo que sí. Acabemos.

GITANA. El par de las tórtolas que heziste creer a la señora que se las habían comido los gatos, ¿dónde se comieron?

CRISTINA. ¡Mirá de qué se acuerda! Aquesso fue antes que mi señor Leonardo se partiesse de esta tierra.

GITANA. Assí es la verdad, pero tú y el moço de los caballos os las comistes en el descanso de la escalera. ¡Ah, bien sabes que digo en todo verdad!

CRISTINA. ¡Mal lograda me coma la tierra si, con los ojos lo viera, dixera mayor verdad.[82]

[EUFEMIA: Leave her, let her go. Be with God, I am in no mood for these antics now.

GITANA: Be calm, gentle lady, be calm, do not weary before thy time, enough is destined to come.

EUFEMIA: I give credit to that. This time thou art right.

CRISTINA: Do not be saddened, lady, all is mockery and lie when those open their mouths.

GITANA: And the little casket with the ablutions you have hidden in the closet for the herbs, is that mockery?

CRISTINA: Alas, lady, she speaks with the mouth of someone who is daunted! Never for a hundred years has the mother who bore me spoken a truer word.

EUFEMIA: Is there such a thing? Can this be possible?

CRISTINA: As we stand here. Say more, sister.

GITANA: I would not want thee to be embarrassed with thy lady in front of you.

CRISTINA: I will not be, for the life of me. What might thou say that can harm my honour?

GITANA: Thou art giving me licence to say it?

---

[82] Lope de Rueda, *Eufemia*, ed. Hermenegildo (1985, 99–100).

CRISTINA: I say yes. Let us end this.

GITANA: The two turtledoves thou madst thy lady believe were eaten by the cats, where were they eaten?

CRISTINA: See how she remembers! That was before my lord Leonardo set off from this land.

GITANA: That is true, but thou and the stable boy ate them sitting on the landing. Thou knowst I am telling the truth!

CRISTINA: May the earth swallow me, with mine eyes open, if there is anything more truthful than this.]

According to Hermenegildo, "enfrentamiento entre Cristina [. . .] y la gitana, deja al descubierto dos conductas tradicionalmente fijadas por el teatro. La criada es ladrona. La gitana es maestra en el arte de la burla y la mentira"[83] [this clash between Cristina . . . and the gipsy uncovers two traditional forms of conduct attached to the theatre. The maid is the crook. The gipsy is the mistress of the art of mockery and deception]. I agree that this scene disqualifies the character of the maid, a fundamental factor which makes the play work, she being the one who is responsible for her mistress's disgrace. Nevertheless, towards the end of the scene, her ingenuous reaction to the prophecy, which portends she will have nine husbands, underlines her gullibility,[84] which explains why she accedes to Paulo's wish to entrust him the hair from her mistress's mole. As for the character of the gipsy, I disagree with Hermenegildo's view. In spite of leaving open the question as to how the gipsy might have known of Cristina's pranks, Lope de Rueda backs up her credibility and thus her other prediction, which is of fundamental importance for the progress of the action.

GITANA. Pues señora, una persona tienes lexos de aquí que te quiere mucho y, aunque agora está muy favorescido de su señor, no pasará mucho que esté en peligro de perder la vida por una traición que le tienen armada. Mas calla, que, aunque sea todo por tu causa,

---

83 See the introduction to his edition of Lope de Rueda, *Eufemia*, ed. Hermenegildo (1985, 33).
84 "CRISTINA. ¿Y de mí no me dizes nada, si seré casada o soltera? GITANA. Muger serás de nueve maridos y todos vivos. ¿Qué más quieres saber? [. . .] CRISTINA. ¡Ay, amarga de mí, señora! ¿Y no vee que me dixo que diz que sería yo muger de nueve maridos y que todos estarían vivos? ¡Ay, malaventurada fui yo! ¿Y cómo puede ser aquello?", Lope de Rueda, *Eufemia*, ed. Hermenegildo (1985, 101) [CRISTINA: And of me thou sayest nothing, if I will be married or not? GITANA: Woman, of nine men will you be the wife, and all alive! What else dost thou want to know? . . . CRISTINA: Such bitterness for me, milady! Did you not hear how she told me that I will be wife to nine men, and all alive? Oh, unfortunate was I! How could this be?].

Dios, que es verdadero juez y no consiente que ninguna falsedad esté mucho tiempo oculta, descubrirá la verdad de todo ello.

EUFEMIA. ¡Ay desventurada hembra! ¿Por causa mía dizes que se verá essa persona en peligro? ¿Y quién podrá ser, cuitada, si no fuesse mi querido hermano?

GITANA. Yo, señora, no sé más, pero pues en cosa de las que a tu criada se han dicho no ha habido mentira. . . Yo me voy.[85]

[GITANA: You see, there is a person far from here who loves you very much and who, although he is now held in great favour by his lord, will shortly be in danger of death because somebody wants to betray him. But don't you worry, although all this may be your fault, the Lord, who is the true judge and will not allow any deceit to remain undisclosed, will uncover the truth of all this.

EUFEMIA: Oh, wretched woman that thou art! Because of me thou sayest this person will be in danger? And how could this be, thou sorrowful person? It can be no other but my dear brother.

GITANA: I, milady, know no more, but perhaps there was no falsehood in what they told your maid. . . I will wend my way. Stay alert, cause if I hear more, I will send you word. God be with you!]

The gipsy has gained Eufemia's confidence,[86] and the audience, together with the protagonist, gives credit to the veracity of the foreboding.[87] This is, obviously, a dramatic device to awaken the audience's curiosity, who will wonder what will happen to Leonardo and how things will work out.

---

85 Lope de Rueda, *Eufemia*, ed. Hermenegildo (1985, 100–101).
86 Cf. the end of the scene: "GITANA. [. . .] Dios te consuele, señora. EUFEMIA. ¿No me dices más en mi negocio y assí me dejas dudosa de mi salud? GITANA. No sé más que dezirte. Solamente tu trabajo no será tan durable que en el tiempo del más fuerte peligro no lo resuelva prudencia y fortuna, que todos remanescáis tan contentos y alegres, cuanto la misericordia divina lo sabe obrar." Lope de Rueda, *Eufemia*, ed. Hermenegildo (1985, 101) [GITANA: . . . May God console you, milady. EUFEMIA: You say no more about my business and leave me troubled about my health? GITANA: I know no more to say. Only that your troubles will not last long, in times of greatest danger prudence and fortune will resolve it, that you will all be happy and merry, divine mercy will bring it to pass].
87 In the introduction to his edition of *Eufemia*, Hermenegildo observes: "La gitana [. . .] queda desrealizada y convertida en figura de índole sobrenatural, de dimensión extrahumana, cuya misión dramática, cuyo rol, es hacer el doble anuncio a Eufemia". (1985, 33) [The gipsy . . . is bereft of reality and is turned into a character of a supernatural drift, of superhuman dimension, whose dramatic mission, whose role it is to make a twofold prediction to Eufemia].

In the second *paso* collected in *El Deleitoso* (1588), the Sevilian playwright plays with the deformation of the inkhorn term *fisiognomía*[88] in the speech of the simpleton Alameda, who uses words like *hilosomía*[89] and *filomancía*.[90] As Amado Alonso (1948) has worked out, Sancho Panza's linguistic distortions go back to the early theatre and above all to Lope de Rueda.[91]

---

[88] As a matter of fact, this is a term of minor presence in 16th century theatre. It is used in the Plautus translation by Timoneda in 1559: "Sosia: No te fatigues, que ya me voy. ¡Por la casa de Apolo juro que cuando miro bien a éste y reconozco mi fisonomía cual yo la he visto en un espejo, él en todo es semejante a mí! El bonete; el vestido, ni más ni menos que yo; el calzado, la estatura y el assiento de la barba, todo es semejante a mí. Sólo en una cosa nos desparecemos como el huevo y la castaña: qu' él es valiente y yo cobarde. Quiero tornarme al puerto, y contar lo que passa a mi amo, si ya por mis pecados no me desconosce también." *Comedia de Anfitrión. Traducción de Plauto*, ed. (1947–1948, I, 263–264) [Sosia: Do not weary of me, I will set off. By the house of Apollo I swear that when I look carefully and recognise my physiognomy, as I have seen it in a mirror, he is like me in all! The bonnet, the dress, neither more nor less than me. His stature and the line of the beard, all is likeness! There is only one thing in which we are apart like the egg and the chestnut: that he is valiant and I'm a coward. I will go back to the harbour and tell my lord what has happened, if, for all my sins, he still knows who I am].

[89] "Pues sepa vuesa merced que, viniendo del monte por leña me la'ncontré junto al vallado del corralejo este diabro de hilosomía", Lope de Rueda, "Compendio llamado 'El Deleitoso'" ed. Sánchez Jiménez & Sánchez Salas (2006, 14) [May your lord know that, coming from the mountain looking for firewood, by the fence of the pen, I met this devil of *hilosomía*].

[90] "¿Y qué se ha de hacer de aquesta filomancía, o qué es?", Lope de Rueda, "Compendio llamado 'El Deleitoso'" ed. Sánchez Jiménez & Sánchez Salas (2006, 14) [And what will become of this filomancía or whatever it is?]. On this aspect see García-Bermejo Giner (2016a, 30–31).

[91] Cf. Veres D'Ocón: "Tales prevaricaciones se derivan de las ideas y preocupaciones culturales del Renacimiento: son como el dializador que pone de manifiesto, con un propósito cómico, los diferentes componentes de esas preocupaciones culturales, disociándolos en dos planos antagónicos y complementarios: el de rusticidad frente al de urbanidad" (1950, 195) [Such perversions of justice derive from the cultural concepts of the Renaissance. They are the diaylizator which lays bare, with a comical intent, the different components of these cultural concerns, dissociating them into two antagonistic and complementary blueprints, that of rusticity in opposition to that of urbanity]. Minic-Vidovic tackles the question from the point of view of Bajtinian carnival, saying: "Al poner en boca de sus simples el latín macarrónico y las prevaricaciones de cultismos [. . .], como, por ejemplo, 'cilicio' por silencio, 'hilosomía' y 'filomancía' por fisonomía, 'melecina' por medicina, etc., Lope de Rueda parodia la superioridad pretendida de los que sirven de tales formas de hablar: el médico, el bachiller, el bachiller, el licenciado y los amos" (2007, 19) [By putting into the mouth of his simpletons the malapropisms and perversion of inkhorn terms . . . such as *cilicio* for *silencio*, *hilosomía* and *filomancía* for *fisionomía*, *melecina* for *medicina*, etc., Lope de Rueda parodies the pretended superiority of those who use this way of speaking: the physician, the scholar, the master and the lords].

Chapter 3
17th century theatre and occultism

1 Palmistry in the theatre of Cervantes

It is well known that Cervantes highly appreciated the theatre of Lope de Rueda[1] and got inspiration from his theatre:[2] "Yo, como el más viejo que allí estaba, dije q ue me acordaba de haber visto representar al gran Lope de Rueda, varón insigne en la representación y en el entendimiento"[3] [I, as the oldest one there, said that I remembered having seen Lope de Rueda on stage, a man distinguished by his works and his understanding]. Cervantes probably knew the comedy *Eufemia* and, as Márquez Villanueva (1985, 744, footnote 5) suspects in connection with his reading of *La gitanilla*, other literary works with palm-reading gipsies.[4]

In the comedy dealing with captivity, *Los baños de Argel* (1601–1602),[5] Cervantes' knowledge of Lope de Rueda's theatre is evidenced by his representation of a colloquy of the Christian captives.[6] In the third of the *ocho comedias*, a recast of *El trato de Argel*,[7] he puts on stage two amorous schemes, one of which

---

[1] See Palacín (1952), Johnson (1981, 96–98), Diago (1992, 51–52) and Rey Hazas (2005, 33–34).
[2] Alonso (1948, 19–20, footnote 45) has studied what impact the linguistic perversions of Rueda's theatre had on Sancho.
[3] See the *Prólogo al lector* in Cervantes: *Comedias y tragedias*, ed. Gómez Canseco (2015, 9).
[4] On the reading of the hand and the forehead in this *novela ejemplar* see Gernert (2016). On Cervantes and the gipsy world, the studies by Starkie (1960), Guasch Melis (1999) and Charnon-Deutsch (2004, 17–44) can be consulted.
[5] "El pequeño debate crítico que ha generado la datación de *Los baños de Argel* abre un arco de composición que abarca desde 1582 a 1614", Baras Escolá (2015, II, 84) in the introduction to his edition of the play [The brief critical debate that the dating of *Los baños de Argel* has triggered off embraces a time span from 1582 to 1614]. After summarizing the present state of the debate, the editor suggests a date 'between the autumn of 1601 and the spring of 1602' (85).
[6] "OSORIO. Antes que más gente acuda, / el coloquio se comience, / que es del gran Lope de Rueda / –impreso por Timoneda–, / que en vejez al tiempo vence ", Cervantes, *Los baños de Argel*, III, vv. 2084–2087, ed. Baras Escolá (2015, 324). [OSORIO: Before more people gather, / may the colloquy start, / which is of the great Lope de Rueda / – printed by Timoneda –, / who in age surpasses time].
[7] On the relationship between *Los baños de Argel* and *El trato de Argel* (and that of both with *Los cautivos de Argel* by Lope) see Casalduero (1951, reed. 1966, 20), Meregalli (1972), Fothergill-Payne (1989), Stackhouse (2000), Castillo (2004) and Rodríguez Rodríguez (2010). On the problem concerning the *moriscos* in *Los baños de Argel* see Irigoyen García (2008), and on the representation of the reality of Algeria see Limami (2006).

Open Access. © 2021 Folke Gernert, published by De Gruyter. This work is licensed under the Creative Commons Attribution-NonCommercial-NoDerivatives 4.0 International License.
https://doi.org/10.1515/9783110695755-004

will be concerning us here, the relationship between Costanza and don Fernando, who are the object of the erotic desires of Halima and her husband Caurali.[8] During the encounter of the lovers in the house of their Algerian mistress, communication between them is frustrated by the insinuations of Halima, who, under the pretext of reading his hand, seeks physical contact with him:

> HALIMA. La blandura o la aspereza
> de las manos nos da muestra
> de la abundancia o pobreza
> de vosotros. Muestra, muestra,
> no las huyas, que es simpleza:
> porque si eres de rescate,
> será ocasión que te trate
> con proceder justo y blando.
> ZARA ¿Qué miras?
>
> COSTANZA. Estoy mirando
> un extraño disparate.
>
> D. FERNANDO. Señora, a mi amo toca
> el hacer esa experiencia,
> aunque a risa me provoca
> que a tan engañosa ciencia
> deis creencia mucha o poca;
> porque hay pobres holgazanes
> en nuestra tierra, galanes
> y del trabajo enemigos.
>
> HALIMA. Estas manos son testigos
> de quién eres; no te allanes.
>
> COSTANZA. (¡Ay, embustera gitana!
> En esas rayas que miras
> está mi desdicha llana.
> ¡Qué despacio las retiras,
> enemigo!)
>
> ZARA. ¿Qué has, cristiana?
>
> COSTANZA. ¿Qué tengo de haber? Nonada.[9]

---

8 On this group of characters which "opera en la dinámica de las relaciones de comedia" [operates in the dynamism of the relations of comedy] see Doménici (2015, 66).
9 Cervantes, *Los baños de Argel*, II, vv. 1087–1113, ed. Baras Escolá (2015, 286–287).

[HALIMA: The blandness or asperity
of a hand shows us
abundance or poverty
in you. Show it, show it,
do not escape, it is simple:
for if you are to be rescued,
it will be advisable
to proceed justly and tenderly.
What are you looking at?

COSTANZA: I am looking at
some strange madness.

D. FERNANDO: Lady, it is my lord
who must make this experience,
though it makes me laugh
that you should give little or much credit
to such a deceitful science;
cause there are poor idlers
in our lands, gallants,
who shy away from work.

HALIMA: These hands witness
to whom you belong; do not escape.

COSTANZA: (Oh, deceitful gipsy!
In these lines that you are looking at
my plain misfortune lies.
How slowly you withdraw them,
enemy!)

ZARA: What is it, Christian?

COSTANZA: Oh, it's nothing, a trifle.]

It is striking that Costanza should call Halima *embustera gitana*, 'deceitful gipsy', associating her rival with a badly-renowned ethnic group,[10] who, in the

---

10 In his study of the Muslim women who exercise authority over their men, Delgado García (2010) makes no mention of Halima and centres his analysis of *Los baños de Argel* on Zahara. On the picture of the Muslim world in *Los baños de Argel* see Canavaggio, who speaks of an "una representación infinitamente más matizada que la deformación caricaturesca a la que nos acostumbran los escritos polémicos de sus contemporáneos" (1987, 129) [infinitely more nuanced representation than the caricature-like deformation to which we are used through the polemical writings of his contemporaries]; also see Morrow, who sets off from the Orientalistic theories of Edward Said and remarks that "los musulmanes se caracterizan por cualidades opuestas a las de los españoles: crueldad, violencia y liviandad, entre otros rasgos negativos"

cultural and dramatic collective imagination, is closely related to the fortune-telling arts. The function of this palmistry scene is different from that of the scenes analysed above: this is a lecherous woman, and, on top of it, a Moor, who makes use of it in order to approach the man she desires.

In *Pedro de Urdemalas* (1615),[11] the last of the *Ocho comedias* by Cervantes, the protean protagonist gives an account of his picaresque biography to Maldonado,[12] the gipsy, finishing the account of his life's voyage with a prediction:

> Es Pedro de Urde mi nombre,
> mas un cierto Malgesí,
> mirándome un día las rayas
> de la mano, dijo así:
> "Añadidle, Pedro, al *Urde*
> un *malas*, pero advertid,
> hijo, que habéis de ser rey,
> fraile y papa, y matachín.
> Y avendraos por un gitano
> un caso que sé decir
> que le escucharán los reyes
> y gustarán de le oír.
> Pasaréis por mil oficios
> trabajosos, pero al fin
> tendréis uno do seáis
> todo cuanto he dicho aquí."
> Y, aunque yo no le doy crédito,
> todavía veo en mí
> un no sé qué que me inclina
> a ser todo lo que oí;
> pues, como de este pronóstico
> el indicio veo en ti,

(2003, 382) [the Muslims are characterised by qualities opposed to those of the Spaniards: cruelty, violence and fickleness, amongst other unfavourable features].

11 In the introduction to his edition of the play, Sáez, concerning the date of the writing or the revision of the comedy, favours a date close to that of publication (2014, II, 146–147).

12 For Sáez, *Pedro de Urdemalas* "constituye la apuesta más firme –y arriesgada– de dar vida dramática al pícaro" (2014, 114) [constitutes the highest – and risky – wager to give dramatic life to the *pícaro*]. On the character's picaresque essence and the classification of the play as a 'picaresque comedy', see Surtz (1980), Müller-Bochat (1984, 231) and Arias Careaga, who argues: "El personaje cervantino no es un pícaro, tampoco es una mera copia de un tipo folklórico; lo que hace Cervantes es servirse de las posibilidades que le ofrecen estos aspectos" (1992, 47) [The Cervantian character is no *pícaro*, nor is it a mere copy of the popular type; what Cervantes does is making use of the possibilities which these aspects offer him]. González Puche allots a number of chapters of his monograph to the character's *genealogía folclórica* (2012, 118–128).

digo que he de ser gitano,
y que lo soy desde aquí.¹³

[My name is Pedro de Urde,
but a certain Malgesí,
looking one day at the lines
of my hand, thus spoke:
"Add, Pedro, to *Urde*
a *malas*, but be alerted,
my son, that you will be king,
friar and pope, and butcher.
And let a gipsy tell you
of a case which, I know,
would make kings listen
and be pleased by what they hear.
You will have to go through
a thousand laborious trades, but
you will end up in one where you
will be all that which I said."
And, although I do not give credit to it,
there is something inside me which inclines me
to believe that I will be all this I have heard.
For, since I see in you this prophecy,
I say I must be a gipsy,
and that from now on I will be.]

As Romo Feito aptly said, this autobiography of Pedro de Urdemalas functions as the "elemento estructurador de toda la obra" (2008, 116)¹⁴ [element which gives structure to the whole play]. It is the sorcerer Malgesí, the Maugis of the *chanson de Maugis d'Aigremont*¹⁵ and the Malagigi of the epic poems of the Italian Renaissance by Pulci, Boiardo y Ariosto, turned into a dramatic character in Cervantes' comedy *La casa de los celos y selvas de Ardenia*, a character who has a gift for the art of palmistry. He reads the lines of the hand of Pedro de Urdemalas,

---

13 Cervantes, *Pedro de Urdemalas*, I, vv. 744–767, ed. Sáez (2015, 824).
14 There is a variety of interpretations of this prediction: Nagy (1981, 276) considers it to be a means of overcoming the condition of the *pícaro* Pedro. Also see Rössner (1989, 49–50), Rey Hazas (2005, 74) and González Puche (2013, 34).
15 Maugis is a kind of *alter ego* of Pedro de Urdemalas, according to the description by Barthelot: "Mais il est avant tout une figure de trompeur, de *trickster*, qui se tire d'affaire dans les situations les plus intenables grâce à sa ruse, et à son art de déguisement." (1995, 322) [But above all he is a deceiver, a trickster, who gets away with the most untenable situations thanks to his cunning, and his art of disguise]. On this character also see Lichtblau (2001) and the edition of *Maugis d'Aigremont* by Vernay (1980). Sarmati (2008, 764) deals with the 'references to the world of the chivalric narrative' in *Pedro de Urdemalas* without mentioning Malgesí.

predicting his future adventures, which, despite Pedro's disbelief, turn out to be right. Just as in the case of the death of the prince Alcaráz in the *Book of Good Love* 123–140, this forecast becomes reality when, during the third day, Pedro de Urdemalas, as an actor, can embody both a king and the pope.[16]

> Llegado ha ya la ocasión
> donde la adivinación
> que un hablante Malgesí
> echó un tiempo sobre mí,
> tenga efecto y conclusión.
> Ya podré ser patriarca,
> pontífice y estudiante,
> emperador y monarca,
> que el oficio de farsante
> todos estados abarca.[17]

> [The occasion has arrived
> where the divination
> that a fortune-teller
> once cast over me
> will finally have effect.
> I could be a patriarch,
> the pontifex or a scholar,
> emperor and monarch,
> cause the trade of the actor
> encompasses them all.]

As Núñez Rivera argues, "con la intervención de la profecía de Malgesí y su cumplimiento a la postre, Cervantes da un aldabonazo final al concepto del determinismo picaresco, burlándose de nuevo de él, ya que la existencia propia no depende de unos orígenes determinados y determinantes, sino que se diseña en

---

[16] For meta-theatricality see Zimic (1977), Rössner (1989), Estévez Molinero (1995, 91–93), Sosa Antonietti (2006), Lewis-Smith (2011), and Enguix Barber (2015, 451–462). In his article on the picaresque lives in Cervantes, Zahareas concludes the paragraph dealing with *Pedro de Urdemalas* saying: "En vista de la ideología estamental respecto a la pureza de la sangre [. . .] Pedro, como artista, manipula la realidad para al fin y al cabo transformarla en teatro: a la notoria 'ilusión' teatral de la realidad histórica él opone el único antídoto accesible a un marginado: la realidad 'histórica' de cómo se hacen las ilusiones: por hombres para hombres" (2001, 470) [In view of the ideology concerning the purity of blood . . . Pedro, as an artist, manipulates reality in order to, in the final analysis, transform it into theatre: to the well-known theatrical "illusion" of historical reality he opposes the only antidote accessible to an outsider: the "historical" reality of how illusions are created: by people for people].

[17] Cervantes, *Pedro de Urdemalas*, III, vv. 2860–2869, ed. Sáez (2015, 895).

instancias más elevadas y ajenas"[18] [with the final intervention of Malgesí's prophecy and its later fulfilment, Cervantes gives a final call to picaresque determinism, once again ridiculing it, since existence itself does not depend on determined and determining origins, but is designed by higher and alien agencies]. As for the tradition of the palm-reading gipsies,[19] Cervantes intersperses only a short remark,[20] but quite deliberately chooses Malgesí as the author of the prophecy, Malgesí, according to Berthelot, being characterised by "dimension ludique [. . .] qui ne résiste jamais au plaisir de se déguiser et de tromper autrui sur son identité" (1995, 324) [a ludic dimension . . . which never resists the desire of disguising itself or of leading others astray with regard to its identity]. Cervantes, who knew the chivalric literature very well, by way of this protean character, adds a new dimension to fortune-telling which the palm-reading gipsy does not have.

Before dealing with Lope's literary work, it is worth mentioning an *entremés* which has been attributed equally to Cervantes or Lope but which was probably written by Gaspar de Barrionuevo.[21] It is *Los habladores* or *Los dos habladores*, a short play in which the impoverished nobleman Roldán badgers a certain Sarmiento, who has had to pay a large amount of money to a nobleman whom he has attacked with a knife and who is asked to attack him again, albeit for less

---

18 Núñez Rivera (2014), *apud* Sáez (2014a, 121).
19 On the gipsy world of *Pedro de Urdemalas* see Estévez Molinero (1995, 91–92). As Rey Hazas (1994, 199) points out with regard to the episode involving Belica, "es posible incluso que se entronquen con el suceso acaecido a una tía del dramaturgo, maría de Cervantes, que mantuvo relaciones amorosas con Don Martín de Mendoza, hijo bastardo de Don Diego Hurtado de Mendoza, Duque del Infantado, apodado 'El Gitano', por ser hijo de una gitana llamada María de Cabrera, la tía de nuestro autor y don Martín tuvieron una hija, llamada Martina, que bien pudiera haber sido el modelo lejano de Belica y Preciosa" [it may even be related to something which had happened to the dramatist's aunt, María de Cervantes, who maintained an amorous relationship with Don Martín de Mendoza, an illegitimate son of Don Diego Hurtado de Mendoza, Duque del Infantado, nicknamed *El Gitano*, for being the son of a gipsy. María de Cabrera, our playwright's aunt, and Don Martín had a daughter, Martina, who may well have been the remote model of Belica and Preciosa].
20 "Silerio ¿Sabéis la buenaventura? / Belica La mala nunca se ignora / de la humilde que levanta / su deseo a alteza tanta, / que sobrepuja a las nubes", Cervantes, *Pedro de Urdemalas*, III, vv. 1672–1675, ed. Sáez (2015, 854) [Silerio: Do you know your fortune? / Belica: The bad fortune is always known / to the humble who raises / his desires to such a height, / that it surpasses the clouds].
21 In his edition of the text, Fernández de Moratín (1838, 501–504) attributes it, without further ado, to Cervantes, an attribution rejected in Baras Escolá's (2012, 196–197) edition of the *entremeses* by Cervantes. Baras Escolá concludes: "Como se ve, todo apunta al entorno de Lope y nada a Cervantes" [As we can see, all points to Lope and his entourage and nothing to Cervantes]. Madroñal suggests authorship of Gaspar de Barrionuevo (1562–ca. 1624), Lope's Toledan friend (1993, 121–122).

money. Amongst other things, Roldán, who is one of the title-giving characters, interprets his interlocutor's physiognomy:

> ROLDÁN. Dice muy bien usted: porque la ley fue inventada para la quietud; y la razón es el alma de la ley; y quien tiene alma, tiene potencias: tres son las potencias del alma, memoria, voluntad y entendimiento: usted tiene muy buen entendimiento; porque el entendimiento se conoce en la fisonomía, y la de usted es perversa, por la concurrencia de Saturno y Júpiter; aunque Venus le mira en cuadrado, en la decanoria del signo ascendente por el horóscopo.[22]
>
> [ROLDÁN: You speak the truth, because the law was invented for peacefulness; reason is the soul of the law; and who has a soul, has faculties: three are the faculties of the soul, memory, will and understanding: you have very good understanding; for the understanding can be told by the physiognomy, and yours is perverse, by virtue of the concurrence of Saturn and Jupiter; although Venus looks at it aslant, in the decan of the ascendant by the horoscope.]

In his speech, Roldán beats about the bush: he picks up a word uttered by Sarmiento in order to associate it with the theory of the three faculties of the soul and to physiognomy and, from there, to judicial astrology. The character's speech is void of meaning and, thus, ridicules the fortune-telling skills.

2 The occult knowledge of Lope de Vega

There are multiple references to science in Lope's theatre, from medicine[23] to astrology.[24] In his comedies, Lope also mentions a number of authorities in occult

---

22 [Cervantes], *"Los dos habladores"*, ed. Fernández de Moratín (1838, 501).
23 Cf. Albarracín Teulón (1954), Sánchez (2005) y Slater (2007, 604–605): "Por un lado, Lope representa una enorme cantidad de saberes populares relativos a plantas y a sus usos medicinales, culinarios y agrícolas. Por otro, Lope nos permite considerar de otra forma la difusión de las ideas desde los textos médicos clásicos y modernos, es decir las ideas de Nicandro, Teofrasto, Galeno, Hipócrates y demás pueden aparecer en un escenario popular, entonces es que tenemos información de que esas ideas tenían una amplia difusión entre los no especialistas". [On the one hand, Lope represents an enormous amount of popular knowledge regarding plants and their medical, culinary and agricultural uses. On the other hand, Lope allows us to view from a different angle the spread of the ideas derived from classical and modern medical texts, i.e. the ideas of Nicander, Theophrastus, Galen, Hippocrates, and others within a popular framework, and it is due to this that we know that these ideas enjoyed an ample diffusion amongst non-specialists].
24 For Lope and astrology see Millé y Giménez (1927), Halstead (1939), McCready (1960), Andrés (1996), Vicente García (2009) and (2011), Pedrosa (2014), as well as Sánchez Jiménez (2014).

sciences: Giovan Battista Della Porta in *El amante agradecido* (about 1602),[25] Agrippa von Nettesheim[26] and Girolamo Cardano in *La boda entre dos maridos* (1595–1601)[27] and the same Cardano[28] and Jean Taisnier[29] in *Servir a señor discreto* (1614–1615).[30] As Caro Baroja (1990, II, 247–250) has found out, the Phoenix has an astrologer for a brother-in-law, Luis de Rosicler, who was not only arrested by the Inquisition in 1605[31] but who had studied mathematics and astrology with the Portuguese João Baptista Lavanha (ca. 1550–1624). As Millé y Giménez (1927, 95) suggests, Lope pursued these matters because of Marta de Nevares' notable superstition. It is striking that the character of Belardo in *Los locos de Valencia* (1591),[32] whom many scholars identify with Lope himself,[33] and who presents himself as *buen estudiante*, 'good student' and *no mal matemático y astrólogo*,[34] 'no poor mathematician and astrologer', should be knowledgeable in metoposcopy.[35]

---

25 "o lee a Bautista Porta / si aquel sahumerio importa", *El amante agradecido*, ed. Sanz & Gómez Martínez (2010, 731, vv. 2294–2295) [or read Bautista Porta / if this perfume matters]. On the dating of the comedy see Morley & Bruerton (1968, 48 and 80) and on the reference to Della Porta see Caro Baroja (1988, 172).
26 See González-Barrera (2018).
27 Felino speaks of *capigorrones* [i.e. poor students who were dressed up with *capa*, cape, and *gorro*, cap] who "cargan de Agripa y Cardano", *La boda entre dos maridos*, ed. Roso Díaz (2002, 831, v. 761) [charge with Agripa and Cardano].
28 "Give your hand / to a man, a new Cardano, / who worked wonders in this", *Servir a señor discreto*, ed. Laplana Gil (2012, 858); Weber de Kurlat (1975, II, 219) punctuates differently: "Give your hand / to a new man, Cardano / who worked wonders in this".
29 "In Juan Tisnerio have I read / what he wrote of this", *Servir a señor discreto*, ed. Laplana Gil (2012, 858 and the comment and footnote at v. 1664, in which he recalls Quevedo's *Sueños*).
30 See the prologue by Laplana Gil in his edition (2012, 761–762). Morley & Bruerton (1968, 268) propose "1610–15 (probably 1610–12) for the date of publication".
31 Also see Granja (1989, 152–153) and Armas (1993b, 5).
32 On the question of dating see González-Barrera (2008).
33 See *Los locos de Valencia*, ed. Aguirre (1977, 316, footnote 99), Tropé (1999, 179), Thacker (2000, 11) and (2002b, 1014) as well as Domènech (2008, 127). Most scholars have focused on the theme of madness – García Lorenzo (1989), Thacker (2002a, 90–106), Flores Martín (2004), Del Conte (2005), Tropé (2008), Aszyk (2009) and Teixeira de Souza (2015) – and, in this context, the relationship to *Orlando furioso*: Thacker (2002b).
34 *Los locos de Valencia*, ed. Tropé (2003, III, 309).
35 "BELARDO. Porque en este tiempo / no me daréis un hombre tan perfecto / que no haya hecho alguna gran locura, / y vos podéis juzgar por vuestro pecho / lo que conozco yo por vuestra frente. / CABALLERO. ¡Jesús! ¿Es este hombre quiromántico?", *Los locos de Valencia*, ed. Tropé (2003, III, 308–309) [BELARDO: For in these days / you don't fine a man who is so perfect / that he has not committed some great madness, / and you can judge by your chest / what I can see by your forehead. / CABALLERO: Goodness! Is this man a chiromancer?].

The manuals dealing with palmistry are materially present in Lope's theatre. In an early comedy, *Los donaires de Matico* (1589–1593/ 1594).[36] one of the characters encounters in another one's saddlebag[37] a number of papers:

"La carta de marear".
¡Donosa cosa! "Recetas
para el dolor de las muelas";
¡damas, si os duelen darélas,
para que lo hagáis secretas!
"Memoria de lo que vi
en Roma que fue notable".
"Forma del monstruo espantable
que de Francia vino aquí".
"Quarenta estancias del Dante".
"Curiosa quiromancía
que compré en Bolonia un día
de un preceptor nigromante".
"Papel que escriví a la Infanta
sobre el premio que gané
quando en la plaça jugué".[38]

["The nautical map".
Amusing matter! "Recipes
for aching of the teeth";
Ladies, if you are prone to them
why be secretive about them?
"Memories of what notable
things I saw in Rome".
"Shape of the frightful monster
which arrived here from France".
"Forty stanzas of Dante".
"Strange palm-reading book
I once bought in Bologna
of a necromancy preceptor".

---

36 On the question of dating see Morley & Bruerton (1968, 241–242), Reyes Peña (1996). Profeti (1998, 73–74) and the edition by Presotto (1994). On the textual history also see Presotto (1992).
37 This is the princess Juana who, after having lost Rujero's love, serves, disguised as a peasant by the name of Matico, serves her former lover Belardo, likewise disguised as a peasant, and searches in her master's saddlebag some papers in which she hopes to find some clarification regarding Rujero's destiny. On the convoluted plot of the comedy see Profeti (1998).
38 *Los donaires de Matico*, ed. Presotto (1994, III, 176, vv. 2425–2442). The editor limits himself in his commentary to some brief observations.

"Paper I wrote to the princess
about the prize I won
when in the square I played".]

The description of the broadsheets is not sufficiently detailed to identify Belardo's reading. He carried with him, besides his personal papers and medical, teratological and poetic texts, a book on palmistry, which he qualifies as "strange". We do not know whether it is a manuscript or a printed text, but we do know that it came from Italy, from Bologna to be precise. This is no petty detail, because, to begin with, it shows us how widely distributed Italian texts of this nature were. Furthermore, it is no accident that Bologna should be mentioned, *the* Italian university, where the professor Alessandro Achillini and his alumnus Bartolomeo della Roca, nicknamed Cocles, who was a notorious necromancer, wrote their studies of palm reading and physiognomy. Likewise, the term *preceptor* alludes to an academic environment.

In the fifth book of Lope's *Arcadia* (1598), Cardenio el Rústico, in the name of Isabella, asks the wise Polinesta for a book, *De suertes*, in order to "para jugar y entretenerse con sus amigas"[39] [play and entertain herself with her friends]. After a detailed description of the *Libro delle sorti e della ventura* by Lorenzo Gualtieri Spirito,[40] the shepherds amuse themselves with playful predictions. After Cardenio has received a disheartening forecast, Polinesta proposes reading his future in his hand:

> –Veamos –dijo Polinesta– qué fuerza e influencia muestran en las líneas y señales de tu mano.
> –Pues ¿en ellas –dijo Cardenio– se conocen por ventura estos sucesos?
> –No disputes –le respondió la sabia– conmigo de la verdad de la quiromancia, que no te sabría decir en lo que es cierta o dudosa. Pero advierte que los miembros principales que rigen y gobiernan el ser de hombre tienen su demostración en la palma de la mano en esta forma: el corazón produce la línea de la vida, que muestra si ha de ser breve o larga y cuáles sus enfermedades e infortunios. Está entre el dedo grueso y el índice el hígado, que es principio de criar y restaurar el cuerpo; hace con la suya y la del corazón un ángulo, y llega al término de la mano, la cual procede de la cabeza; forma con las referidas un triángulo.

---

39 Lope, *Arcadia*, ed. Sánchez Jiménez (2012, 606); also see the edition by Morby (1975, 403–404).
40 It was Morby (1966) who identified as Lope's source the Italian 15th century author, whose play was a bestseller in the following century, both in the Italian original and in the Spanish translation. Also see Lee Palmer (2016), with an ample bibliography, on the book and the (editorial) genre of the book of fortunes in Italy, as well as Peña (1996) on the Spanish translation. On the textualization of this game in the *Arcadia* see Navarro Durán (1984, 361–363) and on the ludic feature of the fortune-telling practices Céard, with special emphasis on Spirito (1982, 407–409).

Llamóse línea capital. La cuarta, que procede de toda su virtud y nace entre el dedo mayor y el índice, es la mensal, llamada así por aquella mesa y espacio que allí forma; las demás no son de consideración respeto de éstas.

Tomándole a este tiempo la mano, vio la línea del corazón larga, gruesa y proporcionada, significadora de la larga vida, y que hacia el monte del dedo grueso salían algunas pequeñas que pronosticaban buenos sucesos, hacienda y honra. Y admirose mucho de que llamándose el Rústico tuviese la línea de la vida y la del hígado tan juntas en sus extremos, pues parece que muestran agudo ingenio. Y díjole que a lo menos no sería mudable, traidor ni envidioso, como lo fuera si del todo estuvieran separadas. Y holgose de ver el fin de la línea mensal sin ramo alguno, por donde coligió estar el Rústico libre de enemigos, porque si rematara en muchas líneas sinificara lo contrario. Díjole por todas, finalmente, notables cosas, con las cuales los pastores quedaron admirados y Cardenio incrédulo, pues, riéndose de la sabia, le dijo que no había más verdad en semejantes ciencias que la voluntad del cielo y las culpas o virtudes de los hombres; porque al paso que procedían en sus ofensas, así los castigaba con sucesos siniestros o, por lo contrario, con los dichosos y prósperos.[41]

["Let's see," said Polinesta, "what power and influence these line and signs of your hand show."

"By chance," said Cardenio, "can those accidents be known by them?"

"Do not debate with me," responded the sage, "the truth of palmistry, for I do not know where it is certain and where it is not. But be forewarned that the principle forces which rule and govern man's life are shown in the palm, thus: the heart produces the line of life, which shows whether life is to be long or not and which ailments and misfortunes it will bring. This other one, between the thumb and the index, shows the liver, which creates and restores the body; it forms an angle together with that of the heart, and reaches the end of the hand, which comes from the head; this one forms a triangle with the others. It is called capital line. The fourth, which comes down right from virtue, grows from the middle finger and the index and is known as the *mensal*, because of the table and the space which it forms there; the others are not so vital as these".

Taking his hand while saying this, she saw that the line of the heart was long and broad and well-proportioned, meaning long life, and that from the mountain of the thumb some lines emerged which promised success, worldly goods and honour. And she was no little surprised to see the lines of the heart and the liver so close together towards their ends in one known as *Rustico*, for this meant great acumen. And she told him that certainly he was not going to be fickle, treacherous or envious, as he would be if they were wide apart. And she was pleased to see the end of the *mensal* without any branches, from which she gathered that the *Rustico* would have no enemies, for if it finished off in many different lines it would mean the contrary. She told him, in conclusion, so many notable things that the shepherds were astonished and Cardenio incredulous, for, laughing at the sage, he told her that there was, in such matters, no truth but the will of the heavens and the vices and virtues of man. For, as they behaved, they were chastised by sinister disasters or rewarded by prosperity and fortune.]

---

41 Lope, *Arcadia*, ed. Sánchez Jiménez (2012, 613–614).

This long speech about the practice of palmistry[42] does not only show Lope's profound knowledge of learned palmistry and of the different lines of the hand but also an acute awareness of the questionable status of this and other fortune-telling practices.

As we shall see, the different allusions to palmistry in Lope's theatre are always allusions to the learned layer of this practice which, more than once, is referred to as a *science* and is not related to the practice of the gipsies and other marginalised groups. Lope tests the dramatic possibilities which palmistry offers.[43]

In *La vuelta de Egipto* (1584),[44] one of his oldest *autos sacramentales*, a scene is interspersed in the dramatic action which is reminiscent of the *Aucto de la huida*

---

42 As Morby observes in his edition of *La Arcadia*, both the fortune-telling episode and Polinesta's palmistry speech were eliminated in the Valentian edition of 1602, 'probably unacceptable for doctor Francisco López de Mendoza, the book's censor' (1975, 453).

43 Isolated scenes including palm-reading are to be found in *La prueba de los ingenios* ("LAURA. ¿No te miraron? / PARIS. De la planta al hombro / y hasta las rayas de la propia mano", ed. Molina 2007, III, 145 [LAURA: Did they not look at you? / PARIS: From head to foot / and even the lines of my hand]); *El arenal de Sevilla* ("LUCINDA. Sois en amor semejantes. / Para esto no es menester / mirar rayas de su mano"), ed. Cornejo (2012, 568, vv. 1880–1882 [LUCINDA: You are equals in love. / To know this you need not / look at the lines of the hand]) and in *Roma abrasada* ("NICETO [. . .] pero lo que yo adivino, / sin rayas de frente o mano, / es que tiene más de humano / tu hijo, que de divino", Gómez & Cuenca Muñoz 1994, II, 265 [NICETO . . . but what I gather, / without line of the forehead or the hand, / is that there is more human matter / in your son than divine]). Also see Gernert (2014c).

44 Cf. Tomillo y Pérez Pastor: "Por precio de 113.900 maravedises se obligó á hacer é hizo en Madrid el año 1584, tres autos: *El Retorno de Egipto. Simón Mago* y otro sacramental á elección del Corregidor de la villa y corte. Si *El retorno de Egipto* es lo mismo que *La Vuelta de Egipto*, este auto será uno de los que Lope dió á Velázquez durante el tiempo que estuvieron en buenas relaciones de amistad, pudiendo además conjeturarse que el poeta escribiría dicho auto poco antes de la fecha de dicho contrato" (1901, 138, footnote 2) [For the price of 113,900 *maravedises* in Madrid in the year 1584 three *autos* were ordered to be made and were made: *El Retorno de Egipto. Simón Mago* and another *sacramental* to be elected by the *Corregidor de la villa y corte*, the chief magistrate of the town and the court. If *El retorno de Egipto* is the same as *La Vuelta de Egipto*, this *auto* must be one of those which Lope gave Velázquez while they maintained a friendly relationship. There is reason to believe that the poet wrote this *auto* shortly before the date of said contract]. As Granja observes in his edition of *Bosque de amor* by Lope, *La vuelta de Egipto* 'might be Lope's oldest preserved auto' (2000, 29). He furthermore remarks with regard to the play: "Es una pieza de poco más de seiscientos versos que llama la atención por su sencillez; en ella un dramaturgo que no había cumplido los veintidós años presenta al Niño Jesús ayudando a la Virgen y a San José en sus tareas caseras cotidianas" (2000, 29) [It is a play of little more than six hundred verses and stands out because of its simplicity; here, a dramatist who was not even twenty-two years of age presents the infant Jesus helping the Virgin Mary and St. Joseph in their everyday household chores].

Egipto from the *Códice de autos viejos*.[45] Contrary to this *auto* and contrary to other dramatic texts of the 16th century, Lope's characters have their own names: Arsinoe and Meroe. And there is no *ceceo* in their speech, and they do not ask for any money when they show up in the Holy Family's abode, where they receive a hearty welcome. Without further ado, one of them reads the child's hand:

> MEROE. Mostrad la mano, os diré
> la buena ventura. A fé
> que esta raya de la vida
> es bien corta y perseguida!
> Tendreis muchos enemigos
> que os han de matar y acer
> en vos notables castigos.
> A fé que os han de vender
> uno de vuestros amigos!
> A los años treynta y tres
> tendreis, niño, una prisión
> por gran trayción y interés.
> Todas estas rayas son
> cruces de la cruz despúes.
> Pero aquesta no entendida
> muestra despues una vida
> perdurable y sempiterna.
>
> ARSINOE. Su madre está un poco tierna.
>
> JESUS. ¡No lloreis madre querida! [. . .]
> Mostrad vos madre la vuestra.
>
> MEROE. Aqui larga vida muestra
> y un transito glorioso,
> mas perdereis vuestro esposo.[46]
>
> [MEROE: Show me your hand, and I will
> read your fortune. By my troth,
> this line of life
> is rather short and strained!
> You will have many enemies
> who will kill you and make you suffer
> some rare chastisement.
> By my troth, you will be betrayed by

---

45 See Rodríguez-Puértolas (1970, 107 and footnote 32).
46 Vega, *Auto de la vuelta de Ejipto*, ed. Restori (1898, 4, vv. 316–340). On this *auto sacramental* of the Phoenix see Herrán Alonso (2010, 630–632)

one of your friends!
At thirty-three years of age,
you, my son, will be in a dungeon
through treachery and conceit.
All these lines are crosses
of the cross which is to come.
But this unfathomable one
shows long and eternal life afterwards.

ARSINOE: His mother is afflicted.

JESUS: Do not weep, dear mother! . . .
Show them your own hand.

MEROE: Here, long life is shown
and a glorious passing away,
but you will lose your spouse.]

The function of this palm-reading scene is the same as in the anonymous *auto* about Christ's infancy. It is a device to tell the story of the Bible, at the same time showing the Virgin Mary's affability in her role as a mother who learns of her child's future misfortune.

The palm-readers in Lope's secular plays tend to be characters who just pretend to possess such knowledge for one reason or another. The gallant men attempt to read the hand of their women in order to be able to approach them, as happens in *De cosario a cosario* (1617–1619)[47] and – with more prominence of palmistry – in the comedy of intrigue *El ausente en el lugar* (ca. 1606).[48] During the second act, Carlos, the rival of the gallant man, characterised by Serralta (2001) as *pre-figurón*, reads his lover Laurencia's hand:

CARLOS. Dadme, señora, la mano.

LAURENCIA. Veisla aquí.

CARLOS. ¡Favor divino!
Hago la cruz y la beso.

LAURENCIA. ¡Quedo! ¿La mano besáis?

---

47 The gallant Mendo relates how he tried to conquer Inés: "Hícele mil trampantojos / astrológicos y vanos / por las rayas de las manos / y los rayos de sus ojos", Vega, *De cosario a cosario*, ed. Ferreras (1992, 153–154) [I played thousands of pranks on her / astrological conceits / by the lines of her hands / and the lines of her eyes]. On this comedy see Grilli (2000), Wright (2002) and Morley & Bruerton (1968, 308) on the question of dating.
48 On the dating of the play see Morley & Bruerton (1968, 287–288).

CARLOS. ¿La cruz no más?

LAURENCIA. Bien entráis.

CARLOS. ¡Jesús, qué estraño suceso!
Aquí se ve claramente
que un hombre en estremo amáis,
de quien mal pagada estáis. . .

LAURENCIA. ¡Que ingenio!

CARLOS. Es cosa excelente.
Esta raya que atraviesa,
es que otra muger llegó
y este galán os quitó.

LAURENCIA. Y aun pienso que a vos os pesa.

CARLOS. Pesábame, pero ya
que desta mano me así,
la que por celos perdí
hoy la venganza me da.

LAURENCIA. ¿Qué decís?

CARLOS. Que aquí se ve
que vengaros intentáis
con otro hombre.

LAURENCIA. Y vos pensáis
que si lo intento podré.

CARLOS. Ya lo estoy aquí mirando,
y me parece que sí.[49]

[CARLOS: Give me your hand, milady.

LAURENCIA: Here it is.

CARLOS: The Heavens be praised!
I make the sign of the cross and give it a kiss.

LAURENCIA: Soft! You kiss my hand?

CARLOS: The cross, no more.

LAURENCIA: A good move.

---

49 *El ausente en el lugar*, ed. Madroñal (2007, II, 486–487).

CARLOS: Heavens, what an affair!
I can clearly see that you are
exceedingly in love with a man
who will not prove worthy of it. . .

LAURENCIA: What banter is this!

CARLOS: An excellent affair.
This line which crosses here
means that another woman came along
and snatched your gallant from you.

LAURENCIA: It seems to me that this saddens you.

CARLOS: It saddens me, but
as through this here hand
I lost what I asked the heavens for,
my mind is set for vengeance now.

LAURENCIA: What do you say?

CARLOS: That I can see
that you try revenge
through another man.

LAURENCIA: And you think that
if I tried I could.

CARLOS: I can see it with mine own eyes,
and it looks like that.]

Carlos does not exert himself much to feign palm-reading skills. He rather insinuates that he is speaking in a key of the amorous embroilment they are both well aware of. He ends up declaring his love. Whereas in *El ausente en el lugar*, palm-reading is used to make physical contact, in other comedies it serves as an excuse if the lovers are caught hand in hand by a father or another person of authority.[50]

---

50 This occurs in a short scene in *Los hidalgos del aldea*, dated by Morley & Bruerton (1968, 337) at between 1608 y 1611, when the earl Albano surprises Finea with Roberto: "FINEA. Pues, dame una mano sola, / ay, si la de esposo fuera. / *(Sale el conde)* / ALBANO. ¿Eres astrólogo acaso? / ROBERTO. Mirar las líneas pudiera, / que Finea me rogó / que le mirase por ellas / si ha de casar con don Blas. / ALBANO. Deja esas vanas quimeras", *Los hidalgos del aldea*, ed. Cotarelo (1916–1930, II, 310) [FINEA: Now, give me just one hand, / alas, would it be that of the spouse. / *(The earl enters)* / ALBANO: Are you perhaps an astrologer? / ROBERTO: The lines observe I may, / Finea prayed me / to look at them to see / if she will marry Don Blas. / ALBANO: End these foolish fantasies]. On this comedy see the studies by Fernández (1988) y Serralta (2003).

In *El desconfiado* (*ca.* 1615–1616),[51] Feliciano pretends to be reading Ana's hand when all of a sudden Lisardo, her father, barges in on them.

> LISARDO. (¿Hombre de la mano asido
> de doña Ana? ¡Hazaña honrada!)
>
> ANA. (¡Mi padre!
>
> FELICIANO. No importa nada.)
>
> ANA. ¡Que soltéis la mano os pido!)
>
> FELICIANO. Esta raya es de la vida
> –tengáis la que yo os deseo–:
> que será bien larga creo,
> pues no hay otra que lo impida.
> Hijos tendréis, serán pocos.
>
> LISARDO. (Esta es la quiromancía.
> ¡Necio quien de ella se fía
> y los que la creen más locos!)
>
> FELICIANO. Venus está favorable,
> y en esta piramidal
> punta. . .[52]

> [LISARDO: (Has he been doña Ana's betrothed?
> What an honourable affair!)
>
> ANA: (My father!
>
> FELICIANO: It does not matter.)
>
> ANA: Let loose that hand, I pray you!)
>
> FELICIANO: This line is the line of life
> – may you be granted what I wish –:
> which will be very long, I believe,
> for there is none other which hampers it.
> Children you will have, few they will be.
>
> LISARDO: (This is palmistry.
> Foolish those who give credit to it
> and more foolish those who believe it!)

---

51 On the question of dating see Morley & Bruerton (1968, 267). Also see Rosado (1971) on this comedy.
52 *El desconfiado*, ed. Rodríguez Rodríguez (2014, 765–766, vv. 639–652).

FELICIANO: Venus is favourable,
and in this pyramid shows herself. . .]

So that the ploy is effective, quite a number of technical terms from palmistry is required. It is remarkable that Lisardo should, for a start, condemn this semiotic practice, calling those foolish who believe in it in order to then allow Feliciano to convince him.

FELICIANO. Dadme, señor, vuestra mano,
así Dios os haga bien,
que quiero ver si también
es con vos mi estudio en vano.

LISARDO. ¿Mi mano?

FELICIANO. Dejad que diga
en qué mi ciencia se funda,
que en gusto a veces redunda.

LISARDO. Vuestro buen término obliga.

ANA. (¿Hay más notable porfía?)

FELICIANO. Vos sois, señor, cuidadoso.

LISARDO. ¿Qué es cuidadoso?

FELICIANO. Celoso.

LISARDO. Conservar mi honor quería.

FELICIANO. Gana tenéis de casaros.

LISARDO. ¿Qué decís?

FELICIANO. Aquesto os digo.

LISARDO. ¡Ya vuestra ciencia bendigo!

FELICIANO. Sólo puede dilataros
este gusto el no tener
casada aquesta señora.

LISARDO. (Aparte me oíd agora.
digo que quiero creer
lo que hasta aquí no he creído).[53]

---

[53] *El desconfiado*, ed. Rodríguez Rodríguez (2014, 765–766, vv. 639–652).

[FELICIANO: Give me your hand, my lord
may the Lord bless you,
for I want to see if in you as well
my studies are in vain.

LISARDO: My hand?

FELICIANO: Let me show
the foundation of my science,
which is wont to give so much pleasure.

LISARDO: Your wise words oblige me.

ANA: (Can there be greater wilfulness?)

FELICIANO: You are cautious, my lord.

LISARDO: What is cautious?

FELICIANO: Jealous.

LISARDO: My honour to guard I wish.

FELICIANO: You want to marry.

LISARDO: What are you saying?

FELICIANO: I am saying it.

LISARDO: I bless your science!

FELICIANO: You can only delay
this pleasure by not having
married that lady.

LISARDO: (Hear me speaking aside now,
saying that I want to believe
what till now I have not believed).]

Thanks to his privileged understanding and his rhetorical qualities he succeeds in manipulating the old man, who comes to believe in the validity of palmistry, to which, incidentally, both refer as a science.

In one of the comedies about the war in Flanders, *Pobreza no es vileza* (1620–1622),[54] we come across a curious dialogue between the jester and a

---

[54] On the date see Morley & Bruerton (1968, 376). The text has been studied by Saunal (1946) and Campbell (1994), who concisely resumes the plot of the war comedy: "La razón del conflicto bélico es la sucesión de don Pedro Enríquez, conde de Fuentes, la gubernatura de tales estados

gallant man. This dialogue is formed in such a way as if both characters were able to read their answers from one another's hand.

> Fabio. Laura me ha puesto en cuidado.
>
> Panduro. Mayor me le ha dado a mi.
>
> Fabio. ¿Este Mendoza es su hermano?
>
> Panduro. No es la palma de la mano
> mas llana.
>
> Fabio. Créolo ansí:
> Mas ya que me la has mostrado
> las rayas te quiero ver.
>
> Panduro. Acá suélese saber
> desto con mayor cuidado.
>
> Fabio. Muestra.
>
> Panduro. ¿Hay raya por ahí
> de que volveré a mi tierra?
>
> Fabio. En acabando la guerra
> lo dice esta raya aquí:
> Y esta muestra que en tu mano
> está una bella muger
> de que puedes disponer
> sin ser melindroso y vano.
> Esta dice que la adoro,
> y esta que la hables por mí
> con este bolsillo aquí
> y cien doblones en oro.

[i.e. Flandes] a la muerte del archiduque Ernesto. En ese contexto tiene lugar la historia novelesca de un soldado español de orígenes nobles, venidos a menos por haber matado a un pretendiente de su hermana Ana. Para evitar un posible deshonor, viaja con ella a Flandes donde ocultan sus identidades y, por necesidad, visten pobremente; la deja encargada a Rosela, hermana del conde Fabio. Éste se enamora y deshonra a Ana mientras Mendoza se encuentra en el campo de batalla". (116) [The reason for the military conflict is the succession of Don Pedro Enríquez, Conde de Fuentes, to the governance of such states [i.e. Flanders] after the death of Archduke Ernesto. In this context the bizarre story of a Spanish soldier of noble origin is set, who has come down in the world for having killed one of his sister Ana's suitors. In order to avoid any dishonour, he travels to Flanders with her where they conceal their identities and, as of necessity, dress poorly. He leaves her to the custody of Rosela, sister to Earl Fabio, who, in his turn, falls in love with Ana and dishonours her while Mendoza is on the battlefield].

PANDURO. Desvialde por mi amor
y sabed que yo también
estudié esta ciencia y bien,
en los libros de mi honor.
Mostrad la mano.

FABIO. ¿Esto sabes?

PANDURO. Esta raya da a entender
que es hija aquesta muger
de padres nobles y graves.
Esta que en esta ocasión
llega tarde ese bolsillo
aunque el metal amarillo
es notable tentación.
Aquí dice que su hermano
vendrá por ella muy presto
si sabe que me habéis puesto
esa blandura en la mano,
porque todo lo corrompe,
que aqueste metal bendito
es como hierba del pito
que las cerraduras rompe.
¡Cuántas rayas hay aquí!
Dicen que os cansáis en vano
pues yo no cerré la mano
cuando los doblones vi.[55]

[FABIO: Laura has put me on guard.

PANDURO: And me even more.

FABIO: Is this Mendoza her brother?

PANDURO: This palm is not
the fullest palm.

FABIO: I believe this,
But as you have shown it to me
I want to see those lines of yours.

PANDURO: Here we go about this
with the highest caution.

---

[55] *Pobreza no es vileza* (1627, II, 62r).

FABIO: Just show it.

PANDURO: Is there a line which says
that I will go back to my soil?

FABIO: When the war is ended
this line here says it.
And it shows a fair woman
by your side of whom
you can dispose
without being finicky or vain.
This line says that I adore her,
and this other that you'll speak on my behalf
with this pocketbook here
and a hundred *doblones* in gold.

PANDURO: Cease for the love of me
and be advised that I also
studied this science well
in the books of my honour.
Show me your hand.

FABIO: You can read it?

PANDURO: This line here purports
that this woman is the daughter
of noble and honest parents.
This one says that this time
that pocketbook will be late arriving
though the golden metal
is a signal temptation.
Here it says that her brother
is to soon come and fetch her
if he knows that you have put
this weakness in my hand,
for it corrupts all,
for this blessed metal
is like the woodpecker's herb,
which breaks the lock.
How many lines there are here!
They say that you are trying in vain
for I did not close my hand
when I saw the *doblones*.]

The construction of the scene is quite ingenious. As Earl Fabio wants to bribe Panduro and pay him his services as a thug, the focus of attention is on the hands in the pockets which are full of money. The audience will have observed with special interest the characters' gestures in order to ascertain whether the jester accepts the bribe or not. The language of palmistry is thus instrumentalised for the sake of scenic efficiency and spectacularity.

In the religious comedy *El rústico del cielo* (1605?),[56] Lope uses palmistry to construct a highly entertaining scene. Its protagonist is friar Francisco, who stands out by his particular simplicity and who is much afraid of a gentleman who wants to examine his hand for signs of sanctity:

CABALLERO. Muestra esa mano.

FRANCISCO. ¡Ay de mi,
para que la quiere!

CABALLERO. Así
la has de tener.

FRANCISCO. ¡Trae cordel! ¡Quiéremela atar!

CABALLERO. ¡Espera! ¡Qué rayas!

FRANCISCO. Ay madre mía.

CABALLERO. Qué estraña fisionomia,
qué simplicidad sincera.
Aspecto tienes, hermano,
de ser un santo.

FRANCISCO. ¿Quién, yo?

CABALLERO. Tu pues, y por si, o por no,
te quiero besar la mano.

FRANCISCO. ¡Ay, que me muerde![57]

[GENTLEMAN: Show me your hand.

FRANCISCO: Alas,
what does he want it for?

CABALLERO: Like this
you are to hold it.

FRANCISCO: He brings a cord! He wants to tie me!

CABALLERO: Hold! What lines!

---

56 On the question of dating see Morley & Bruerton (1968, 60 y 294).
57 *El rústico del cielo*, ed. Gómez & Cuenca Muñoz (1997, I, 404–405).

FRANCISCO: Goodness me.

CABALLERO: What strange physiognomy,
what sincere simplicity.
You, brother, have the looks
of a saint.

FRANCISCO: Who, me?

CABALLERO: Yes, you. And be it yes or no,
I will kiss your hand.

FRANCISCO: Woe on me, he will bite me!]

Besides making the audience laugh, this palmistry scene serves to once again highlight the outstanding ingenuousness of the protagonist.

The character who is of outstanding importance for the dramatization of the occult sciences is that of the *capigorrón*.[58] As Antonio Liñán y Verdugo tells us in his *Guía de forasteros que vienen a la corte* (1620), these poor scholars had a reputation for being swindlers:

> Hay otro modo y suerte de gentes, que se llaman capigorras, los cuales con hábito de hombres estudiosos y de escuelas, se entretienen en esta Corte vanamente; unos haciéndose astrólogos, sacando pronósticos de las cosas por venir, anunciando sucesos, levantando figuras, haciéndose oráculos, siendo la verdad que en toda su vida abrieron libro ni estudiaron proposición de Astrología. Otras veces se hacen conocedores fisonómicos, declaran

---

58 On knowledge of the occult see also a romance by Lobo Lasso de la Vega in which a maid scolds her suitor for his dedication to the occult arts: "Señor estudiante, déxese de eso, / no me taña ni cante las de don Bueso. / Dexe el astrolabio, también la esfera / que no soy matemática, ni estrellera, / que es moneda batida en tierra extranjera / que aunque todos la miran nadie la quiere; / hábleme en Castellano, si algo quisiere, / que una onza, el de a ocho tiene de peso. / Señor estudiante, déxese de eso, / no me taña ni cante las de don Bueso. // No me trate de versos, ni su misura, / que a la olla no ponen ni dan gordura, / ni de mi nacimiento de alzar figura, / que antes no como de eso sino de echallas; / pídeme las manos, no quiero dallas, / que es para chiromántico travieso. / Señor estudiante, déxese de eso, / no me taña ni cante las de don Bueso", *Manojuelo de romances*, ed. González Palencia & Mele (1942, 19–20) [Master student, desist / don't ring, don't sing those airs of Don Bueso. / Leave alone the astrolabe and the sphere / for I am no mathematician and no stargazer either, / for this is a coin minted in a distant land / which no one wants but all gaze at; / speak to me in Castilian words, if you desire something, / for this has weight, a weight of eight ounces. / Master student, desist / don't ring, don't sing those airs of Don Bueso. // Don't give me verses, nor their measure, / for they add nothing to the stew and give no fat, / nor have they ever set my birth horoscope / for I would rather hurl them off than taste of them; / if you ask for my hands, I will not give them, / this is matter for palm-reading rogues. / Master student, desist / don't ring, don't sing those airs of Don Bueso].

por las rayas de manos cuando se hallan entre gente ignorante y fáciles de persuadir, como son mujeres, adonde muy á lo gitano les venden el gato por liebre, diciéndoles desde una mentira hasta ciento.[59]

[There are people of a different sort and nature, known as *capigorras,* who, with the semblance of studious and scholarly men, give themselves to the most vain diversions here at court, professing to be astrologers, making prophecies of things to come, foretelling events, by drawing up star charts or consulting oracles. They have in truth never opened a single book in their lives, nor have they studied the clauses of Astrology. At other times they profess knowledge of physiognomy and gather things from the lines of the hand when unlettered and gullible people like women are present. In the way of gipsies, they pull wool over their eyes and tell them any number of lies, from one to a hundred.]

In the comedy of intrigue *La boda entre dos maridos* (1595–1601),[60] the protagonists are two scholars from Salamanca, Febo and Lauro, united by a sincere friendship.[61] The latter appears in the first scene of the play accompanied by his servant Pinabel,[62] like this, according to the stage directions: "*Lauro caballero en calzas y en jubón, con buen cuello, aunque estudiante, y Pinabel, capigorrón, en cuerpo*"[63] [*Lauro, gentleman in breeches and doublet, with a good collar, though a scholar, and Pinabel, loafer, capigorrón, in bodice*]. At the end of the first act, the jester has to make use of his capacities as a trickster[64] when he is in danger of being punished by the father of his lord's lover and by his servants Felino y Tebano.[65] While he tries to dazzle Prudence with a speech in Latin (" Señor, ego

---

59 *Guía de forasteros que vienen a la corte,* ed. Simons (1980, 189). On this description of the *capigorrones* also see Caro Baroja (1990, II, 252).
60 On the question of dating see Morley & Bruerton (1968, 294).
61 The plot gets its inspiration from *Decameron* X, 8, whose protagonists are the students of philosophy, Gisippo and Tito Quinzio. On Boccaccio's recast see Megwinoff (1981), Calvo (1997) and Roso Díaz (1999), who also considers other sources. The close relationship between the two men has been studied by scholars like González-Ruiz (2009) in homoerotic terms.
62 On this character cf. Roso Díaz (1999, 390), who observes: "Pinabel responde al tipo del gracioso. Se caracteriza por ser servidor fiel, por su cobardía, por ser embustero, por ser consejero de su amo, por ser perezoso y dormilón y por ser narrador o comentarista de sucesos importantes" [Pinabel corresponds to the type of the jester. He is characterised by being a faithful servant, by his cowardice, by being a trickster, by being his master's advisor, by being lazy and sleepy, and by being the narrator and commentator of important events].
63 *La boda entre dos maridos,* ed. Roso Díaz (2002, 813).
64 It is no coincidence that this character should be named like the traitor of the French cause, friend to Ganelon in the *Chanson de Roland* and malicious adversary of Bradamante in *Orlando furioso.*
65 See the interpretation of the scene by Magnaghi (2014, 169–173).

sum pauper scolasticus"⁶⁶ [Sir, I am just a poor scholar]), he feigns to do palmistry with the domestics:

> PINABEL. Quedo: y si no me dan, les daré a entrambos,
> porque soy quiromántico espantoso,
> dos cédulas, que valen mil escudos.
>
> FELINO. ¿Es alguna de amor, por vida mía?
>
> PINABEL. La una es para amor, y otra de juego.
>
> TEBANO. Ésa quiero.
>
> FELINO. Yo esotra.⁶⁷

> [PINABEL: Soft: and if you don't give me, I will give both of you,
> for a frightful palmreader am I,
> two cards, worth a thousand escudos.
>
> FELINO: By my troth, is one of them for love?
>
> PINABEL: One's for love, the other one's for game.
>
> TEBANO: I want that one.
>
> FELINO: I the other.]

The cards mentioned induce Lope to entertain his audience with some outlandish speeches in an invented language. This language has been examined by Magnaghi (2014, 171–173):

> TEBANO. Está atento:
> cédula para ganar.
>
> FELINO. Titón, Tirín, Tulimán. . .
> Nombres del gran Turco son.
>
> TEBANO. Birlimboto, Escotillón,
> Xerlín, Girón, Carimán.
>
> FELINO. El leyó en el Araucana.
>
> TEBANO. ¿Que con esto ganaré
> si juego?

---

66 *La boda entre dos maridos*, ed. Roso Díaz (2002, 828, v. 636).
67 *La boda entre dos maridos*, ed. Roso Díaz (2002, 831, vv. 746–752).

Felino. Yo no lo sé

Tebano. Probar quiero esta mañana.

Felino. Prueba en poco.

Tebano. ¿Y si me pico?

Felino. Escucha leeré la mía,
que si es verdad, este día
yo me caso y tú eres rico.
Rimoteros, Caratrafa.

Tebano. Espíritus son. No leas;
mas ¿qué importa? No los creas.

Felino. Serpentimurrio, Engarrafa.

Tebano. ¿Engarrafa? Ése, sin duda,
es algún diablo corchete.

Felino. Matacan del cochoflete,
apio, murta, salvia y ruda.
Tebano. ¿Dice más?

Felino. Coscoscriscas,
tuf, tuf.[68]

[Tebano: Stay attentive:
card to win.

Felino: Titón, Tirín, Tulimán. . .
Names of the great Turk they are.

Tebano: Birlimboto, Escotillón,
Xerlín, Girón, Carimán.

Felino: He read in the Araucana.

Tebano: What will I win
if I play?

Felino: I don't know.

Tebano: I want to try it this morning.

---

[68] *La boda entre dos maridos*, ed. Roso Díaz (2002, 832, vv. 769–792). Also see the interpretation of this scene as a parody of epodic therapy by Sánchez (2005, 228–229).

FELINO: Try a little.

TEBANO: What if I get stung?

FELINO: Listen, I'll read mine,
for if it's true, this day
I will marry and you will be rich.
Rimoteros, Caratrafa.

TEBANO: Spirits they are. Don't read;
but what does it matter? Just do not believe it.

FELINO: Serpentimurrio, Engarrafa.

TEBANO: Engarrafa? That one, no doubt,
is some devilish brace.

FELINO: Matacan del cochoflete,
leek, myrtle, sage and rue.

TEBANO: Does it say more?

FELINO: Coscoscriscas,
tuf, tuf.]

Rather than for some cheap laughter at the cost of the two shy servants, Lope exploits this language to characterise the *capigorrones* in the manner of Liñán y Verdugo:

FELINO. [. . .] estos capigorrones,
siempre estudian invenciones
en toda Universidad.
Danse a la quiromancía,
y a las rayas de la mano;
cargan de Agripa y Cardano,
y estudian hechicería.
Que con estos embelecos
las mujeres los admiten
para que a amarlas se inciten
algunos amantes secos.[69]

---

[69] *La boda entre dos maridos*, ed. Roso Díaz (2002, 831–832, vv. 756–766). On the offices of the *capigorrones* cf. Nemtzov (1946, 69): "Otro medio que ellos tienen para ganarse la vida es vender oraciones. El vulgo tenía cierto respeto a estos estudiantes-pícaros y estaba convencido de que los gorrones poseían conocimientos de magia y les compraban los papelitos que vendían suponiéndolos tener poderes curativos o mágicos" [Another means which they have to make a living is selling prayers. People had a certain respect for these student-picaros and

[FELINO: . . . those loafers,
at their University invent
all manner of things.
they dwell on palmistry
and the lines of the hand;
they load themselves with Agripa and Cardano,
and study witchcraft.
For with such dupes
the women own up to them
and allow them to incite them
with love for withered lovers.]

The theatre as a mirror of life puts on stage contemporary customs and problems. The extensive motif of the student in whose academic curriculum the dark arts were also included, studied at the chairs of the universities of Salamanca or Toledo, is perhaps an indication that there were many professors like Bartolomé Barrientos (ca. 1520–1576), master of liberal arts in Salamanca.

The professor from Salamanca was known as a palmist according to the testimony of the sorcerer from Toledo, Amador de Velasco, who was prosecuted by the Inquisition in 1576. On this occasion he maintained that "había en España más de diez mil conocedores de la chiromancia " [there were more than ten thousand people in Spain who knew about palmistry], amongst them "el maestro Barrientos, que tenía aguas, licores y libros de todas partes, del cual se decía que miraba los hurtos en un espejo o en un caldero de agua y que había hecho unos sigilos para que los aguadores no pasasen por su calle, a pesar de todo lo cual nunca fue penitenciado por la Inquisición, ni en público ni en secreto"[70] [the master Barrientos, who had water, liquor and books from all over, of whom it was said that he saw thefts in a mirror or in a cauldron of water, and that he had put up some secret signs so that the water carriers would not pass through his street, in spite of all which he was never imprisoned by the Inquisition, neither in public nor in secret].

In most cases, Lope's palmists are men, almost always of a high social standing or linked to the academic world. One exception is the comedy *Lo que hay que fiar del mundo* (about 1610)[71] about the captivity of a group of Christians in

---

were convinced that they had knowledge of magic, so they would buy the papers they sold assuming they had curative or magical powers].

70 See Cirac Estopañán (1942), the chapter "El licenciado Velasco y su recetario mágico" [The bachelor Velasco and his magic recipes] in Caro Baroja (1990, I, 287–333), Gagliardi (2007, 9) as well as the chapter "Amador de Velasco – El maestro de brujo" [Amador de Velasco – The Wizard's Master], in Rey Bueno (2007a, 9–34).
71 On the question of dating see Morley & Bruerton (1968, 349).

Constantinople. In it, the Turkish lady Marbelia, wife of the Grand Turk, offers to read the future in Leandro's hand in order to make his wife Blanca jealous:

> MARBELIA. Dejemos de argumentar.
> O una mano me has de dar
> o has de ver mi atrevimiento.
> Dámela, por lo que sé
> de conocer por la mano,
> y si has de ser rey persiano,
> por las rayas te diré,
> y aun si has de heredar también
> el imperio de Selín.[72]

> [MARBELIA: Let's stop arguing.
> Either you give me your hand
> or you will see my boldness.
> Give it to me, for what I know
> to be known by the hand,
> and if you are to be the King of Persia,
> I'll tell you by the lines of your hand,
> and even if you are to inherit
> the empire of Selin.]

In spite of his misgivings – palmistry "[no] es ciencia que entre cristianos / se cree"[73] [is not a science that among Christians / is believed] – Leandro lets himself be convinced that Marbelia can read his destiny in his hand:

> MARBELIA. Muestra.
>
> LEANDRO. ¿Cuál quieres?
>
> MARBELIA. Dame la diestra.
>
> LEANDRO. ¡Ay!
>
> MARBELIA. No importa que te apriete,
> que es porque salgan las rayas.
>
> LEANDRO. ¡Suéltame! Basta mirar
> las rayas; comienza a hablar.[74]

---

72 *Lo que ay que fiar del mundo*, ed. Sánchez Laílla & Laplana Gil (2013, 450, vv. 2432–2440).
73 *Lo que ay que fiar del mundo*, ed. Sánchez Laílla & Laplana Gil (2013, 450, vv. 2443–2444).
74 *Lo que ay que fiar del mundo*, ed. Sánchez Laílla & Laplana Gil (2013, 450–451, vv. 2448–2454).

[MARBELIA: Show it.

LEANDRO: Which do you want?

MARBELIA: Give me the right one.

LEANDRO: Oh!

MARBELIA: Never mind that I squeeze you,
it is so that the lines come out.

LEANDRO: Let go of me! It suffices to look
at the lines; start speaking!]

Like the gallants in other comedies by Lope, the Turkish lady takes advantage of her physical proximity to declare herself to Leandro: "¿Qué diré / que penetre tus oídos? / Digo: mi bien que te adoro"[75] [What shall I say / that penetrates your ears? / I say: by my troth, I adore you]. In this compromising situation Blanca appears, and her husband tries to save face by saying: "De un moro / Marbelia, Blanca, aprendió / la ciencia de adivinar"[76] [From a Moor, Blanca / Marbelia learned / the science of foreseeing]. The link of this divinatory practice with a non-Christian woman has nothing to do with the female characters of Calderón, bearers of occult knowledge, with a clear doctrinal intention. What is to be trusted in the world lacks the ideological and theological implications that the staging of the occult arts and astrology in the theatre of Calderón entails.

2.1 *Servir a señor discreto* (1614–1615)

While in many of Lope's comedies isolated scenes, micro sequences, of a chiromantic theme are introduced, *Servir a señor discreto* is one of the few comedies in which the chiromantic and physiognomic prognosis affects the macro structure of the play. The author of the prediction is Severo, a true astrologer, who is presented at the end of the second act by a companion on his way to the protagonist, Don Pedro:

ESTEBAN. Por todo el camino
viene en círculos hablando

---

75 *Lo que ay que fiar del mundo*, ed. Sánchez Laílla & Laplana Gil (2013, 451, vv. 2457–2459).
76 *Lo que ay que fiar del mundo*, ed. Sánchez Laílla & Laplana Gil (2013, 451, vv. 2462–2464).

y cielo y tierra enfadando;
que es escolar imagino.⁷⁷

[ESTEBAN: All the way
he talks in circles,
defying heaven and earth;
he is a scholar, I guess.]

Severo is an educated man, not only a real astrologer but also a palm reader and physiognomist who reads Don Pedro's face:⁷⁸

SEVERO. [. . .] Yo os amé luego que os vi,
y por la fisionomía
he visto bien que algún día
os acordaréis de mí,
porque habéis de ser dichoso!

PEDRO. ¿Dichoso yo?

SEVERO. Dad la mano
a un hombre, nuevo Cardano,
que fue en esto milagroso.

PEDRO. En Juan Tisnerio he leído
lo que de aquesto escribió.
para que sepáis que yo
también estudiante he sido,
mas no he tenido por cierta
ninguna adivinación.

---

[77] *Servir a señor discreto*, ed. Laplana Gil (2012, II, 855, vv. 1608–1611). Esteban takes up his story again, saying: "Si llegamos a un lugar, / quiere que sea a tal hora; / si salimos al aurora, / luego se quiere parar / porque reina no sé quién, / aunque Santurno le llama, / ¡qué santo!, y con mala fama, / no sé si lo piensa bien" (856, vv. 1620–1631) [If we arrive at a place, / he wants it to be at such and such a time; / if we leave at dawn, / then he wants to stop, / because I do not know who reins then, / although he calls him Santurno, / what a saint!, and with a bad reputation, / I do not know if he judges well].

[78] The link between physiognomy and astrology can also be found in the palatine comedy *El amigo por fuerza* (1599), where the funny old *guardadamas* (i.e. lady attendant) Hortensio answers jokingly to the interrogation of his mistress, Lisaura: "No / que soy astrologo yo / y entiendo fisonomía", *El amigo por fuerza*, ed. Pontón y Laplana Gil (2002, I, 967, vv. 682–684) [No / I am an astrologer / and I understand physiognomy]. See on the date the prologue by Laplana Gil in the edition *El amigo por fuerza*, ed. Pontón y Laplana Gil (2002, 925). Lanuza-Navarro (2014, 209) notes about this scene: "The association of astrology and physiognomy could not be clearer; Hortensio is an astrologer, therefore he understands physiognomy".

> Severo. Eso con la religión
> y con la verdad concierta.⁷⁹
>
> [Severo: . . . I loved you the moment I saw you,
> and by your physiognomy
> I saw that one day
> you will remember me,
> because you are to be blessed!
>
> Pedro: I, blessed?
>
> Severo: Shake hands
> with a man, a new Cardano,
> who has worked wonders in this.
>
> Pedro: In John Tisnerio I read
> what he wrote about this.
> Thus you can see that I
> have been a scholar myself,
> but I have not yet had
> my fortune told.
>
> Severo: This with religion
> agrees and with the truth.]

The conversation that takes place on the subject of prediction is of great informative value in terms of the dissemination of the relevant European authorities in Spain and also in terms of the scientific status of the physiognomic sciences as it relates to the academic world. While Don Pedro is sceptical about the effectiveness of the divinatory arts, Severo insists not only on their veracity but also, and this is important, on their compatibility with Catholic dogmas. Don Pedro, in turn, insists on the Orthodox position, rejecting both physiognomy and palmistry ("the face and the hand") because "lo impide la fe que adoro"⁸⁰ [it is forbidden by the faith I adore], evidently because it is at odds with the dogma of free will. After contrasting these diametrically opposed positions, Severo predicts the future to Don Pedro:

> Yo sólo os sabré decir
> y esto teneldo por cierto,
> que de solamente un puerto
> el bien os ha de venir.⁸¹

---

79 *Servir a señor discreto*, ed. Laplana Gil (2012, II, 858, vv. 1655–1668).
80 *Servir a señor discreto*, ed. Laplana Gil (2012, II, 859, vv. 1678–1679).
81 *Servir a señor discreto*, ed. Laplana Gil (2012, II, 860, vv. 1689–1692).

[I will only tell you this,
and of this you can be certain,
that from one port only
the good can come to you.]

and also to his servant Giron:

Tú sirves con grande amor,
puesto que te enojas luego:
sólo te digo, está atento,
que harás tu sangre ajedrez.[82]

[You serve with passion,
since you get angry later:
I'm just telling you, be careful,
do not allow your blood to turn into chess.]

If we read these predictions in relation to the debate on the effectiveness and legality of divination, Severo would be the winner, because he is right in all his predictions. However, this should not be overrated and the comedy should not be interpreted as Lope's plea for the occult sciences. Rather, the Phoenix plays with the dramatic possibilities offered by the typical figurative language of predictions in order to increase tension. The audience will easily relate the word *puerto*, 'port', to Pedro Silvestre's rival, the shipowner, but this turns out to be a red herring. The puzzle is only solved when, in the third act, the Count of Palma, a nobleman with the surname of Puertocarrero,[83] appears on the scene. Like a *Deus ex machina*, he arranges don Pedro's life.[84] The servant Giron, in his turn, marries Elvira, Doña Leonor's mulatto maid, with whom he will have children of both colours of a chess board.

Lope exploits the dramatic possibilities offered by the reading of body signs and above all of the hand in order to create highly effective scenes.

---

82 *Servir a señor discreto*, ed. Laplana Gil (2012, II, 861, vv. 1699–1702).
83 For the historical identification of this character see the introduction by Weber de Kurlat (1975, 21).
84 Pedro reminds the audience of the prognosis when he tells the count of his adventures prior to his arrival in Madrid: "En el camino hallo un hombre / que por la fisionomía / del rostro y viendo en mis manos / ciertas señales o líneas, / me dijo, señor, que estaba / el remedio de mi vida / en un puerto", *Servir a señor discreto*, ed. Laplana Gil (2012, III, 885, vv. 2261–2267) [On the road I found a man / who by the physiognomy / of my face and seeing in my hands / certain signs or lines, / told me, sir, that he was / the remedy of my life / in a port].

2.2 Body readings between mockery and truth

> Las partes por quien se conoce el ingenio están delineadas de la naturaleza en el rostro, y así la invidia y los demás vicios; generalmente se ha de tener que los miembros que están en su proporción natural cuanto a la figura, color, cantidad, sitio y movimiento señalan buena complexión natural y buen juicio, y los que no tienen debida proporción y las demás referidas partes, que la tienen perversa y mala.[85]

> [The parts by which ingenuity is known are delineated by nature in the face, and thus envy and other vices; generally it is thought that the members which are in their natural proportion as to figure, colour, quantity, place and movement indicate a good natural constitution and good judgement, and those which have no due proportion and the other features referred to signify a perverse or evil character.]

This is what Lope says in the dedication of the comedy *Los españoles en Flandes* (1597–1606) to Cristóbal Ferreira de Sampayo, in which he also cites the "excelente fisiónomo Filomenes"[86] [excellent physiognomist Philomenes]. In another paratext, the dedication of the comedy *Virtud, pobreza y mujer* (1612–1615)[87] to the poet Giambattista Marino, Lope alludes to the fashion of making a physiognomic judgment based on paintings:

> Debe á mi amor y inclinacion a vuesa Señoría justamente tanto favor, que haya tenido deseo de mi retrato; que puesto que la pluma lo es del alma, después de haberla leido en el entendimiento, tengo por honra grande hacer estimacion de los exteriores instrumentos; y obediente al señor Auditor, dejé copiar á los pinceles de Francisco Yaneti, florentin, en estos años las ruinas de los días al declinar la tarde, cuyas primeras flores *aut morbo aut aetate deflorescunt*. Si ha llegado el lienzo, podrá vuesa Señoría con juicio fisionómico reconocer fácilmente si corresponde á su voluntad quien esas señas tiene.[88]

> [My love and reverence for your honour is such that I feel it is a great favour that you should have desired my portrait, and since the pen is that of the soul, after having read it in my mind, I hold it as an honour to make an estimate of the external instruments; and in obedience to the lord Auditor, I have ordered the brushes of Francisco Yaneti, a Florentine, to copy the ruins of the days at the decline of the afternoon whose first flowers *either disease or age do wilt*. If the canvas has arrived, you will, with physiognomic judgement, easily be able to see if he who has these traits corresponds to your wishes.]

---

85 Vega, *Los españoles en Flandes*, ed. Cortijo Ocaña (2014, 925). On the dating of the comedy see Morley & Bruerton (1968, 322).
86 Vega, *Los españoles en Flandes*, ed. Cortijo Ocaña (2014, 925) as well as footnote 5 on the link with physiognomic studies.
87 On the dating of the comedy between 1612 and 1615 see Morley & Bruerton (1968, 269).
88 Vega, *Virtud, pobreza y mujer*, ed. Hartzenbusch (1860, 211).

As Canonica de Rochemonteix (2000) argues, the Italian artist Francesco Giannetti made a portrait of Lope, now lost, at Marino's request. However, the canvas never arrived and was not included in the *Gallery* of the Neapolitan poet, as was possibly planned.[89]

In his writings, Lope uses the term *physiognomy* with some frequency,[90] an indication of the physiognomic awareness on the part of both the author and his characters. Its use is of particular interest in *La hermosura de Angélica:*

> El sustentar que la color del oro,
> la nieve de la cara y la blandura
> hacen cobarde el alma de Medoro
> más evidente enseña tu locura
> que, puesto que se muestre en el decoro,
> de la esterior humana arquitectura
> muchas veces se engañan los jüicios
> hechos por fisionómicos indicios.[91]

> [Holding that the colour of gold,
> the snow on the face and its softness
> make Medoro's soul a coward
> clearly your folly proves,
> for, as decorum shows,
> by the human exterior architecture

---

89 See Marino, *La Galeria*, ed. Pieri (2005, 262), who, as Canonica de Rochemonteix (2000) also observes, includes Garcilaso as the only Spanish poet in the section of the *poeti volgari*,
90 In the *Arcadia*, mention is made of "una doncella la cual, aunque no era de tan agudo ingenio como la segunda, era más vistosa, así en el rostro, fisionomía y proporción de la persona como en la riqueza de los vestidos", ed. Sánchez Jiménez (2012, 622) [a maiden who, although not as sharp-witted as the second one, was more eye-catching, both in the countenance, the physiognomy and the proportion of the person as in the richness of her clothes]. In the second act of the comedy *Los amigos enojados y verdadera amistad*, Renato says to the Duke: "Pues ya no te conocía / que hasta la philosomía / disfigura una traición" (1603, without pagination) [What now, I didn't recognise you any more / for even philosomy / disfigures a betrayal]. In the tragedy *La inocente sangre*, Doña Ana asks Morata: "¡Jesús! ¿Que vos sois Poeta?" [Almighty! What are you, a poet?] and the jester answers: "¿No tengo fisionomía / poetil?" (ed. Hartzenbusch 1860, 365) [Don't I have a poetical / physiognomy?]. In the "Advertimiento al Señor Lector", which serves as a prologue to *Rimas humanas y divinas del licenciado Tomé de Burguillos*, it says: "su fisionomía dirá ese retrato que se copió de un lienzo en que le trasladó al vivo el catalán Ribalta, pintor famoso entre españoles de la primera clase" (ed. Cuiñas Gómez 2008, 111–112) [his physiognomy will be told by this portrait, which was copied from a canvas onto which he was brought in verisimilitude by the Catalan Ribalta, a famous painter of the first class amongst the Spaniards]. Also see the entries for *fisionomía, fisionómico, fisiónomo, fisonomía* and *fisonómico* in the *Vocabulario completo de Lope de Vega by* Fernández Gómez (1971).
91 Vega, *La hermosura de Angélica*, VI, 13, vv. 97–104, ed. Trambaioli (2005, 333).

many times the judgements are beguiled
which are made by physiognomic signs.]

In the cited octave, the Phoenix questions the validity of this semiotic practice while subordinating Medoro's body to a reading in a physiognomic key.

In a whole series of works by the Phoenix, there are descriptions of the human body that are susceptible to interpretation in a physiognomic key, and those are sometimes carried out by the fictional characters. This is the case in *La Dorotea* (1632), when the maid Clara talks to her lady Marfisa about the physical appearance of her rival:

MARFISA. No es tan hermosa como dicen [. . .] Es muy de caras redondas. ¿Cómo le va de color?

CLARA. Trigueño claro.

MARFISA. ¿El cabello?

CLARA. Algo crespo, efecto de aquel color.

MARFISA. Si fuera hombre, fuera atrevida y cobarde.

CLARA. ¿Quién te lo ha dicho?

MARFISA. Yo lo he leído.[92]

[MARFISA: She's not as beautiful as they say . . . Her face is very round. How's her colour?

CLARA: A little swarthy.

MARFISA: Her hair?

CLARA: A little frizzy, effect of that colour.

MARFISA: If she were a man, she would be bold and cowardly.

CLARA: Who told you?

MARFISA: I read it.]

---

[92] Vega, *La Dorotea* I, 6, ed. McGrady (2011, 64–65 and additional footnote 65,395, 551–542). Also see Morby, who, in his commentary to his edition (1968, 114, footnote) argues that "the association of frizzy hair with cowardice or shyness is quite common," quoting Della Porta and Cortés. On the roundfaces see the examples collected by Herrero García (1925, 157–158). In *Dorotea*, Lope puts the word *physiognomy* into the mouth of the protagonist, who exclaims: "In your wall of discernment some rare wreckage did the rich Indian cause with his liberal physiognomy", Vega, *La Dorotea* I, 2, ed. McGrady (2011, 28).

This dialogue not only shows the characters' awareness of the legibility of the human body, but also provides us with an interesting piece of information about the dissemination of physiognomic knowledge which, as bookish knowledge ("I read it"), was within the reach of a woman of a certain social level. Thanks to the inventories of wills compiled by Dadson (1998), we know of two readers of physiognomic texts in the time of Lope: Antonia de Ulloa, Countess of Salinas, had "un libro yntitulado finosomia natural enquadernado en pergamino"[93] [a book entitled natural physiognomy bound in parchment], and Isabel Montero, who kept among her possessions the physiognomic books of Cortés and Della Porta as well as the *Examen de ingenios* by Huarte de San Juan.[94] Likewise, it may have been a reading facilitated by female access to male libraries, as has been demonstrated by Cruz (2011).

In the theatre of the Phoenix there are also characters on stage who defend the physiognomic principles. This is the case in *El marqués de las Navas* (1624).[95] At the beginning of the first act, the marquis talks with the noblemen don Filipe and don Enrique and with the witty Mendoza about how to judge women:

> Don Filipe. ¡Gallardas son las mujeres!
>
> Marqués. Siempre juzgáis por los talles.
>
> Don Filipe. La bizarría procede
> Del talle.
>
> Don Enrique. Y ¿no de la cara?
>
> Mendoza. Cara que no puede verse,
> ¿Qué ha de llamar por el talle?
>
> Marqués. No es el que menos enciende.
>
> Mendoza. ¡Que siempre Vueseñoría
> Por lo singular se pierde!
>
> Don Filipe. La bizarría del cuerpo
> Muestra que el alma contiene
> Todas las partes iguales;
> No el rostro, que el rostro puede
> Ser hermoso, y no tener
> La perfección que se debe

---

[93] On the inventory of 1605 cf. Dadson (1998, 433), who notes: "Probably it is Jerónimo Cortés, *Phisionomia y varios secretos de naturaleza*, Madrid, Pedro Madridgal, 1598".
[94] See the inventory of 1629 in Dadson (1998, 461–490).
[95] On the dating of the comedy see Morley & Bruerton (1968, 68 and 97).

A sí mismo en las demás
Partes que el cuerpo contiene.

Mendoza. Y ¿qué importa que una dama
Tenga el cuerpo diligente,
Derecho como una lanza.
Bizarro como un alférez.
La cintura que en un puño
Pueda apretarse y cogerse,
Las caderas como en Flandes,
Las piernas como un jinete,
Si el rostro puede ser molde
De hacer diablos para el jueves
En que el despensero cuelgan
Que afrentó los calabreses?
¡Vive Dios, que es de mal gusto
Quien tal opinión tuviere!
Que no puede enamorar
La boca donde los dientes
Sobre los asientos riñen
Como hidalgos montañeses.
La cara es mayor indicio
Del alma, que en ella vense
Las costumbres como en mapa;
Luego á los cuerpos prefiere.[96]

[Don Filipe: Gallant are the women!

Marquis: You always judge by the figure.

Don Filipe: The splendour proceeds
From the figure.

Don Enrique: Not from the face?

Mendoza: Face that can't be seen,
What should it say about the figure?

Marquis: It is not what least ignites the fire.

Mendoza: Your lordship is always
diverged by singularities!

Don Filipe: The body's splendour
shows that the soul contains

---

[96] Vega, *El marqués de Navas*, ed. Menéndez Pelayo (1902, 5).

all parts equal;
not the face, for the face can
be beautiful and not have
the perfection that
the other parts have
which the body contains.

MENDOZA: And what does it matter that a lady
holds her body rigid,
straight as a lance,
brave like an ensign.
The waist that in a fist
can be held and squeezed,
hips like in Flanders,
legs like a rider,
if the face can serve as a mould
to make figures of the devil for Maundy Thursday
on which they hang the traitor Judas
what insulted the Calabrese?
By Heavens, this is tasteless,
who would have such an opinion!
For a mouth cannot incite love
where the teeth quarrel
about the place they have,
like the Cantabrigian noblemen
The face is the major sign
Of the soul, for in it one sees
the habits as in a map;
So it must be preferred to the body.]

In a mixture of taunts and truths, the men raise the question of whether the face or the body of a woman is more indicative of her character and how important the beauty or ugliness of the figure and face are. It is the character of the jester who defends the legibility of the face (a "map") and therefore the conceptual basis of physiognomy.

In *Los Melindres de Belisa* (1606–1608),[97] the young protagonist rejects all the suitors presented to her by her mother and uncle. As Fiadino observes, "[l]as causas de los rechazos [. . .] son todas fútiles y ligadas a la apariencia física: pecan de ser calvo, tuerto, de barba oscura, manco, de pies grandes y uñas oscuras, vestir hábito de Santiago, tener ojos grandes o los bigotes caídos, ser

---

[97] On the dating of the comedy see Morley & Bruerton (1968, 362) as well as León, who, in the prologue of his edition (2007, 1469–1471), dates the play between 1606 and 1610.

francés o portugués. . ." (2000, 508)[98] [the causes of the rejections . . . are all futile and linked to physical appearance: they suffer from being bald, one-eyed, with a dark beard, one-armed, with large feet and dark nails, dressed in the habit of Santiago, having big eyes or fallen moustaches, being French or Portuguese. . .]. Eliso, one of her suitors, tells his servant Fabio how the capricious girl judges men by their physiognomy:

> ELISO. Un hombre desechó porque tenía
> un lunar en la cara, y por bermejo
> a un caballero.
>
> FABIO. Mas razón tenía.
>
> ELISO. ¿Por qué?
>
> FABIO. Por lo que dicen del pellejo.[99]
>
> [ELISO: A man discarded because he had
> a mole on the face, and for being red-haired
> a gentleman.
>
> FABIO: But I was right.
>
> ELISO: Why?
>
> FABIO: Because of what they say about the skin.]

The information that the text provides about Belisa's physiognomic knowledge is rather scarce. The bad reputation of the redheads was proverbial,[100] and the apprehension about them shared by Fabio and the protagonist is not necessarily explained by physiognomic studies.

It is striking that the Phoenix was particularly interested in the outward appearance of historical figures such as Sigismund Báthory (1572–1613), the central character of the comedy *El prodigioso príncipe transilvano*,[101] or Muley Xeque (1566–1621), called Felipe de África, a Saadian prince who was baptised

---

98 On this comedy see Hesse (1971), Schalk (1973), Fiadino (2000), Vaiopoulos (2001), Serralta (2003), Walde Moheno (2005), Cornejo (2007), Carrión (2015) and Sileri's metric study (2007).
99 Vega, *Los melindres de Belisa*, ed. León (2017, 1495, vv. 347–351); concerning this point, see González Ollé (1981, 161) and, in passing, Vaiopoulos (2001, 138).
100 See Herrero García (1925, 158–163) and González Ollé (1981).
101 The description of the Christian prince is introduced through a portrait that Mahomet receives along with a letter from his opponent: "MAHOMET. ¿Vióse atrevimiento igual? / ¡Oh, terrible deacato! / Dadme el retrato. ¡Ah, retrato / de aquel falso original! / ¿Qué dios te anima y levanta /

in El Escorial in 1593.[102] In the comedy *El bautismo del Príncipe de Marruecos* (1593–1603),[103] a servant describes the face of the Moorish sovereign to the knight Juan Ruiz de Velasco:

> JUAN. ¿Hasle visto alguna vez?
>
> CRIADO. Sí, señor.
>
> JUAN. ¿Que señas tiene?
>
> CRIADO. La majestad que conviene
> para un príncipe de Fez:
> modesto rostro y moreno,
> de cabello rizo y alto,
> alegre de ojos y falto
> de barba, fornido y lleno
> fuerte, ligero y galán,
> a pie y a caballo airoso,
> llano, humilde y generoso.[104]

> [JUAN: Have you ever seen him?
>
> SERVANT: Yes, sir.

---

contra el poder otomano? / ¡Oh, mozo arrogante y vano! / ¡Por Alá, pintado espanta! / ¡Qué barba le pintan! / SINÁN. ¡Brava / barba, catadura y talle. / MAHOMET. Tú no acabas de miralle, / ni yo de admirarme acabo", Vega, *El prodigioso príncipe transilvano* I, ed. Cotarelo and Mori (1916, 379) [MAHOMET: Has ever such boldness be seen? / Oh, dreadful contempt! / Give me the portrait. Ah, portrait / of that false original! / What god encourages you and arouses you / against the Ottoman power? / Oh, youth, so arrogant and vain! / What terrifying painting, by Allah! / What a beard they paint on him! / SINAN: Ferocious / beard and figure and size. / MAHOMET: You do not stop looking at it, / nor do I stop wondering at myself]. On the uncertain authorship and historical background of this comedy cf. Rambaud Cabello (1995), González Cuerva (2006, 288: "Segismundo parece una mezcla de genio y locura, epilepsia y lunatismo, dueño de una rica sensibilidad musical pero también con tintes sombríos, como apropiarse de los bienes de sus enemigos tras presenciar su masacre" [Segismundo seems to be a mixture of genius and insanity, epilepsy and lunacy, owner of a rich musical sensibility but with dark shades, too, like appropriating his enemies' possession after witnessing their massacre]) as well as Sâmbrian (2012) and (2016).

102 As Torres Martínez observes, Lope was present at the ceremony and 'must have met the novice and somehow communicated with him' (2009, 717). He also dedicates a sonnet to him ("Alta sangre real, claro Felipe"). On the historical character see Oliver Asín (1955, reed. 2008), Guastavino Gallent (1956), Sánchez Ramos (2010) and Bunes Ibarra and Alonso Acero (2011).

103 These are the dates proposed by Morley & Bruerton (1968, 50 and 233). On this comedy see Swislocki (1999) and Romanos (1999) and (2001).

104 Vega, *El bautismo del Príncipe de Marruecos* III, ed. According to Albarracín Teulón (1954, 15), those are the characteristics of a perfect gentleman.

JUAN: What semblance does he have?

SERVANT: The majesty suitable
for a prince of Fez:
modest face and dark hair,
curly, long hair,
bright-eyed and no beard,
stocky and plump,
strong, light and gallant,
on foot and on horseback,
plain, humble and generous.]

This description goes back in part to Muley Xeque's description in *Relación de las fiestas celebradas en Valencia con motivo del casamiento de Felipe III* by Felipe de Gauna: "hes gentil hombre y de buen rostro y disposición, haun ques hun poco moreno, y el cabello de la cabessa crespo y pocas barbas, y su persona vestido a la española"[105] [He is a gentle man with a good face and disposition, though he is rather darkish, and his hair rather curly and he doesn't have much beard and is dressed like a Spaniard]. The chronicler contrasts the sheik's gentleness and good disposition with his typically Moroccan physical appearance by means of the adverse conjunction.

Lope wrote this comedy probably at the request of Felipe de África himself,[106] who – according to Pedraza Jiménez – needed a 'letter of introduction to Christian society' (2012, 18). Belloni suspects that Muley Xeque wanted to "aprovecharse del potente medio teatral y dejarse conocer como 'nuevo' príncipe cristiano frente al heterogéneo público del corral" (2014, 91)[107] [take advantage of the powerful theatrical medium and make himself known as a "new" Christian prince in front of the heterogeneous public of the corral]. This is of great relevance when it comes to interpreting the Sheik's bodily features. Lope insists on

---

105 Felipe de Gauna, *Relación de las fiestas celebradas en Valencia con motivo del casamiento de Felipe III*, ed. Carreres Zacares (1926–1927, I, 214), also quoted by Oliver Asín (1955, reed. 2008, 160–161), Guastavino Gallent (1956, 120–121), Alonso Acero (2009, 267–271) and in Vega, *El bautismo del Príncipe de Marruecos* III, ed. Pontón (2012, 945, footnote).
106 See Pedraza Jiménez (1997, 137–140) and Belloni (2014).
107 "Desde esta perspectiva, entonces, podríamos definir la obra, según una terminología actual, como el resultado de una acción de comunicación estratégica muy refinada para lograr consenso y acrecentar consecuentemente su reputación, su honra. A fin de cuentas, su condición de morisco, aunque ilustre, necesitaba una aceptación" (Belloni 2014, 91) [From this perspective, then, we could define the play, according to current terminology, as the result of a highly refined act of strategic communication, aimed at achieving consensus and consequently increase its reputation, and its honour. Ultimately, his condition of an, albeit illustrious, *morisco* needed acceptance].

Felipe's condition as a Moor through the typical physiognomic signs such as, first of all, the frizzy hair, which used to be interpreted as a sign of the evil character that was attributed to this ethnic group. However, Felipe's virtuous acts belie this interpretation and Muley Xeque is presented as an exemplary and positive character in spite of the corporal determinism. But there is more to it. *El bautismo del Príncipe de Marruecos* was written and performed at a moment of particular fear towards the Turkish enemy and their potential allies within the Kingdom,[108] in which the positive representation of a Muslim could be a problem, were it not for the ideological burden of the play, as described by Belloni:

> [. . .] la comedia lopesca no pretendía contar la historia personal de un moro cualquiera, sino celebrar la conversión de un ilustre príncipe musulmán, heredero al trono de Marruecos. De esta manera, la victoria del cristianismo asumiría una acepción aún más significativa y la obra se convertiría en una artimaña de innegable e inmediato éxito a nivel social, primero, y luego también a nivel político. (2014, 94)

> [. . . Lope's comedy did not seek to tell the personal story of just any Moor, but to celebrate the conversion of an illustrious Muslim prince, heir to the throne of Morocco. In this way, the victory of Christianity would assume even more significance, and the play would become a ruse of undeniable and immediate success on, first of all, a social and, then, on a political level, too.]

The physiognomic profile of the Muley Xeque fits perfectly in this context: Lope combines the body signals indicative of ethnicity that have strong negative connotations (brown skin, frizzy hair[109] and lack of facial hair) with positive signals such as tall stature or cheerful eyes.

---

108 "Felipe III, en 1609, determinó la solución del controvertido argumento político [i.e. la cuestión morisca, FG] a través del decreto de la expulsión definitiva de los hispano-musulmanes. [. . .] Mientras Lope componía la obra encargada por Muley, las esferas gubernamentales estaban preconizando una definitiva conclusión del problema. La derrota definitiva del Islám nacional tuvo entonces que atrasarse hasta el primer decenio del siglo XVII" (Belloni 2014, 94). [Felipe III, in 1609, determined the solution of the controversial political question (i.e. the Moorish question, FG) through the decree of the definitive expulsion of the Hispanic Muslims. . . While Lope was composing the play commissioned by Muley, the governmental spheres were pushing for a definitive settlement of the problem. The definitive defeat of national Islam had then to be delayed until the first decade of the 17th century].
109 "Los cabellos crespos denotan rudeza de ingenio y simpleza en el varón, y en la mujer, desvergüenza y atrevimiento", Cortés, ed. Saguar (2017, without pagination). [Frizzy hair denotes rudeness of wit and simplicity in the male, and, in the female, shamelessness and daring]. As is well known, Cortés falls back on Michael Scott: "Cuius capilli sunt multum crispi significant hominem duri ingenii: aut multae simplicitatis seu utrumque", *Liber Phisionomiae*, Porsia (2009, 200) [Whose hair is very frizzy, this means a man with rudeness of wit or of great simplicity or both of them]. This interpretation continues in the Pseudo-Cocles where we read: "Cuius capilli

But physiognomy also played other roles in Lope's work. The masculine and at the same time intriguing aspect of the Amazons is described in some detail in the comedy *Las justas de Tebas y reina de las amazonas* (before 1596).[110] In another mythological comedy about a warlike conflict between the Amazons and the Greek heroes Hercules, Jason and Theseus,[111] *Las mujeres sin hombres* (1613–1616),[112] we find descriptions of the physical aspect of the three Greek heroes in the mouth of a jester in the service of Theseus. After having been taken prisoner by the *viragos*, Fineo informs Antiopía, the queen of the Amazons, about his companions. Speaking of Hercules, he remembers some of his twelve labours, but the Amazon is more interested in his physical appearance:

ANTIOPÍA. ¿Tiene buen talle?

FINEO. Es robusto.

ANTIOPÍA. ¿Qué es lo que robusto llamas?

---

sunt multum crispi, significant hominem duri ingenii, aut multe simplicitatis, sive utrunque etc.". *Physiognomiae et Chiromantiae Compendium* (1536, without pagination) [Whose hair is very frizzy, this means a man with rudeness of wit or of great simplicity or both of them, etc.]. Polemón interprets curly hair as a sign of cowardice and desire ("Know that the curliness of the hair indicates cowardice and desire", ed. Hoyland 2007, 431) and Adamatius interprets it (1544, 68) as a sign of shyness ("Virum crispo capillo, timidum ac fraudulentum dicito" [A man with frizzy hair is said to be shy and fraudulent]). Also see the English translation by Repath (2007, 525). The curly hair of Rampín, a character from *La Lozana Andaluza* has, however, a favourable meaning, since the manuals available before 1528 – the *Physiognomonica* (ed. Calvo Delcán & Martínez Manzano 1999, 46), Rasis (ed. Förster 1893, II, 163) and the *Secretum secretorum* (ed. Förster 1893, II, 198) – interpret curly hair as a sign of boldness.

110 It is the servant Drusus who gives an ample description of the beauty of the amazon Abderite, his master's sister: "Es tanta su perfección, / que a naturaleza excede. / El cuerpo tiene gentil, / entre robusto y brioso; / el brazo, blanco y nervioso, / que cubre un velo sutil: / su rostro a la nieve iguala; / mirando a sus ojos / que airados, despiden fuego, / y, mansos, blando regala, con unas vivas centellas / roban las prendas mejores [. . .] / Una madeja vistosa / de cabello negro, y tal, / que como palio real / cubre la frente espaciosa", Vega, *Las justas de Tebas I*, ed. Gómez & Cuenca Muñoz (1993, 745) [Her perfection is so great, / that it exceeds nature. / The body is gentle, / between robust and sturdy; / the arm is white and tense, / and is covered by a subtle veil: / her face is equal to snow; / looking into her eyes / which, angry, give off fire, / and, if meek, flatter, with bright sparks / break your vows [. . .] / An ornate mane / of black hair, and such, / that like a royal cloak / covers the airy forehead]. On the dating of the comedy see Morley & Bruerton (1968, 248 and 590).

111 On the classical sources of the comedy see García Fernández (2006). The theme of the Amazons in Lope has been studied by Cabrero Aramburo (2006) and Trambaioli (2006). McGaha (1991) has proposed a feminist reading of the play.

112 Those are the dates suggested by Morley & Bruerton (1968, 365–366)

FINEO. Hombre fornido de miembros,
trabado y ancho de espaldas.[113]

[ANTIOPÍA: Is he of good size?

FINEO: He's sturdy.

ANTIOPÍA: What do you call sturdy?

FINEO: A man with strong limbs,
muscular, with broad shoulders.]

The same dialogical scheme is repeated when speaking of Theseus: Fineo mentions his victory over the Minotaur, but Antopía wants to know "what man" he is. The servant emphasises that his master 'is of excellent size and has a fine face'.[114] This description corresponds to what characterises these heroes in mythology: Hercules is the incarnation of strength while Theseus makes Ariadne and her sister Phaedra fall in love with him. From a physiognomic perspective, Jason's description is the most interesting:

FINEO. Mediano cuerpo,
brío, gentileza y gracias,
y agudeza en hombre rubio.

ANTIOPÍA. Pues, ¿a los rubios les falta?

FINEO. No digo tal; mas lo rubio
se atribuye a cosas bajas;
que yo he visto barbinegros
con cuatro dedos de escarcha.
Quiere decir que Jasón
es brioso.[115]

[FINEO: Medium body,
spirit, gentleness and grace,
and sharpness in a fair man.

ANTIOPÍA: What, do fair men lack it?

FINEO: I do not say so; but the fair
is assigned to low things;

---

113 Vega, *Las mujeres sin hombres*, ed. García Fernández (2008, 193, vv. 779–782).
114 Vega, *Las mujeres sin hombres*, ed. García Fernández (2008, 193, v. 790).
115 Vega, *Las mujeres sin hombres*, ed. García Fernández (2008, 194, vv. 809–818).

for I've seen blackbeards
with gold leaf four fingers thick
Which means that Jason
is spirited.]

For Cortés, light or fair hair indicates rather negative character traits, although none of them would rule out sharpness of mind: "Los que tienen los cabellos royos naturalmente son invidiosos, soberbios, maldicientes y engañosos, pero el sabio y prudente lo domina todo"[116] [Those with fair hair are naturally envious, haughty, foul-mouthed, and deceitful, but the wise and prudent masters everything]. Della Porta, who distinguishes four shades of fair hair, – "capelli biondeggianti" [blondish hair], "capelli molto biondi, biancheggianti" [very blond and whitish hair], "capelli biondi" [blond hair] and "capelli biondi rossi" [red-blond hair][117] – says of men with light fair hair:

> Il color de' capelli biondo biancheggiante qual si vede ne' Sciti, dimostra rozzezza, malignità e rusticità: da Palemone. E Adamanzio dice altramente di Palemone: il capello molto biondo biancheggiante, qual è il color de' Celti, dimostra ignoranza, rozzezza e rusticità. Aristotele ne' *Problemi*: sono così di aspetto come di costumi ferini quelli che abitano sotto il gran caldo e freddo. La cagion è questa: che il temperamento non solo giova al corpo, ma all'animo ancora. Gli eccessi muovono così la distemperanza del corpo come della mente, e la pervertono. [. . .] Nerone fu di capello biondeggiante, cioè di biondo che va al bianco, e però riluvevano in lui quei costumi rozzi e ferini.[118]

> [The colour of light fair hair, as seen in Scythians, shows roughness, malignancy and rusticity: Polemonic. And Adamantius says otherwise of Polemon: very light and white hair, which is the colour of the Celts, shows ignorance, roughness and rusticity. Aristotle in the *Problems*: those who dwell under the great heat and cold are of such appearance well as of feral habits. The cause is this: that temperament is not only of benefit to the body, but also to the soul. The excesses thus move the distemper of the body as well as the mind, and pervert it. . . . Nero had fair hair, that is to say blond hair that goes white, and yet those coarse and feral habits shone through him.]

According to the same Neapolitan scholar, "i capelli né molto neri né molto duri faran l'uomo ingegnoso; e questo color de' capelli Aristotele dà all'ingegnoso nella sua figura"[119] [hair which is neither very black nor very hard will make an ingenious man; and this colour of hair Aristotle attributes to the outward appearance of the ingenious]. The collation of these theories shows Lope's and his characters' familiarity with them, but, at the same time, the Phoenix questions

---

116 Cortés, *Fisonomía natural*, ed. Saguar (2017, without pagination).
117 See Della Porta, *Della fisionomia dell'uomo*, ed. Paolella (2013, 413–416).
118 Della Porta, *Della fisionomia dell'uomo*, ed. Paolella (2013, 415).
119 Della Porta, *Della fisionomia dell'uomo*, ed. Paolella (2013, 413).

the import of corporal determinism with a character whose way of being contradicts the corporal signs.

In the Byzantine comedy[120] *La doncella Teodor* (1610–1612),[121] Lope de Vega brings onto the stage the medieval legend of the wise maiden.[122] In this comedy, it is Fenicia, one of the wise daughters of the philosopher Beliano, who asks Teodor, "¿Qué partes ha de tener / una perfecta mujer?"[123] [What parts should / a perfect woman have?]. The answer is the same as in the medieval tradition:

> TEODOR. Si son esteriores partes
> y en dieciocho las repartes,
> desta manera han de ser:
> corta en tres y larga en tres,
> en tres blanca y en tres roja,
> en tres gruesa y flaca en tres.[124]

> [TEODOR: If they are external parts
> and you divide them up into eighteen,
> this way they have to be:
> short in three and long in three,
> in three white and in three red,
> in three thick and in three thin.]

At the request of Fenicia, Teodor explains which parts are to be short (mouth, nose and feet), long (body, neck and fingers), red (cheeks, lips and gums),

---

120 On this dramatic subgenre see González-Barrera (2005), Fernández Rodríguez (2017) and Madroñal (2011).
121 On the dating of the comedy see Morley & Bruerton (1968, 314) and the introduction to the edition by González-Barrera (2007, 169).
122 On medieval sources see Valero Cuadra (1994) (1997), Jerez-Gómez (2010, 253–255) and Mochón Castro (2012, 101–104). The history of the motif has been studied by Darbord (1995) and Parker (1996); González-Barrera has dealt with the printed diffusion of *La historia de la doncella Teodor* and proposes that "Lope leyó la edición impresa que conocemos como P [i.e. Sevilla, Jacobo Cromberger, 1526–1528] o, al menos, otra basada en este testimonio" (2007, 439) [Lope read the printed edition that we know as P [i.e. Sevilla, Jacobo Cromberger, 1526–1528] or, at least, another one based on this testimony].
123 Vega, *La doncella Teodor* III, ed. González-Barrera (2007, 276, vv. 3063–3064). See also the edition by González-Barrera (2008).
124 Vega, *La doncella Teodor III*, ed. González-Barrera (2007, 276, vv. 3065–3070). See on this 'canon of perfect feminine beauty' Albarracín Teulón (1954, 10–11) and Valero Cuadra (1997, 36–37 and 86). González-Barrera (2007, 441–442) compares the *mouvance* of the inventories in the different printed testimonies. On a reading of comedy from the point of view of genre studies see Case (1994).

white (face, teeth and hands), wide (shoulders, wrists and hips) and black (eyes, eyelashes and eyebrows). In addition to the brief questions, Fenicia intersperses this on the subject of black eyes:

> FENICIA. Aunque son vivos,
> mucho en los negros te engañas,
> verdes son nobles y altivos
> y azules, color de cielo.[125]

> [FENICIA: Though they are vivid,
> much you can be deceived by black eyes,
> Greens are noble and haughty
> and blue ones, colour of the sky.]

As González-Barrera aptly observes, this description does not correspond to the canon of beauty of the 17th century.[126] Through the intertextual relationship with medieval history, the aesthetic preferences of the model are updated.

In the historical tragedy[127] *El Duque de Viseo* (1608–1609)[128] there is a brief humorous dialogue between the duke and his squire Brito,[129] in which the jester ridicules physiognomic science:

> VISEO. ¿Sois poeta?
>
> BRITO. ¿No se ve?

---

125 Vega, *La doncella Teodor* III, ed. González-Barrera (2007, 277, vv. 3090–3095).
126 González-Barrera (2007, 439–440): "The preferred qualities have an evident oriental origin, as is evidenced, for example, by their division into groups of three, but it does not correspond to the canon of beauty of the time of the caliphate of Baghdad and, of course, it does not resemble the Petrarchan ideal – fair and bright-eyed –, dominating the Renaissance, although we do find more than one coincidence with the prototype of the woman of the Golden Age".
127 As Calderón notes in the introduction to the edition of *El duque de Viseo*, ed. Calderón (2005, 1033), the play "is based on two historical facts: the execution of the third Duke of Braganza in Évora, on June 23rd 1483, and the assassination of the Duke of Viseo, in Setúbal, on August 23rd 1484. Most of the studies of the play address its historical background and its political message: Gigas (1917), González del Valle (1973), Alborg (1981), Álvarez Sellers (1995), Gagnon-Riopel (2002), Campbell (2007) and (2010), Oleza (2013), Domínguez Matito (2015) and Teixeira de Souza (2016).
128 On the dating of the comedy see Morley & Bruerton (1968, 318) and the introduction to the edition of *El duque de Viseo*, ed. Calderón (2005, 1033).
129 On the character of Duke González's squire see del Valle, who observes: "It is within the thematic context to which I have briefly referred that the figure of Brito acquires importance within *El duque de Viseo*. In spite of Brito being a character of low class, we can observe in him a wisdom that reminds us of a Sancho Panza" (1979, 104).

VISEO. ¿Adónde?

BRITO. En el sobrescrito

VISEO. Pues ¿tienen fisonomía
particular los poetas?

BRITO. ¿Luego no?

VISEO. ¡Cosas secretas!

BRITO. ¿No se conoce en la mía?
Lo primero, ha de tener
un poeta la cabeza
sobre el hombro, porque es pieza
en que consiste el saber;
junto al cabello, la frente;
la nariz en la mitad
de la cara.

VISEO. Eso es verdad.

BRITO. ¿Y cómo! Verdad patente.
La boca es de grande efeto
que esté. . .

VISEO. Mira lo que dices.

BRITO. . . . debajo de las narices
para que sea discreto
y para comer también.

VISEO. ¡Lindas señas![130]

[VISEO: Are you a poet?

BRITO: Can't you see?

VISEO: Where?

BRITO: In what is overwritten.

VISEO: What, do poets
have a physiognomy of their own?

---

[130] *El duque de Viseo*, ed. Calderón (2005, III, 1116, vv. 2266–2285).

BRITO: Why not?

VISEO: Secret matter!

BRITO: Can't you see it in me?
First of all, a poet must have
his head on his shoulder,
for it is the part
in which knowledge resides;
next to the hair, the forehead;
the nose in the middle
of the face.

VISEO: That is true.

BRITO: And how! Obvious truth.
The mouth is of such great effect
that it . . .

VISEO: Heed what you say.

BRITO: . . . should be under the nose
in order to be discreet
and in order to eat, too.

VISEO: Fine signs those are!]

It should be remembered that shortly before, when the duke and his servant, disguised as villains, had bumped into a student astrologer on their way, Brito was particularly sceptical about the scientific validity of astrology: "Pues discreto / yo os probaré con efeto / que es falsa la ciencia vuestra"[131] [Now, you wit, / I will prove to you with effect / that your science is false]. As in other plays by Lope, this comedy questions scientific principles which manifest themselves among servants and subaltern characters.

3 Tirso de Molina and physiognomy

In the dramatic work of Tirso de Molina (1579–1648)[132] we find neither references to palmistry nor scenes in which the characters' hands are read. Still, the term

---

131 *El duque de Viseo*, ed. Calderón (2005, III, 1113, vv. 2177–2179).
132 On astrology in Tirso de Molina see Halstead (1941).

physiognomy occurs repeatedly, especially to refer to someone's external appearance.[133] In the theatre of the Mercedarian, we also find signs of physiognomic consciousness, as those we have identified in Lope. They can also be found in Mira de Amescua.[134] In the comedy *El vergonzoso en palacio* (1604–1611)[135] the servant Tarsus says to his unfaithful lover Melissa:[136] "Aunque lloréis un diluvio / tenéis el cabello rubio: / no hay que fiar de ese pelo. / Ya os conozco que sois fina"[137] [Even if you cry a flood of tears / your hair is fair: / one cannot trust that hair. / I know you and that you are pretty dangerous]. The typical colour of the

---

133 Thus in *El amor médico* ("ESTEFANÍA. ¡Qué dello que os parecéis / a vuestro hermano! Tenéis / su misma fisonomía; / ninguna diferencia hay / en los dos; quedo admirada", ed. Oteiza 1999, 813, 3144–3148) [ESTEFANÍA: How much like your brother! You have / the same physiognomy; / there is no difference / in the two; I am admired], in *Doña Beatriz de Silva* ("MELGAR. [. . .] conocióme / en la tal fisonomía /don Pedro Pereira [. . .]", ed. Tudela 1999, 987–988, vv. 3090–3092) [MELGAR: . . . By such a physiognomy / Don Pedro Pereira / knew me . . .] and in *Por el sótano y el torno* ("POLONIA. Repare vuesa merced / en esta fisonomía, / y verá la diferencia / de la dama parecida. / Mire esta aguileña cara, / las rosas destas mejillas, / los rasgos de aquellos ojos, / la nariz no tan prolija, / y conocerá su engaño". ed. Palomo 2005, 576 [POLONIA: Note, my lord, / this physiognomy, / and you will see the distinction / of this lady / Look at this sharp face, / the roses on these cheeks, / the features of those eyes, / the nose not very long, / and you will know her machinations]).
134 In *El arpa de David* (1610) by Mira de Amescua (1577–1644), Jonatás, the son of King Saul, recognises David's royal condition by reading the body of that Old Testament character: "Miro en tu fisonomía, / David, aspecto real; / si fueses rey, yo sería, / pues soy tu amigo, tu igual", Mira de Amescua, *El arpa de David*, ed. García Sánchez (2001, 138, vv. 1095–1098) [I see royal appearance / in your physiognomy, David; / if you were king, I would be, / for I am your friend, your equal].
135 On the dating of the comedy see Labarre (1981) and the introduction to the edition by Oteiza (2012, 149–152).
136 On this comedy see Glenn (1965), Conlon (1985) and (1988), Florit Durán (1991), (2000) and (2001), Frenk (1994), González (1996), Beat Rudin (1997), Dartai-Maranzana (2002), Armas (2006b), Oteiza (2009), Berruezo Sánchez (2011) and Yoon & Na (2016). On its characterization as a palatine comedy see Dixon (1995). The scene of rustic lovers has received very little critical attention.
137 Molina, *El vergonzoso en palacio* I, ed. Oteiza (2012, 15, vv. 234–237) The editor notes in her commentary of these verses that "en este contexto no se refiere al cabello rubio, canon de belleza femenina, sino al rojizo, tradicionalmente mal visto, por asociarse al traidor Judas" [in this context she does not refer to fair hair, part of the canon of feminine beauty, but to reddish hair, traditionally frowned upon because it is associated with the traitor Judas]. Although in the additional footnote she quotes verses 235–236 of Pujasol's book ("de los cabellos rubios como el azafrán, señal de ser el hombre desalmado y cruel ["with fair hair like saffron, a sign of being a heartless and cruel man]), she neglects the physiognomic implications (2012, 266). Likewise, in the editions of Ayala (1971, 55, footnote to verse 250), Hesse (1983, 48, footnote 17) and Rull (1986, 71, footnote to verses 249–250) reference is made to the bad reputation of redheads, of which González Ollé (1981, 154) also speaks with regard to this passage.

Petrarchan lady's hair appears in the mouth of the jester in a physiognomic key with strong negative connotations. As Jerónimo Cortés says, fair-haired people tend to be 'deceitful' (ed. Saguar 2017, without pagination).

In *Quien calla otorga* (1620–1624),[138] a continuation of *El castigo del penseque*,[139] there is a scene in which the reading of the body has a certain prominence. At the end of the second act, the jolly Chinchilla is in the garden with Doña Brianda. This ugly old woman tries to take advantage of the darkness in order to conceal her unattractiveness and offer herself without detours in marriage to Don Rodrigo's servant, who, in order to make fun of her, pretends to be indecisive:

> CHINCHILLA. Ahora bien, para que diga
> de sí o no, dame esa mano.
>
> BRIANDA. De esposa os la doy.
>
> CHINCHILLA. ¡Qué fría,
> qué flaca y que floja está!
> Y, en fin, para ser francisca,
> ¡qué de nudos de cordón
> traen los dedos por sortijas!
> ¡Vive el cielo que parecen
> manojo de disciplinas
> o espárragos de Portillo,
> si no son de cañafístola!
>
> BRIANDA. No hagas caso de las manos,
> que aunque me desacreditan,
> lo demás es de manteca.
> Toca la fisonomía.
>
> CHINCHILLA. Carirredonda pareces.
>
> BRIANDA. ¿Pues es malo?
>
> CHINCHILLA. ¡En redondillas
> me enamoras, vive Dios!
> ¡Ay!
>
> BRIANDA. ¿Qué ha sido?

---

[138] On the dating of this comedy see the introduction to the edition by Zugasti (2013, 46).
[139] On both comedies and the relationship between them see Mandrell (2003).

CHINCHILLA. ¡Antojadiza!

BRIANDA. Traigolos por el sereno
de noche.

CHINCHILLA. ¿Y te melindrizas?
¡Bueno! ¿Son negros o zarcos?

BRIANDA. Negros.

CHINCHILLA. ¿Mucho?

BRIANDA. Como endrinas.

CHINCHILLA. Pues serán espadas negras,
que por ser amor esgrima
se ha puesto, por no lisiarme,
antojos por zapatillas.

BRIANDA. ¿Qué buscas?

CHINCHILLA. Lo que no hallo:
la narigación.

BRIANDA. ¿No atinas
con ellas?

CHINCHILLA. No

BRIANDA. Aquestas son.

CHINCHILLA. ¡Estas! ¿Romas?[140]

[CHINCHILLA: How now, for me to say
yes or no, give me that hand of yours.

BRIANDA: As your wife, I give it to you.

CHINCHILLA: How cold,
How skinny, how slack it is!
And, anyway, to be frank,
what knotty cords those fingers
have for rings!

---

140 Molina, *Quien calla, otorga*, ed. Zugasti (2013, 369–371, vv. 1925–1954).

By Heaven, they feel like
a bundle of whips
or like Portillo asparagus,
if they're not fistulas of reed!

BRIANDA: Never mind my hands,
for even though they discredit me,
the rest is purest butter.
Touch the physiognomy.

CHINCHILLA: A round face you seem to have.

BRIANDA: Is that bad?

CHINCHILLA: In swirling quatrains
you make me fall in love, by God!
Ouch!

BRIANDA: What was that?

CHINCHILLA: You wear glasses!

BRIANDA: I wear them to protect me from the cold and damp of the night.

CHINCHILLA: Are you quibbling?
Well! Are they black or blue?

BRIANDA: Black.

CHINCHILLA: Very black?

BRIANDA: Like sloes.

CHINCHILLA: Black (i.e. uncut) swords they must be,
because love is swordplay
she has put on, in order not to maim me,
glasses as a sword protection.

BRIANDA: What do you search?

CHINCHILLA: What I can't find:
the nose.

BRIANDA: Can't you
find it?

CHINCHILLA: No.

BRIANDA: Here it is.

CHINCHILLA: This? A snub!]

After the jester continues to make jokes about the absence of a nose in Doña Brianda,[141] this scene, which functions as a 'burlesque counterpoint',[142] is interrupted by the arrival of Don Carlos. The encounter of the two secondary characters in the darkness of the garden allows to bring on stage in a plausible way the description of the woman's physical peculiarities with a great comic potential. Chinchilla touches Doña Brianda's hands and face, asking her about what he discovers by touch. This ploy allows us to specify some details that can be read in a physiognomic key. Like Dulcinea and Sansón Carrasco, Brianda has a round face[143] and is snub-nosed,[144] two characteristics which not only serve to describe a rather unattractive woman, but also indicate a libidinous and dumb woman.

---

[141] "CHINCHILLA. ¡A Roma me voy por todo! / Por Dios, si te arromadizas / roma dama que no topes / qué tirar, sino es con pinzas. / ¡Mona hay que las trae mayores! / BRIANDA. ¿Pensabas que era judía? / CHINCHILLA. No, mas redonda, y sin ellas, / cara tienes de buñiga. / Sutiles jinetes son / los antojos, pues encima / pueden tenerse, aunque vayan / a la jineta o la brida. / ¿Hay tal esterilidad / de narices en las Indias? / Puedes pretender por chata / una plaza de cacica. / ¡Válgate el diablo por roma!", Molina, *Quien calla, otorga*, ed. Zugasti (2013, 372–373, vv. 1956–1972) [CHINCHILLA: I will go to Rome for all of this! / Heavens, if you catch a cold / my snubber lady not to come upon / tweezers you will need to get at it. / There are monkeys who have larger ones! / BRIANDA: Did you think I was a Jew? / CHINCHILLA: No, but round, and without them, / you have a face like a cow-patty. / Subtle riders are those glasses, / because they can stay on top / with short or long stirrups. / Is there any such sterility of noses in the Indies? / You can claim with your snub nose / to get a post as chieftain. / Go to hell for being a snub!]. Translator's note: The play on words based on homophony with *Roma* (name of the Italian city), *nariz roma* (flat nose) and *arromadizarse* (catching a cold) cannot be rendered in English.

[142] Thus Zugasti (2013, 69) characterises this scene in the introduction to his edition.

[143] On round faces in the Golden Age of Spanish literature see Herrero García (1925, 157–158). According to Cortés, "los que tienen el rostro muy menudo y redondo son simples, flacos, tímidos y de poca memoria" (ed. Saguar 2017, without pagination) [the ones with very small and round faces are simple, thin, shy and have little memory].

[144] On the snub nose as a sign of lasciviousness see the chapter about *La Lozana Andaluza* in Gernert (2018b, 270–272).

4 Body signs in Rojas Zorrilla

In the hagiographic comedy *Santa Isabel, reina de Portugal*[145] by Francisco de Rojas Zorrilla (1607–1648), the comical Tarabillo,[146] servant to Ramiro and favourite to the queen, enters the stage at the beginning of the first act in front of the king and is introduced by his favourite Carlos:

> Es un lacayuelo
> [. . .] De humor nuevo
> se hace astrólogo, y podrás
> con él divertir el tiempo
> un rato.[147]

---

[145] The comedy was published in the *Primera parte de sus comedias* (1640) and was probably performed in 1635. On the controversy over dating see the prologue of the Arenas Cruz edition (2011, 13–14). According to Pedraza Jiménez (2005, 970), it is rather a palatial comedy than a comedy of saints: "Rojas Zorrilla se aparta de forma clara y consciente de las fuentes hagiográficas con la decidida voluntad de crear una pieza dramática que no se ciñe a los tópicos y esquemas estructurales de la comedia de santos. Prescinde, en gran medida, de la misión didáctica propia del género que se empeña en difundir las verdades de la fe mediante excursos más o menos pertinentes" [Rojas Zorrilla clearly and consciously departs from the hagiographic sources with the fierce determination to create a drama that will not stick to the clichés and structural patterns of the comedy of saints. He dispenses, to a great extent, with the didactic mission proper to the genre, which strives to spread the truths of the faith through more or less relevant excursuses]. Sánchez speaks of "la double dimension religieuse et profane de l'œuvre" (2008, 225) [the twofold religious and profane dimension of the play].

[146] On this character see Sánchez (2008, 232, footnote 17: "La seule tonalité légère de l'œuvre est apportée par les interventions de ce personnage, bouffon médiéval [. . .] plutôt que traditionnel *gracioso*. Il atténue la tension des moments les plus dramatiques et évite que la pièce ne sombre dans la tragédie" [The only light tone in the play is provided by the interventions of this character, a medieval buffoon . . . rather than the traditional *gracioso*. He alleviates the tension of the most dramatic moments and prevents the play from sinking into tragedy]) and Duro Rivas (2011, 168–169): "Como en todas las comedias, en esta existe un personaje que es el gracioso, en este caso Tarabilla, un criado. A través de sus discursos se observa el ingenio cómico de Rojas Zorrilla, pues son una sucesión de 'disparates' que provocan la risa del espectador. Se hace pasar por astrólogo, y su presencia supone un toque de humor en medio de la tragedia" [As in all comedies, in this one there is a funny character, in this case Tarabilla, a servant. In his speeches we can appreciate Rojas Zorrilla's comical skills, as they are a succession of "absurdities" that provoke the laughter of the audience. Tarabilla pretends to be an astrologer, and his presence gives a touch of humour to the tragedy, right in the middle of it].

[147] Rojas Zorrilla, *Santa Isabel, reina de Portugal*, ed. Arenas Cruz (2011, 39, vv. 124–129).

[He's a lackey.
. . . On a whim
feigns to be an astrologer, and you can
while away some time with him.]

This introduction arouses the monarch's curiosity. He invites the jester to speak to him of his astrological skills,[148] giving Tarabilla the chance to make a funny speech about the predictions he is able to make:

Notable; y porque lo veáis
pronósticos son aquestos
Descubre una pretina de papeles.
de los años que han pasado,
porque de los venideros
yo pienso que no hay ninguno
que pueda afirmar lo cierto,
y esto lo hemos visto todos.[149]

[Quite notable; and so that you can see
these are the forecasts
Taking out a bundle of papers
about the past years,
because of the coming years,
I don't think there is anyone
who can claim to be certain,
but this we have all seen.]

After negating in the manner of Rabelais the possibility to know the future, he takes out a book and comments on the ideas of this *lunario nuevo*, which contains platitudes about the constellations[150] and, in the second chapter,

---

148 "En esto de astrología / diz que sois grande sujeto?", Rojas Zorrilla, *Santa Isabel, reina de Portugal*, ed. Arenas Cruz (2011, 40, vv. 149–150) [In this matter of astrology / they say you're a master?].

149 Rojas Zorrilla, *Santa Isabel, reina de Portugal*, ed. Arenas Cruz (2011, 40, vv. 151–158).

150 "Mas este es Lunario nuevo / *Saque un libro.* / de lo que ha de suceder / el año que viene. Empiezo: / 'La mayor señal de agua, / conforme dice Ruperto, / es no tener para vino; / y cuando estuviere Venus / con Géminis, que es un signo / mezclado con los ungüentos, / es que está Venus herida / y es Géminis el remedio; / si Júpiter está en Libra / es que vive de tendero; / si la Luna está en cabeza / de Dragón, será muy cierto / que el dragón tiene cabeza; / ítem, si hubiere en el cielo / cometa, según Nebrija / pronostica, mil encuentros / de reyes en las barajas / todas las veces que hay juego. / Si el sol estuviere en Piscis / y algo salado el aspecto, / es señal que está de viernes: / será año de pocos huevos, / habrá melones, pepinos, / médicos. . .', con que protesto / que morirá mucha gente / si no los matan a ellos–", Rojas Zorrilla, *Santa Isabel, reina de Portugal*, ed. Arenas Cruz (2011, 40–42, vv. 158–186). [But this is the new Lunario / *Takes out*

about omens.[151] The third chapter of the book is about physiognomy and says:

> "El que tuviere el aspecto
> con frente chica y arrugas
> en ella, dice Marcelio,
> que tendrá cara de mico
> si tiene pequeño el gesto;
> el que tuviere la boca
> en almíbar –decir quiero
> en humedad, como balsa–
> con perdigones a trechos
> que va lloviendo razones
> y va escupiendo concetos,
> que habrá menester traer
> enjugador, pues con esto,
> si hablaba de regadío,
> hablará en secano luego;
> ítem, el que fuere bizco
> viene a valer por dos tuertos,
> pues no se sabe de qué ojo
> de los dos viene a ser ciego;
> ítem. . .".[152]

---

a book / of what is to happen / next year. I will start: / "The surest sign of water, / as Ruperto says, / is not to have money for wine; / and when Venus / is with Geminis, which is a sign / mixed with ointments, / then Venus is wounded / and Gemini is her remedy; / if Jupiter is in Libra / then he makes his living as a shopkeeper; / if the Moon is in the head / of the Dragon, it will be very certain / that the dragon has a head; / item, if there is in the sky / a comet, that, according to Nebrija / predicts a thousand encounters / of kings in the cards / every time there is a game. / If the sun is in Pisces / and its appearance is somewhat salty, / it is a sign that it is Friday: / it will be a year of few eggs, / there will be melons, cucumbers, / physicians. . .', with which I protest / that many people will die / if they are not killed].

151 "Va el capítulo segundo, / que trata de los agüeros: / 'El que al salir de su casa / encontrare tabernero, / tendrá un día muy aguado; / y el que sin llevar dineros / fuere a buscar qué comer, / se volverá sin traerlo; / el que encontrare algún zurdo / por la mañana, protesto / que no hará cosa a derechas; / ítem, aquel que riñendo / se le cayere la espada, / tendrá por mejor agüero / que caérsele la cara'", Rojas Zorrilla, *Santa Isabel, reina de Portugal*, ed. Arenas Cruz (2011, 42, vv. 187–201) [Here is the second chapter, which deals with omens: / "He who when he leaves his house / meets an innkeeper, / will have a very bad day; / and he who without money / goes out in search of food, / will return without it; / he who meets a left-handed person / in the morning, I protest / will do nothing right; / he who quarrels / and drops his sword, / will have as his best omen / that his face drops].

152 Rojas Zorrilla, *Santa Isabel, reina de Portugal*, ed. Arenas Cruz (2011, 42–43, vv. 204–223).

["Whoever has a small forehead
and wrinkles in it, says Marcelio,
will have a face like a monkey
if he has a small face
the one with the mouth
in syrup – I want to say
in treacle, like a pond –
with pellets in stretches
raining down reasons
and spitting out conceits,
so that you need to bring
a duster, for with this,
if he was talking about irrigation before,
he'll be speaking of dry land later;
item, whoever is cross-eyed
is worth two one-eyeds,
for it is not known from which
of the two eyes he will be blind;
item. . .".]

Tarabilla is interrupted by the king, who is becoming tired of the servant's gibberish. In this brief and amusing interlude that delays the first meeting between the monarchs, Rojas Zorrilla ridicules the principles of physiognomic discourse in gross platitudes.[153]

5 Occult knowledge in Juan Ruiz de Alarcón

Juan Ruiz de Alarcón (1580/1582–1639) is probably the playwright of the Golden Age who has given most space to magic,[154] astrology[155] and occult knowledge.[156] The author "fue un gran aficionado a la magia y que conocía el mundo libresco en que se teorizaba"[157] [was a great lover of magic and knew the bookish world

---

153 Also see Lanuza-Navarro, who observes: "Tarabilla pokes fun at astrological-physiognomic assertions, but also parodies the style of astrologer's annual prognostications" (2014, 209).
154 See Vetterling (1980), González Fernández (2011) and Bermann (2016).
155 See Espantoso-Foley (1964). As far as the textualization of astrological knowledge is concerned, the comedy *El dueño de las estrellas* is particularly interesting, since it raises the problem of free will, as has been studied by Espantoso-Foley (1972, 91–98), Parr (1974) and Reichenberger (1991).
156 See Espantoso-Foley (1967) and (1972).
157 On the dating of the play see the introduction to his edition of *Quien mal anda en mal acaba* by Martínez Blasco (1993, 1).

in which it was theorised]. As Espantoso-Foley notes, in one quarter of his dramatic work he 'used the occult sciences as a basis for argument' (1967, 319). This researcher emphasises that the novo-Hispanic playwright "conocía muy a fondo las posibilidades artísticas y dramáticas que la nigromancia, adivinaciones, astrología y otras prácticas relacionadas con el ocultismo poseen para el desarrollo de una trama" (1967, 319) [has in-depth knowledge of the artistic and dramatic possibilities that necromancy, divinations, astrology and other practices related to the occult have for the development of a plot]; they show his attempts to reconcile this theatrical resource with orthodoxy.[158]

In *Quien mal anda en mal acaba* (before 1620),[159] the Morisco Román Ramírez, disguised as a physician,[160] tries to find out the causes of his beloved Aldonza's illness by reading the body signs:

> Si de las manos confiero
> las líneas, con las señales
> del rostro, de vuestros males,
> señora, entender espero
> la verdadera ocasión.[161]

---

[158] Espantoso-Foley (1967, 319): "Es importante notar que cuando Alarcón se refiere a alguna práctica del ocultismo, invariablemente presenta una explicación sacada de los teólogos sobre dicho asunto; en esta forma deja aclarado que a pesar de utilizar la teoría de las ciencias ocultas él era ortodoxo; esto era no sólo explicable sino necesario en aquella época de disciplina inquisitorial [. . .] las explicaciones de Alarcón reflejan claramente las doctrinas de S. Agustín, de Sto. Tomás y de los escritos de los 'teólogos del ocultismo' del siglo XVI, Francisco de Vitoria, Martín de Castañega, Pedro Ciruelo, Francisco de Osuna, y del siglo XV, Lope de Barrientos. Alarcón incorpora estas doctrinas en forma sutil y artística, sin recalcarlas. De esta manera, evita que lo didáctico sobrepase a lo artístico". [It is important to realise that when Alarcón refers to some practice of occultism, he invariably presents an explanation on said subject borrowed from theologians; in this way he clarifies that, in spite of using the theory of occult sciences, he was orthodox; this was not only explicable but necessary in an age of inquisitorial discipline . . . Alarcón's explanations clearly reflect the doctrines of St. Augustine, of St. Thomas and of the writings of the "theologians of the occult" of the 16th century, Francisco de Vitoria, Martín de Castañega, Pedro Ciruelo, Francisco de Osuna, and of the 15th century, Lope de Barrientos. Alarcón incorporates these doctrines in a subtle and artistic way, without highlighting them. In this way, he prevents the didactic from overtaking the artistic].
[159] On the question of dating, see Martínez Blasco's introduction to his edition of *Quien mal anda en mal acaba* by Martínez Blasco (1993, 1).
[160] On the character of the fake physician see González García (2005) and on the pact with the devil Fernández Rodríguez (2007) and Bermann (2016, 35–38).
[161] *Quien mal anda en mal acaba*, ed. Martínez Blasco (1993, 104, vv. 788–792). See Bermann (2016, 26) on this point.

[If from your hands I confer
the lines, with the signs
of the face, of your ills,
milady, their true cause
I hope to understand.]

The servant Tristan cautiously points out the illegality of this method for both Orthodoxy and for its Catholic beliefs:

Señor doctor, no quisiera
que esta cura adoleciera
de la Santa Inquisición. [. . .]
No me vayas
a la mano, porque he oído
decir, que está prohibido
adivinar por las rayas.
Y yo soy, aunque me ves,
en lo demás tan humano,
un Católico Cristiano,
testarudo aragonés.[162]

[Master physician, I would not want
this cure to suffer
from the Holy Inquisition. . . .
Don't go
for my hand, for I have heard
it say that it is forbidden
to read the lines.
And I am, for all that,
otherwise so very human,
a Christian Catholic,
a headstrong Aragonese.]

As a matter of fact, Ramón, at the end of the play, is condemned by the Inquisition, so that, as Bermann notes, "el autor señala la nulidad y el carácter efímero tanto de los deseos mundanos como de todo lo creado por magia" (2016, 38) [the author points out the nullity and ephemeral nature of both worldly desires and everything created by magic]. It has been known since González Palencia (1929–1930)[163] that the plot of the comedy was inspired by the trial

---

162 *Quien mal anda en mal acaba*, ed. Martínez Blasco (1993, 104, vv. 793–803). Also see Espantoso-Foley (1967, 323) on this point.
163 Without relating it to the comedy, González Palencia renders information about the physiognomic knowledge of the Moriscos: "Y que en la fisonomía de él conoce este confesante si es flemático, colérico, melancólico o sanguino. Y que en lo que este conoçe ser uno colérico es

against the Morisco magician of the same name which took place in Toledo in 1600[164] and was included by Martín del Río in the expanded edition of his *Disquisiciones*, published in Mainz (1603, 183–185).[165]

5.1 *La cueva de Salamanca* (1617–1620)

One of the central characters of Alarcon's *La cueva de Salamanca* (1617–1620)[166] is the elderly scholar Enrico, who was identified by Fernández-Guerra[167] as the

---

cuando tiene el labio bajo morteçino de color; y si es flemático tiene todo el dicho labio muy colorado y el rostro encendido; y el sanguino, en que tiene las venas del rostro muy açules y gruesas, y es melancólico, en que tiene el rostro de color çetino algo oscuro, y el párpado de abajo de los ojos un poco grueso" (1929–1930, reissued 1942, 251) [And so it is that by his physiognomy this confessor knows if he is phlegmatic, choleric, melancholic or sanguine. For it is known that somebody is choleric when he has a flabby lower lip; and if he is phlegmatic, said lip is fully red and he has a burning countenance; and the sanguine is known by the very blue and thick veins of his face, and the melancholic by his greenish and somewhat dark skin, and rather heavy eyelids under the eyes].

164 See Caro Baroja (1992, I, 339–353), the introduction to the edition of *Quien mal anda en mal acaba* by Martínez Blasco (1993, 35–53) and Díaz Migoyo (2004).

165 It is also included as a facsimile by Martínez Blasco in the introduction to his edition of *Quien mal anda en mal acaba* (1993, 25).

166 On the dating of the play see Campbell (1989, 11) and on this comedy in general González (1993), Prian Salazar (1993), Whicker (1997), Josa (2001), García-Valdés (2008) and Vargas de Luna (2009).

167 Cf. Fernandez-Guerra y Orbe (1871, 177): "Hace Girón nuestro D. Juan al marqués (pues nunca se detuvo en pesquisas geográficas ni históricas), y le finge discípulo de Merlín en Italia, y compañero allí de un cierto Enrico, francés, que en Salamanca enseña las artes mágicas; figura principal en el drama. Al retocarle se le vino a la memoria el célebre matemático y fisiónomo Enrico Martin, diestro, como el de la comedia, en sacar por las señales del rostro las ocultas inclinaciones del alma." [Girón turns our Don Juan into the marquis (since he never entertained himself with geographical or historical researches), and pretends he is a disciple of Merlin in Italy, and a companion there of a certain Enrico, a Frenchman, who teaches the magic arts in Salamanca; he is the main character in the drama. When he revised the text, the famous mathematician and physiognomist Enrico Martin came to his mind, skilled, like the one in comedy, in extracting the hidden inclinations of the soul from the signs of the face"], and also the *Introduction* of the edition of the *Obras completas of Juan Ruiz de Alarcón* de Millares Carlo (1957, 385–386): "La figura central de la comedia es la del mago Enrico, francés de nación, que llegado poco menos que misteriosamente a la ciudad del Tormes, no tarda en convertirse en ídolo de la clase estudiantil. Fernández Guerra supuso que al retocar Alarcón su obra, se le vino a la memoria el célebre matemático y fisiónomo Enrico Martínez, 'diestro como el de la comedia, en sacar por las señales del rostro las ocultas inclinaciones del alma'. Nuestro autor debió de tener ocasión de conocer a Martínez, que residía en la capital de México, donde se le tenía

German mathematician Enrico Martínez.[168] In I, viii this character relates his life to Don Diego and Don Juan, whom he has given shelter in his tiny house. He presents himself as a native of France and, following university studies in Paris,[169] a disciple of the magician Merlin, "un eminente / en las ciencias varón"[170] [an eminent

---

generalmente por francés, aunque era, en realidad, (386) alemán, desde 1589 -antes de su primer viaje a España- y de tratarle más tarde, pues de las prensas del célebre autor del desagüe, que tanto impresionó la mente de Alarcón, salió en 1609 la tesis doctoral de su hermano Don Pedro." [The central character of the comedy is the magician Enrico, a Frenchman, who arrived mysteriously in the city of the river Tormes and soon became an idol of the student population. Fernández Guerra supposed that when Alarcón revised the play, the famous mathematician and physiognomist Enrico Martínez came to his mind, "as skilful as the one in comedy, in removing the hidden inclinations of the soul through the signs of the face". Our author must have had the opportunity to meet Martínez, who had lived in the capital of Mexico, where he was generally considered to be French, although he actually was German (386) since 1589 – before his first trip to Spain – and later must have had the opportunity to socialise with him, since from the printing press of the famous author of the drainage, which so impressed Alarcón's mind, came out his brother Don Pedro's doctoral thesis in 1609]. This identification is generally accepted by researchers such as Concha (1981, 769) or Campbell (1989).

168 See Maza (1943) on the life and works of this scholar, who – as he tells us in his *Reportorio de los tiempos* – was the author of a treatise on physiognomy, the publication of which he announces in said book: "El segundo es un Tratado de Fisionomía de rostros en que se declara la causa natural de las varias inclinaciones humanas, enseñase como se podrá por medio de la fisionomía y de los actos que cualquier niño hace a ciertos tiempos de su edad rastrear algo de su complexión y natural inclinación para conforme a ello elegirle ejercicio en que se ocupe." (1606, 277) [The second is a Treatise on the Physiognomy of Faces, in which the natural cause of the various human predispositions is declared, and it is demonstrated how it will be possible, by means of physiognomy and the actions that any child performs at certain stages, to ascertain aspects of his complexion and natural inclination, in order to choose the occupations which he is to exercise]. There is no record of a printed edition of the book, which Martínez should have finished by the time he was writing the *Reportorio*, since he says: "No puse este referido Tratado de Fisionomía en este presente libro porque ocupa más lugar del que aquí se le pudiere dar, y ser grande el coste de la impresión en estas partes y muy poca la salida que los libros tienen." (1606, 277) [I did not include this *Tratado de Fisionomía* in this book because it takes up more space than it could be allowed here, and the cost of printing these passages is high, and the profit from the books is very low].
169 Ruiz de Alarcón, *La cueva de Salamanca*, ed. García-Valdés (2013), 114, vv. 363-364: "En la niñez, las artes liberales / me dieron en París honrosa fama" [In childhood, the liberal arts / gave me honourable fame in Paris].
170 Ruiz de Alarcón, *La cueva de Salamanca*, ed. García-Valdés (2013), 114, vv. 379-380). Also see Enrico's eagerness to know: "llevé conmigo mis inclinaciones, / que en cualquiera región, cualquiera estado / aprender siempre más fue mi cuidado" (114, vv. 376-378) [I carried with me my inclinations, / for in any region, any state / to learn more was always my concern].

man / in the sciences] in Italy. Thanks to this master, he has received an excellent formation in the occult sciences:

> Aprendí la sutil quiromancía,
> profeta por las líneas de las manos;
> la incierta judiciaria astrología,
> émula de secretos soberanos;
> y con gusto mayor, nigromancía,
> la que en virtud de caracteres vanos
> a la naturaleza el poder quita,
> y engaña, al menos, cuando no la imita.[171]

> [I learned the subtle art of palmistry,
> a prophet by the lines of the hands;
> the uncertain judicial astrology,
> imitator of sovereign secrets;
> and with greater taste, necromancy,
> which by virtue of vain characters
> robs nature of its power,
> and cheats, at least, when it doesn't imitate it.]

In I, iii the Marquis of Villena[172] enters the stage. He expresses to Don Juan and Don Diego his desire to study in the famous cave of Salamanca, which seems to be located in Enrico's house. The character of the Marquis is marked, like Enrico, by his interest in the occult sciences, acquired, once again, thanks to the magician Merlin:

> Enseñóme los efetos
> y cursos de las estrellas,
> que el entendimiento humano
> hasta los cielos penetra;
> las quirománticas líneas,
> con que en la mano a cualquiera
> de su vida los sucesos
> escribe naturaleza.
> Supe la fisonomía,
> muda, que habla por señas,
> pues por las del rostro dice
> la inclinación más secreta;
> sutiles eutropelías
> con que las manos se adiestran,

---

[171] Ruiz de Alarcón, *La cueva de Salamanca*, ed. García-Valdés (2013, 115, vv. 387–394).
[172] On the character of the Marquis in *La cueva de Salamanca* see Vetterling (1980, 238) and Marcos Celestino (2004).

y a la vista más aguda
engaña su ligereza.
De números y medidas
las demonstraciones ciertas
por matemática supe
y supe por arismética.
Estudié en cosmografía
el sitio, la diferencia,
longitud y latitud
de los mares y las tierras.
Y por remate de todo
la arte mágica me enseña,
de cuyo efeto las causas
no alcanza la humana ciencia,
pues con caracteres, vemos,
y con palabras ligeras,
obra prodigios que admira
la misma naturaleza.[173]

[He showed me the effects
and courses of the stars,
for human understanding
even the heavens penetrates;
the lines of the palm,
for in the hand of anyone
his life's events
are written by nature.
I knew the mute physiognomy,
which speaks in signs,
by those of the face it tells
the most secret inclinations;
subtle eutrapelias
with which the hands are trained,
and deceive the sharpest glance
by their lightness.
Of numbers and measures
the true proofs
by mathematics I learnt
and by arithmetic.
I studied cosmography
the place, the difference,

---

173 Ruiz de Alarcón, *La cueva de Salamanca*, ed. García-Valdés (2013, 129–130, vv. 697–728). Millares Carlo edits more aptly: 'with vain characters' (1957, 410, v. 725). Espantoso-Foley (1972, 87) and Lanuza-Navarro (2014, 208–209) take up this scene without elaborating on the reference to physiognomy.

> the longitude and the latitude
> of the seas and of the lands.
> And to top it all off
> the magic art it teaches me,
> the causes of whose effects
> are not attained by human science,
> for with symbols
> and with light words,
> it works wonders to the admiration
> of nature itself.]

In this comedy we encounter two magicians who go back to historical models, one contemporary, the other medieval: Enrico Martinez and Enrique de Villena. Both claim to have studied magic with Merlin, a literary character. As for their knowledge, Campbell observes:

> Además, quizá lo más importante, los conocimientos de los magos (u hombres de ciencia) no van en una sola dirección. Es decir, estudian ciencias naturales (fisionomía, matemáticas, cosmología, pero también saben artes mágicas, demoníacas (quiromancia, nigromancia, astrología judiciaria). No hay límites para el conocimiento y ello provoca una confusión entre lo aceptable y lo pecaminoso. (1989, 13)

> [Furthermore, and perhaps most importantly, the knowledge of the magicians (or men of science) does not move in only one single direction. That is to say, they study natural sciences (physiognomy, mathematics, cosmology), but they also know magical, demonic arts (chiromancy, necromancy, judicial astrology). There are no limits to knowledge; and this causes a confusion between the acceptable and the sinful.]

The play ends with an academic-style debate on the legitimacy of magic; both of them, dressed in Estudio's academic gown, take a stand. Enrico, with a blue tasselled cape from his philosophical studies, defends this "science" against a Dominican friar who, with his white tasselled surplice, is the representative of Theology. According to Darst, it is "la más sucinta y bien organizada descripción del asunto en la literatura dramática del Siglo de oro" [the most succinct and well organised description of the subject in the dramatic literature of the Golden Age], characterised by the researcher as 'a summary compendium of Renaissance thought on *magia naturalis*' (1970, 31).[174] Enrico's discourse, in syllogistic form, makes use of the minor proposition *Magic is natural* and the major proposition *All natural science is lawful*.[175] In his reply, the theologian distinguishes three

---

[174] Also see Campbell (1989, 12).
[175] Ruiz de Alarcón, *La cueva de Salamanca*, ed. García-Valdés (2013, 211–212, vv. 2416–2424); also see García-Valdés' commentary on these verses.

types of magic – natural, artful and diabolic – and concedes that the first two – unlike the third – are lawful. He then disproves all the arguments put forward by Enrico, who, in the end, declares himself convinced. The investigator rules that magic is a reprehensible practice. Therewith, all the knowledge previously described in detail, amongst them physiognomy and palmistry, are condemned.

6 Agustín Moreto and Lope's model of hand reading

In the second half of the 17th century, the device of reading the hand on stage, which had been in use in the new comedy since Lope, is still met with. In his comedy *De fuera vendrá*,[176] a recast of the cloak and sword comedy in the manner of Lope, *¿De cuándo acá nos vino?*,[177] Agustín Moreto (1618–1669) proves to be an attentive reader of the chiromantic scenes of the Phoenix. In his play, Lisardo and the ensign Aguirre, veterans of the war in Flanders, back in Spain, seduce the young Francisca and her maid Margarita, who live in the house of Cecilia, the lady's aunt, a widow who is jealous of her niece's youth.[178] On the second day, the matron surprises the two men in the lady's room, a predicament from which the young man and his companion seek to escape by pretending to read in her hands:

> ALFÉREZ. ¡Hola, la tía! Al remedio:
> esta raya os significa
> inclinada por estremo
> a beber; y en el beber
> habéis de tener un riesgo.
>
> MARGARITA. Bien decís, y éste es el trago
> que me amenaza
>
> LISARDO. Convento
> significa aquesta raya.
> Que habéis de ser monja es cierto.

---

176 On the complicated question of the dating of this comedy, see the prologue of the edition by Gavela García (2010, 5). It places the composition of the text between two historical events referred to, 1653 and 1654, and a performance in 1600.
177 For Lope's recasting see Moreto Exum (1981).
178 Exum (1983, 4) describes Cecilia as a caricatured character and as 'parody of the role of the lady of comedy', while Gavela García (2007) characterises her as a *figurona*, i.e. a 'figurehead', a 'hefty woman'.

DOÑA FRANCISCA. Vos me dais muy buenas nuevas
porque eso es lo que deseo;
que yo estoy tan bien hallada
con este recogimiento
en que me tiene mi tía,
que ésa es la elección que tengo.[179]

[ENSIGN: Attention, the aunt! To the remedy:
this line means
strongly inclined
to drink; and in the drink
there will lie some danger.

MARGARITA: You are saying well, and this is the liquor
which threatens me.

LISARDO: Convent
this line means.
That you will be a nun is certain.

DONA FRANCISCA: You give me very good news
because that is what I desire;
for I am so well placed
in this seclusion
in which my aunt has me,
that that is the choice I have.]

The comedy of the scene lies in the fact that the two women relate in a buffoonish way what the gallants read in their hands to the unpleasant situation at the aunt's house. The ensign who plays the part of the clown ridicules the curiosity of the widow, who takes seriously what she is hearing without realizing the irony:

VIUDA. ¿Qué es eso?

ALFÉREZ. Curiosidades
que allá en Flandes aprendemos.

VIUDA. ¿En Flandes saben de manos?

ALFÉREZ. Pues, ¿ahora dudáis de eso?
Sin saber quiromancia,
no puede uno ser sargento.

VIUDA. ¿Y ha de ser monja Frazquita?

---

179 Moreto, *De fuera vendrá*, ed. Gavela García (2010, 78, vv. 1375–1383).

LISARDO. Tres señales tiene de ello.[180]

[WIDOW: What's that?

ENSIGN: Curiosities
that we in Flanders learn.

WIDOW: Do they know about hands in Flanders?

ENSIGN: Now, you do not doubt it?
Without knowing palmistry,
you can't be a sergeant.

WIDOW: And she has to be a nun, Frazquita?

LISARDO: She has three signs for it.]

In his reworking of Lope's comedy, Moreto uses other dramatic resources of the Phoenix, such as this episode of reading the hand on stage to entertain his audience.

Likewise, in Moreto's play we find isolated references to physiognomy that are indicative of a certain scientific curiosity on the part of the playwright. The tangled love affair in the palatine comedy *Lo que puede la aprehensión* (1648–1653)[181] stems from the fact that a Duke fell in love with Fenisa just by hearing her sing. At the beginning of the second act, while they are waiting for the lady to arrive, the Duke and his servant Camilo wonder what she will be like physically. A dialogue between mockery and truth takes place about the nature of love and the reasons for infatuation. The point of view of the jester is based on the theories of sympathy and of the humours:

CAMILO. Bien pudiera ser hermosa,
y no darte gusto a ti,
que para el gusto, señor,
nunca es la dama más bella
la que lo es, sino aquella
que le parece mejor;
y esto va en la simpatía

---

180 Moreto, *De fuera vendrá*, ed. Gavela García (2010, 78–79, vv. 1389–1397).
181 On the dating of the play see Domínguez Matito in the introduction to his edition of the comedy (2010, 401).

que [a] los humores conviene:
la que más de mi humor tiene
es la mejor para mía.¹⁸²

[CAMILO: She might well be beautiful,
and not please you,
for, milord, for the taste
never the fairest lady is
the one, but the one
that you deem best for you;
and this lies in the affection
that to the humours is convenient:
the one that has most of my humours
is the best for me.]

As Domínguez Matito aptly comments with reference to Huarte de San Juan, "los humores deben estar en equilibrio, para que se produzca una armoniosa y eficaz relación entre los sexos ha de darse una correspondencia entre los humores de los hombres y las mujeres" (2010, 478, footnote to verse 1088)¹⁸³ [the humours must be in balance, so that a harmonious and effective relationship between the sexes is produced there must be a correspondence between the humours of men and women]: Camilo solely talks about the ideas of the *Examen de los ingenios* in order to make fun of them by instantly introducing the topic of food:

No hay perfección que aproveche,
que hay muchos hombres, señor,
a quien les sabe mejor
abadejo que escabeche:
esto es cosa averiguada.
Yendo un día solo a vellas,
yo, entre muchas damas bellas,
escogí una corcovada,
y buscando las razones,
vi que era mi inclinación,
porque parecía melón,
y me muero por melones.¹⁸⁴

[There is no perfection which satisfies,
for there are many men, milord,

---

182 Moreto, *Lo que puede la aprehensión*, ed. Domínguez Matito (2010, 478, vv. 1081–1090). The editor explains the term *sympathy* by quoting the definition from the *Diccionario de Autoridades*.
183 Also see Huarte de San Juan, *Examen de los ingenios*, ed. Serés (1989, 601–627) on this point.
184 Moreto, *Lo que puede la aprehensión*, ed. Domínguez Matito (2010, 478–479, vv. 1091–1102).

who prefer the taste of pollack
to that of pickle:
this is a proven fact.
Going off alone one day to see them,
I, among many beautiful ladies,
chose a hump,
and looking for the reasons,
I saw it was my inclination,
because it looked like a melon,
and I'm dying for melons.]

The servant then refutes the duke's theory of the possibility of falling in love by hearsay:

CAMILO. Ésas son falsas razones,
porque lo que es simpatía,
se ve en la fisonomía,
y no en las otras acciones.
¿Cada día por la calle
no se ven damas tapadas
tan airosas, y aliñadas
que arrebatan con el talle?[185]

[CAMILO: Those are false reasons,
because true affection
is seen in physiognomy,
not in other matters.
Does one not see in the street
every day veiled ladies
so gracefully attired
that they seize you with their size?]

Like other playwrights such as Ruiz de Alarcón, Moreto transforms the stage into a space of thought – a *Denkraum* in Walter Benjamin's sense – that allows for the discussion of scientific theories and philosophical ideas.

---

[185] Moreto, *Lo que puede la aprehensión*, ed. Domínguez Matito (2010, 479–480, vv. 1111–1116).

Chapter 4
Calderón and the condemnation of the divinatory arts on the stage

Calderón, in a series of dramas of different genres, condemns the divinatory arts from an orthodox stance and shows on the stage how the human being is able, thanks to his free will, to triumph over astral or corporal determinism. The position of the playwright towards astrology is well known,[1] although he approached the question from different stances, in accordance with each dramatic genre. In the early cloak-and-dagger comedy *El astrólogo fingido*[2] the heavenly science is openly mocked,[3] and the character who pretends to be an astrologer disqualifies himself by declaring himself a disciple of the physiognomist Giovanni Battista Della Porta.[4] Calderón's concern with this question is evident from his earliest plays onwards; thus, in *La devoción de la cruz*,[5] the cross-shaped birthmarks of the twins Julia and Eusebio are visible signs of their propensity towards violence. But thanks to their willpower they triumph over physiognomic determinism. The ending of the play equals a refutation of the epistemological basis of physiognomic thinking.[6]

---

[1] On astrology in Calderón see Lorenz (1961), Hurtado Torres (1983), Thiengo de Moraes (2003) and Vicente García (2014).
[2] The time of writing of Calderón's play, printed in 1632, is usually assumed to be between 1623 and 1625, as can be gathered from the introduction in the edition by Rodríguez-Gallego (2011, 11–12) and Vitse (2005, 345). It is therefore contemporary to the papal bull of Gregory XV and is situated at a historical moment of renewed interest in the struggle against the divinatory arts.
[3] See Gernert (2017a).
[4] "Llegué a Nápoles, adonde / por ventura conocí / a Porta, de quien la fama / contaba alabanzas mil", *El astrólogo fingido*, ed. Rodríguez-Gallego (2011, 254, vv. 1063–1166) [I arrived in Naples, where / by chance I met / Porta, of whom fame / told a thousand praises]. In Gernert (2017a), I argued against the interpretation of the reference to the Neapolitan scholar as an *effet de réel*, as proposed by Hurtado Torres (1983, 930) and Schizzano Mandel (1990, 163). On the play with the authorities on astrological and occult matters in Calderón and the French rewritings of his work see Gernert (2017a) and (in press). The hypothesis of Rodríguez Cuadros and Tordera Sáez (1983, 213) and (1985, 47), rejected by Schizzano Mandel (1990, 166), is not sustained.
[5] According to Sáez, the time of writing is definitively between 1622–1623' (2010, 217). Also see the edition of the play by Sáez (2014).
[6] See Gernert (2014a).

1 Body signs in Calderón's early work: *La devoción de la Cruz* (1622–1623)

"The more cruel the tragedies, the more exquisite they are", says Pierre de Laundun in his *L'art poétique français* of 1598.[7] Like the seigneur d'Aigaliers, other French poetological treatises such as Jean de la Taille's *L'art de la tragédie* (1572),[8] as early as the 16th century stressed that violence is an essential ingredient of tragedy, equating the art of Melpómene with the staging of cruelties. Almost at the same time we find comparable approaches in Spain, amongst theorists like Pinciano as well as amongst authors who reflect on their own literary practice.[9] May that definition of tragedy suffice which Carlos Boyl offers in his romance addressed at "a un Licenciado que deseaba hacer comedias" [a scholar who wishes to make comedies]:

> La tragedia es todo Marte,
> todo muertes, todo guerras,
> que por eso a las desgracias
> las suelen llamar tragedias.[10]

---

7 *L'art poétique français*, ed. Dedieu (1909, 160).

8 Jean de la Taille holds that tragedy "ne traicte que de piteuses ruines des grands Seigneurs, que des inconstances de Fortune, que bannissements, guerres, pestes, famines, captivitez, execrables cruautez des Tyrans, et bref, que larmes et miseres extremes." *De l'art de la tragédie*, ed. Forsyth (1968, 3–4) [does not deal with the petty misfortunes of the grand Lords, but with the waywardness of Fortune, with banishments, wars, plagues, famine, captures, with tyrants' execrable cruelties, in short, with tears and extreme misery].

9 See also Juan de la Cueva, who, in his *Exemplar poético* (ed. Reyes Cano 1986, 108, v. 1800) links tragedy with "sucessos espantables" [terrifying events]. With regard to the Spanish perspective, the following should also be consulted: Sánchez Escríbano & Porqueras (1972); the studies by Newels (1974, 107–124), Canavaggio (1988, 181–195), as well as the three volumes by Álvarez Sellers (1997, especially, for the Spanish Renaissance perspective, I, 1–192 and, for the Spanish Baroque perspective I, 211–340). I have not been able to consult the most recent publication by Fuente & Pérez-Magallón (2008).

10 The romance is included in *Norte de la poesía española* (1616, without pagination, vv. 7–20). Accessible online: http://opacplus.bsb-muenchen.de/search?oclcno= 165688290 (visited on 1.6.2011). Also see Lupercio Leonardo de Argensola who, at the beginning of his *Alejandra*, puts the following self portrait into the mouth of one of his characters, the personification of tragedy: "Estas tocas sangrientas y corona, / y la lucida espada de dos cortes / os descubre mi nombre, que es Tragedia", ed. Giuliani (2009, 7) [This bloody cape and crown / and the shining spade of two blades / make you discover my name, which is Tragedy].

> [Tragedy is all Mars,
> all dead, all wars,
> which is why misfortunes
> are wont to be called tragedies.]

Such is the spirit which dominates the scene from the beginning of the emergence of the tragic genre in the baroque period. Its evolution is well known, but it must be borne in mind if one is to understand the extremes this genre reaches at the height of its splendour in the 17th century. What is remarkable about violence in Calderón's works and, above all, in *La devoción de la Cruz* is the fact that Calderón does not confine such deaths and misfortunes to tragedy but finds them a place in works not easily classified on account of their happy ending[11] (happy in religious terms) like *La devoción de la Cruz*, which ends with these words uttered by Curcio:[12]

> Y con el fin
> de tan grande admiración,
> *La devoción de la Cruz*
> da felice fin su autor.[13]

> [And thus,
> With so wonderful a close,
> Happily the author endeth
> The devotion of theCross.]

---

[11] See Sáez (2012).

[12] The genre of the play is controversial. On account of its happy ending, Benabu (1988, 214) argues, rejecting Parker's (2000) classification: "Al salirse del marco de la obra, o, por decirlo en otras palabras, al quitarse la máscara, el actor que ha representado el papel de Curcio hace tomar conciencia al público que lo que han presenciado es una obra de teatro y que la fuerza del mal que han visto personificado en Curcio, no sólo que queda destrozada dentro de la obra sino que no es más que una ilusión, puesto que el mismo actor que la ha representado viene ahora a desengañarle al público calificando el final de *felice*. Esto asegura al público que lo que ha visto en escena es el triunfo del bien y la frustración del mal, y que el efecto propio de tal victoria es el deleite." [When leaving the frame of the play or, in other words, when dropping his mask, the actor who has played the part of Curcio makes the audience aware that what they have seen is a theatre play and that the forces of evil which they have seen personified in Curcio are not only destroyed within the play but that they are a figment of the imagination, given that the very actor who has played him is now able to break the illusion, telling the audience that the ending is *felice*. This assures the audience that what they have seen on stage is the victory of virtue and the defeat of evil, and that a victory of this kind results in delight]. See also Strosetzki (2001, 133).

[13] Calderón, *La devoción de la cruz*, ed. Sáez (2014, 345–346, vv. 2573–2576); English translation MacCarthy (1861, 316). Also see the edition by Delgado (2000) and the doctoral thesis by Hernández González (2002), who proposes a comparative study and edition of *La cruz en la sepultura* and *La devoción de la cruz*.

In spite of its comforting finish for its contemporary audience, this play lends itself particularly well as an object of study at a Congress dedicated to the analysis of violence in Calderón,[14] because, as Delgado observes, the acts of violence it contains "anuncian los múltiples y variados episodios que tendrán lugar en su producción posterior." (2009, 99)[15] [herald the multiple and variegated episodes which take place in its later production]. It goes without saying that said brutality cannot be an aim in itself, but must be understood within the framework of the system of beliefs of its author and his time. The aforementioned scholar proposes a reading of the play in the light of Seneca, particularly his *De la ira y De la clemencia*[16] as well as through his Christianization by St. Augustine, St. Bernard of Clairvaux and St. Thomas Aquinas.[17]

In the present study, I will propose a complementary reading of the play, a reading which, in my view, has not yet received the attention it deserves and which is apt to shed some light on the meaning of the use of violence in a work with a happy ending, which separates it from a distinctly tragic text, and its provenance. It is well known that Julia and Eusebio, the twins, the protagonists of *La devoción de la Cruz*, are both born with a red cross of blood on their chest,[18] and that, right after their birth, they are abandoned in the mountains. After being separated, they both develop a violent personality,[19] which induces them to become

---

14 As a matter of fact, Sáez (2014b) put forward a highly interesting view regarding the link between power and violence in *La devoción de la Cruz*.
15 The abundance of violent acts is underlined by Taulhade (1909, 83 and further). It was precisely the play's "violence exacerbée" [exacerbated violence] which interested Marcel Herrand, responsible for the Festival d'Angers in 1953, as recorded by Schmidt (1992, 196). This is also interesting because Herald himself requested a translation of Calderón from none other but Albert Camus; cf. for *La Dévotion à la Croix*, besides the aforementioned study by Schmidt (1992), Cots Vicente (2003, 138–139), and Esseni (2002, 85–96), a study including a CD with photos of the first production. The monograph by Bandera & Girard (1975) limits itself to the study of *La vida es sueño*. For the 'the masculine world of violence' in Calderón, see O'Connor (1988, 89–94).
16 For the range of cruelty in Seneca in medieval thinking see Baraz (1998).
17 "*La devoción de la cruz* contiene una dialéctica sostenida entre dicha violencia o, para ser más exactos, entre la crueldad que la define y la clemencia y la misericordia a las que aspira nuestro dramaturgo." Delgado (2009, 99) [*La devoción de la cruz* contains a dialectics upheld between this violence or, more precisely, the cruelty which defines it and the mercy and compassion which our author aims to convey].
18 Scholars have put forward various interpretations of the birthmarks. Burton observes that "because they bear the same birthmark they share a common identity, even as they retain their own individual personality" (1994, 18).
19 This is how Eusebio describes himself: "bello infante era en los brazos / del ama, cuando mi fiera / condición, bárbara en todo, / dio de sus rigores muestra, / pues con solas las encías, / no sin diabólica fuerza, / partí el pecho de quien tuve / el dulce alimento y ella / del

great sinners, although, in spite of their crimes, in the end they are saved thanks to their devotion to the cross which is inscribed in their bodies.[20] They are birthmarks which – besides being a popular motif spread by chivalrous novels[21] – are the subject matter of physiognomy, a pseudoscience which has an established position within the scientific system of the Renaissance, only to enter into a serious crisis in the wake of the Council of Trent. Its case is similar to that of other disciplines, such as astrology, which from the point of view of analogical thought propose an interpretation of diverse signs that imply a determinism of an astral or corporal nature.

Its presence in Calderonian comedy must, it seems to me, be seen as the staging of the conflict between predeterminism and free will,[22] a debate the

---

dolor desesperada, / y de la cólera ciega, / en un pozo me arrojó", Calderón, *La devoción de la cruz*, ed. Sáez (2014, 238–239, vv. 255–265) [Still a tender infant, lying / In my nurse's arms, my wicked / Nature, which was wholly savage, / Gave a sample of its wildness; / Since but with my gums, their weakness / By a demons power assisted, / I cut through the tender bosom / Out from which my sweet food trickled:– / She, made desperate by the anguish, / And by sudden anger blinden, / Down into a deep well threw me,] translation MacCarthy (1861, 316)].

Amezcua Gómez (1982, 126) points out the character's mischievousness. Julia becomes a bandoleer in the third act and turns into an excessively violent character who kills various people. Huerta Calvo (1999, 182) stresses the importance of the female character of the play, describing Julia as a "vigoroso espíritu femenino que se ve abocado fatalmente al ejercicio de la violencia y de la crueldad" [vigorous feminine spirit, who finds herself inevitably heading for the exercise of violence and cruelty]. For an interpretation of this scene, see Smieja (1973, 37–39); with regard to the role of the woman in Calderón and especially this play, one should consult Rey Hazas (2003).

20 Actually Honig (1961, 83) characterises the play as "a religious thriller, a lesson in heavenly clemency steeped in blood and spiced with incest."
21 On this point see the entry for "birthmarks" in Thompson (1932, H525), on the birth of princesses and the recognition on account of birth marks, see (1932, H51.1).
22 Examining Antoon Frans Wouthers' Dutch translation, *Devotie van Eusebius* (1665), Sullivan observes that, for Calderón, the "libre albedrío [. . .] gozaba de una *indiferencia activa* por la que la voluntad podía resistir a los influjos celestiales o diabólicos" (1980, 734) [free will enjoyed an *active indifference* through which the will could withstand the celestial or diabolical influences"]. Cardona Castro (1988, 125) insists on the importance of 'the Tridentine free will', comparing Calderón's play with Schiller's *Die Räuber*. Also see the inspiring interpretation by Teuber (2008, 411): "Vielmehr erweist sich Eusebios Erlösung, wenn man denn eine theologische Begrifflichkeit bemühen will, nicht als Frucht einer verdienten erworbenen Gnade (*gratia acquisita*), sondern als Geschenk einer umsonst verliehenen Gnade (*gratia gratis data*). Dann wäre *La devoción de la cruz* und dann wären vermutlich auch andere Räuberstücke der Epoche Orte zwischen dem Heiligen und dem Profanen, zwischen göttlicher Providenz und menschlicher Kontingenz, wo die göttliche Vorhersehung als rein zufällig und der reine Zufall doch auch als gnädige Fügung erscheinen können. Ein kontroverses Kernstück der tridentinischen Theologie wäre damit, wenn nicht zur Disposition gestellt, so doch zum Gegenstand

scientists of the time dealt with, as can be gathered from the paratexts of many physiognomic studies. Like astrology in *La vida es sueño*,²³ physiognomy in *La devoción de la Cruz* provides the scientific background which, at first sight, explains the violent behaviour of the protagonists. Nevertheless, the dramatic *dénouement* constitutes a highly orthodox rejection of the epistemological basis of physiological thinking in favour of salvation, a result of Eusebio's own actions, enabling him to overcome his inclination towards violence through his determination to embrace virtue.

---

der Problematisierung gemacht und zur Verhandlung freigegeben: die berühmte Lehre von der Rechtfertigung des Sünders aus den guten Werken." [Eusebio's salvation turns out to be, if one is to use theological terminology, not as the fruit of mercy deservedly acquired (*gratia acquisita*), but as a gift of mercy freely granted (*gratia gratis data*). If so, *La devoción de la cruz* and similar plays of the robbery genre from that period would be sites set between the Holy and the Profane, between divine providence and human contingency, in which divine providence might appear arbitrarily and yet be perceived as divine foreordination. A controversial key play of the Tridentine theology would then, if not discarded, at least be up for discussion: the famous doctrine of the justification of the sinner through good works]. At his time, Muñoz y Manzano (1881, 26–27) insisted on the "consorcio [. . .] establecido hábil y magistralmente entre la fatalidad y el libre albedrío" [partnership . . . skilfully and shrewdly established between fate and free will], arguing: "Existía por entonces una creencia muy arraigada, aunque no muy ortodoxa por cierto. No se había desterrado todavía del orden de ideas, *el influjo de los astros*, ni de la esfera social el oficio del *astrólogo*, y Calderón al admitir aquella creencia no hizo más que conformarse con el modo de ser de su tiempo, así como al presentar en sus comedias tipos que profesasen semejante teoría, no hizo más que copiar la época. En el drama que nos ocupa hay lucha y lucha encarnizada entre un hombre libre y su mala estrella. Sólo aquel genio [. . .] pudo combinar dos elementos tan incompatibles." [There was at the time a deeply rooted albeit not at all orthodox belief. The influence of the stars had not been discarded yet from the order of ideas, nor had the astrologer disappeared from society, and Calderón, admitting this belief, did nothing but acquiesce to the way of life of his time. By presenting in his comedies characters who professed such a theory, he simply replicated his period. In the play which concerns us here, there is a fight, a fierce fight, between a free man and his evil star. Only that his genius . . . achieved in making those incompatible elements compatible].

23 Calderonian criticism of astrology is well known, both in a comic key as in *El astrólogo fingido* and in a serious form in *La vida es sueño*, where the action refutes the veracity of Basilio's astrological predictions. For the function this science acquires in Calderón's theatre, see Lorenz (1961), Armas (1983), Hurtado Torres (1983), Schizzano Mandel (1990), Thiengo de Moraes (2003), Zambrana Ramírez (2009) and Vicente García (2014). Cf. also the bibliographical index by Hurtado Torres (1984).

1 Body signs in Calderón's early work: *La devoción de la Cruz* (1622–1623) — **149**

1.1 Birth marks and analogical thinking

In order to fully understand the meaning and the implications of the motif, one must bear in mind that physiognomy was a pseudoscience deeply rooted in the collective imagination of the time. It studies human beings' (and, at times, animals') outer appearance in order to draw conclusions about their character, disposition and destiny.[24] To this end, birth marks, just like other bodily characteristics, could be interpreted as *signaturas*, i.e. markers of the analogy between macrocosm and microcosm.[25] The Swiss physician and astrologer Theophrastus Phillippus Aureolus Bombastus von Hohenheim, better known as Paracelsus,[26] developed this idea in "De signatura rerum naturalium", one chapter in his nine-volume *De natura rerum*.[27] It was, however, his disciple Oswaldus Crollius who, in his *Tractatus de signaturis*,[28] spread his master's ideas. His influence is attested by his being quoted by Michel Foucault:

> Il faut que les similitudes enfouies soient signalées à la surface des choses; il est besoin d'une marque visible des analogies invisibles. Toute ressemblance n'est-elle pas, d'une même coup, ce qui est le plus manifeste et ce qui est le mieux caché? [. . .] Il n'y a pas de ressemblance sans signature. Le monde du similaire ne peut être qu'un monde marqué.[29]

---

24 For the history of this science and its ample bibliography cf. Gernert (2018b).
25 For more details, cf. Rico (1970). With regard to the theatre, Varey (1987, 10) observes: "Una de las creencias fundamentales que forman la base de muchas de las obras teatrales aquí estudiadas es la de la necesidad imprescindible de jerarquías, la manera en que el microcosmos – tanto la naturaleza como la sociedad humana – necesariamente refleja el macrocosmos." [One of the fundamental beliefs which form the basis of many theatre plays studied here is that of the indispensable need for hierarchies, the way in which the microcosm – nature as well as human society – necessarily reflects the macrocosm].
26 On the theory of signs see Maclean (2002, 324).
27 Liber X says with regard to signs in physiognomy: " Da ist aber von nöten, daß ir dieselbigen nach Phisionimischer Kunst wissen suerkennen, unnd der Kunst signata wol underricht seit, unn durch aufwendige zeychen den inneren Menschen erkennen" (Paracelsus 1584, 80r) [This, however, must be: that you recognise this same by physiological art, and that you be well instructed in the art of the *signata*, so you can by conspicuous signs recognise the inner man].
28 This treatise is accessible online thanks to the *gallica* server of the French National Library: http://gallica.bnf.fr/ark:/12148/bpt6k65570z.image.r=Crollius.f2.langEN (visited on 3.3.2011).
29 Foucault (1966, 41). This form of analogical thinking has been equally interpreted in terms of Christianity, as Henry relates: "An important element of symbolic magic, for example, involved the reading of the *signatures* of things. It was supposed that God, at the Creation, had left physical clues about the secret workings of things, and these were the signatures" (2008, 9).

[It is necessary for hidden similarities to be reflected in the surface of things; a visible mark for the invisible analogies is required. Is not all similarity, after all, both highly obvious and deeply hidden? . . . There is no similarity without *signatura*. The world of the similar can only be a marked world.]

The popularity of these ideas in the 16th century is reflected in the literature of the time and even in such a widespread genre as the chivalrous novels.[30] A good example is the anonymous *Lepolemo* (1521), especially because of the birthmark which appears in this book, parallel in function to those of Calderon's play. Its protagonist, who is also known as the *Caballero de la Cruz* (i.e. the Knight of the Cross), has a birthmark which carries a prophetic charge. Prior to his conversion to Christianity, a magician announces to him that he will fall in love with a Christian woman having a mole in the same place as he, the knight, himself.[31] The prediction of the Moorish fortune-teller comes true in a passage of chapter CXLIV, which gives an account of " de cómo el cavallero de la Cruz fue a hablar con la infanta Andriana por las rejas de las ventanas del jardín"[32] [how the Caballero de la Cruz comes to talk to the infant Andriana through the bars of the garden window]. Here, reference is made once again to the mole being a sign of the predetermined nature of the relationship which is to unite Lepolemo and the infant:

[. . .] y teniéndole la infanta de la mano, al rayo de la lumbre viole la señal que el Caballero de la Cruz tenía en el brazo que parecía a la suya y díjole: "Mi señor, este lunar vos me lo habéis hurtado", y sacó su brazo y mostrole el suyo que ninguna diferencia había del uno al otro y díjole: "Señor, paréceme que Dios nos señaló a los dos de una señal para ser los dos una persona mesma".[33]

---

30 For further details see Gernert (2013a).

31 "Y más has de saber que, aunque hasta agora tu corazón no está seguro de servir ninguna dama, que verná tiempo que te dará gran pasión de amores una de las más hermosas doncellas de los cristianos. El dónde será, no te lo quiero decir, sólo que cuando la verás la primera vez, sentirás gran alteración de tu corazón, y para que más claro conozcas la que ha de ser señora de tu libertad, tiene un lunar leonado a la entrada del brazo derecho, en el mesmo lugar que tú tienes otro. Este te dará mucha pena, pero al fin alcanzarás virtuosamente el fin deseado." *Libro del invencible caballero Lepolemo* I, xliv (1550?, XLIIv) [And further you will have to know that, although your heart has not been sure to serve any dame, that the time will come when one of Christianity's fairest maidens will give you passionate love. Where this will be I will not reveal, only that when you see her for the first time, you will feel a great change to your heart, and so that you more clearly know who will be the lady of your liberty, she has a tawny mole up in her right arm, just where you have yours. This will give you much pain, but in the end you will virtuously reach the desired end]. I transcribe from the copy preserved in the Biblioteca Histórica de la Universidad de Valencia (BH R-1/157), accessible thanks to the server http://trobes.uv.es (visited on 3.3.2011).

32 *Lepolemo* I, cxliv (1550?, CIVv).

33 *Lepolemo* I, cxliv (1550?, CVv).

1 Body signs in Calderón's early work: *La devoción de la Cruz* (1622–1623) — 151

[. . . and the infant holding his hand, in a ray of light saw the birth mark which the Caballero de la Cruz had in the same place as she herself and spoke thus: "My Lord, this mole you have stolen from me" and saying this, brought forward her arm and showed him her mole, and it not showing any difference to hers, said to him, "Sir, it appears to me that God has marked us with one single sign to tell us that we are one and the same."]

It is highly significant that Andriana should interpret these moles as signs of divine origen or – in other words – as individualising marks. In the light of this episode, which looks like an inversion of the configuration in *La devoción de la Cruz*, it seems fair to read Calderon's play from the point of view of the contemporary theory of the birthmarks which abundantly occur in the literature of the Golden Age. May it suffice to mention Don Quijote[34] and, as for the theatre, Lope de Rueda's *Comedia llamada Eufemia*.[35] I will not go further into the history of the motif, but rather expose the conceptual background which explains the different forms of textualisation of an idea proceeding from the contemporary scientific discourse of Calderón's time. The religious implications of this motif are concisely summed up by Delpech:

> On voit en effet fleurir, aux XVIe et XVIIe siècles, alors que la physiognomonie s'efforce de concilier astrologie, théorie humorale et libre-arbitre imposé par l'Église, toute une *littérature métoposcopique* où ces diverses tendances sont plus ou moins explicitement ou insensiblement réabsorbées, assimilées par le raisonnement analogique et alignées sur les schémas traditionnels de la pensée divinatoire. (1990, 30)

> [During the 16th and the 17th centuries, as physiognomy reconciles itself with astrology, the theory of the humours and the free will imposed by the church, an entire *metoposcopical literature* flourished, in which these various tendencies were more or less explicitly or imperceptibly reabsorbed, assimilated by analogical reasoning and aligned with the traditional schemas of thinking.]

These interpretations of this French scholar are also reflected in *La devoción de la Cruz*, as I will show with the help of a few examples.

---

34 Cervantes makes fun of the chivalrous motif of these physical signs in chapter 13 of *Don Quijote*.
35 As studied in chapter 1.4., in this comedy, one of the characters, Paulo, mentions "un pedaço de un cabello que le nasce del hombro izquierdo en un lunar grande". *Las cuatro comedias*, ed. Hermenegildo (2001, 108) [a bit of a hair which appears in a large mole on the left shoulder].

1.2 Calderón and the signatures: Julia's and Eusebio's birthmarks

During the first beats of the first act, speaking to his brother Lisardo, Eusebio does not only describe his birthmark but also ponders on its meaning.[36] This sign is, just like that in *Lepolemo*, a mark whose interpretation is the pith of the dramatic dénouement,[37] both for the characters themselves and for the audience. Little by little, it is revealed what the "causa secreta"[38] [secret cause] was which Eusebio mentions. During the second act, Curcio[39] gives his friend Otavio an account of the details of the labours of his wife Rosmira[40] but, as critics have pointed out, the birthmark only gains significance when Eusebio is

---

36 He says, "y la que yo tengo impresa / en los pechos, pues los cielos / me han señalado con ella / para públicos efetos / de alguna causa secreta. / Pero aunque no sé quién soy, / tal espíritu me alienta, / tal inclinación me anima / y tal animo me fuerza, / que por mí me da valor / para que a Julia merezca, / porque no es mas la heredada, / que la adquirida nobleza." Calderón, *La devoción de la cruz*, ed. Sáez (2014, 241–142, vv. 334–346) [And of which I bear the impress / On my breast; since Heaven math mark'd me / With that symbol's mystic image, / Thus to publish the effects / Of a cause that yet lies hidden. / Thus though ignorant who I am, / Such a spirit doth incite me, / Such an impulse animates me, / Such a glow of courage fires me, / That I feel I'm not unworthy / To love Julia, and to win her; / Since nobility is equal / Wether self-born or transmitted, translation MacCarthy 1861, 227].

37 See also Sloane (1977, 304): "But if society negates him and will not let him be *quien es*, if he is no one at all socially, he is aware that he has been mysteriously isolated by heaven in opposite fashion, made special, marked again and again protected by the Cross, permitted to live while others are allowed to die [. . .]. He senses that his life is part of a divine plan."

38 After having leapt over the walls of the monastery, Eusebio said to Julia, "no es amor quien vive en mí, / causa más oculta fue", Calderón, *La devoción de la cruz*, ed. Sáez (2014, 298, vv. 1544–1545) [Love no more impelleth me– / I some subtler law obey, translation MacCarthy 1861, 273].

39 Delgado (2009, 101) focuses on the character of Curcio, who, for him, is "el personaje que más se destaca por su violencia y crueldad" [the character who stands out most because of his violence]. Amongst the commentators of the play there are various who consider the father as the bearer of the tragic action, Parker (1949, 403–410) and (2000) being one of them. According to McKendrick (1989, 316–317), Curcio's tragic has its roots in his incapacity to perceive reality correctly. For an update of the studies of this paternal character, see Sáez (2010, 219–222).

40 "[. . .] que su parto / había sido aquella tarde / al mismo pie de la cruz, / y, por divinas señales / con que al mundo descubría / Dios un milagro tan grande, / la niña que había parido / dichosa con señas tales / tenia en el pecho una cruz / labrada de fuego y sangre", Calderón, *La devoción de la cruz*, ed. Sáez (2014, 289–290, vv. 1378–1387) [. . . the birth having / On that very evening happen'd / At the foot of that same Cross. / And for proofs divinely patent, / By whose means would God discover / To the world so great a marvel, / On the newborn baby's bosom, / Happy to be thus so mark'd there, / Was a Cross of blood and fire, translation MacCarthy 1861, 267].

about to violate his own sister. Thanks to this birthmark, he does not commit the crime, which would have been made worse by incest.[41] As for the meaning of the cross, Eusebio comes to be more explicit when interpreting it as a divine message:

> tantos temores me causa
> la cruz que he visto en tu pecho.
> Señal prodigiosa ha sido,
> y no permitan los cielos,
> que, aunque tanto los ofenda,
> pierda a la cruz el respeto;[42]

> [So much fear that Cross hath caused me
> Which thy breast reveal's and show'd me:
> Sign prodigious! sacred symbol!
> And the heavens allow me nowhere,
> Though I so offend, to fail in
> Reverence for a sign so holy.]

---

41 "Mujer, ¿qué intentas? / Déjame, que voy huyendo / de tus brazos, porque he visto / no sé qué deidad en ellos", Calderón, *La devoción de la cruz*, ed. Sáez (2014, 301, vv. 1597–1599) [Woman, leave me, / For I fly those arms that sold me, / Having seen but now within them / Some, I know not what, God's token, translation MacCarthy 1861, 275]. The incestuous love between the siblings has been interpreted repeatedly from a Freudian point of view, above all from *Totem and Taboo*, suggested, at his time, by Rank (1974, 550–554) and, more recently, by Amezcua Gómez (1982, 121–138) and by Sáez (2013). Hesse (1973) interprets the play from a psychological point of view, specifically from the point of view of the problem of alienation, while Kartchner (1999) carries out his investigation on the basis of Derridean ideas, finding a homoerotic undertone in the scene between Menga and Gil from the beginning of the play.

42 Calderón, *La devoción de la cruz*, ed. Sáez (2014, 301, vv. 1606–1610); English translation MacCarthy (1861, 275–276). See the interpretations by Friedman (1982, 136–137: "Given the opportunity to win Julia, Eusebio flees from the Cross on her chest, revering it, almost precognitively, as a sign of his imminent salvation. [. . .] In viewing the Cross as the means of his own redemption, Eusebio connects signifier with signified; he begins to think symbolically"), McKendrick (1989, 316–317: "Pero tan ciego está Eusebio hacia el estado de cosas que en seguida trata de persuadir a Julia por medio de chantaje a cometer un acto de sacrilegio. Como su padre, trata de someter la realidad a sus propias percepciones, con sus propios deseos. Pero la realidad no quiere someterse y la cruz en el pecho de Julia simboliza la insuperabilidad de la verdad." [But Eusebio is so blind to the state of affairs that he immediately tries to persuade Julia, blackmailing her, to commit a sacrilegious act. Like his father, he tries to adapt reality to his own ideas, to his own wishes. But reality does not want to submit itself, and the cross on Julia's chest symbolises the impossibility to overcome the truth]) and Burton (1994, 21: "Eusebio obeys a law of his own making when he recoils at the sight of Julia's birthmark. He takes the cross, the outward sign of an external deity, into himself.").

It should be borne in mind that Calderón, accepting the use of those signs as a form of communication of a divine nature, does not commit any contradiction or heterodoxy, in so far as these signs do not provide any information regarding the salvation or condemnation of his soul, not even regarding any mortal danger he may be incurring. They are elements which allow him to take a free decision with the help of some complementary information, to make up for his ever-deceptive senses. In this regard, one should remember the so-called "Juicios de Eusebio" [Judgements of Eusebio], though their attribution to Calderón is rather doubtful. Leaving the problem of authorship aside, we are witness to judicial astrology being called into question.[43] Eusebio's short dialogue with an astrologer questions the ability of this interpretative *techné* to provide its owner with any information on what destiny[44] has in stall for him. This is what gives rise to Eusebio coming on stage at the beginning of the third act, after a comical interlude,[45] and give vent to his feelings of despair in a short monologue:

> Sin gozar, al fin, dejé
> la gloria que no tenía,
> mas no fue la causa mía,
> causa mas secreta fue,
> pues teniendo mi albedrío
> superior efeto, ha hecho,
> que yo respete en tu pecho

---

43 See in the context of this episode McKendrick (1989, 320): " Tanto el astrólogo como el pintor han usurpado el papel de Dios, la última realidad. Eusebio en su papel de juez hace que conozcan de nuevo esta realidad. De la misma manera que Eusebio lleva por su cuerpo la señal de la cruz [. . .], él es también el que aquí distingue entre ilusión y la verdad." [Both the astrologer and the painter have usurped the role of God, the ultimate reality. Eusebio in his role as judge makes them see this reality again. In the same way as Eusebio has the sign of the cross on his chest . . . it is he who here distinguishes between illusion and reality].
44 "Si pudo tu ciencia ver / tanto, ¿por qué no previno / lo que en aqueste camino / te había de suceder?", *Apéndice* II, vv. 57–60, in Calderón de la Barca, *La devoción de la Cruz*, ed. Delgado (2000, 266) [If your art could see / as much, why did you not foresee / what in this path / was to happen to you?]. Immediately afterwards, the brigand disproves in a highly didactic manner the astrologer's forecast, addressing the astrologer, who sees himself destined to die by the hands of Eusebio, with these words: "Vete libre, porque así / conozcas de tu ignorancia / el error; que desde el suelo / no se ha de medir el cielo, / que es infinita distancia", *Apéndice* II, vv. 57–60, in Calderón de la Barca, *La devoción de la Cruz*, ed. Delgado (2000, 266) [Go, you are free, because thus / you will of your ignorance / know your mistake, for from the earth / you cannot measure the sky / which is infinite in distance."
45 I am referring to the repetition of the theme of the cross in a comic vein at the beginning of the last act, when the jester Gil comes on stage "*con muchas cruces, y una muy grande al pecho*", Calderón, *La devoción de la cruz*, ed. Sáez (2014, 311) [with numerous Crosses, and with a large one on his breast, translation MacCarthy 1861, 281] as the stage direction says.

la cruz que tengo en el mío.
Y pues con ella los dos,
¡ay, Julia!, habemos nacido,
secreto misterio ha sido
que lo entiende solo Dios.⁴⁶

[But the glory I repell'd,
Fled the untasted joy I sought,
Not through mine own strength me-thought,
No, some secret force compell'd
Since my will I could resign
To that mightier power protecting,
On the beauteous breast respecting
That same Cross that's stamp'd on mine.
Then, since Heaven was pleased to send
Thee and me thus sign'd to earth,
Some strange mystery marks our birth
Gold alone doth comprehend.]

The researchers have proposed a reading here which goes back to Aristotelian-Thomistic ideas.⁴⁷ Thus, Delgado refers to the 'Aristotelian and scholastic concept of cause and effect', by which he explains the attitude of Eusebio, who can only restrain his instincts in order not to assault his unknown sister thanks to divine providence. According to the editor, the "mensaje central de la obra [. . .] gira en torno al concepto de interacción y cooperación entre la gracia divina y el libre albedrío con vistas a la salvación final del ser humano"⁴⁸ [the play's central

---

46 Calderón, *La devoción de la cruz*, ed. Sáez (2014, 311, vv. 1804–1815); English translation MacCarthy (1861, 275–276). See Varey (1987, 283): "En el cuadro primero del Acto III estamos de vuelta en el monte. Haciendo uso de su libre albedrío, Eusebio se da cuenta de que las cruces que llevan Julia y él en el pecho son indicio de una suerte misteriosa" [In the first scene of the third act we are back in the mountains. Making use of his free will, Eusebio realises that the crosses which Julian and he have in the bodies are a sign of a mysterious fortune].
47 See, for example, Entwistle (1948, 474): "For Calderón, however, the situation was simpler than for a professed theologian. Thomist apophthegms represented for him simply the agreed truths of Catholic doctrine, the *asentados principios* so often cited in his autos; these truths provided him also, by a system of masterly inferences in or from the Summa, with his philosophy, psychology, cosmography, jurisprudence and other sciences."
48 See Calderón de la Barca: *La devoción de la Cruz*, ed. Delgado (2000, 217, footnote) and also O'Connor (1986, 365). "Aunque el drama depende particularmente del mito de la redención de la humanidad, encierra en sí, mayormente, el mito arquetípico de toda la tradición judeocristiana: la revelación de Dios como una presencia personal y amorosa que se manifiesta en el tiempo y en la historia." [Although the drama depends especially on the myth of the redemption of humanity, it encloses, chiefly, the archetypical myth of the Judaeo-Christian tradition: the revelation of God as a personal and loving presence manifesting itself in time and history].

message revolves around the concept of interaction and cooperation between divine grace and free will concerning the final salvation of the human being]. Friedman, in turn, underlines the underlying perception of the truth which Eusebio is capable of since he knows how to distinguish between reality and appearance.[49] Burton also argues along these lines, highlighting the human being's difficulty in perceiving the ultimate divine cause and his limited perspective.[50] In this sense, the final anagnorisis poses the problem of the correct interpretation of the signs, given that it is again the birthmark which Curcio discovers when he looks at the wound in Eusebio's chest:

¿Qué señal divina y bella
es esta, que al conocella,
toda el alma se turbó?[51]

---

49 Friedman (1982, 132): "The linguistic facet of the dichotomy is embodied in Curcio's refusal to abstract the significance of transcendent signs, as opposed to Eusebio's consciousness (through acknowledgement of a secret cause) of the supremacy of signs". ("The other side of the metaphor: an approach to *La devoción de la cruz*"). A different interpretation is put forward by Amezcua Gómez (1982, 121): "Y es que el protagonista une extrañamente lo diabólico –la transgresión impía de lo sagrado– con su marca de elegido por Dios *para públicos efectos / de alguna causa secreta*, con lo santo; Eusebio es presa de la fatalidad de la predestinación divina, tanto como de la ciega pasión del incesto que lo arrastra de un crimen a otro mayor." [The point is that the protagonist strangely unites the diabolicalness – the impious transgression of the sacred – with his hallmark of chosen by God *to make public / some secret cause*, with saintliness; Eusebio is the prisoner of the fatality of divine preordination as well as of the blind passion of the incest, which drives him from one criminal act to yet another, graver one].
50 "[. . .] if from the point of view of God causes have certain effects, from the point of view of man effects have certain causes. Since effects are not identical to their causes, proceeding from effect to cause offers man only an imperfect knowledge of God. Such is the case for Eusebio who, although he has a birthmark in the form of a cross and had witnessed its powerful effects, is ignorant of the source of its power." (Burton 1994, 15–16).
51 Calderón, *La devoción de la cruz*, ed. Sáez (2014, 335, vv. 2339–2341); English translation MacCarthy (1861, 306). As he recognises his son, Curcio says: "[. . .] ¡Ay, hijo mío, / pena y gloria en verte siento! / Tú eres, Eusebio, mi hijo, / si tantas señas advierto, / que, para llorarte muerto / ¡qué justamente me aflijo! / [. . .] / en el lugar que te he hallado. / Donde cometí el pecado / el cielo me castigó, / y aqueste lugar previene / información de mi error; / pero ¿cuál seña mayor / que aquesta cruz que conviene / con otra que Julia tiene? / Que no sin misterio el cielo / os señaló, porque al suelo / fuerais prodigio los dos." Calderón, *La devoción de la cruz*, ed. Sáez (2014, 336, vv. 2354–2374) [O my long-lost son! I feel / Pain and pride in seeing thee. / Thou, Eusebio, art my son,– / This a thousand proofs have said; / Ah / that I must mourn thee dead, / Ere thy life hath well begun. / What my soul by brooding on / Had divined, thy words make clear, / That thy mother left thee here, / In the place where I stand o'er thee; / Where I sinn'd to her who bore thee, Falls the wrath of Heaven severe. / Yes, delusion disappereth, / All the more this place I see; / But what greater proof can be / Than that thy breast also

[But what mark, divine and fair,
Is this sign my hand lays bare,
Which to see, my soul moves so?]

What stands out in our play, besides the frequent use of the word *prodigio*,[52] is the fact that the twins feel they belong to this category for having been "mysteriously" marked by the heavens.[53]

1.3 *La devoción de la Cruz*: a prodigious history?

Thus, the meaning of the play seems to be clearly determined by concepts which form part of the teratology[54] of the literature of the age, which interprets the birth of beings, for some reason deformed or exceptional, as monsters, in the literal sense of the word. As Vega Ramos concisely defines:

> Los sucesos que se producen *contra natura* se llaman *monstra, ostenta, portenta, prodigia*: San Agustín, en el *De civitate Dei*, precisa que se les nombra *monstra*, de *monstrare*, porque muestran alguna cosa, a la que significan; se llaman *ostenta*, de *ostendere, portenta*, de *portendere*, y *prodigia* porque dicen en la lejanía *(porro dicere)*, esto es, porque predicen las cosas futuras *(De Civ. Dei*, XXI.8). Los monstruos, prodigios y portentos son medios por los que Dios manifiesta su presencia y su poder. (1995, 225)

> [The incidents which happen *contra natura* are called *monstra, ostenta, portenta, prodigia*: St. Augustine, in *De civitate dei*, specifies that they are called *monstra*, which derives from *monstrare*, because they show something, something to which they give meaning; they are called *ostenta, portenta*, derived from *ostendere* and *portendere* respectively, and *prodigia* because they speak at a distance, *(porro dicere)*, i.e. they predict future events *(De Civ. Dei*, XXI.8). The monsters, the prodigies, the portents are means by which God shows his presence and his power.]

---

beareth / The same Cross that Julia weareth? Not without some mystery / Heaven has mark'd you out to be / The world's wonder thus, ye two, translation MacCarthy (1861, 307)].

52 According to the *Diccionario de Autoridades*, a prodigy is not only a "sucesso extraño que excede a los límites regulares de la naturaleza" [strange event which transgresses the ordinary limits of nature], but is also used to denote a miracle.

53 See, for example, Eusebio saying this speaking to Lisardo: "Oíd prodigios que admiran / y maravillas que elevan", Calderón, *La devoción de la cruz*, ed. Sáez (2014, 236–237, vv. 211–212) [Hear the wonders most astounding, / Hear the marvels most surprising, translation MacCarthy (1861, 224)] and "Si fue prodigioso el parto, / no lo fue menos la estrella" Calderón, *La devoción de la cruz*, ed. Sáez (2014, 238, vv. 251–252) [If my birth was so prodigious, / Nothing less so was my life's star, translation MacCarthy (1861, 225)].

54 For further details cf. Genert (2013b).

Later on, the aforementioned critic explains the function of the prodigies as an immediate divine message, without the mediation of its messengers, the clerics:

> Dios habla a través de la monstruosidad: o, en otros términos, el monstruo es *la manifestación singular de la voluntad de pre-significar de Dios*. El prodigio es el lenguaje escogido por la divinidad para comunicarse con los hombres, y ese lenguaje adopta la forma de emblemas vivos o representaciones analógicas que deben ser cuidadosamente interpretados. (Vega Ramos 1995, 235)
>
> [God speaks through monstrosity, or, in other words, the monster is *the singular manifestation of God's will to pre-signify*. The prodigy is the language chosen by divinity in order to communicate with man, and this language adopts the form of living emblems or analogical representations which must be carefully interpreted.]

In order to return to the question of possible sources of Calderon's play, it should be remembered that this form of thinking has its origin in the literary genre of the so-called prodigious histories, created in France by authors such as Pierre Boaistuau, Claude Tesserant or François de Belleforest. In 1603, a Spanish translation of one of these compilations was published in Madrid under the title of *Historias Prodigiosas y Maravillosas*, quoted above as one of the possible sources of the play by Valbuena Prat.[55] The distinguished editor also adduces a quotation from the Spanish translation about the meaning of the cross:

> La cruz es una señal que nos trae a la memoria la grande obligación que todos tenemos de estar siempre contemplando en Aquél que por salvarnos estuvo en ella pendiente. Y también es señal de tal vigor, que todas las veces que se nos aparece nos predice grandes significados que algunos son de contento, dicha y victoria; y otros de tribulación, fatiga y congoja.[56]

---

55 Cf. his edition of *La devoción de la cruz* (1931, 35–36) "En un libro traducido del francés, de Bovistau, que muy bien puede haber leído Calderón [. . .] hay un curioso capítulo *De la milagrosa impresión de la señal de la cruz que en un árbol se vió en Bretaña, en la diócesis de Renes*, en que además del suceso del encabezamiento se relatan otras apariciones y señales de cruces maravillosas." [In a book translated from French, by Bovistau, which Calderón may well have read . . . there is an intriguing chapter, *De la milagrosa impresión de la señal de la cruz que en un árbol se vió en Bretaña, en la diócesis de Renes*, in which, besides this event, an account is given of other apparitions and signs of marvellous crosses]. See also Neugaard (1973, 1): "Possible sources mentioned by Valbuena include the *Historias prodigiosas* [. . .] In this work there appears a chapter which deals with tales of miraculous appearances of the sign of the cross, generally on clothing or trees". Other scholars have not paid attention to Valbuena Prat's interpretation. Nevertheless, recently the important influence which such and other collections of prodigious histories exerted has received more attention. Given that prolific writers like Pierre Boaistuau enjoyed a large audience, it does not come as a surprise that don Pedro, as Andrés (2004) has demonstrated, is amongst them.

56 Boaistuau (1603, 256v–257r). Cf. the recent edition of the French text by Bamforth and Céard (2010).

[The cross is a sign which brings to mind the important obligation we all have to always contemplate in Him who, in order to save us, was hanged on it. And it is a sign of such might that, every time that we see it, it entails important messages, be they messages of joy, of luck, of victory, be they messages of suffering, of weariness, of anguish.]

Thus, from the point of view of Calderón's contemporaries, the cross did not carry an exclusively and automatically positive meaning,[57] but it could be a sign of future misfortunes, as is the case with Eusebio's and Julia's birthmarks. Besides the aforementioned chapter "Of the miraculous impression of the sign of the cross which was seen in a tree in Brittany, in the diocese of Renes", we must bear in mind the overall intention of the book, summarised by the translator, Pescioni, in the prologue, "Al cristiano lector" [To the Christian reader]. It is because of "nuestras corruptas y abominables vidas [. . .] que continuamente Dios nos muestra por medio de varias señales y prodigios [que] nos advierten y amonestan que nos emendemos [. . .]"[58] [our depraved and abominable lives . . . that God speaks to us, by means of various signs and prodigies, (which) warn us and admonish us to change our ways . . .]. Hence, we understand why Eusebio interprets as signs of divine wrath a series of phenomena in the sky which he perceives after having attempted to violate Julia:[59]

¿No ves la esfera del fuego
poblada de ardientes rayos?
¿No miras sangriento el cielo,

---

57 On this point see Martínez (2008, 307): "Eusebio deutet sein Leben als Exempel und das Kreuz als Zeichen und Instrument christlicher Heilsgeschichte. Mit dieser Hypostasierung des Kreuzes folgt Calderón [. . .] der nachtridentinischen Theologie, z.B. eines Fray Alonso de la Cruz in seinen *Discursos evangélicos y espirituales* (1599). Dieser Kreuzestheologie zufolge präsentiert das Kreuz realiter Christus, so dass der Gläubige in der Verehrung (*devoción*) des Kreuzes in unmittelbare Berührung mit dem Heiligen tritt und auf entsprechende Wundertaten hoffen darf." [Eusebio interprets his life as an example and the cross as a sign and instrument of the Christian doctrine of salvation. With the hypostasis of the cross, Calderón is in line with the theology following the Council of Trent, as expressed, for instance, by Fray Alonso de la Cruz in his *Discursos evangélicos y espirituales* (1599). According to this doctrine, the cross represents Christ in reality, so that the devotee, in the devotion of the cross (*devoción*) comes into direct contact with the saint and can thus hope for corresponding miracles].
58 Boaistuau (1603, without pagination).
59 Also see chapter VII of the third part, "De una maravillosa claridad y en medio della una lança de fuego que se vio en tierras de Perigort el año de 1577" (Boaistuau 1603, 265 onwards): The description of these signs of divine wrath also spread through the accounts of events. See, for example: *Declaración de las señales y monstruos espantables que han aparecido en el ayre encima de la Villa de La Rochela* (Valencia, 1621), published anew by Ettinghausen (1995, N° XVII).

> que todo sobre mí viene?
> ¿Dónde estar seguro puedo,
> si airado el cielo se muestra?⁶⁰
>
> [See you nowhere
> Red bolts peopling all the night wind?
> Do you not behold the gory
> Heavens that open to o'erwhelm me?
> Where can I be safe, if o'er me
> Heaven displays its awful anger?]

The translator of the aforementioned play by Boaistuau did not only translate the histories but added three tales of his own creation, all of them set in Spain. Of these, we are mainly interested in the second, "De un monstruo que el año de 1563 nació en Jaén"⁶¹ [Of a monster which was born in Jaén in 1563]. It tells the tale of a maid of a virtuous lady, who was violated by a priest and, when giving birth to the child who was the outcome of this rape, secretly brought into the world a creature with three faces "que estavan situados de la suerte como algunos pintores suelen figurar la santísima Trinidad"⁶² [arrayed in such a way as, in the works of certain painters, is the Holy Trinity]. This prodigy made the midwife spread the story so that the priest in the end received his just punishment. In this light, we can consider by way of analogy the birthmarks of Julia and Eusebio as a visible sign of Curcio's crime, or rather of Rosmira's innocence.⁶³

The period in which the play was written grants special attention and meaning to this kind of incident, in line with the interpretation offered above that they are heralds of divinity. News of the prodigious births of monsters⁶⁴ was spread by way of accounts of events and broadsheets, precursors of journalism which circulated all kinds of news stories and which have only recently become the object of the academic interest they deserve. It is worth remembering, in order to finalise this inventory of possible sources which Calderón might have had in mind when

---

60 Calderón, *La devoción de la cruz*, ed. Sáez (2014, 302–303, vv. 1625–1630); English translation MacCarthy (1861, 276).On this scene, see Delgado (1997, 57): "Given that the fire witnessed by Eusebio is merely an illusion, unseen by Ricardo and Celio, it is unlikely that it would be perceived by the audience, particularly since Calderón does not suggest any special effects to make such manifestation visible".
61 Boaistuau (1603, 398r–400r).
62 Boaistuau (1603, 399v).
63 This is how Andrist (1989, 37) reads this scene: "The cross birthmark on the infant's chest testifies to the innocence of her mother". She interprets the violence in Calderón following René Girard's anthropological approach and considers the twins' mother as *bouc émissaire*".
64 On monstrosity in *La vida es sueño* see Armas (1989).

writing this play, the cases of certain creatures born with the sign of the cross in order to contextualise what Mariscal (1981) rightly called the "icono central y motivo estructurante"[65] [central icon and structuring motif]. In 1628, Barcelona saw the publication of a *True account of a monstrous child, who in the city of Lisbon was born on the 14*th *of April of the year 1628.*[66] Both the illustration and the author of the account emphasise that "en el pecho traía la señal de la Santa Cruz de carne, y colorada, hecha del ordinario modo que pintan las demás cruces, una de las mayores monstruosidades que en este monstruo considero y hallo" [on his chest he showed the sign of the Holy Cross, in flesh, red, in such a form as crosses are commonly painted, one of the major monstrosities which in this monster I consider and find]. The divine message conveyed by this birthmark is none too obvious, and the account offers different readings of the intention of "la magestad de Dios, quizá para pronóstico de pena de tantos y tan graves pecados con que los hombres a su Hacedor tienen offendido e irritado o quizá para pronóstico de algunos bienes que ha de hacer a la Cristianidad" [the majesty of God, perhaps as a forecast of the pains for so many and such grievous sins with which the humans have offended and angered their divine Maker, or perhaps as a forecast of some good which he will do for Christianity]. At the end of the account, Portuguese astrologers are mentioned who make forecasts concerning the significance of this monstrous child. The author of this tale, with regard to the significance of the cross, observes: "digamos que este monstruo por tener la Santa Cruz en el pecho significa y pronostica exaltación y dilatación de la Santa Fe Católica. Plegue al Cielo sea assí" [We hold that this monster, for having the Holy Cross on his chest, means and foreshadows the exaltation and the divulgence of the Holy Catholic Creed. May the Heavens grant that it comes to pass].

For all this, the most famous sample of the deformed creature with a cross is no doubt the so-called Ravenna monster. It is a winged monster, born on the eighth of March 1512 in said city, son of a nun and a monk. Its story is spread all over Europe by way of broadsheets, a prodigy to which Boaistuau dedicates one of his histories. In Spain, there is no record of such broadsheets to spread the news of the amazing case of Ravenna, but, as is evidenced by its being mentioned in the *Guzmán de Alfarache*, the history was well known at the end of

---

[65] Mariscal (1981, 349). In this article, Mariscal underlines the "índole visual del teatro barroco" [visual character of baroque theatre] and its "énfasis sobre un refuerzo visual del texto" (1981, 341) [emphasis on the visual reinforcement of the text].
[66] *Relación verdadera de un monstruoso Niño, que en la Ciudad de Lisboa nació a 14, del mes de Abril, Año 1628 la qual en una carta ha embiado de Madrid Sebastián de Grajales Ginovés a un mercader d'esta ciudad, junto con la efigie verdadera del dicho monstruo la qual se sacó de una que embiaron a la Magestad del rey nuestro Señor*, facsimile in Ettinghausen (1995, N° XVII).

the 16th century, thanks to the Spanish translation of Boaistuau's histories.⁶⁷ It is not too fanciful to believe that for Calderón and *La devoción de la Cruz* Mateo Alemán's explanation of the "cruz bien formada" [well-formed cross] which the creature had in his belly was of special importance: "la cruz en el vientre [significaba], que si, reprimiendo las torpes carnalidades, abrazasen en su pecho la virtud, les daría Dios paz y ablandaría su ira"⁶⁸ [the cross in his belly (meant) that, if they suppress all inept carnal appetite and embrace virtue, God would grant them peace and relent in his wrath].

In accordance with the rigorous scholastic spirit which inspire and underlie Calderón's texts, this early and not easily classified play corresponds to the logic built on post-Tridentine principles that today, at first sight, do not have the rigour which they used to have. To reconstruct this episteme and its possible sources of inspiration is a task requiring a renewed *tolle lege* (*Confesiones* 8, 12, 28s), not only in printing but in the great Book of Creation, in which he sought signs with which to obey the mandate to celebrate the mystery of Salvation.

2 Predetermination and free will

2.1 *La vida es sueño* (1635)

In *La vida es sueño* (1635), the most emblematic example of anti-superstitious Calderonian criticism, he depicts the orthodox position of the post-Tridentine Church regarding astrology: As King Basilio had foreseen, his offspring Segismundo is prone to wrath and hardly knows how to control himself.⁶⁹ However, thanks to

---

67 See "Capítulo quadragesimoprimo. De un monstruo que nació en Ravena poco tiempo antes que fuesse saqueada", Boaistuau (1603, 156r) [Capítulo quadragesimoprimo. De un monstruo que nació en Ravena poco tiempo antes que fuesse saqueada].
68 Alemán, *Guzmán de Alfarache*, ed. Rico (1983, 122–124). On Boaistuau as a source of Alemán see Cros (1967, 135–147).
69 On the day of Segismundo's birth, a whole series of bad omens were produced: "Llegó de su parto el día / y, los presagios cumplidos, / [. . .], / / nació en horóscopo tal, / que el sol, en su sangre tinto, / entraba sañudamente / con la luna en desafío; / y siendo valla la tierra, / los dos faroles divinos / a luz entera luchaban, / ya que no a brazo partido. / El mayor, el más horrendo / eclipse que ha padecido / el sol, después que con sangre / lloró la muerte de Cristo, / éste fue; porque, anegado / el orbe entre incendios vivos, / presumió que padecía / el último parasismo", *La vida es sueño*, ed. Morón (1984, 98, vv. 676–695). [Now, come the day the child was born, / These omens proved to be correct, / . . . / Spheres inauspiciously aligned / Provoked the scarlet-blooded sun / To challenge the cold moon to duel / And turned the heavens rubicund. / With all the earth their battleground, / The two celestial lanterns gleamed / In

his free will, he manages to overcome his inclinations, finally becoming a worthy monarch.[70] According to LaRubia-Prado *"Life is a Dream* goes on to establish an ironic distance from Basilio's epistemological position, a position that will be progressively eroded as the play moves towards its conclusion" (2002, 380). The vicissitude is only possible because Basilio himself questions his own prediction. It is thanks to his doubting that he embarks on the path of learning. In the final analysis, as Brioso has clearly perceived, this is a scientific experiment:

> El experimento y el conocimiento conjetural de la lectura de los signos constituyen dos formas de conocimiento que representan dos tecnologías diferentes del saber y dos temporalidades diferentes: el saber astrológico de la antigüedad y el saber experimental naciente en la modernidad. El experimento además agrega una tercera variable a la lucha de saberes que se presencian en la obra: el antiguo saber de las estrellas, la cristiana noción de libre albedrío y la ciencia moderna con su peculiar noción de pronóstico y su distintiva concepción de la naturaleza. (Brioso 2004, 60)

> [The experiment and the conjectural knowledge of the reading of signs constitute two forms of knowledge that represent two different methods of acquiring knowledge and two

---

savage combat perched on high, / Both beaming bright as they could beam. / The longest and most horrible / Eclipse that ever dis transpire– / Besides the one that dimmed the globe / The day Our Lord was crucified– / Occurred next. As the planet sensed / itself engulfed in living flames, / It must have thought the throes of death / Were making its foundation shake. Translation Racz 2006, without pagination].

70 Regalado (1995, I, 487) poses the problem in terms of order and disorder: "Calderón opone al orden determinista de Basilio lo imprevisible y aleatorio, consecuencia de la naturaleza de las cosas, de la libertad del hombre y del ajetreo azaroso del mundo social. Ante el sistema estático de correspondencias y simpatías que ordenan el universo de Basilio, Segismundo introduce el desorden, el movimiento y la incertidumbre. Calderón esgrime frente a la racionalidad despótica de Basilio una retórica de probabilidades, asumiendo que la ignorancia de los eslabones que unen los acontecimientos se suplen con causas imaginarias y falsas dictadas por un apetito insaciable de certidumbre. Segismundo, víctima del determinismo impuesto por el experimentador, asume desde el escepticismo, la incertidumbre como criterio de su comportamiento." [Calderón opposes to Basilio's deterministic order the unpredictable and random, a consequence of the nature of things, of the freedom of man and the random hustle and bustle of the social world. In the face of the static system of correspondences and sympathies which order Basilio's universe, Segismundo introduces disorder, movement and uncertainty. Calderón wields against Basilio's despotic rationality a rhetoric of probabilities, assuming that the ignorance of the links that unite the events are supplanted by imaginary and false causes dictated by an insatiable appetite for certainty. Segismundo, a victim of the determinism imposed by the experimenter, accepts, from the point of view of scepticism, uncertainty as a criterion of his behaviour]. This problem has been studied by Dunn (1953), Armas (1983) and (2001), Chem Sham (1998), Andueza (2000), Aylward (2002), LaRubia-Prado (2002), Santibáñez (2002), Sears (2002), Brioso (2004), Brewer (2011) and Sosa-Velasco (2011). On alchemy in *La vida es sueño* see Armas (1992).

different time frames: the astrological knowledge of antiquity and the experimental knowledge emerging in modernity. The experiment also adds a third variable to the struggle for knowledge, which can also be found in the play: the ancient knowledge of the stars, the Christian notion of free will and modern science with its peculiar notion of prognosis and its distinctive conception of nature.]

From this perspective, the ambivalence of the character becomes evident. On the one hand, Basilio appears as an acknowledged sage,[71] thus boasting about his studies:

> Ya sabéis que son las ciencias
> que más curso y más estimo,
> matemáticas sutiles,
> por quien al tiempo le quito,
> por quien a la fama rompo
> la jurisdicción y oficio
> de enseñar más cada día;
> pues cuando en mis tablas miro
> presentes las novedades
> de los venideros siglos,
> le gano al tiempo las gracias
> de contar lo que yo he dicho.[72]

> [For well you know, the sciences
> Are what we've loved and cherished most,

---

[71] In his famous monologue he insists on this: "ya sabéis que yo en el mundo, / por mi ciencia he merecido / el sobrenombre de docto", *La vida es sueño*, ed. Morón (1984, 96, vv. 604–606) [For well you know, men have bestowed / On us the epithet of "wise", translation Racz (2006, without pagination)]. Cascardi proposes to identify Basilio with Galilei: "Basilio [. . .] is a scientist in the literal sense. He seeks and would be content with empirical knowledge. He wants to verify his astrological predictions and so arranges test circumstances for his son. If his costume seems medieval, his science is coincident with Renaissance concepts of scientific method. He might be Galileo, convinced of the reduction of nature to geometry and mathematics. He works from observation to theory to practice" (1984, 13). Mujica compares the wise king to scholars criticised from the viewpoint of scepticism: "Basilio, the astrologer-sage, represents the kind of thinking that Sanches criticises in *Quod nihil scitur* when he attacks dogmatic scientists who put language, reason and the senses at the service of a premise." (1990, 27) [Basilio, the astrologer-sage, represents the kind of thinking that Sanches criticises in *Quod nihil scitur* when he attacks dogmatic scientists who put language, reason and the senses at the service of a premise]. Vivalda (2008, 385) observes from the perspective of political theory that for the time 'a scientific king represented, to a large extent, an absurd king'. Armas (2006a) compares the character of the king astrologer in Lope and in Calderón.

[72] *La vida es sueño*, ed. Morón (1984, 96, vv. 612–623); English translation Racz (2006, without pagination).

Fine mathematic formulae
By which we've robbed Time of its role,
Foreseeings what the future holds,
The only source of its renown,
And oresaged mor events each day.
Fir when our charts reveal accounts
Of incidents set to occur
In centuries still unbegun,
The dupe is dull chronology
As we glimpse first what's yet to come.]

In addition to astrology, Basilio is committed to mathematics, which, at the time of Calderón, referred to another scientific realm than today:

> During Calderón's time, mathematics was part of the same "discipline" as astrology. Despite the fact that the astrological dimension of his "subtle mathematics" is not a legitimate science nowadays, there is no doubt that Basilio's methods, as well as his basic attitude of transcending contingency, are clearly scientific. (LaRubia-Prado 2002, 37)[73]

On the one hand, therefore, the king is characterised by his commitment to practices which could be considered scientific and by his optimism regarding the effectiveness and validity of these disciplines. On the other hand, it is the astrologer king himself who ends up realizing the weakness of his epistemological foundations and regrets his initial credulity:

> Es la última y tercera,
> el ver cuánto yerro ha sido
> dar crédito fácilmente
> a los sucesos previstos;
> pues aunque su inclinación
> le dicte sus precipicios,
> quizá no le vencerán,
> porque el hado más esquivo,
> la inclinación más violenta,
> el planeta más impío,
> sólo el albedrío inclinan,
> no fuerzan el albedrío.[74]

---

[73] Also see Brewer (2011, 490–491) and be reminded that Jean Taisnier's study of the divinatory arts is entitled *Opus mathematicum octo libros complectens: innumeris propemodum figuris idealibus manuum et physiognomiae*. On ironic comparisons of Basilio with mathematical authorities such as Thales and Euclid see Presberg (2001, 113).

[74] *La vida es sueño*, ed. Morón (1984, 100–101, vv. 780–792); English translation Racz (2006, without pagination). On the identification of the "most unholy planet" with Saturn see Armas (1988b).

[To third and final point entails
Determining to what extent
A person errs to readily
By trusting in foretold events,
For though our heir may be disposed
To outbursts and imetuous acts,
This bent is but a tendency.
The direst fate, we know for fact,
Much like the rashest temperament
Or strongest planetary pull.
May boast some influence on free will
But cannot make man bad or good.]

Basilio is a much more complex character than he might seem at first glance.

> El desengaño del Rey demuestra que la nueva visión científica exagera la capacidad del hombre para interpretar de manera matemática, es decir, empírica y conclusiva, tanto los grandes signos celestiales como las más cotidianas señales de identidad personal, realzando así la necesidad de una filosofía moral basada en la recta razón escolástica y capaz de abarcar todas las peripecias de una vida caótica y contingente. (Brewer 2011, 488)

[The King's delusion shows that the new scientific world view exaggerates man's ability to interpret in a mathematical, that is, empirical and conclusive way, both the great celestial signs and the more everyday signs of personal identity, thus enhancing the need for a moral philosophy based on proper scholastic rationality and capable of encompassing all the vicissitudes of a chaotic and contingent life.]

In the light of these reflections, Basilio – as the bearer of divinatory knowledge – plays a role of paramount importance in disapproving of astrology as a science and the scientific methodology on which it is based.

2.2 *Apolo y Climene* (1661) and *El tesoro escondido* (1679)

From the perspective opened up by this reappraisal of the king's character in *La vida es sueño*, we must also reconsider the figure of the magician in the mythological comedy *Apolo y Climene* (1661), which presents a similar starting point:[75] The magician Fitón had prophesied to King Admeto that his daughter Climene would have a love affair with Apollo and that she would give birth to Phaeton who, in turn, would lose control over the chariot of the sun with the well-

---

[75] On this point see Valbuena-Briones (1988, 176) and Gutiérrez Carbajo (2002, 219 and 226). Hernández Araico characterises Climene as 'a kind of Segismundo who regrets her lack of freedom' (2002, 253).

known dire consequences.[76] Just like Basilio, Admeto locks up his daughter to prevent the fateful prediction from coming true. However, Apollo seduces Climene, and in a second mythological comedy (*El hijo del sol, Faetón*) the prophecy will be fulfilled.[77] In contrast to what happens in *La vida es sueño*, the mytheme on which the comedy is based[78] prevents Climene, unlike Segismundo, from dominating her own proclivities. The strategy of disqualifying the divinatory arts is different in mythological comedy. The author of the prophecy is not the king himself,[79] but an evil wizard who arranges things so that in the end his predictions come true.[80] There is no doubt that Fitón's non-magical stratagems lead to the predicted outcome, thus reconciling the fatalism inherent in myth with free will. As Admeto himself says: "el entendimiento es / tan absoluto monarca / que con leyes de

---

76 Just as in *La vida es sueño*, the birth of Climene is accompanied by a series of bad omens: "El fausto felice día / que todos a verla clara / luz del sol nacen, nació / Climene a no verla, a causa / de que interpuesta la Luna, / entre él y la tierra estaba / lidiando un letal eclipse / con tan desigual batalla, / que de las doradas luces / triunfaban las sombras pardas. / No en este horóscopo, en este / crisis solamente, infausta / la previno el cielo, pues, / bien como víbora humana, / nació reventando el seno / de las maternas entrañas, / falseándome en que una muera / el gozo de que otra nazca", *Apolo y Climene*, ed. Neumeister (2010, 1078) [On that magnificent happy day / when all are born seeing / the splendid light of the sun / Climene, not seeing it, because / that the moon was placed / between her and the earth / fighting a lethal eclipse / in such an unequal battle, / that over the golden lights / the brown shadows triumphed. / Not by this horoscope, by this / crisis only, unfortunate crisis / was she forewarned by heaven, for, / just like a human viper, / she was born bursting the flesh / of her mother's womb, / falsifying me in that one's dying / brings forth the bliss of another's birth].
77 On the character of Fitón and his performance in this comedy see Narinesingh (1982. 163–170).
78 On the rewriting of the myth see Gómez Mingorance (1983). Armas (1986) relates mythological comedy to Botticelli's *Primavera*. Hernández Araico reads this comedy in a political key (1987).
79 Although he has a keen interest in the occult sciences, Admeto is only apprentice to the magician Fitón: "Yo, que ya sabéis cuán docto / discípulo de las varias / ciencias de Fiton logré / en sus estudios la sabia / astrología, observando / el punto de tan estrañas / señales, las anteví / tan opuestos, y contrarias / al transcurso de su vida, / que no hubo estrella de cuantas / ya benévolas inducen, / ya retrógradas arrastran, / que no influyese en Climene / infortunios, y desgracias", *Apollo and Climene*, ed. Neumeister (2010, 1078). [I, who you know how learned / a disciple I was / of Fitón's various sciences / attained the studies of the wise / astrology, observing / the point of such strange / signs, I foresaw them / so opposite, and contrary / to the course of his life, / that there was no star amongst all which / induce benevolence, / or drag backwards, / that did not inflict on Climene / misfortunes, and calamities].
80 "(¡Qué ajenos de mis motivos / su seguridad presumen, / sin saber que van a fin / solo de que se consume / lo que ya dije una vez! / Pues si la hallaran, no dude / que con su muerte mintiera / mi estudio)", *Apollo and Climene*, ed. Neumeister (2010, 1149) [(How unaware of my motives / their safety they presume, / not knowing that their sole aim / is to see consumed / what I once said! / For if they find it, do not doubt / that with its death it would belie / my scholarship)].

albedrío / sobre las estrellas manda"[81] [understanding is / so absolute a monarch / that by laws of freewill / it overrules the stars]. In this way, those divinatory practices that Fitón uses are discredited:

> No sé si quiromancía
> fue la que le habló en las rayas
> de la mano, o en el aire
> la eteromancía en fantasmas;
> la nigromancía, no sé
> si en cadáveres o estatuas;
> si la piromancía en fuego
> o si la hidromancía en agua;
> porque solo sé que lleno
> de espíritus que le inflaman,
> cuando son suyas las voces,
> y no suyas las palabras.[82]

> [I don't know if it was palmistry
> which spoke to him about the lines
> of the hand, or divination
> of ghosts in the air;
> or necromancy, be it
> in corpses or in statues;
> if pyromancy in the fire
> or hydromancy in the water;
> for I only know that
> with spirits inflamed
> are his voices when they are his
> but his are not his words.]

In *El tesoro escondido* (1679),[83] one of his last *autos sacramentales*, Idolatry, one of the allegorical characters that escort the quest for Paganism, is characterised as engaging in the same divinatory practices as Fitón:

> Para eso
> de que con su afecto cumplas,
> ¿qué es menester ausentarte,
> sabiendo que no hay ninguna
> mágica ciencia de cuanta

---

81 *Apolo y Climene*, ed. Neumeister (2010, 1077–1078).
82 *Apolo y Climene*, ed. Neumeister (2010, 1079).
83 On this point also see the introduction to Lauer's edition of *El tesoro escondido* (2012, 7–8), as well as Farm (1997), Lauer (2003a), (2003b), (2012) and (2014) along with Gilbert (2008) on this *auto sacramental*.

explícitamente intrusas
dejó enseñadas Balam,
en que implícita no incurra
la idolatría de Oriente,
donde en siria frase suya
magos a sus sabios llama
la fama, que los gradúa?
Y siendo así que en el fuego,
–cuando a los dioses consulta,
el imperio de mi voz–
la piromancia ejecuta;
la heteromancia en el aire;
la hidromancia en la espuma
del mar; la nigromancia,
de la tierra en sepulturas
de cadáveres, que yertos
responden a mis preguntas;
y en fin, la quiromancia
en las lineadas arrugas
de la mano, en balde admiras,
extrañas y dificultas
que ese pueblo te revele,
te informe, advierta e infunda
lo que de la estrella sabe
y del tesoro barrunta.[84]

[So that
with her affection to comply,
do you need to go away,
knowing that there is no
magical science amongst
the explicitly intrusive
which Balam taught
in which the idolatry
of the Orient does not implicitly intrude,
where not fame, who calibrates them,
in in Syrian her wise men
calls "magicians"?
And this being like that
in the fire – when she consults the gods,
the command of my voice –
pyromancy executes;
heteromancy in the air;
hydromancy in the froth

---

84 *El tesoro escondido*, ed. Lauer (2012, 100–101, vv. 367–396).

of the sea; necromancy,
of the earth in graves
of corpses, who stiffly
answer my questions;
and finally, palmistry
in the lines of the wrinkles
in the hand, in vain you're admired,
you're puzzled, you're dismayed by
what this folk may reveal,
may disclose, may forewarn, and may instil in you
what from the star it knows
and from the treasure may conjecture.]

The condemnation of divinatory practices works, in both the comedy and the *auto sacramental*, through the negative character, be it an evil wizard or the personification of idolatry.

3 Women as bearers of occult knowledge in Calderón

One of the strategies adopted by Calderón in his fight against divination is the creation of female characters who are bearers of the forbidden knowledge.[85] Don Pedro tests this resource in different dramatic genres such as mythological comedy, chivalrous comedy and *auto sacramental*.

3.1 *El mayor encanto, amor* (1635)

The mythological play *El mayor encanto, amor* (1635)[86] begins with Ulysses' arrival on the island of a Circe,[87] who is not only the Homeric magician but also a

---

[85] See Gernert (2017c).
[86] The comedy was first performed during the night of San Juan in 1635 at the Palacio del Retiro, see Shergold (1958), Whitaker (1997) and, for the context of the premiere, Ulla Lorenzo (2014). The play has been read in a political key by some researchers – Armas (1986c), (2000), (2011) and (2013); Greer (1989) and (1992); Hernández Araico (1993), Aercke (1994) and, from another perspective, by Sáez (2014), who proposes an identification of Circe with the Count-Duke of Olivares, who seduces Ulysses /Felipe IV and keeps him captive in his palace. This interpretation is called into question by Fernández Mosquera in the introduction to his edition of *El mayor encanto, amor* (2007, XXV–XXVI) and in Fernández Mosquera (2008a) and (2008b). See Neumeister (2013) on the key interpretations of Calderón's mythological plays.
[87] On the rewriting of the myth see Fischer (1981) and Grilli (2009); the importance of anagnorisis has been studied by Pascual Barciela (2012).

scandalously erudite woman[88] who has studied mathematics, philosophy and astrology[89] and who proudly displays her hermetic knowledge:

> pues pasando a más empeños
> la ambición de mi albedrío,
> el canto entiendo a las aves,
> y a las fieras los bramidos,
> siendo los dos para mí
> agüeros o vaticinios;
> cuantos pájaros al aire
> vuelan, ramilletes vivos,
> dando a entender, que se llevan
> la primavera consigo,
> renglones son para mí
> ni señalados, ni escritos.
> La armonía de las flores,
> que en hermosos laberintos
> parece que es natural,

---

[88] "Prima nací de Medea / en Tesalia, donde fuimos / asombro de sus estudios / y de sus ciencias prodigio, / porque enseñadas las dos / de un gran mágico, nos hizo / docto escándalo del mundo, / sabio portento del siglo, / que en fin las mujeres, cuando / tal vez aplicar se han visto / a las letras, o a las armas, / los hombres han excedido", *El mayor encanto amor*, ed. Fernández Mosquera (2007, 29, vv. 604–615) [Being of Medea's kindred, / I with her, a child, was rear'd / In Thessalia as a sister, / Where we were its school's amazement, / And the wonder of its science; / For being there well taught, we two, / By a greatly-skill'd magician, / We became the learned marvel / Of the world, a lore-enlighten'd / lamp portentous to the age, / For 'tis ascertain'd that women, / When to letters or to arms / They woth resolute will apply them, / Oftentimes surpass the men, translation MacCarthy 1861, 42]. For an interpretation of Circe's knowledge in a feminist key see Hernández (2002).

[89] "No te digo que estudié / con generoso motivo / matemáticas, de quien / la filosofía principio / fue, no te digo que al cielo / los dos movimientos mido, / natural, y rapto, siendo / ambos a un tiempo continuos; / no te digo que del sol / los veloces cursos sigo, / siendo cambiante cuaderno / de tornasoles, y visos. / no que de la luna observo / los resplandores mendigos, / pues una dádiva suya / los hace pobres o ricos; / no te digo, que los astros, / bien errantes, o bien fijos, / en ese papel azul / son mis letras; solo digo / que esto, aunque es estudio noble, / fue para mi ingenio indigno [. . .]", *El mayor encanto amor*, ed. Fernández Mosquera (2007, 29, vv. 622–643) [I say nothing of the zeal, / Trusth inspired, with which I studied / Mathematics, on whose base / All philosophy is builded / Or with what success I measured, / With a scientific niceness, / The two movements of the sky, / Each by days and years divided, / Both continous at one time. / I say nought of my untired / Watching of the sun's swift's course, / As it oped its ever-shifted / Gold-emblazon'd book of light, / Or the moon's poor pauper brightness, / Begg'd for from the sun, like alms, Since its poverty and riches / Are his beams, refused or given. / I say nothing of the fixed / Or flow-moving orbs on high / Being to me but letters written / On the heaven's cerulean page. / This alone I say, this singly, / That the study of the science, / Noble though it be, seem'd worthless / To my mind . . ., translation MacCarthy 1861, 43].

sé yo bien que es artificio,
pues son imprenta en que el cielo
estampa raros avisos.
Por las rayas de la mano
la quiromancia examino,
cuando en ajadas arrugas
de la piel el fin admiro
del hombre; la geomancía
en la tierra cuando escribo
mis caracteres en ella;
y en ella también consigo
la nigromancía, cuando
de su centro, de su abismo,
hago abrirse las entrañas
y abortar a mis gemidos
los difuntos, que responden
de mi conjuro oprimidos.[90]

[To my mind that sought the highest,
Since its free flight, soaring ever
In pursuit of new achievements,
Learn'd what meant the bird's sweet ditties,
And the howlings of the wild-beasts,
They to me becoming patent
Auguries or prophesyings.
When the rich-plumed birds sweep by me
Like to living nosegays lifted
High in air, the tidings telling
Of the sweet spring they bear with them,
They to me are secret ciphers,
Legible although unwritten.
Then the harmony of flowers,
In wild beauteous mazes mingled,
Though so natural it seemeth,
Well I know is artificial;
Since upon their lovely leaves
Rare advices heaven imprinteth.
By the lines upon the hand
Palmistry's strange lore delight's me,
When the destiny of man
In the skin's poor wither'd wrinkles
I can see. And geomancy
On the earth, when I inscribe there

---

90 *El mayor encanto amor*, ed. Fernández Mosquera (2007, 30–31, vv. 644–675); English translation MacCarthy (1861, 43–44).

My mysterious characters;
And with it I also mingle
Pyromancy [i.e. Necromancy], when from out
Earth's far centre, its abysses,
I command its womb to ope
And with groans bring forth the buried
Dead, who answer all I ask,
To my magic spell submitted.]

Researchers have approached this monologue by Circe from the perspective of gender studies and have stressed that the knowledge of the sorceress belongs to the male domain. Frederick A. de Armas observed that "[s]he can certainly be included among the male women [. . .] and more appropriately, would fall under the heading of "scholar" since in her early years our enchantress became "docto escándalo del mundo" [. . .] which led to men's envy" (1981, 209).[91] According to Matas Caballero the "ideario feminista de Circe se manifiesta, entre otros aspectos, en la proclamación orgullosa que ella muestra de su sabiduría [. . .] un arsenal de saberes que constituye la base doctrinal de su poder y que le facilita la autocomplacencia de considerarse superior y capaz de dominar a los hombres" [feminist ideology of Circe is manifested, among other aspects, in the proud ostentation that she makes of her wisdom [. . .] an arsenal of knowledge that constitutes the doctrinal base of her power and that facilitates her self-complacency, allowing her to consider herself superior and capable of dominating men]. Fernández Mosquera, in his turn, insisted on her "valor como mujer sabia y educada en las ciencias y en las artes, malas y buenas"[92] [value as a wise woman educated in the sciences and in the arts, both good and bad]. Regalado is one of the few researchers who underline the fact that Circe's knowledge is occult knowledge.[93] Ellis – after comparing the Calderonian Circe with her Homeric model – specifies that "she moved on from more traditional studies to the darker

---

91 In Armas (2000), the American researcher relates the knowledge of the magician to a painting by the Italian Renaissance painter Dosso Dossi.
92 See the introduction to his edition of *El mayor encanto, amor* (2007, XXVI). On Circe's charms also see DiPuccio (1987).
93 See Regalado (1995, II, 217): "Circe, caracterizada por un saber enciclopédico y virtuosa de las 'ciencias prohibidas', esgrime frente a su deseado adversario, el 'retórico griego', un arte dialéctico en el que imbrica sofismas y estratagemas, potente combinación de ingenio y sensualidad que la configuran como una libertina que actúa con 'libertad de conciencia'." [Circe, characterised by an encyclopaedic and masterly knowledge of the 'forbidden sciences', wields against her chosen adversary, the 'Greek rhetorician', a dialectical art in which she interweaves sophistry and stratagems, a powerful combination of ingenuity and sensuality that makes her a libertine who acts with 'freedom of conscience'].

arts mostly associated with divination: ornithromancy, quiromancy, pyromancy, necromancy" (2010, 148) and argues convincingly that the interest of the play lies in staging an epistemological conflict arising from the antagonism between Circe and Ulysses:

> Clearly the struggle between the two is going to be a battle of wits: Who has the greater knowledge? This creates a dynamic in the play of opposing and competing philosophies in which dependence on natural philosophy and the occult sciences, seen through the lens of philosophical scepticism, must ultimately fail, while the tenets of moral philosophy lead to triumph. (Ellis 2010, 148)

In other words: the occult sciences throughout the comedy prove their ineffectiveness, and the status of the sorceress as a 'depositary of supreme science' (Saura 2003, 171) is questioned. Through the character of the mythological sorceress, Calderón accomplishes a condemnation of the *artes manticae*.

3.2 *Los encantos de la culpa* (1645)

The profoundly negative evaluation of the character of Circe becomes evident in *Los encantos de la Culpa* (1645),[94] an *auto sacramental* in which she is transformed into the allegory of guilt and becomes the cause of the perdition of Man, symbolised by Ulysses in the eschatological sense. Arellano characterises it, in fact, as "símbolo de la tentación, la mujer malvada y lasciva que incita al pecado y a los vicios, los cuales transforman a los hombres en bestias" (2011, 177) [symbol of temptation, the wicked and lewd woman who incites to sin and vices which transform men into beasts]. Like the Circe of the mythological feast, the Culpa of the *auto sacramental* flaunts her hermetic knowledge, which is the same as in *El mayor encanto, amor*,[95] only presented in another order:[96]

> La Nigromancia verás
> ejecutada, saliendo
> a mi conjuro obedientes

---

94 For the rewriting of the myth in *Los encantos de la culpa* see LeVan (1982) and García Manzano (1986). The dramatic structures and the role of the dreamlike have been studied by Gilbert (2006), (2007) and (2010).
95 Hence, probably, the use of the word *chiromancy* where it should say *pyromancy* because of the context.
96 Ellis perceives the same conflict in the *auto* as in the comedy, regarding the types of knowledge embodied by Ulysses and Circe which – according to him – "can be understood in terms of her pursuit of both forbidden and impossible knowledge, attempting to know and master what the sceptics called 'incerta natura'" (2010, 161).

de sus sepulcros los muertos
(*Aparte.*)
–cadáver es el que peca,
pues me obedece; no miento–.
La grande quiromancía
verás, cuando en vivo fuego
en los papeles del humo
caracteres de luz veo
(*Aparte*)
–¿qué fuego no enciendo yo?,
no es engaño, pues lo enciendo–.
Titubear verás caducos
uno y otro polo, haciendo
que desplomados se caigan
sobre todo el universo
–no será la vez primera
que yo estremecí su imperio–.
El idioma de las aves
verás, que yo sola entiendo
siendo el canto vaticinio
y siendo el graznido agüero.
De las flores te leeré
estos escritos cuadernos,
donde la naturaleza
escribió raros misterios.[97]

[Necromancy shalt thou see,
Tried and tested to the farthest; –
So that, yielding to my spells,
From their graves the dead will answer:–
(*Aside*)
Yes, for dead in fin is he
Who doth yield to my advances.–

---

97 *Los encantos de la culpa*, ed. Escudero (2004, 211–213, vv. 816–841); English translation MacCarthy (1861, 185). On this point cf. Martínez Torrón (1983, 709): "La Culpa invita al Hombre a disfrutar de sus palacios y estudios ocultos. Se insiste con ello en el carácter de hechicera de Circe, exagerando su poder de seducción. recuérdese la batalla inquisitorial de la época contra brujería. La Culpa le indica que verá apagado el sol a un soplo de su aliento, las estrellas desclavadas de octavo firmamento, la Nigromancia, la Quiromancia, el idioma de las aves, la escritura de las flores, músicas, manjares, jardines, regalada cama para el tacto." [Culpa invites Man to enjoy her palaces and occult practices. In this way, Circe's role of a sorceress is insisted upon, her power of seduction being exaggerated. We should remember the inquisitorial battle of the time against witchcraft. Culpa announces that the sun will be extinguished with a single blow of her breath, the stars will be dislodged from the eighth firmament, necromancy, chiromancy, the language of the birds, the writing of flowers, music, food, gardens a soft bed of touch].

Pyromancy, too, will show thee
How upon the red flames' sparkles,
How upon the curling smoke-wreaths,
Knowledge there inscribed I gather:
(*Aside*)
Lit by me does ever crackle--
Thou wilt see the poles of Heaven
Tremble at my dread commandments,
As if down about to fall
On the world's disturbed axes:-
Not the first time will it be
That its kingdom I have shaken.-
All the language of the birds
Wilt thou learn, by *me* sole master'd-
Both their sweet prophetic warble
And their harther augural crackle.
On the flowers, too, wilt thou read,
As upon illumined parchment,
Natures mysteries and marvels.]

Unlike in the mythological comedy, Culpa here insists that these are forbidden sciences:

Verás mis grandes estudios,
mis admirables portentos
examinarás, tocando
de mi ciencia los efectos.
¿Por qué piensas que me llaman
la Circe de estos desiertos?
Porque ciencias prohibidas,
que son leyes que yo tengo,
con mis estudios alcanzo,
con mis vigilias arreglo.[98]

[Thou wilt see my deep researches,-
Thou my wonders wilt examine,-
All the secrets of my science
Will be bared to five thee answer.
Wherefore, thinkest thou, the Circe
Of these desert wastes they call me?
'tis because forbidden knowledge
(*That* sole law I have untrampled)

---

[98] *Los encantos de la culpa*, ed. Escudero (2004, 208–209, vv. 794–807); English translation MacCarthy (1861, 184).

I, by application, reach to,–
I, by mighty studies, master.]

The *auto sacramental* is much more direct in its condemnation of the divinatory arts, and researchers such as Flasche,[99] Egido[100] and Martinengo[101] have emphasised how this relates with the post-Tridentine condemnations.

---

[99] "Verbotene Wissenschaften [. . .] sind es, die dem zuhörenden Ulises vorgeführt werden [. . .] Mit verbotenen Büchern beschäftigt sich das Konzil von Trient nicht viele Jahrzehnte vor Calderón [. . .] Verbotene Wissenschaften fand Calderón in den Handbüchern seiner Zeit ausführlich erörtert. Exempla für Mantik aus verschiedenen Sphären der Schöpfung hatte Calderón beständig vor Augen." Flasche (1968, 29) [It is forbidden sciences . . . that are presented to the attentive Ulises . . . Not many decades before Calderón had the Council of Trent dealt with forbidden books . . . Calderón found forbidden sciences discussed in detail in the manuals of his time. He had specimens of manticism from different spheres of creation constantly before his eyes].

[100] "Calderón mostraba lo evidente en esto como en toda el área de los 'encantos' que, ya desde el título, apelaban a artificios prohibidos y magia, a deslumbres de la razón por medio de apariencias y engaños. 'Encantamiento' no era sino el objeto o apariencia, 'que por arte mágica se pone a la vista, o se hace para fingir y manifestar como real y existente lo que en sí no es. De forma que la puesta en escena equivalía a cuanto la maga podía con su ciencia oculta." Egido (1982, 68–69) [Calderón showed the obvious in this as in the whole area of the "charms" which, from the title on, appealed to forbidden artifices and magic, to the dazzling of reason by means of appearances and deceptions. 'Enchantment' was nothing but the object or appearance, 'which by magic is placed in view, or is made to pretend and manifest itself as real and existing, which in itself it is not'. So putting it on stage was equal to what the sorceress could do with her occult science].

[101] "En cualquier cao, el centro de gravedad del monólogo reside en el fragmento [. . .] en el que Circe-Culpa enumera sus habilidades mágicas, su profunda experiencia de las que llama 'ciencias prohibidas' [. . .] La referencia a unas 'ciencias prohibidas' merece especial atención: a diferencia de la comedia donde las facultades mágicas de la protagonista se integraban (se diría que armoniosamente) en un conjunto de 'encantos' del cual formaban parte también los atractivos femeninos, aquí se alude claramente al signo diabólico que en la opinión corriente de la época caracterizaban dichas facultades, cuyo ejercicio por tanto prohibía terminantemente la Iglesia tridentina." Martinengo (2000, 214) and (2001, 113–114) [In any case, the centre of gravity of the monologue resides in the fragment . . . in which Circe-Culpa enumerates her magical skills, her profound experience of what she calls 'forbidden sciences' . . . The reference to the 'forbidden sciences' deserves special attention: unlike the comedy, in which the protagonist's magical skills were integrated (one might say harmoniously) into a set of 'charms' of which female attractions were also a part, here there is a clear allusion to the diabolical character of these skills, the exercise of which was therefore strictly forbidden by the Tridentine Church].

3.3 *Los tres mayores prodigios* (1636)

Like the *auto sacramental Los encantos de la Culpa*, the mythological comedy *Los tres mayores prodigios* (1636)[102] is closely linked to *El mayor encanto, amor*.[103] Premiered only a year later, this comedy has also been interpreted in a political key, proposing an identification of the main character of the sorceress Medea with the Count-Duke Olivares.[104] Like Circe and Culpa (i.e. Guilt) personified, Medea is presented as a scholarly woman and bearer of hermetic knowledge:[105]

> [. . .] yo soy
> la sabia y docta Medea,

---

102 As Fernández Mosquera points out in the introduction to his edition of the comedy, it 'was premiered on the night of Saint John in 1636, a few months before the edition of the *princeps*' (2007, LXXIX). On the staging see Rose (1994) and Rull Fernández (2005), and for the prologue Schizzano Mandel (1988). Many researchers of the play like Watson (1971), Colahan (1983) and Edwards (1984) have focused on the character of Hercules.
103 Cf. the introduction by Fernández Mosquera: "Por otro lado, al tratarse de fiestas cortesanas de tema mitológico, coinciden en el tratamiento de los personajes y también en el significado, además de tener en común rasgos estilísticos que en más de un caso provocan coincidencias intertextuales muy llamativas. Claro ejemplo de esto último serán los monólogos de Circe [. . .] y de Medea [. . .]. Mismo estilo, similar tono para idénticos versos que subrayan una muy parecida caracterización relacionada con el peso del personaje femenino principal, el cual se puede entender en clave de reivindicación femenina, rasgo que habrán de destacar quienes quieren ver en Calderón un autor heraldo de la modernidad." (2007, LXXIX–LXXX) [On the other hand, as they are court festivals with a mythological theme, they coincide in the treatment of the characters and also in the content, as well as having stylistic features in common that in more than one case cause very striking intertextual coincidences. A clear example of the latter are the monologues of Circe . . . and of Medea . . . Same style, similar tone for identical verses that underline a very similar characterization related to the weight of the main female character, which can be understood in the key of female vindication, a feature that should be highlighted by those who want to see in Calderón an author who is a herald of modernity].
104 Hernández Araico speaks, in fact, of "a current of opposition to the politics of Olivares that finds opposition in *Los tres mayores prodigios*" (1991, 85), a position that is rejected by Fernández Mosquera in the introduction to his edition of the comedy (2007, LXXX–LXXXI). Rose proposes instead "to re-examine the play and determine if *Los tres mayores prodigios* falls within the confines of comedy" (1997, 247).
105 On the parallels in the construction of the main character in both comedies see Trambaioli (1995, 231–232: "Nada más fácil, por lo tanto, para Calderón que construir y dramatizar en la segunda comedia una Circe-Medea que, aun manteniéndose dentro de la tradición de la Medea mitológica, presenta algunos rasgos específicamente acentuados de la hechicera hermanastra" [Nothing is easier, therefore, for Calderon than to create and dramatise in the second comedy a Circe-Medea that, while remaining within the tradition of the mythological Medea, presents some specifically accentuated features of the sibling-sorceress]); Fernandez Mosquera's introduction to his edition of *Los tres mayores prodigios* (2007, XXVI) as well as Lara Alberola (2010, 184):

a cuyo mágico estudio
son caracteres y letras
en la campaña las flores
y en el cielo las estrellas.
De la astrología pasando
a la magia, el aura mesma
puntado libro es que ocultos
secretos me manifiesta.
La nigromancia examino
en cadáveres que encierra
el centro, cuando a mi voz
los esqueletos despiertan;
la piromancia, que en fuego
ejecutó su violencia,
me escribe en papeles de humo
varias cifras con centellas.
A mis mágicos conjuros
todos los infiernos tiemblan
y sus espíritus tristes,
sus lóbregas sombras negras,
sus profundos calabozos,
oprimidos de la fuerza
del encanto, a mis preguntas
dan equívocas respuestas,
a cuyo estudio entregada,
a cuyo ejercicio atenta,
es mi patria aqueste monte
y mi palacio esta selva.[106]

[. . . I am
the wise and learned Medea,
to whose magical study
the flowers of the field
and the stars of the sky
are symbols and letters.

"Calderón aprovecha la descripción de Circe de *El mayor encanto, amor* para definir a la Medea de *Los tres mayores prodigios*. Hay una conexión clara entre ambos textos. El autor vuelve a dibujar a una hechicera sabia, una estudiosa, una experta en las artes mágicas, consideradas una *ciencia*. Medea domina la astrología, la nigromancia, la piromancia, los conjuros infernales y los elementos de la naturaleza, en la que ha construido su refugio." [Calderon uses the description of Circe of *El mayor encanto, amor* to define the Medea of *Los tres mayores prodigios*. There is a clear connection between both texts. The author redraws a wise sorceress, a scholar, an expert in the magical arts, considered to be a science. Medea masters astrology, necromancy, pyromancy, infernal spells and the elements of nature, in which she has built her refuge].
106 *Los tres mayores prodigios*, ed. Fernández Mosquera (2007, 1025–1026, vv. 615–644).

From astrology to
magic, the aura itself
is a dotted book which hidden
secrets reveals to me.
Necromancy I practice
in bodies that the centre
encloses, when by my voice
the skeletons wake up;
pyromancy, that in the fire
executed its violence,
is writing for me on papers of smoke
different codes with sparks.
At my magic spells
all hells tremble,
and their sorrowful spirits,
their dreary black shadows,
their deep dungeons,
forced by the strength
of my spell, to my questions
give equivocal answers,
to whose study committed,
to whose exercise attentive I am,
my home is this mountain,
my palace this forest.]

Just like the Calderonian Circe, his Medea knows how to read in the book of nature and decipher the signatures of things. The divinatory practices mentioned are astrology, necromancy and pyromancy.

3.4 *El jardín de Falerina* (1649)

A third Calderonian comedy uses a female character to condemn the occult sciences. I am referring to the magician Falerina, inspired by the *Orlando inamorato* and the *Orlando furioso*.[107] In *El jardín de Falerina* (1649),[108] a *zarzuela*, it is a negative female character that shares many features with the evil magicians of

---

107 On the tradition of that character see Trambaioli (2008).
108 It is a comedy sung in two acts, probably performed in the Alcazar of Madrid on June 25th, 1649. On the date of the premiere see the introduction to the edition by Ruano de la Haza (2010, XXVI) and, on music in the new genre of *zarzuela*, Pacheco y Costa (2003).

mythological plays[109] and that – like the Circe of *El mayor encanto, amor* – is transformed into the allegory of Guilt in the homonymous *auto sacramental*.[110] At the beginning of the play, Marfisa and Lisidante call for the wise woman while presenting her as the bearer of hermetic knowledge:

> LISIDANTE. ¡Oh tú, de aquestos montes
> que el mar en desiguales horizontes
> une y desune, oráculo divino. . .
>
> MARFISA. ¡Oh tú, destas montañas peregrino
> ídolo humano, a cuyo docto anhelo
> es el abismo intérprete del cielo. . .
>
> LISIDANTE. Tú, que sabia la gran piromancía
> escribes en pirámides de fuego.
>
> MARFISA. Tú, que en el aire a tus conjuros ciego,
> das a las aves la heteromancía. . .
>
> LISIDANTE. Tú, que en sepulcros la nigromancía
> ejecutas. . .
>
> MARFISA. Y en agua
> la hidromancía, en quien fragua
> su asombro.
>
> LISIDANTE. En quien esmera su portento. . .

---

109 See Aszyk (2007, 110–111). Hernández Araico compares the three characters from the point of view of a criticism of the Count-Duke of Olivares: "Ya en 1635, el montaje espectacular de *El mayor encanto, amor*, con el motivo también de la maga Circe que hechiza al héroe en un palacio de maravillosos jardines refleja ambiguamente la crítica de brujería contra el conde-duque por embelesar a Felipe IV con diversiones superfluas. La maga Medea en *Los tres mayores prodigios* de 1636 también remite a dicha crítica contra don Gaspar. *El jardín de Falerina* cierra, pues, una especie de círculo de ilusionismo teatral calderoniano donde se vislumbra la crítica contra el poder hechiceril del privado junto con la alabanza de la fuerza y lealtad de la monarquía española." (2008, 399) [As early as 1635, the spectacular staging of *El mayor encanto, amor*, with the motif of the sorceress Circe who bewitches the hero with a palace with wonderful gardens, ambiguously reflects the criticism of witchcraft directed against the Count-Duke for entrancing Felipe IV with superfluous amusements. The sorceress Medea in *Los tres mayores prodigios* of 1636 also recalls this criticism of Don Gaspar. *El jardín de Falerina* encloses, then, a kind of circle of Calderonian theatrical magic where the criticism of the private power of sorcery is displayed together with the praise of the strength and loyalty of the Spanish monarchy].
110 See Aszyk (2007, 111). On the function of Culpa in this *auto* see Cardona Castro (1997, 32) and Mata Induráin (2006, 291) and on her "diabolic sciences" Díaz Balsera (1994, 148).

MARFISA. El cielo.

LISIDANTE. El mar. . .

MARFISA. La tierra.

LISIDANTE. El fuego.

MARFISA. El viento.

LISIDANTE. Tú, que a líneas divides
los ámbitos del sol, que a dedos mides. . .

MARFISA. Tú, que a rumbos las sombras de sus huellas
le pisas a la luna, y las estrellas
le cuentas una a una. . .

LISIDANTE. Anticipada voz de la fortuna. . .

MARFISA. Futuro vaticinio de la fama. . .

LOS DOS. ¡Mágica Falerina![111]

[LISIDANTE: Oh you, from these mountains
that the sea in uneven horizons
unite and disunite, divine oracle. . .

MARFISA: Oh you, pilgrim of these mountains,
human idol, whose learned desire
is the abysmal interpreter of heaven. . .

LISIDANTE: You, who the great pyromancy
wisely write in pyramids of fire.

MARFISA: You, who give heteromancy
to the birds of the sky, blind to your spells. . .

---

111 *El jardín de Falerina. Comedia*, ed. Ruano de la Haza (2010, 771, vv. 1–23). In collaboration with Francisco de Rojas Zorrilla and Antonio Coello Ochoa, Calderón had also written a comedy in three acts of the same title that was premiered on January 13th, 1636. The play, in which there are no references to occult sciences, was edited by Pedraza Jiménez and González Cañal (2010) and studied by Aubrun (1966) and Pedraza Jiménez (2003) and (2009). Much later, for the Feast of Corpus Christi in 1675, Calderón wrote an *auto sacramental* entitled *El jardín de Falerina*, edited by Galván and Mata Induráin (2007) and studied by Pollin (1968), Díaz Balsera (1994), Cardona Castro (1997), Villarino Martínez (2005), Mata Induráin (2006) and Coduras (2010). Like the collaborative comedy, this play makes no reference to the occult.

LISIDANTE: You, who in sepulchres necromancy
execute. . .

MARFISA: And in the water
hydromancy, in which it forges
its wonders.

LISIDANTE: In which it exerts its portents. . .

MARFISA: The sky.

LISIDANTE: The sea. . .

MARFISA: The land.

LISIDANTE: The fire.

MARFISA: The wind.

LISIDANTE: You, who in lines divide
the spheres of the sun, which with fingers you measure. . .

MARFISA: You, who tread on the moon's traces. . .
and the stars
count one by one. . .

LISIDANTE: Anticipated voice of fortune. . .

MARFISA: Future prophecy of fame. . .

BOTH: Magic Falerina!]

The presentation of Falerina's knowledge – pyromancy, heteronomy, necromancy and hydromancy – is structured according to the four elements, which generally play a major role in Calderon's work.[112] When it becomes known, at the end of the play, that Marfisa and Ruggiero are brothers, Falerina's charm loses its effectiveness and the magician commits suicide. As Aszyk observes, "[d]esaparece así el

---

[112] On the four elements in Calderón see Wilson (1936) and, with regard to the four elements in *El mayor encanto amor*, Grilli, who comments: "Empezaremos por decir que el número cuatro no es un azar métrico, sino que corresponde a un rasgo permanente de la comedia. Ésta establece su pasaje alrededor de los cuatro elementos: agua, aire, tierra, fuego que son, para así decirlo, la base sobre la cual se aplica la cultura físico-matemática de Circe." (2009, 81) [We will begin by saying that the number four is not a metric chance, but corresponds to a permanent feature of this comedy. It establishes its passage around the four elements: water, air, earth, fire which are, so to speak, the basis to which the physical-mathematical culture of Circe is applied].

mal identificado con las 'diabólicas ciencias', a saber, con la magia reconocida como negra, condenada por las autoridades eclesiásticas en España" (2007, 112) [this is how the evil identified with the 'diabolic sciences', i.e. with magic identified as black, condemned by the ecclesiastical authorities in Spain, disappears].

The knowledge of the Calderonian sorcerers and sorceresses does not correspond to the imaginary of the mythological[113] or chivalrous tradition but coincides with those practices that were persecuted in the time of Calderón:

El mayor encanto, amor (1635): [heteromancy], palmistry, geomancy, necromancy

Los tres mayores prodigios (1636): astrology, necromancy, pyromancy

Los encantos de la culpa (1645): necromancy, palmistry [pyromancy]

El jardín de Falerina (1649): pyromancy, heteromancy, necromancy and hydromancy

Apolo y Climene (1661): palmistry, heteronomy, necromancy, pyromancy and hydromancy

El tesoro escondido (1679): pyromancy, heteromancy, hydromancy, necromancy, pyromancy

Over the years, Calderón has combined the very elemental *mancies*, those which interpret fire, water, earth and air, with necromancy and palmistry. It is striking that he never speaks of aeromancy, supplanting it by ornithomancy. Geomancy is mentioned only once and is almost always replaced by necromancy. The playwright never tires of equipping certain evil characters with knowledge of the mantic arts, which had been forbidden since the bull *Coeli et Terrae Creator Deus* by Sixtus V.

4 Calderón and physiognomy

Physiognomy is not usually mentioned in the lists of forbidden divination arts in Calderón. There is, however, a burlesque reference to the reading of body signs in the courtly comedy of chivalric genre[114] *Hado, y divisa de Leonido, y de*

---

113 It is striking that the Calderonian Medea should dispense with the facet of infanticide of the mythological character.

114 The comedy repeats the situation presented in *La vida es sueño* and *Apolo y Climene*: The magician Argante locks up the wild young Marfisa to protect her from her fate of killing or being killed by a beloved person. In fact, she unwittingly duels herself with Leonido, whom she loves, without knowing that he is her twin brother. Antonucci characterises the comedy as a

Marfisa (1680).[115] In this, his last secular play, Calderón intersperses a burlesque scene of an entertaining nature, in which a soldier tries to convince the servant Merlin[116] to escort him into battle:

> MERLÍN. Ni amigo sin miedo yo.
>
> SOLDADO 1°. Ya sé que esa es falsedad,
> que vuestra fisonomía
> muestra grande valentía.
>
> MERLÍN. ¿Mi frisoni qué? Mirad
> lo que decís; que a fe mía
> que la que os dio aquesa muestra
> será la frisona vuestra
> mas no la frisona mía;
> que en mi vida conocí
> à esa señora.
>
> SOLDADO 1°. Dejemos
> las burlas y refresquemos.[117]

[MERLÍN: Nor am I a friend and neither without fear.

"compendium", in which many motifs from the playwright's previous work reappear, including that of the "astrólogo incapaz de contrastar un oráculo" (2014, without pagination) [astrologer unable to counteract an oracle]. Becker, in his turn, speaks of "una antología de sus temas, asuntos y argumentos favoritos desde 1630, así como de sus personajes y papeles" (2006, 54) [an anthology of his favourite themes, subjects and plots since 1630, as well as his characters and roles] and emphasises the parallels with *La vida es sueño* (2006, 55 and 58–59). As in *El jardín de Falerina* there are parallels with the epic poems of Boiardo and Ariosto, see Trambaioli (2008).

115 Antonucci (2014, without pagination): "*Hado y divisa de Leonido y Marfisa* fue representada en la Corte, en marzo de 1680, para celebrar las bodas entre Carlos II y María Luisa de Orleans: fue la última obra de tema profano compuesta por Calderón, que moriría al año siguiente." [*Hado y divisa de Leonido y Marfisa* was performed at Court, in March 1680, to celebrate the wedding between Charles II and Marie-Louise of Orleans: it was the last play with a profane theme written by Calderón, who would die the following year]. For the performance of the play, also see Tardón Botas (2001) and Tobar (2015) as well as Rodrigues Vianna Peres (2013) on the *La tía*, an *entremés*.

116 On Merlin's role as a jester and on his role in the comedy see Meixell (2008). According to the aforementioned researcher, the character "symbolises intuitive knowledge and those insights rendered through a non-rational approach to wisdom" (2008, 79).

117 *Hado y divisa de Leonido y Marfisa*, ed. Ruano de la Haza (2010, 158).

SOLDIER 1: But I know that this is false,
for your physiognomy
shows great courage.

MERLÍN: My *frisonee* what? Heed what you say;
for, by my faith,
what gave you this proof
was your *freesona*
not mine;
for in all my life I have
not met that lady.

SOLDIER 1: Let's stop. . .
this banter and brace ourselves.]

The typical cowardice of the jester gives rise to a jocular dispute, in which Merlín cleverly misinterprets the cultism *physiognomy* and dismisses the interpretation of the soldier, who considers him to be a brave person.

Like Lope in some comedies, like Moratín, Rojas Zorrilla or later Juan Vélez de Guevara,[118] Calderón speaks of physiognomy in a comical context, in which the character of the jester provokes the laughter of the audience either because of his knowledge of this semiotic practice or because of his unfamiliarity with the term.

---

118 In the *zarzuela Los celos hacen estrellas* (1672) by the playwright Juan Vélez de Guevara (1611–1675), son of the author of *El Diablo cojuelo*, the comical Momo speaks to Juno of the devastating effects of jealousy: "Tú eres, Juno, la primera / que te ofendes a ti misma, / sin reparar que los celos / de qualquiera paz son cisma, / de qualquier veldad vltraje, / ciçaña de qualquier dicha. / Siempre ha de estar la celosa / rostrituerta, desabrida, / y lo rostrituerto causa / en quien se precia de linda / vn gran defecto, pues queda / con mala fisonomia." Vélez de Guevara, *Los celos hacen estrellas*, ed. Varey & Shergold (1970, 28) [You are, Juno, the first / to offend yourself, / without noticing that jealousy / means division for peace, / outrage for beauty, / guile for joy. / The jealous must always be / crookfaced, dishevelled, / and the crooked face makes her / think herself fair / a grave defect, for she is still left / with a foul physiognomy].

Chapter 5
Divination and marginalised women on stage

In the Spanish theatre of the 16th and 17th centuries, the character of the diviner is usually male. Female fortune tellers are oftentimes palm reading gipsy women or the mythological heroes of the Calderonian theatre. On the Spanish stage we very rarely find the type of marginalised women who are capable of reading body signs and interpret the outward appearance of others as Francisco Delicado's *Lozana Andaluza* or the female rogue Justina do.[1] There are some 'daughters' of Celestina, who, unlike Rojas' matchmaker, also practise palmistry like *El encanto es la hermosura y el hechizo sin hechizo*, begun in 1654 by Agustín de Salazar y Torres and then finished and published by his pupil Juan de Vera y Tassis.[2] The go-between herself characterises chiromancy as fraud:

> por mentir a lo gitano
> a todos la mano tomo,
> y me voy por ella, como
> por la palma de la mano;[3]

> [for lying like a gipsy
> everyone's hand I take,
> and I go for her, like
> through the palm of the hand;]

We do not have historical documentation about the knowledge of women like the aforementioned in Spain,[4] but the case of Antonia la Ferrarese, prosecuted by the Florentine Inquisition in 1567, recorded by Castelli (2006, 511), is interesting in this context. When she arrived at Florence, this illiterate woman carried a placard with her which said: "Signori, in questa città una donna astrologa guardandovi alla phinosomia et alla mano saprà dire del passato et del avvenire in parte. Sto alloggiato allo albergo al canto del Giglio"[5] [Ladies and Gentlemen, in this city a woman astrologer looking at your phinosomy and hand will be able to tell you about the past and partly the future. I'm staying at the hotel close to the Lily]. Asked about her knowledge by the Inquisitors, she says that she learned this practice from her

---

1 See the chapter on pimps and sorceresses in Di Pinto's (2016, 34–40) article on marginal characters in the Golden Age scene in which there is no mention of divinatory practices.
2 See Lara Alberola (2010, 131).
3 Salazar y Torres, *El encanto es la hermosura y el hechizo sin hechizo*, ed. O'Connor (1994, 26).
4 For divination in early modern Germany see Coy (2020).
5 Text cited in Prosperi (1986, 120–121) and Castelli (2006, 511 and 519).

first husband and chose the term 'astrology' because, according to her, people do not know what 'phinosomia' is: "Che ho detto di sopra quello ne ho imparato et ho facto dire astrologia perché ci sono di molte persone che non intendono che uol dire phisionomia"[6] [That I said before what I learned about it and I said astrology because there are many people who do not understand that it means phisionomy].

1 Female diviners in 17th century France: The *affaire des poisons*

The so-called *affaire des poisons*, the most intriguing scandal of the France of the *Ancien Régime*, in which members of the high nobility were involved,[7] provides us with reliable documentation about the knowledge of divinatory practices of women of lower social background. During the investigations and trials from 1675 onwards, many marginalised women were arrested, interrogated and even tortured, women who were engaged in precisely the same businesses as Celestina and Lozana.[8] The most famous of them, Catherine Deshayes, called *La Voisin*, was arrested in March 1679 and executed in February of the following year. The

---

6 See the transcript of the interrogation (Archivio di Stato di Firenze, Nunz. 842. Costituito, 5 aprile 1567) *apud* Castelli (2006, 511 and 519–520).

7 I will not go into the details of the case of the poisons and will refer instead to the historiographic studies by Nass (1898), Funck-Brentano (1900), Mongrédien (1953), Mossiker (1969), Petitfils (1977), Lebigre (2001), Chautant (2002), Mollenauer (2002) and (2007), Somerset (2006) as well as Quétel (2010).

8 Funck-Brentano (1900, 104–105) characterises the persecuted "witches" in the context of the *affaire de poisons* like this: "A la magie noire ou blanche les sorcières joignent la médecine et la pharmacie. Elles ont des drogueries avec des fioles innombrables: sirops, juleps, onguents, baumes, émollients d'une variété infinie [. . .] Le plus souvent aussi la sorcière était sage-femme, mais, de même que, dans ce monde étrange, sous la droguiste se cachait l'empoisonneuse, que l'alchimiste était doublé du faux-monnayeur, derrière la sage-femme apparaissait la faiseuse d'anges." [The witches combine black or white magic with medicine and pharmacy. They have dispensaries with innumerable vials: syrups, potions, ointments, balms, softeners of an infinite variety. Most often the witch was also a midwife, but, likewise, in this strange world behind the pharmacist was hidden the poisoner, the alchemist was doubled by the counterfeiter, behind the midwife appeared the abortionist]. Chautant (2002, 119) notes with regard to *La Voisin*: "Mais elle ne cantonnait pas dans les seuls domaines de la chiromancie et de la physionomie. Il lui arrivait parfais de mettre à profit ses talents de guérisseuse" [But she was not confined to the fields of palmistry and physiognomy. Sometimes she was perfectly capable of using her healing skills].

immense documentation generated by the case of the poisons contains valuable information about the skills of the fortune-tellers.[9] Not only *La Voisin*,[10] but also other women of the same ilk (*La Vigoureux*,[11] *La Bosse*,[12] etc.) admit in the interrogations that they are committed to palmistry and physiognomy, although Lebigre suspects that they call with the "nom pompeux de 'physionomie' l'art de percevoir les désir, les tensions, les espoirs que trahissent les visages et les attitudes" (2001, 85) [pompous name of *physiognomy* the art of perceiving the desires, tensions, spirits which are revealed in faces and attitudes]. The French historian is surely not wrong with her interpretation of these women's abilities. However, we also have evidence of a handwritten treatise that belonged to *La Voisin* and was probably compiled by herself:[13]

> En prétendant que le fond de son art était la physionomie, la Voisin disait vrai. Elle en avait fait une étude approfondie. Nous trouvons sur ce sujet mille et une notes dans son dossier et un Traité de physionomie appuyé sur six inébranlables colonnes: 1re la sympathie entre l'esprit et le corps; 2° les rapports entre les animaux raisonnables et irraisonnables; 3° la diversité de l'un et de l'autre sexe; 4° la diversité des nations; 5° le tempérament des corps; 6° la diversité de l'âge; et ne pas s'appuyer sur un seul signe, car souvent les hommes sont attaqués de quelque défaut que la force de leur esprit, avec le secours de la grâce, peut assurément vaincre. Quand la comtesse de Beaufort de Canillac vint consulter la devineresse, "la dame lui ayant voulu donner sa main sans se démasquer, elle lui dit qu'elle ne se connaissait point aux physionomies de velours, et sur cela la dame ayant ôté son masque". La Voisin avoua qu'elle lisait bien plus sur les visages que dans les lignes de la main, "étant assez difficile de cacher une passion ou une inquiétude considérable". Elle n'était pas seulement physionomiste mais finement psychologue et c'est par là qu'elle donnait un fondement à sa sorcellerie. (Funck-Brentano 1900, 121–122)[14]

---

9 The documents preserved in the Bastille were published in the 19th century in 19 volumes by Ravaisson (1866–1904)

10 There is more documentation on *La Voisin's* palmistry in Ravaisson (1866–1904, V, 260, 266, 275, 319, 337, 370, 469, 481, 502 y VI, 54); physiognomy is only mentioned in Ravaisson (1866–1904, V, 281 and 457).

11 On the palmistry skills of *La Vigoureux* see Ravaisson (1866–1904, V, 160, 172, 215, 217, 220, y 429).

12 On *La Bosse* and palmistry see Ravaisson (1866–1904, V, 234 y 284)

13 See *Annexe 6* in Chautant (2002, 306–314), which reproduces the *Traicté de physionomie* del Ms 10, 357, fol. 665–673 of the *Bibliothèque de l'Arsenal*.

14 On this point also cf. Funck-Brentano (1900, 120): "La Voisin raconta très ingénument à La Reynie les débuts de sa carrière. À présent son mari ne faisait plus rien. Il avait été marchand joailler, puis boutiquier sur le Pont-Marie. Il avait perdu ses boutiques et alors, voyant son époux ruiné, 'elle s'était attachée à cultiver la science que Dieu lui avait donnée'. – 'C'est la chiromancie et la physionomie, dit-elle, que j'ai apprises dès l'âge de neuf ans'." [*La Voisin* told *La Reynie* very ingeniously about the beginning of her career. At present her husband was no longer doing anything. He had been a jewellery merchant, then a shopkeeper on the Pont-

[By claiming that the basis of her art was physiognomy, *La Voisin* was telling the truth. She had made a thorough study of it. We find a thousand and one notes on this subject in her file and a Treatise on Physiognomy based on six solid columns: 1st the harmony between the mind and the body; 2nd the relations between reasonable and unreasonable animals; 3rd the diversity of the sexes; 4th the diversity of nations; 5th the temperament of bodies; 6th the diversity of age; and do not rely on a single sign, for often men are beset by a certain defect which the strength of their spirit, with the help of gracefulness, can overcome. When the Countess de Beaufort de Canillac came to consult the soothsayer, "the lady having wanted to show her hand without unveiling herself, she told her that she did not at all know about velvet physiognomy, and that at that point the lady had removed her veil". *La Voisin* confessed that she read much more out of faces than out of the lines of the hand, it "being rather difficult to hide a major passion or anxiety". She was not only a physiognomist but also a fine psychologist, and it was through this that her sorcery had a strong foothold.]

As opposed to "magicians" like *La Bosse*, who were illiterate,[15] we know of others who read and owned libraries: According to Chautant, *La Voisin* 'was interested in alchemy, owned twenty-five works of occult science'[16] and 'kept a skeleton at home' (2002, 115) in order to know how many bones the human body had. In a letter to abbot Nicaise we read of "une Duval, qui a été arrêtée pour cause de magie, dont on dit qu'elle tient école et en avait une grande bibliothèque"[17] [a Duval, who was arrested for magic and who was said to have a school equipped with a large library]. *La Vigoureux* was interrogated on January 4th, 1679 and answered the question "Si elle-même ne se mêle pas aussi de deviner?" [Does she herself not meddle with divination?] thus: "–À la vérité, elle s'en est mêlée quelquefois, et elle a même eu quelques livres de chiromancie dont elle se servait comme elle pouvait"[18] [To tell the truth, she has meddled with it a few times, and she even had a few books of chiromancy that

---

Marie. He had lost his shops, and then, seeing her husband ruined, "she had set out to cultivate the science that God had given her". – "It's palmistry and physiognomy," she says, "that I learned at the age of nine"].

15 See Chautant (2002, 121).
16 The French researcher emphasises, moreover, the role of the printing press for the spread of occultism: "L'importance donnée aux ouvrages et aux manuels révéla le rôle de l'imprimerie ainsi que l'essor de la diffusion des livres dans le domaine de la magie. L'édition contribua, dans une certaine mesure, à la popularité de occultisme" Chautant (2002, 1215) [The importance given to books and manuals revealed the role of the printing press as well as the rise in the diffusion of books in the field of magic. Publishing contributed, to some extent, to the popularity of occultism].
17 *À l'abbé Nicaise. Ce 14 mars 1680*, apud Ravaisson (1866–1905, VI, 191). On this particular aspect, also see Chautant (2002, 115).
18 *Interrogatoire de La Vigoureux. L'an 1679, le 4 janvier, à Vincennes*, apud Ravaisson (1866–1905, V, 158–159). On this point also see Chautant (2002, 115).

she used as best she could]. In the same interrogation, *La Vigoureux* said that she did not know whether *La Bosse* was also involved in divining: "bien est vrai qu'elle regardait souvent dans la mains des gens, et qu'elle leur disait ce que lui venait dans l'esprit" (Ravaisson 1866–1905, V, 158–159) [It is true that she often looked at people's hands and told them what came into her mind]. Historical documentation reveals that there were women who were seriously pursuing the study of the occult arts, while others, curiously enough those who do not have access to book culture, pretend to have the same knowledge.

The Bastille documents also tell us of men who knew about the occult arts[19] such as Lesage, one of *La Voisin*'s collaborators, of whom Madame Dufontet, a friend of the Duke of Luxembourg, says that "he was knowledgeable in the physiognomy of the hand". In the same interrogation, Lesage himself says that he "vint lui demander si elle voulait qu'il lui regardât dans la main, parce qu'il s'y connaissait, et en physionomie, disant qu'il savait sur cela des merveilles, et que les femmes étaient quelquefois curieuses"[20] [he came and asked her if she wanted him to read her hand, because he knew how to do it, and that he knew wonders about physiognomy, and that women were sometimes curious to know]. This account clarifies, on the one hand, how suspicious characters like Lesage entered the houses of the nobility; and, on the other hand, it informs us about the female clientele of these individuals.

---

19 A certain Gobert Ferrandinier is interrogated because he had tried to hide a bag full of forbidden books and manuscripts, among them the studies of palmistry of sieur de Peruchio and of Indagine: "Qui, il a un livre de Peruchio, le livre de Roussille, et le livre d'Indagine, et plusieurs manuscrits dont aucuns sont de sa main, et ce sont de ces secrets et des fables qui lui ont été donnés et desquels il ne s'est jamais servi". Interrogation of Gobert. May 7, 1679, in Vincennes, apud Ravaisson (1866–1905, V, 358–359) [He has a book by Peruchio, the book by Roussille, and the book by Indagine, and several manuscripts, none of which by his hand, and these are secrets and fables that were given to him and which he has never used]. Also see Chautant (2002, 144). Abbot Lefranc – being asked "S'il se mêle pas de curiosité?" [if he meddles with curiosities] – admits: "Il se mêle de les savoir et de les enseigner, et depuis a dit qu'il ne se mêle point de les démonter ni de les pratiquer. Il sait la néomance [sic], la chiromancie, la physionomie", *Interrogatoire de l'abbé Lefranc. Du 9 juillet 1680, à Vincennes, apud* Ravaisson (1866–1905, V, 240) [He meddles in knowing and teaching them, and later he said that he does not at all meddle in showing or practising them. He knows neomance [sic], palmistry, physiognomy].
20 *Inerrogatoire de Madame Dufontet. Du28 janvier 1680, à Vincennes, apud* Ravaisson (1866–1905, VI, 112–113).

2 La Voisin – a real soothsayer on the scene in *La Devineresse* (1679)

Catherine Deshayes, called *La Voisin*, immortalised as Madame Jobin[21] in the comedy *La Devineresse* (1679),[22] written in collaboration by Thomas Corneille (1625–1709) and Donneau de Visé (1638–1710).[23] As the authors remember in the prologue to the reader ("Au lecteur") of the printed edition, the play premiered on 19 November 1679 at the Théâtre Guénégaude, had an immense success: "Le succès de cette Comédie a esté si grand, qu'il s'en est peu veu de semblables. On y a couru, & on y court encor tous les jours en foule"[24] [The success of this comedy was so great that you seldom saw anything comparable. People came in droves and still do]. The comedy rotates around Madame Jobin, who deceives a whole series of people with her tricks until the Marquis, a skeptical character, exposes her to the entire eyes of the world. At the very beginning of the play, the Marquis tries to convince the widow he wants to marry that Madame Jobin is a cheater:

> LE MARQUIS. [. . .] Il est vray, Madame, que vous m'auriez épargné ce deguisement, si vous donniez moins dans les artifices de vostre Devineresse, qui ne vous dit toutes les fadaises qui vous font peur, que pour attraper vostre Argent.

---

21 "La devineresse, qui est le principal personnage de la pièce, n'était autre que la Voisin, de qui Corneille et Visé déformèrent légèrement le nom en appelant leur devineresse Mme Jobin. On trouve dans la comédie l'écho des réponses que la sorcière fit devant les commissaires de la Chambre ardente, ce qui indique l'intervention de Nicolas de La Reynie. Le principal compère de la Voisin s'appelait Du Buisson, celui de Mme Jobin s'appelle Du Clos. Les pratiques sont les mêmes, mais ridiculisées par les auteurs, qui font de leur Mme Jobin une simple intrigante qui n'a d'autre préoccupation que d'attraper les écus des bonnes gens. Par le fond du caractère, nous sommes donc loin de la terrible devineresse de la Villeneuve-sur-Gravois." (Funck-Brentano 1900, 303) [La devineresse, who is the main character of the play, was none other than *La Voisin*, whose name Cornelius and Aimee slightly distorted when they called their soothsayer *Mrs. Jobin*. We find in the comedy the echo of the declarations that the sorceress made in front of the commissioners of the *Chambre ardente*, which points to an intervention on the part of Nicolas de La Reynie. *La Voisin*'s main companion's name was Du Buisson, while that of Mrs. Jobin's is Du Clos. The practices are the same, but ridiculed by the authors, who make their Mrs Jobin a mere schemer whose only concern is to snatch some coins off righteous people. At the core of the character, we are thus far away from the terrible diviner of Villeneuve-sur-Gravois].

22 The play was first published by Yarrow (1971) and, more recently, by Prest (2007). On *La Devineresse*, also see the studies by Paige (2000), Steinberger (2003), Poirson (2004), Clarke (2006), Prest (2007), Rudall (2010), Brooks (2014) and Gernert (2017a).

23 On this author see Vincent (1987).

24 Cf. *La Devineresse*, ed. Prest (2007, 30).

LA COMTESSE. Vous me croyez donc sa Dupe?

LE MARQUIS. Est-ce que vous ne luy donnez rien?

LA COMTESSE. Il faut bien que chacun vive de son Mestier.

LE MARQUIS. Le mestier est beau de parler au Diable, selon vous s'entend, Madame; car je ne suis pas persuadé que le Diable se communique aisément. A dire vray, j'admire la plûpart des Femmes. Elles ont une délicatesse d'esprit admirable; ce n'est qu'en les pratiquant qu'on en peut avoir, & elles ont le foible de courir tout ce qu'il y a de Devins.

LA COMTESSE. Ce sont tous Fourbes?

LE MARQUIS. Fourbes de Profession, qui ne sçavent rien, & qui ébloüissent les Crédules.[25]

[MARQUIS. . . . It is true, Madam, that you would have spared me this disguise, if you had given less heed to the artifices of your Soothsayer, who only tells you all the nonsense that frightens you, to seize your money.

COUNTESS. You think I'm her dupe?

MARQUIS. Aren't you giving him anything?

COUNTESS. Everyone has to live off his profession.

MARQUIS. It is beautiful to speak to the Devil, according to you, Madam; for I am not persuaded that the Devil communicates himself easily. To tell you the truth, I admire most women. They have an admirable delicacy of spirit; just by relating to them you'll be a beneficiary of this, and they have a weakness for running to all kinds of fortune tellers.

COUNTESS. Are they all swindlers?

MARQUIS. Professional swindlers, who know nothing, and who cheat the gullible.]

The audience has been aware of the fact that Madame Jobin is an imposter since the opening scene.[26]

Like her historical model, the protagonist of the dramatic adaptation practices chiromancy[27] and physiognomy. In the second act, she reads the lines in

---

25 Cf. *La Devineresse* I. 5, ed. Prest (2007, 38–39).
26 As Wörsdörfer correctly observes, "wird die Hauptfigur in *La Devineresse* also gerade nicht durch ihre magische Kompetenz etabliert, sondern von vornherein als schauspielernde Betrügerin gebrandmarkt und entlarvt" (2019, 238) [the main character in *La Devineresse* is not established by her magical competence, but is branded and exposed as an acting fraud from the start].
27 Cf. *La Devineresse* I. 6, ed. Prest (2007, 41): "MME JOBIN [. . .] je n'aimerois pas qu'on dist dans le Monde que je me mesle de plus que de regarder dans la main" [MME JOBIN . . . I wouldn't want people to spread the news that I'm involved in anything other than reading palms].

the hand of a marquess who accuses her of cheating on people and wants to put her to the test:

> MME JOBIN. Il me faudroit plus d'adresse pour cela que pour leur dire la verité.
>
> LA MARQUISE. Voyons si vous pourrez me la dire. Voila ma main.
>
> MME JOBIN. Toutes les lignes marquent beaucoup de bonheur.
>
> LA MARQUISE. Passons, cela est general.
>
> MME JOBIN. Vous estes Veuve, & parmy beaucoup d'Amans que vous avez, il y en a un qui vous touche plus que les autres, quoy qu'il soit le plus jaloux. [. . .]
>
> LA MARQUISE. C'est quelque chose que cela.
>
> MME JOBIN. Il est absent depuis quelque temps, & vous l'avez assez maltraité pour craindre que l'éloignement ne vous le dérobe.
>
> LA MARQUISE. Cela peut estre.[28]

> [MME JOBIN. I would need more skill for that than to tell them the truth.
>
> MARQUESS. Let's see if you can tell me. Here's my hand.
>
> MME JOBIN. All lines show plenty of bliss
>
> MARQUESS. Anyway, this is general.
>
> MME JOBIN. You are a widow, and among the many lovers you have, there is one who touches you more than the others, no matter how jealous he may be.
>
> MARQUESS. That's something.
>
> MME JOBIN. He's been out of town for some time, and you've treated him badly enough to fear that being away from you might take him away from you.
>
> MARQUESS. That may be.]

The fortune teller knows her customer's circumstances from the outset and pretends to read this information from the lines of her hand, a trick of which the audience is fully aware.

On another occasion in the third act, Mme Jobin asks the countess to remove her mask, because it is her face rather than her hands that provides her with informatio n: "Je m'arreste plus aux traits du visage qu'aux lignes des mains"[29] [I am more interested in the features of the face than in the lines of

---

28 *La Devineresse* II, 10, ed. Prest (2007, 74).
29 *La Devineresse* III, 4, ed. Prest (2007, 95). Clarke (2006, 227) compares this scene with what *La Vigoureux* allegedly said to Madame Poulaillon.

the hand]. Although Madame Jobin knows about physiognomy and chiromancy and other practices that could be considered effective in the 17th century, what the piece highlights is the ingenuity of the deceptions and the naivety of her clients. In spite of the fact that the protagonist is a character of utmost modernity, she uses magical objects like a mirror or an enchanted sword that do not have to do with real accusations[30] but come from the literary imaginary, in the former case from the Calderonian comedy *El astrólogo fingido* (1623–1625).[31] In this context, it should be remembered that Thomas Corneille wrote an adaptation of this comedy under the title of *Le feint astrologue* (1651). *La Devineresse* is, like Calderón's early comedy, a play of entertainment that is characterised, as Folger rightly points out by "una aparente o presunta falta de profundidad filosófica" (2017, 97) [an apparent or alleged lack of philosophical depth]. Rodríguez-Gallego (2017, 234) shows by the example of this comedy that Calderón "no era, o no era únicamente, ese autor serio, grave y ceñudo solo amigo de tragedias sangrientas, dramas filosóficos y autos sacramentales, sino también uno de los más hábiles constructores de universos lúdicos y de ingeniosos enredos" [was not, or was not only, that serious, serious and somber author who was only a friend of bloody tragedies, philosophical dramas and *autos sacramentales*, but also one of the most skilful builders of playful universes and ingenious entanglements]. It probably was this "funny" Calderón who may have influenced *La Devineresse* in the playful approach to the fictionalization of a fortune teller. The two French authors do not care much about alerting their audience to the danger of the magic arts. Their comedy premiered the same year as theologian Jean Baptiste Thiers published his *Traité des superstitions* which shows that the papal bulls

---

30 See Yarrow in the introduction to his critical edition (1971, XVI-XVII): "La façon dont les auteurs ont traité leur sujet est intéressante. Ils ont écarté tout le côté criminel, sacrilège, macabre et répugnant des véritables devineresses. Mme Jobin ne s'occupe pas d'avortements, ne vend pas des poisons, ne fait pas célébrer de messes noires; le diable qu'elle fait paraître à ses clients est un *bon diable* en chair et en os [. . .] Mme Voisin a donc été transformée en fourbe, en une espèce de Mascarille ou de Scapin; aussi ingénieuse que les valets de Molière, elle n'est guère plus méchante". [The way the authors treated their subject is interesting. They dismissed the entire criminal, sacrilegious, macabre and repulsive side of true fortune tellers. Mrs. Jobin does not do abortions, does not sell poisons, does not celebrate black masses; the devil she makes her clients see is a good devil in the flesh. . . Mme Voisin has thus been transformed into a deceiver, into a kind of Mascarille or Scapin; as ingenious as Molière's valets, she is not much more wicked]. Also see Brooks (2014, 275): "Fausse enchanteresse, magicienne frauduleuse, elle n'est pas dotées des sinistres caractéristiques de la Voisin, celles d'être bel et bien une meurtrière, une avorteuse, une empoisonneuse, une diseuse de messes noires [. . .]". [False enchanter, fraudulent magician, she is not endowed with the sinister characteristics of La Voisin, those of being a murderer, an abortionist, a poisoner, a celebrator of black messes . . .].
31 See Gernert (2017a, 257).

against the magical arts by Sixtus V (*Coeli et Terrae Creator Deus*, 1586), Gregory XV (*Omnipotentis Dei*, 1623) or Urban VIII (*Inscrutabilis iudiciorum*, 1631) were not able to eradicate divinatory practices:

> Le Concile Provincial de Toulouse en 1590 ordonne que l'on punisse rigoureusement selon les Canons de l'Église tous les sorciers, soit ecclésiastiques, soit laïques; et que l'on avertisse souvent le peuple de ne pas se servir de leur art, de ne pas leur demander des remèdes dans les maladies et de ne pas consulter les trompeuses divinations des diseurs d'horoscopes. Il ordonne aussi ensuite aux confesseurs et aux prédicateurs, de déraciner des esprits des fidèles par fréquentes exhortation et par de bonnes raisons, les vaines pratiques qui se sont introduites dans l'Église par l'ignorance et la simplicité des hommes, pour chasser les maladies d'une manière superstitieuse. (Thiers 1697, 50–51)[32]

> [The Provincial Council of Toulouse in 1590 orders that all sorcerers, both ecclesiastical and lay, be rigorously punished according to the Canons of the Church; and that the people be often warned not to use their art, not to ask them for cures for illnesses and not to consult the deceptive divinations of the horoscope tellers. It also orders confessors and preachers to uproot from the minds of the faithful, by frequent exhortation and with good reasoning, the vain practices which have entered the Church through ignorance and the simplicity of men, in order to drive out diseases with superstition.]

These warnings are not reflected in the comedy, which is a long way distant from the clearly dogmatic intention of many of Calderon's works.

---

32 See for Thiers' anti-superstitious treatise Cameron (2010, 287–290).

Epilogue

There's no art To find the mind's construction in the face (Macbeth)[1]

The starting point of my study was a revision of the ancient and medieval physiognomic manuals that shared the European book market in the Golden Age with an enormous number of recently created books on disciplines that were considered to be attached to the aforementioned physiognomy, linked to the reading of the body and the hand. It was necessary to determine in some detail which were the different ancient and medieval texts – from Aristotle to Michael Scott – dedicated to the interpretation of body signs in order to trace their diffusion – both in the original Greek and Latin and in the different vernacular translations – in early modern times and thus document the surprising continuity of classical and medieval physiognomic thought. Its knowledge and use lasted longer than one might think; and this is because in spite of the advent of the Cartesian dualist concept, which with the separation of body (*res extensa*) and soul (*res cogitans*) invalidates the conceptual basis said semiotic practices, the legibility of the human body did not cease to be an attractive idea for most of the 17th century. Those materials provided me with a documentary basis to be able to rethink the way in which the golden theatre represents the human body and the extent to which the external aspect of a character is indicative of its interiority and therefore meaningful. A large number of authors from different fields (in the first instance theologians, but also jurists and many scholars with an academic background in medicine) were determined to condemn or defend physiognomy and to differentiate it from palmistry and metoposcopy. The complex casuistry in which these authors explain themselves is by no means homogeneous, although some arguments such as free will are quite frequently repeated. The controversy about the legitimacy and validity of the reading of the body is also developed on stage where a wide variety of positions are orchestrated. The physiognomists and chiromancers that swarm through the golden theatre draw the attention of the spectators to the complexity of the textual (and extratextual) world, but also to the instability of the knowledge they embody. The characters who are bearers of occult knowledge often become spokesmen for the scepticism of their creators and, as the post-Tridentine struggle against any kind of deterministic

---

1 Shakespeare, *Macbeth* I, 4, vv. 11–12, ed. Braunmuller (1997, 119).

approach becomes more insistent, they are increasingly instrumentalised in the fight against heterodoxy; in this sense, the defence of Catholic orthodoxy on the stage reaches its peak in the Calderonian theatre. Physiognomic determinism had to clash with don Pedro's obstinacy in repeatedly staging the dogma of free will with images of great dramatic and aesthetic force.

Bibliography

Primary sources

Adamantius. *Adamantii Sophistae Physiognomicon*. Basel: Robert Winter, 1544.
Alemán, Mateo. *Guzmán de Alfarache*. Ed. Francisco Rico. Barcelona: Planeta, 1983.
Anonymous. "Aucto de finamiento de Jacob." *Colección de autos, farsas y coloquios del siglo XVI*. Ed. Léo Rouanet. Barcelona / Madrid: L'Avenç / M. Murillo, 1901. Vol. 1. 200–216.
Anonymous. "Aucto de la huida a Egipto." *Colección de autos, farsas y coloquios del siglo XVI*. Ed. Léo Rouanet. Barcelona /Madrid: L'Avenç / M. Murillo, 1901. Vol. 2. 374–387.
Anonymous. *Libro del invencible caballero Lepolemo*. Sevilla: Francisco Pérez, [1550?], available online http://trobes.uv.es (visited on 3.3.2011).
Aretino, Pietro. "Lo Ipocrito." *Edizione Nazionale delle opere di Pietro Aretino. Vol. 3. Teatro 2*. Ed. Giovanna Rabitti, Enrico Garavelli and Carmine Boccia. Roma: Salerno, 2010. 153–338.
Argensola, Lupercio Leonardo de. *Tragedias*. Ed. Luigi Giuliani. Zaragoza: Prensas Universitarias, 2009.
Ariosto, Ludovico. *Le commedie. Volume primo*. Ed. Andrea Gareffi. Torino: UTET, 2007.
Aristotle (attributed). *Fisiognomía. Fisiólogo*. Ed. Carmen Calvo Delcán and Teresa Martínez Manzano. Madrid: Gredos, 1999.
Aristotle (attributed). *Fisiognomica. Anonimo Latino, De physiognomonia liber*. Ed. Giampiero Raina. Milano: Rizzoli, 1993, ²1994.
Aristotle (attributed). *Fisiognomica: testo greco a fronte*. Ed. Maria Fernanda Ferrini. Milano: Bompiani, 2007.
Aristotle (attributed). *Le Secret des Secrets. Traduction du XVe siècle*. Ed. Denis Lorée. Paris: Champion, 2017.
Aristotle (attributed). "Physiognomonica." Aristotle. *The Complete Works of Aristotle (The Revised Oxford Translation)*. Ed. Jonathan Barnes. Princeton: Princeton UP, 1984.
Aristotle (attributed). *Physiognomonica. Aristoteles – Werke in deutscher Übersetzung*. Ed. Sabine Vogt. München: Oldenbourg Akademie-Verlag, 1999. Vol. 18.
Aristotle (attributed). *Physiognomonica. Translatio Bartholomaei de Messana*. Ed. Lisa Devriese. Turnhout: Brepols, 2019.
Aristotle (attributed). *Secreto de los secretos. Poridat de las poridades. versiones castellanas del Pseudo-Aristóteles Secretum Secretorum*. Ed. Hugo O. Bizzarri. Valencia: Universitat, 2010.
Aristotle (attributed). *The Secreto de los secretos. A Castilian version*. Ed. Philip B. Jones. Potomac: Scripta Humanistica, 1995.
Biondo, Michelangelo. *Conoscenza dell uomo dall aspetto esteriore*. Ed. Lucia Rodler. Roma: Vignola, 1995.
Boaistuau, Pierre. *Histoires prodigieuses*. Ed. Stephen Bamforth and Jean Céard. Genève: Droz, 2010.
Boaistuau, Pierre. *Historias Prodigiosas y Maravillosas*. Trans. Andrea Pescioni. Madrid: Sánchez, 1603.
Boccaccio, Giovanni. *Decameron*. 2 vol. Ed. Vittore Branca. Firenze: Le Monnier, 1951.
Boyl, Carlos. "Del mismo don Carlos Boil a un Licenciado que deseaba hacer comedias. Romance." *Norte de la poesia española*. Valencia: Felipe Mey, 1616.
Bruno, Giordano. *Candelaio*. Ed. Isa Guerrini Angrisani. Milano: Rizzoli, 1976.

Bruno, Giordano. "Candelaio." *Opere italiane di Giordano Bruno*. Ed. Giorgio Bárberi Squarotti. Torino: UTET, 2002. Vol. 1.
Calderón de la Barca, Pedro. *"Apolo y Climene." Comedias IV*. Ed. Sebastian Neumeister. Madrid: Castro, 2010. 1039–1162.
Calderón de la Barca, Pedro. *El astrólogo fingido*. Ed. Fernando Rodríguez-Gallego. Madrid / Frankfurt: Iberoamericana / Vervuert, 2011.
Calderón de la Barca, Pedro. *El jardín de Falerina. Auto sacramental*. Ed. Luís Galván and Carlos Mata Induráin. Pamplona / Kassel: Universidad de Navarra / Reichenberger, 2007.
Calderón de la Barca, Pedro. *"El jardín de Falerina. Comedia." Comedias V*. Ed. José María Ruano de la Haza. Madrid: Castro, 2010. 769–834.
Calderón de la Barca, Pedro, Antonio Coello Ochoa, and Francisco Rojas Zorrilla. *El jardín de Falerina*. Ed. Felipe B. Pedraza Jiménez and Rafael González Cañal. Barcelona: Octaedro, 2010.
Calderón de la Barca, Pedro. *"El mayor encanto, amor." Comedias II*. Ed. Santiago Fernández Mosquera. Madrid: Castro, 2007. 9–106.
Calderón de la Barca, Pedro. *El tesoro escondido*. Ed. A. Robert Lauer. Kassel: Reichenberger, 2012.
Calderón de la Barca, Pedro. *"Hado y divisa de Leonido y Marfisa." Comedias V*. Ed. José María Ruano de la Haza. Madrid: Castro, 2010. 85–232.
Calderón de la Barca, Pedro. *La devoción de la Cruz y el Mágico Prodigioso*. Ed. Ángel Valbuena Prat. Madrid: Espasa-Calpe, 1931.
Calderón de la Barca, Pedro. *La devoción de la cruz*. Ed. Ángel Valbuena-Prat. Madrid: Espasa-Calpe, 1931.
Calderón de la Barca, Pedro. *La devoción de la cruz*. Ed. Manuel Delgado. Madrid: Cátedra, 2000.
Calderón de la Barca, Pedro. *La devoción de la cruz*. Ed. Adrián J. Sáez. Madrid / Frankfurt: Iberoamericana / Vervuert, 2014.
Calderón de la Barca, Pedro. *La vida es sueño*. Ed. Ciriaco Morón. Madrid: Cátedra, 1984.
Calderón de la Barca, Pedro. *Los encantos de la culpa*. Ed. Juan Manuel Escudero. Pamplona / Kassel: Universidad de Navarra / Reichenberger, 2004.
Calderón de la Barca, Pedro. *"Los tres mayores prodigios." Comedias II*, Ed. Santiago Fernández Mosquera. Madrid: Castro, 2007. 989–1125.
Calderón de la Barca, Pedro. *Life is a Dream*. Trans. Gregary J. Racz. New York: Penguin Book, 2006.
Calderón de la Barca, Pedro. "Love, the greatest enchantment." "The sorceries of sin." "The devotion of the Cross". Trans. Denis Florence MacCarthy. London: Longmann, 1861.
Calvete de Estrella, Juan Cristóbal. *El felicíssimo viaje del muy alto y muy poderoso príncipe don Phelippe*. Ed. José Luis Gonzalo Sánchez-Molero and Paloma Cuenca Muñoz. Madrid: Sociedad Estatal para la Conmemoración de los Centenarios de Felipe II y Carlos V, 2001.
Campanella, Tommaso. *Dalla metaphysica. Profezia, divinazione, estasi*. Ed. Germana Ernst. Soveria Mannelli (Catanzaro): Rubbettino, 2007.
Campanella, Tommaso, *Del Senso delle cose e della magia*. Ed. Antonio Bruers. Bari: Laterza, 1925.
Cervantes, Miguel de. *Comedias y tragedias*. 2 vol. Ed. Luis Gómez Canseco. Madrid: RAE, 2015.
Cervantes, Miguel de. *Entremeses*. Ed. Alfredo Baras Escolá. Madrid: RAE, 2012.
Cervantes, Miguel de. *"Los baños de Argel."*. Ed. Alfredo Baras Escolá. *Comedias y tragedias*. Ed. Luis Gómez Canseco. Madrid: RAE, 2015. Vol. 1. 241–361.

[Cervantes, Miguel de]. *"Los dos habladores." Orígenes del teatro español*. Ed. Leandro Fernández de Moratín. Paris: Baudry, 1838. 501–504.
Cervantes, Miguel de. *"Pedro de Urdemalas."* Ed. Adrián J. Sáez. *Comedias y tragedias*. Ed. Luis Gómez Canseco. Madrid: RAE, 2015. Vol. 1. 795–906.
Cicero, Marcus Tullius. *Sobre la adivinación. Sobre el destino. Timeo*, trad. Ángel Escobar. Madrid: Gredos, 1999.
Cicero, Marcus Tullius. *Über die Wahrsagung = De divinatione. Lateinisch – deutsch*. Ed. Christoph Schäublin. Darmstadt: Wissenschaftliche Buchgesellschaft, 1991.
Cocles, Bartolomeo. *Absolutissima ratio chiromantiae*. Strasbourg: Johann Albrecht, 1536.
Corneille, Thomas, and Jean Donneau de Visé. *La devineresse*. Ed. Philip J. Yarrow. Exeter: University, 1971.
Corneille, Thomas, and Jean Donneau de Visé. *La devineresse, ou les faux enchantemens*. Ed. Julia Prest. London: MHRA, 2007.
Cortés, Jerónimo. *Fisonomía natural y varios secretos de naturaleza*. Ed. Amaranta Saguar. Trier: Romanica Treverensis, 2017, available online http://hispanistik.uni-trier.de/v-machine/JeronimoCortes/FisonomiaNatural.xml (visited on 14. 6.2020).
Corvo de Mirandola, Andrea. *Arte de Chiromantia*. Ed. M.ª Isabel de Páiz Hernández. Salamanca: Q ediciones, 2006.
Crollius, Oswaldus, *Traicté des signatures*, Lyon, Pierre Drobet, 1624, available online http://gallica.bnf.fr/ark:/12148/bpt6k65570z.image.r=Crollius.f2.langEN (visited on 3.3.2011).
Cueva, Juan de la. *Exemplar poético*. Ed. José María Reyes Cano. Sevilla: Alfar, 1986.
Della Porta, Giovan Battista. *De ea naturalis physiognomoniae parte quae ad manuum lineas spectat libri duo*. Ed. Oreste Trabucco. Napoli: Edizioni Scientifiche Italiane, 2003.
Della Porta, Giovan Battista. *De humana physiognomonia libri sex – volume I*. Ed. Alfonso Paolella. Napoli: Edizioni Scientifiche Italiane, 2011.
Della Porta, Giovan Battista. *Della fisionomia dell'uomo libri sei – volume II*. Ed. Alfonso Paolella. Napoli: Edizioni Scientifiche Italiane, 2013.
Donatus, Aelius. "De comoedia." *Aeli Donati qvod fertvr Commentvm Terenti*. Ed. Paul Weßner. Leipzig: Teubner, 1902. Vol. I. 22–31.
Dovizi da Bibbiena, Bernardo. *La Calandria*. Ed. Carlo Téoli. Forni: Bologna, 1974.
Erasmo, Desiderio. *Moria de Erasmo Roterodamo*. Ed. Jorge Ledo and Harm den Boer. Leiden: Brill, 2014.
Förster, Richard (ed.). *Scriptores physiognomonici Graeci et Latini*. 2 vol. Leipzig: Teubner, 1893.
Fontaine, Charles. *Epitome des trois premiers livres de Artemidorus*. Lyon: Jean de Tournes, 1546.
Garzoni, Tomaso. *La piazza universale di tutte le professioni del mondo*. Ed. Paolo Cherchi and Beatrice Collina. Torino: Einaudi, 1996.
Giovio, Paolo. *Elogia*. Roma: Istituto Poligrafo dello Stato, 1972.
Guillén de Ávila, Diego. *"Égloga ynterlocutoria." Sieben spanische dramatische Eklogen*. Ed. Eugen Kohler. Dresden: Buchdruckerei des Waisenhauses in Halle an der Saale, 1911. 236–265.
Gundissalinus, Dominicus. *De divisione philosophiae*. Ed. Alexander Fidora. Freiburg: Herder, 2007.
Hartlieb, Johannes. *Das Buch der verbotenen Künste*. Ed. Falk Eisermann and Eckhard Graf. München: Diederichs, 1998.

Hoyland, Robert (ed.). "A new edition and translation of the Leiden Polemon." *Seeing the face, seeing the soul: Polemon's physiognomy from classical antiquity to medieval Islam.* Ed. Simon Swain. Oxford: Oxford UP, 2007. 329–463.

Huarte de San Juan, Juan. *Examen de ingenios para las ciencias.* Ed. Guillermo Serés. Madrid: Cátedra, 1989.

Hugh of San Victor. *Didascalicon de studio legendi. El afán por el estudio.* Ed Carmen Muñoz Gamero and María Luisa Arribas Hernáez. Madrid: Biblioteca de Autores Cristianos, 2011.

Laundun d'Aigaliers, Pierre de. *L'art poétique français.* Ed. Joseph Dedieu. Toulouse: Siège des Facultés libres, 1909.

Lichtenberg, Georg Christoph. *Schriften und Briefe.* Vol. 1: *Sudelbücher, Fragmente, Fabeln, Verse.* Ed. Franz H. Mautner. Frankfurt am Main: Insel, 1983.

Liñán y Verdugo, Antonio. *Guía y avisos de forasteros que vienen a la Corte.* Ed. Edison Simons. Madrid: Ed. Nacional, 1980.

Lobo Lasso de la Vega, Gabriel. *Manojuelo de romances.* Ed. Ángel González Palencia and Eugenio Mele. Madrid: Saeta, 1942.

Marino, Giambattista. *La Galeria.* Ed. Marzio Pieri. Lavis (Trento): La Finestra, 2005.

Martínez, Enrico. *Reportorio de los tiempos y historia natural desta Nueva España.* México: En la emprenta del mesmo autor, 1606.

Marzio da Narni, Galeotto. *Chiromanzia (Chiromantia perfecta).* Ed. Mario Frezza. Napoli: Pironti, 1951.

Mey, Aurelio, *Norte de la poesía española*, Valencia, Felipe Mey, 1616, available online: http://opacplus.bsb-muenchen.de/search?oclcno=165688290 (visited on 1.6.2011).

Mira de Amescua, Antonio. "El arpa de David." Ed. Concepción García Sánchez. *Teatro completo.* Ed. Agustín de la Granja. Granada: Universidad, 2001. Vol. 1. 97–206.

Molière. *Œuvres complètes.* 2 vol. Ed. Georges Forestier. Paris: Gallimard, 2010.

Molière. "The Forc'd Marriage." *Select Comedies of Mr. de Molière in French and English.* London: John Watts, 1732. Vol. 7.

Molière. *The Miser (L'Avare).* Trans. Charles Heron Wall, London / New York: Ward / Lock & Bowden, 1894.

Molina, Tirso de. "Doña Beatriz de Silva." Ed. Manuel Tudela. *Cuarta parte de comedias I.* Ed. Ignacio Arellano. Pamplona: Instituto de Estudios Tirsianos, 1999. 833–1152.

Molina, Tirso de. "El amor médico." Ed. Blanca Oteiza. *Cuarta parte de comedias I.* Ed. Ignacio Arellano. Pamplona: Instituto de Estudios Tirsianos, 1999. 651–832.

Molina, Tirso de. *El castigo del penseque. Quien calla, otorga.* Ed. Miguel Zugasti. Madrid: Cátedra, 2013.

Molina, Tirso de. *El vergonzoso en palacio.* Ed. Francisco de Ayala. Madrid: Castalia, 1971.

Molina, Tirso de. *El vergonzoso en palacio.* Ed. Everett W. Hesse. Madrid: Cátedra, 1983.

Molina, Tirso de. *El vergonzoso en palacio.* Ed. Enrique Rull Fernández. Madrid: Cátedra, 1986.

Molina, Tirso de. *El vergonzoso en palacio.* Ed. Blanca Oteiza. Madrid: RAE, 2012.

Molina, Tirso de. "Por el sótano y el torno." *Obras completas.* Ed. María del Pilar Palomo. Madrid: Castro, 2005. Vol. 4. 477–580.

Moreto, Agustín. "De fuera vendrá." *Comedias de Agustín Moreto. Primera parte de comedias II.* Ed. Delia Gavela García. Kassel: Reichenberger, 2010. 3–180.

Moreto, Agustín. "Lo que puede la aprehensión." *Comedias de Agustín Moreto. Primera parte de comedias IV.* Ed. Francisco Domínguez Matito. Kassel: Reichenberger, 2010. 399–590.

Palmireno, Juan Lorenzo. "Octavia." *Palmyreni Fragmenta. Fragmentos del teatro escolar de Palmireno (1562–1567).* Ed. Julio Alonso Asenjo. *TeatrEsco* 0 (2003): without pagination.

Paracelsus. *De Natura Rerum*. Straßburg: Jobin, 1584.
Pérez, Juan. *Teatro latino escolar. "Suppositi – Los supuestos" de Juan Pérez 'Petreyo' (ca. 1540)*. Ed. Antonio Cortijo Ocaña. Pamplona: Universidad de Navarra, 2001.
Peucer, Kaspar. *Commentarius de praecipuis divinationum generibus*. Wittenberg: Johann Krafft, 1553.
Porsia, Franco (ed.). *Antiche scienze del corpo. Il "Liber Phisionomiae" di Michele Scoto*. Taranto: Chimenti, 2009.
Pujasol, Esteban. *El sol solo, y para todos sol*. Madrid: Tres Catorce Diecisiete, 1980.
Pujasol, Esteban, *El sol solo, y para todos sol*. Madrid: Magalia, 2000.
Rabelais, François. *Pantagrueline prognostication pour l'an 1533*. Ed. Michael A. Screech. Genève: Droz, 1974.
Rapisarda, Stefano, and Rosa Maria Piccione (ed.). *Manuali medievali di chiromanzia*. Roma: Carocci, 2005.
Ricci, Agostino. *I tre tiranni*. Ed. Anna Maria Gallo. Milano: Il Polifilo, 1998.
Rhasis, Mohammed. *L'Almansore. Volgarizzamento fiorentino del XIV secolo*. Ed. Rosa Piro. Firenze: Sismel. Edizioni del Galluzzo, 2011.
Rhasis, Mohammed, *Liber medicinalis Almansoris. Edizione critica del volgarizzamento Laurenziano (Plut. LXXIII. Ms. 43)*. Ed. Mahmoud Salem Elsheikh. Roma: Aracne, 2016.
Río, Martín Antonio del. *Disquisitionum magicarum libri sex*. Mainz: Johann Albin, 1603.
Rojas, Fernando de (and 'antiguo autor'). *La Celestina. Tragicomedia de Calisto y Melibea*. Ed. Francisco J. Lobrera, Guillermo Serés, Paloma Díaz-Mas, Carlos Mota, Íñigo Ruiz Arzálluz and Francisco Rico. Barcelona: Crítica, 2000.
Rojas Zorrilla, Francisco de. "Santa Isabel, reina de Portugal." Ed. Elena Arenas Cruz. *Obras completas*. Ed. Felipe B. Pedraza Jiménez, Rafael González Cañal and Gemma Gómez Rubio. Cuenca: Universidad de Castilla-La Mancha, 2011. Vol. 3. 11–128.
Rueda, Lope de. *Compendio llamado "El Deleitoso" de Lope de Rueda, seguido del coloquio "Prendas de amor" (Logroño, 1588)*. Ed. Santiago U. Sánchez Jiménez and Francisco J. Sánchez Salas. Logroño: Instituto de Estudios Riojanos, 2006.
Rueda, Lope de. *Las cuatro comedias: Eufemia, Armelina, Los engañados, Medora*. Ed. Alfredo Hermenegildo. Madrid: Taurus, 1985.
Rueda, Lope de. *Las cuatro comedias*. Ed. Alfredo Hermenegildo. Madrid: Cátedra, 2001.
Ruiz de Alarcón y Mendoza, Juan. *La cueva de Salamanca. La prueba de las promesas*. Ed. Celsa Carmen García-Valdés. Madrid: Cátedra, 2013.
Ruiz de Alarcón y Mendoza, Juan. *Obras completas*. Ed. Agustín Millares Carlo. México: Fondo de Cultura Economica, 1957.
Ruiz de Alarcón y Mendoza, Juan. *Quien mal anda en mal acaba*. Ed. Ángel Martínez Blasco. Kassel: Reichenberger, 1993.
Sachs, Hans. "Die Rockenstuben." *Ausgewählte Fastnachtspiele*. Ed. Karl Pannier. Leipzig: Reclam, 1898. 27–36.
Salazar y Torres, Agustín, Juan de Vera Tassis y Villarroèl and Sor Juana Inés de la Cruz. *El encanto es la hermosura y el hechizo sin hechizo. La segunda Celestina*. Ed. Thomas Austin O'Connor. Binghamton: Medieval and Renaissance Texts and Studies, 1994.
Sánchez González de Herrero, María de las Nieves, and María de la Concepción Vázquez de Benito (ed.). *Tratado de fisonomía. Tratado de la forma de la generación de la criatura*. Salamanca: DLE. Artículos del Departamento de Lengua Española, 2009.
Scott, Michael. *Liber Particularis. Liber Physionomie*. Ed. Oleg Voskoboynikov. Firenze: Sismel. Edizioni del Galluzzo, 2019.

Shakespeare, William. *Macbeth*. Ed. A. R. Braunmuller. Cambridge: Cambridge UP, 1997.
Stelluti, Francesco (ed.). *Della fisionomia di tutto il corpo umano di Signor Giovanni Battista Della Porta ora brevemente in tavole sinottiche ridotta*. Roma: Vitale Mascardi, 1637.
Taille, Jean de la. "*De l'art de la tragédie.*" *Saul le furieux*. Ed. Elliott Forsyth. Paris: Didier, 1968.
Timoneda, Juan de. "*Comedia de Anfitrión. Traducción de Plauto.*" *Obras*. Madrid: Sociedad de Bibliófilos Españoles, 1947–1948. Vol. 1. 249–292.
Timoneda, Juan. "*Comedia llamada Aurelia.*" *Obras*. Ed. Eduardo Juliá Martínez. Madrid: Sociedad de bibliófilos españoles, 1948. Vol. 3. 153–216.
Tricasso, Patrizio, and Bartholomaeus Cocles. *Comentarios clarísimos sobre la quiromancia de Cocles hechos por Tricasso de Mantua*. Ed. Eustaquio Sánchez Salor and Elisa Ruiz García. Mérida: Editorial Regional de Extremadura, 2000.
Tuetey, Alexandre (ed.). *Journal d'un bourgeois de Paris. 1405–1449*. Paris: Champion, 1881.
Vega, Lope de. *Los amigos enojados y verdadera amistad*. Lisboa: Pedro Crasbeeck, 1603.
Vega, Lope de. *Arcadia, prosas y versos*. Ed. Antonio Sánchez Jiménez. Madrid: Cátedra, 2012.
Vega, Lope de. "*Auto de la vuelta de Ejipto.*" *Degli "Autos" di Lope de Vega Carpio*. Ed. Antonio Restori. Parma: R. Pellegrini, 1898. 1–7.
Vega, Lope de. "*De cosario a cosario.*" *Tres comedias madrileñas*. Ed. Juan Ignacio Ferreras. Madrid: Comunidad de Madrid, 1992.
Vega, Lope de. "*El amante agradecido.*" Ed. Omar Sanz and María Dolores Gómez Martínez. *Comedias de Lope de Vega. Parte X*. Ed. Ramón Valdés and María Morrás. Lérida: Milenio, 2010. Vol. 2. 633–767.
Vega, Lope de. "*El amigo por fuerza.*" Ed. Gonzalo Pontón and José Enrique Laplana Gil. *Comedias de Lope de Vega. Parte IV*. Ed. Luigi Giuliani and Ramón Valdés. Madrid: Gredos, 2002. Vol. 2. 925–1080.
Vega, Lope de. "*El arenal de Sevilla.*" Ed. Manuel Cornejo. *Comedias de Lope de Vega. Parte XI*. Ed. Laura Fernández and Gonzalo Pontón. Madrid: Gredos, 2012. Vol. 2. 461–612.
Vega, Lope de. "*El ausente en el lugar.*" Ed. Abraham Madroñal. *Comedias de Lope de Vega. Parte IX*. Lérida: Milenio, 2007. Vol. 1. 419–535.
Vega, Lope de. "*El bautismo del Príncipe de Marruecos.*" Ed. Gonzalo Pontón. *Comedias de Lope de Vega. Parte XI*. Ed. Laura Fernández and Gonzalo Pontón. Madrid: Gredos, 2012. Vol. 2. 793–960.
Vega, Lope de. *El bosque de amor. El labrador de la Mancha (autos sacramentales inéditos)*. Ed. Agustín de la Granja. Madrid. CSIC, 2000.
Vega, Lope de. "*El desconfiado.*" Ed. José Javier Rodríguez Rodríguez. *Comedias de Lope de Vega. Parte XIII*. Ed. Natalia Fernández Rodríguez. Madrid: Gredos, 2014. Vol. 1. 713–841.
Vega, Lope de. "*El duque de Viseo*". Ed. Manuel Calderón. *Comedias de Lope de Vega. Parte XI*. Ed. Victoria Pineda and Gonzalo Pontón. Madrid: Gredos, 2005. Vol. 2. 1033–1160.
Vega, Lope de. "*El marqués de Navas.*" *Obras de Lope de Vega publicadas por la RAE*. Ed. Emilio Cotarelo y Mori. Madrid: Sucesores de Rivadeneyra, 1894. Vol. 4. 477–506.
Vega, Lope de. "*El prodigioso príncipe transilvano*". *Obras de Lope de Vega publicadas por la RAE*. Ed. Emilio Cotarelo y Mori. Madrid: Tipografía de la Revista de Archivos, Bibliotecas y Museos, 1916. Vol. 1. 369–421.
Vega, Lope de. "*El rústico del cielo.*" *Comedias XIII*. Ed. Jesús Gómez and Paloma Cuenca Muñoz. Madrid: Turner, 1997. 393–499.
Vega, Lope de. *La Arcadia*. Ed. Edwin S. Morby. Valencia: Castalia, 1975.

Vega, Lope de. "*La boda entre dos maridos.*" Ed. José Roso Díaz. *Comedias de Lope de Vega. Parte IV*. Lérida: Milenio, 2002. Vol. 2. 793–923.
Vega, Lope de. "*La doncella Teodor.*" Ed. Julián González-Barrera. *Comedias de Lope de Vega. Parte IX*. Ed. Marco Presotto. Lérida: Milenio, 2007. Vol. 1. 167–304.
Vega, Lope de. *La doncella Teodor*. Ed. Julián González-Barrera. Kassel: Reichenberger, 2008.
Vega, Lope de. *La Dorotea*. Ed. Edwin S. Morby. Valencia: Castalia, 1968.
Vega, Lope de. *La Dorotea*. Ed. Donald McGrady. Madrid: RAE, 2011.
Vega, Lope de. *La hermosura de Angélica*. Ed. Marcella Trambaioli. Pamplona / Madrid / Frankfurt am Main: Universidad de Navarra / Vervuert, 2005.
Vega, Lope de. "*La inocente sangre.*" *Comedias escogidas*. Ed. Juan Eugenio Hartzenbusch. Madrid: Rivadeneyra, 1860. Vol. 4. 349–372.
Vega, Lope de. "*La prueba de los ingenios.*" Ed. Julián Molina. *Comedias de Lope de Vega. Parte IX*. Lérida: Milenio, 2007. Vol. 1. 41–164.
Vega, Lope de. "*Las justas de Tebas.*" *Comedias I*. Ed. Jesús Gómez and Paloma Cuenca Muñoz. Madrid: Turner, 1993. 739–816.
Vega, Lope de. *Las mujeres sin hombres*. Ed. Óscar García Fernández. León: Secretariado de Publicaciones, 2008.
Vega, Lope de. "*Lo que hay que fiar del mundo.*" Ed. Luis Sánchez Laílla and José Enrique Laplana Gil. *Comedias de Lope de Vega. Parte XII*. Ed. José Enrique Laplana Gil. Madrid: Gredos, 2013. Vol. 2. 339–484.
Vega, Lope de. *Los donaires de Matico*. Ed. Marco Presotto. Kassel: Reichenberger, 1994.
Vega, Lope de. "*Los españoles en Flandes.*" Ed. Antonio Cortijo Ocaña. *Comedias de Lope de Vega. Parte XIII*. Ed. Natalia Fernández Rodríguez. Madrid: Gredos, 2014. Vol. 2. 909–1108.
Vega, Lope de. "*Los hidalgos de aldea.*" *Obras de Lope de Vega publicadas por la RAE*. Ed. Emilio Cotarelo y Mori. Madrid: Tipografía de la *Revista de Archivos, Bibliotecas y Museos*, 1916–1930. Vol. 6. 288–323.
Vega, Lope de. *Los locos de Valencia*. Ed. José Luis Aguirre. Barcelona: Aubí, 1977.
Vega, Lope de. *Los locos de Valencia*. Ed. Hélène Tropé. Madrid: Castalia, 2003.
Vega, Lope de. "*Los melindres de Belisa.*" Ed. Jorge León. *Comedias de Lope de Vega. Parte IX*. Lérida: Milenio, 2007. Vol. 3. 1467–1600.
Vega, Lope de. "*Pobreza no es vileza.*" *Parte veinte de las Comedias de Lope de Vega Carpio*. Madrid: Juan González, 1627.
Vega, Lope de. *Rimas humanas y divinas del licenciado Tomé de Burguillos*. Ed. Macarena Cuiñas Gómez. Madrid: Cátedra, 2008.
Vega, Lope de. "*Roma abrasada.*" *Comedias VIII*. Ed. Jesús Gómez and Paloma Cuenca Muñoz. Madrid: Turner, 1994. 207–306.
Vega, Lope de. *Servir a señor discreto*. Ed. Frida Weber de Kurlat. Madrid: Castalia, 1975.
Vega, Lope de. "*Servir a señor discreto.*" Ed. José Enrique Laplana Gil. *Comedias de Lope de Vega. Parte XI*. Ed. Laura Fernández and Gonzalo Pontón. Madrid: Gredos, 2012. Vol. 1. 759–918.
Vega, Lope de. "*Virtud, pobreza y mujer.*" *Comedias escogidas*. Ed. Juan Eugenio Hartzenbusch. Madrid: Rivadeneyra, 1860. Vol. 4. 211–232.
Vélez de Guevara, Juan. *Los celos hacen estrellas*. Ed. John E. Varey and Norman D. Shergold. London: Támesis Books, 1970.
Vernay, Philippe (ed.). *Maugis d'Aigremont, chanson de geste*. Berne: Francke, 1980.
Vicente, Gil. *As obras de Gil Vicente*. 5 vol. Ed. José Camões. Lisboa: Universidad, 2002.

Vicente, Gil. *"Auto de las Gitanas:" Teatro castellano*. Ed. Manuel Calderón. Barcelona: Crítica, 1996. 263–273.
Vincent of Beauvais, *Speculum Naturale*, Venice, Hermann Liechtenstein, 1494, available online http://daten.digitale-sammlungen.de/~db/0005/bsb00056560/images/ (visited on 29.5.2020).

Secondary sources

Aercke, Kristiaan Paul Guido. "El rey planeta: *El mayor encanto* amor." *Gods of play baroque festive performances as rhetorical discourse*. Albany: State of New York UP, 1994. 139–164.
Agrimi, Jole. *Ingeniosa scientia nature. Studi sulla fisiognomica medievale*. Firenze: Sismel. Edizioni del Galluzzo, 2002.
Aguirre Felipe, Javier. *Historia de las itinerancias gitanas de la India a Andalucía*. Zaragoza: Institució Fernando el Católico, 2008.
Akasoy, Anna. "Arabic physiognomy as a link between astrology and medicine." *Astro-Medicine astrology and medicine, East and West*. Ed. Charles Burnett and Ronit Yoely-Tlalim. Firenze: Sismel. Edizioni del Galluzzo, 2008. 119–142.
Albarracín Teulón, Agustín. *La medicina en el teatro de Lope de Vega*. Madrid: CSIC, 1954.
Alborg, Concha. "El Teatro como propaganda en dos tragedias de Lope de Vega: *El Duque de Viseo* y el *Castigo sin venganza*." *Lope de Vega y los orígenes del teatro español*. Ed. Manuel Criado del Val. Madrid: EDI-6, 1981. 745–754.
Alonso, Amado. "Las prevaricaciones idiomáticas de Sancho." *Nueva Revista de Filología Hispánica* 2 (1948): 1–20.
Alonso Asenjo, Julio. "El nigromante en el teatro prelopista." *Comedias y comediantes. Estudios sobre el teatro clásico español*. Ed. Manuel Vicente Diago Moncholi and Teresa Ferrer. València: Universitat, 1991. 91–108.
Alonso Asenjo, Julio. "Los elementos mágicos del teatro de J. Lorenzo Palmireno." *La comedia de magia y de santos*. Ed. Francisco Javier Blasco, Ricardo De La Fuente Ballesteros, Ermanno Caldera and Joaquín Álvarez Barrientos. Gijón: Júcar, 1992. 33–50.
Alvar, Carlos. *Traducciones y traductores. Materiales para una historia de la traducción en Castilla durante la Edad Media*. Alcalá de Henares: Centro de Estudios Cervantinos, 2010.
Álvarez Sellers, María Rosa. "Formas renacentistas para una ideología barroca: el duque de Viseo, una tragedia de Lope de Vega de inspiración portuguesa." *Quaderns de filologia* 1 (1995): 69–86.
Álvarez Sellers, María Rosa. *Análisis y evolución de la tragedia española en el Siglo de Oro: La tragedia amorosa*. 3 vol. Kassel: Reichenberger, 1997.
Amezcua Gómez, José. "Naturaleza y cultura. *Totem y tabú* en *La devoción de la Cruz*." *Calderón, apóstol y hereje*. México: Difusión cultural UAM, 1982. 121–138.
Andrés, Christian. "Aspectos astrológicos en el teatro de Cervantes y de Lope de Vega." *Studia aurea*. Ed. Ignacio Arellano, Carmen Pinillos, Marc Vitse and Frédéric Serralta. Pamplona: Universidad de Navarra, 1996. Vol. 2. 23–32.
Andrés, Christian. "La metáfora del *theatrum mundi* en Pierre Boaistuau y Calderón." *Criticón* 91 (2004): 67–78.

Andrist, Debra D. *Deceit plus desire equals violence: a Girardian study of the Spanish "comedia"*. New York: Lang, 1989.
Andueza, María. "Libertad / destino en *La vida es sueño* de Calderón de la Barca." *Revista de la Universidad de México* 591 (2000): 88–95.
Annus, Amar (ed.). *Divination and interpretation of signs in the ancient world*. Chicago: Oriental Institute of the University of Chicago, 2010.
Antonucci, Fausta. "*Hado y divisa de Leonido y Marf*isa: obra última y compendio de la dramaturgia palatina de Calderón." *e-Spania* 18 (2014): without pagination.
Aphek, Edna, and Yishai Tobin. *The semiotics of fortune-telling*. Amsterdam: Benjamins, 1989.
Arellano, Ignacio. "Magos y prodigios en el escenario del Siglo de Oro." *En torno al teatro del Siglo de Oro*. Ed. José Juan Berbel. Almería: Instituto de Estudios Almerienses, 1996. 13–36.
Arellano, Ignacio. "El motivo del viaje en los autos sacramentales de Calderón, I: los viajes mitológicos." *Revista de Literatura* 73 (2011): 165–182.
Arias Careaga, Raquel. "*Pedro de Urdemalas*: otro ejemplo de libertad cervantina." *Annali di Ca' Foscari* 31 (1992): 43–59.
Armas, Frederick A. de. "The hunter and the twins: astrological imagery in *La Estrella de Sevilla*." *Bulletin of the Comediantes* 32 (1980): 11–20.
Armas, Frederick A. de. "Metamorphosis in Calderón's *El mayor encanto, amor*." *Romance Notes* 22 (1981): 208–212.
Armas, Frederick A. de. "The serpent star: Dream and horoscope in Calderón's *La vida es sueño*." *Forum for Modern Language Studies* 19 (1983): 208–223.
Armas, Frederick A. de. "El planeta más impío: Basilio's role in La vida es sueño." *Modern Language Review* 81 (1986a): 900–911.
Armas, Frederick A. de. "The betrayal of a mystery: Botticelli and Calderón's *Apolo y Climene*." *Romanische Forschungen* 92 (1986b): 304–323.
Armas, Frederick A. de. *The return of Astraea: an astral-imperial myth in Calderón*. Lexington: Kentucky UP, 1986c.
Armas, Frederick A. de. "The king's son and the golden dew: alchemy in Calderón's *La vida es sueño*." *Hispanic Review* 60 (1992): 301–319.
Armas, Frederick A. de. "*El sol sale a medianoche*: amor y astrología en *Las paredes oyen*." *Criticón* 59 (1993a): 119–126.
Armas, Frederick A. de. "The critical tower." *The Prince in the tower*. Ed. Frederick A. de Armas. Lewisburg / London / Mississauga / Cranbury: Bucknell UP / Associated UP, 1993b. 3–14.
Armas, Frederick A. de. "The enchantments of Circe: Dosso Dossi and Calderón's *El mayor encanto, amor*." *Calderón. Protagonista eminente del barroco europe*. Ed. Theo Reichenberger and Kurt Reichenberger. Kassel: Reichenberger, 2000. Vol. 1. 175–192.
Armas, Frederick A. de. "Segismundo / Philip IV: The politics of astrology in *La vida es sueño*." *Bulletin of the Comediantes* 53 (2001): 83–100.
Armas, Frederick A. de. "El rey astrólogo en Lope de Vega y Calderón." *El teatro clásico español a través de sus monarcas*. Ed. en Luciano García Lorenzo. Madrid: Fundamentos, 2006a. 119–134.
Armas, Frederick A. de. "Isis y el silencio hermético en *El vergonzoso en palacio* de Tirso de Molina." *Tirso, escuela de discreción*. Ed. Blanca Oteiza and Eva Galar. Pamplona: Instituto de estudios Tirsianos, 2006b. 9–26.
Armas, Frederick A. de. "Claves políticas en las comedias de Calderón: el caso de *El mayor encanto amor*." *Anuario Calderoniano* 4 (2011): 117–144.

Armas, Frederick A. de. "Timantes y la pintura que habla en *El mayor encanto, amor.*" *Anuario Calderonian* Extra 1 (2013): 97–113.
Armas, Frederick A. de. *La astrología en el teatro clásico europeo (siglos XVI–XVII)*. Madrid: Antígona, 2017.
Armstrong, A. M. "The methods of the Greek physiognomists." *Greece and Rome* 5 (1958): 52–56.
Arnaudo, Marco. "Alla palestra dell'intelletto: Una lettura del *Candelaio* di Giordano Bruno." *Italica* 84 (2007): 691–707.
Arróniz Báez, Othón. *La influencia italiana en el nacimiento de la comedia española*. Madrid: Gredos, 1969.
Aszyk, Urszula. "El jardín mágico y la magia del teatro: notas sobre la fiesta teatral palaciega *El jardín de Falerina.*" *Theatralia* 9 (2007): 107–122.
Aszyk, Urszula. "*Los locos de Valencia* de Lope de Vega: un paradigmático intento de dramatización y teatralización del discurso de la locura a finales del siglo XVI." *Itinerarios* 10 (2009): 45–63.
Aubrun, Charles V. "Une anticipation de Calderón: La television magique dans *El jardin de Falerina.*" *Homenaje: Estudios de filologia e historia literaria lusohispanas e iberoamericanas publicados para celebrar el tercer lustro del Instituto de Estudios Hispanicos, Portugueses e Iberoamericanos de la Universidad Estatal de Utrecht*. Den Haag: Van Goor Zonen, 1966. 51–59.
Autuori, Adele. "Testo latino e testo arabo della fisiognomica di Muhammad ibn Zakariya al-Razi." *Annali dell'Istituto Universitario Orientale di Napoli* 44 (1984): 29–40.
Aylward, E. T. "A question of values: The spiritual education of Segismundo in Calderón's *La vida es sueño.*" *Bulletin of the Comediantes* 54 (2002): 339–372.
Badaloni, Nicola. "I fratelli Della Porta e la cultura magica e astrologica a Napoli nel '500." *Studi Storici* 1 (1960): 431–448.
Balbiani, Laura. *La magia naturalis di Giovan Battista della Porta: lingua, cultura e scienza in Europa all'inizio dell'età moderna*. Bern: Lang, 2001.
Baltrusaitis, Jurgis. *Aberrations: quatre essais sur la légende des formes*. Paris: Oliver Perrin, 1957.
Bandera, Cesáreo, and René Girard. *Mimesis conflictiva: ficción literaria y violencia en Cervantes y Calderón*. Madrid: Gredos, 1975.
Baraz, Daniel. "Seneca, ethics, and the body: the treatment of cruelty in medieval thought." *Journal of the History of Ideas* 7 (1998): 195–215.
Barr, Alan. "Extension and excision: Imagistic and structural patterns in Giordano Bruno's *Il candelaio.*" *Texas Studies in Literature and Language* 13 (1971): 351–363.
Bartolomé Luises, Montserrat. "La crítica de Bruno en el *Candelaio* y los *Dialoghi Italiani.*" *Philosophica* 33 (2009): 119–158.
Barton, Tamsyn S. *Power and knowledge: astrology, physiognomics, and medicine under the Roman Empire*. Ann Arbor: Michigan UP, 1994.
Basile, Bruno. "*Riflessi dell'anima*. La fisiognomia prima e dopo Della Porta." *La "mirabile" natura. Magia e scienza in Giovan Battista Della Porta (1615–2015)*. Ed. Marco Santoro. Pisa / Roma: Fabrizio Serra, 2016. 57–70.
Baumbach, Sybille. *Let me behold thy face: Physiognomik und Gesichtslektüren in Shakespeares Tragödien*. Heidelberg: Winter, 2007.

Baumbach, Sibylle. "Scrutinizing Interfaces: Physiognomy as a Travelling Concept." *Travelling Concepts, Metaphors, and Narratives*. Ed. Sibylle Baumbach, Beatrice Michaelis and Ansgar Nünning. Trier: Wissenschaftlicher Verlag Trier, 2012a. 95–114.

Baumbach, Sybille. "Voice, face and fascination: The art pf physiognomy in *A midsummer night's dream*." *Shakespeare Survey* 65 (2012b): 77–91.

Beat Rudin, Ernst. "Variedades de teatralidad en Tirso de Molina: *El vergonzoso en palacio* y *La fingida Arcadia*." *El teatro dentro del teatro: Cervantes, Lope, Tirso y Calderón*. Ed. José Manuel. López de Abiada, Pedro Ramírez Molas and Irene Andres Suárez. Madrid: Verbum, 1997. 111–126.

Becker, Danièle. "*Hado y divisa de Leonido y de Marfisa*: adios a las tablas palaciegas de Calderón." *El siglo de Oro en escena. Homenaje a Marc Vitse*. Ed. Odette Gorsse and Frédéric Serralta. Toulouse: PUM, 2006. 53–63.

Belloni, Benedetta. "Lope de Vega y el encargo aprovechado. Algunas reflexiones sobre *El bautismo del Príncipe de Marruecos*, pieza de corte histórico-político." *Páginas que no callan: historia, memoria e identidad en la literatura hispánica*. Ed. Alejandro García-Reidy, Luis María Romeu Guallart and Eva Soler Sasera. València: Universitat, 2014. 89–100.

Benabu, Isaac. "*La devoción de la Cruz* y su *felice* fin." *Hacia Calderón*. Ed. Hans Flasche. Stuttgart: Steiner, 1988. 212–220.

Benedettini, Riccardo. "*Il Negromante* de l'Arioste traduit par Jean de La Taille." *Italique* 13 (2010): 81–104.

Bennett, Jolynn. "Antonio Pellegrini's translation of the *Moriae Encomium*." *Erasmus Studies* 4 (1984): 37–52.

Bergdolt, Klaus, and Walther Ludwig (ed.). *Zukunftsvoraussagen in der Renaissance*. Wiesbaden: Harrassowitz, 2005.

Bermann, Anne-Katrin. "*Por la mágica ciencia se causan tantos excesos*: Magia y moral en las comedias de Juan Ruiz de Alarcón." *Esoterismo y Brujería en la Literatura del Siglo de Oro*. Ed. María Luisa Lobato, Javier San José and Germán Vega. Alicante: Biblioteca Virtual Miguel de Cervantes, 2016. 23–44.

Berruezo Sánchez, Diana. "Amor, humor y equívocos en *El vergonzoso en palacio* de Tirso de Molina." *Anagnórisis* 3 (2011): 38–52.

Berthelot, Anne. "Maugis d'Aigremont, magicien ou amuseur public." *Burlesque et dérision dans les épopées de l'Occident médiéval*. Ed. Bernard Guidot. Paris: Les Belles Lettres, 1995. 321–332.

Biow, Douglas. "Manly matters: The theatricality and sociability of beards in Giordano Bruno's *Candelaio* and sixteenth-century Italy." *Journal of Medieval and Early Modern Studies* 40 (2010): 325–346.

Bizzarri, Hugo O. "Difusión y abandono del *Secretum secretorum* en la tradición sapiencial castellana de los siglos XIII y XIV." *Archives d'Histoire Doctrinale et Litteraire du Moyen Age* 63 (1996): 95–137.

Bizzarri, Hugo O. "Le *Secretum secretorum* en Espagne: de traité médical à miroir de prince." *Trajectoires européennes du "Secretum secretorum" du Pseudo-Aristote (XIIIe–XVIe siècle)*. Ed. Jean-Yves Tilliette, Margaret Bridges and Catherine Gaullier-Bougassas. Turnhout: Brepols, 2015. 187–214.

Blasi, Nicola De. "Bastiano di Francesco." *Dizionario Biografico degli Italiani* 7 (1970). http://www.treccani.it (visited on 9. 4.2020).

Bloch, Raymond. *La divination. Essai sur l'avenir et son imaginaire*. Paris: Fayard, 1991.

Blum, Paul Richard. "*Qualitates occultae*: zur philosophischen Vorgeschichte eines Schlüsselbegriffs zwischen Okkultismus und Wissenschaft." *Die okkulten Wissenschaften in der Renaissance*. Ed. August Buck. Wiesbaden: Harrassowitz, 1992. 45–64.
Blumenberg, Hans. *Die Lesbarkeit der Welt*. Frankfurt am Main: Suhrkamp, 1981.
Bouchet, Alain. "J.-B. Della Porta et la physiognomonie aux XVIe et XVIIe siècles." *Cahiers Lyonnais d'Histoire de la Médecine* 2 (1957): 13–42.
Boudet, Jean-Patrice. *Entre science et nigromance: astrologie, divination et magie dans l'Occident médiéval (XIIe–XVe siècle)*. Paris: Publications de la Sorbonne, 2006.
Boudet, Jean-Patrice, Martine Ostorero, and Agostino Paravicini Bagliani (ed.). *De Frédéric II à Rodolphe II. Astrologie, divination et magie dans les cours (XIIIe–XVIIe siècle)*. Firenze: Sismel. Edizioni del Galluzzo, 2017.
Boys-Stones, George. "Physiognomy and ancient psychological theory." *Seeing the face, seeing the soul: Polemon's physiognomy from classical antiquity to medieval Islam*. Ed. Simon Swain. Oxford: Oxford UP, 2007. 19–124.
Brasswell-Means, Laurel. "A new look at an old patient: Chaucer's *Summoner* and medieval physiognomia." *The Chaucer Review* 25 (1991): 266–275.
Brewer, Brian. "Las matemáticas sutiles o los límites del saber en *La vida es sueño*." *Bulletin of Spanish Studies* 88 (2011): 487–522.
Briggs, E. R. "Galeoto Marzio da Narni (1427?–1497?)." *Aspects du libertinisme au XIIe siècle. Actes du colloque international de Sommières*. Paris: Vrin, 1974. 75–84.
Brioso, Jorge. "¿Cómo hacer cosas con los enigmas? *La vida es sueño* o el drama del desengaño." *Bulletin of the Comediantes* 56 (2004): 55–75.
Brooks, William. "*La Devineresse* dans la *Notice nécrologique* de Thomas Corneille par Jean Donneau de Visé." *Thomas Corneille. Colloque international à l'occasion du tricentenaire de Thomas Corneille*. Ed. Myriam Dufour-Maître. Rouen: PU Rouen-Le Havre, 2014. 271–286.
Brunel, Magali. "*Sans la science, la vie est presque une image de la mort*: la place du discours scientifique dans l'esthétique verbale de Molière." *Littératures Classiques* 85 (2014): 155–170.
Buck, August (ed.). *Die okkulten Wissenschaften in der Renaissance*. Wiesbaden: Harrassowitz, 1992.
Bujanda, Jesús Martínez de. *Index de l'Inquisition Espagnole: 1551, 1554, 1559*, Sherbrooke / Genève: Centre d'études de la Renaissance Université de Sherbrooke / Droz, 1984. Vol. 5.
Bujanda, Jesús Martínez de. *Index de l'Inquisition Espagnole: 1583, 1584*, Sherbrooke / Genève: Centre d'études de la Renaissance Université de Sherbrooke / Droz, 1993. Vol. 6.
Bujanda, Jesús Martínez de. *Index des livres interdits. Thesaurus de la littérature interdite au XVIe siècle*. Sherbrooke / Genève: Centre d'études de la Renaissance Université de Sherbrooke / Droz, 1996. Vol. 10.
Bujanda, Jesús Martínez de, and Marcella Richter. *El índice de libros prohibidos y expurgados de la Inquisición Española (1551–1819)*. Madrid: Biblioteca de Autores Cristianos, 2016.
Bunes Ibarra, Miguel Ángel de, and Beatriz Alonso Acero. "Los Austrias y el norte de África: Muley Xeque en la corte de Felipe II." *De Maŷrit a Madrid Madrid y los árabes, del siglo IX al siglo XXI*. Ed. Daniel Gil Flores and Maria Dolores Algora Weber. Barcelona: Casa Árabe / Lunwerg, 2011. 98–107.
Buono Hodgart, Lia. "*Candelaio*: La commedia di un filosofo." *The Renaissance Theatre: Texts, Performance, Design, I: English and Italian Theatre*. Ed. Christopher Cairns. Aldershot: Ashgate, 1999. 160–167.

Burnett, Charles. "The earliest Chiromancy in the West." *Journal of the Warburg and Courtauld Institutes* 50 (1987): 192–195.

Burnett, Charles. "Michael Scott and the transmission of scientific culture from Toledo to Bologna via the court of Frederick II Hohenstaufen." *Micrologus* 2 (1994): 101–126.

Burnett, Charles. *Magic and divination in the Middle Ages. Texts and techniques in the Islamic and Christian worlds.* Aldershot: Variorum, 1996.

Burnett, Charles. "Filosofía natural, secretos y magia." *Historia de la ciencia y de la técnica en la corona de Castilla.* Ed. Luis García Ballester Valladolid, Junta de Castilla y León, 2002. Vol. 1. 95–144.

Burton, Grace. "The creation of myth in Calderón's *La devoción de la Cruz.*" *Revista de Estudios Hispánicos* 21 (1994): 9–24.

Cabrero Aramburo, Ana. "La figura de la Amazona entres obras de Lope de Vega." *"Scripta manent". Actas del I Congreso Internacional Jóvenes Investigadores Siglo de Oro.* Ed. Carlos Mata Induráin and Adrián J. Sáez. Pamplona: Universidad de Navarra, 2006. 61–69.

Cacho Blecua, Juan Manuel. "Las figuras de *Poridat de las poridades.*" *Revista de Poética Medieval* 30 (2016): 47–54.

Calderón, Manuel, and Joana Lloret Cantero. "La comunicación no verbal en los autos y en las farsas de Gil Vicente." *Actas do IV Congresso da Associação Hispânica de Literatura Medieval.* Ed. Aires Augusto Nascimento and Cristina Almeida. Lisboa: Cosmos, 1993. Vol. 3. 313–317.

Calvo, Sonsoles. "*La boda entre dos maridos*: Lope de Vega y Boccaccio." *El teatro italiano.* Ed. Joaquín Espinosa. València: Universitat, 1997. 117–123.

Cameron, Euan K. *Enchanted Europe. Superstition, reason, and religion 1250–1750.* Oxford: Oxford UP, 2010.

Camões, José. "El espacio escénico en el teatro de Gil Vicente: Invención e integración." *Los albores del teatro español.* Ed. Felipe B. Pedraza Jiménez and Rafael González Cañal. Cuenca: Universidad de Castilla-La Mancha, 1995. 155–172.

Campbell, Ysla. "Magia y hermetismo en *La cueva de Salamanca.*" *Texto y espectáculo.* Ed. Barbara Mujica. Lanham: UP of America, 1989. 11–24.

Campbell, Ysla. "Las conquistas del oro: honor y apariencia en *Pobreza no es vileza* de Lope de Vega." *El escritor y la escena.* México: Universidad Autónoma de Ciudad Juárez, 1994. 115–123.

Campbell, Ysla. "Del ser al deber ser: *El Duque de Viseo.*" *Teatro de Palabras* 1 (2007): 29–45.

Campbell, Ysla. "*El duque de Viseo* y *Las políticas* de Justo Lipsio." *Nuevos caminos del hispanismo.* Ed. Pierre Civil and Françoise Crémoux. Madrid / Frankfurt: Iberoamericana / Vervuert, 2010. Vol. 2, without pagination.

Campopiano, Michele. "La circulation du *Secretum secretorum* en Italie: la version vernaculaire du manuscrit de Florence, Biblioteca Nazionale Centrale, Magliabecchi XII. 4." *Trajectoires européennes du "Secretum secretorum" du Pseudo-Aristote (XIIIe–XVIe siècle).* Ed. Jean-Yves Tilliette, Margaret Bridges and Catherine Gaullier-Bougassas. Turnhout: Brepols, 2015. 243–256.

Canavaggio, Jean. *Cervantes.* Madrid: Espasa-Calpe, 1987.

Canavaggio, Jean. "La tragedia renacentista española: Formación y superación de un género frustrado." *Literatura en la época del Emperador.* Ed. Víctor García de la Concha. Salamanca: Universidad, 1988. 181–195.

Canonica de Rochemonteix, Elvezio. "Lope y los literatos italianos enla corte de Felipe III." *Anuario Lope de Vega* 6 (2000): 61–74.

Caputo, Cosimo. "La struttura del segno fisiognomico (G. B. Della Porta e l'universo culturale del Cinquecento)." *Il Protagora* 22 (1982): 63–102.

Cardona Castro, Ángeles. "Temas coincidentes en Calderón y Schiller: *La devoción de la Cruz* y *Die Räuber*." *Hacia Calderón*. Ed. Hans Flasche. Stuttgart: Steiner, 1988. 118–129.

Cardona Castro, Ángeles. "Iniciación al estudio de *El jardín de Falerina*, auto sacramental de Calderón." *Divinas y humanas letras, doctrina y poesía en los autos sacramentales de Calderón*. Ed. Ignacio Arellano, Carmen Pinillos, Blanca Oteiza and Juan Manuel Escudero. Kassel: Reichenberger, 1997. 25–43.

Cardoner, Antonio. "La fisiognomía hasta el siglo XIX." *Revista de Dialectología y Tradiciones Populares* 27 (1971): 81–95.

Cardoso Bernardes, José Augusto. "Pastores y filósofos en la corte de Portugal: La palabra velada en el teatro de Gil Vicente." *Studia Aurea* 4 (2010): without pagination.

Caro Baroja, Julio. *Historia de la fisiognómica: el rostro y el carácter*. Madrid: Istmo, 1988.

Caro Baroja, Julio. *Vidas mágicas e Inquisición*. 2 vol. Barcelona: Circulo de Lectores, 1990.

Caro Baroja, Julio. *Jardín de flores raras*. Barcelona: Círculo de Lectores, 1993.

Carrión, Gabriela. "*Burlas en tiempo de tantas veras*: Violence and humor in Lope de Vega's *Los melindres de Belisa*." *Bulletin of the Comediantes* 67 (2015): 15–31.

Casalduero, Joaquín. *Sentido y forma del teatro de Cervantes*. Madrid: Aguilar, 1951; reedition Madrid: Gredos, 1966.

Cascardi, Anthony J. *The limits of illusion. A critical study of Calderón*. Cambridge: Cambridge UP, 1984.

Case, Thomas E. "Parody, gender and dress in Lope's *La doncella Teodor*." *Bulletin of the Comediantes* 46 (1994): 187–206.

Castelli, Patrizia. "La chiromanzia tra divinazione e scienza normativa tra Medioevo ed Età Moderna." *L'art de la Renaissance entre science et magie*. Ed. Philippe Morel. Roma: Académie de France à Rome, 2006. 495–526.

Castillo, Moisés R. "¿Ortodoxia cervantina?: un análisis de la *La gran sultana*, *El trato de Argel* y *Los baños de Argel*." *Bulletin of the Comediantes* 56 (2004): 219–240.

Cavallo, Jo Ann. "The *Candelaio*: A hermetic puzle." *Canadian Journal of Italian Studies* 15 (1992): 47–55.

Céard, Jean. "Jeu et divination à la Renaissance." *Les jeux à la Renaissance*. Paris: Vrin, 1982. 405–420.

Cecioni, Giorgo. "Il *Secretum secretorum* attribuito ad Aristotele e le sue redazioni volgari." *Il Propugnatore* 2 (1889): 72–102.

Chalkomatas, Dionysios. *Ciceros Dichtungstheorie*. Berlin: Frank & Timme, 2007.

Chandezon, Christophe, Véronique Dasen, and Jérôme Wilgaux. "Dream Interpretation, Physiognomy, Body Divination." *A companion to Greek and Roman sexualities*. Ed. Thomas K. Hubbard. Oxford: Blackwell, 2013. 297–313.

Charnon-Deutsch, Lou. *The Spanish Gypsy*. University Park: Pennsylvania State UP, 2004.

Chautant, Gisèle. *Croyances et conduites magiques dans la France du XVIIe siècle d'après l'affaire des poisons*. Villeneuve d'Ascq: PU du Septentrion, 2002.

Chem Sham, Jorge. "La fuerza ilocutiva de la profecía en *La vida es sueño*." *Anuario de Estudios Filológicos* 21 (1998): 57–72.

Cirac Estopañán, Sebastián. *Aportación a la historia de la Inquisición española: los procesos de hechicería de Castilla la Nueva*. Madrid: Instituto Jerónimo Zurita, 1942.

Clarke, Jan. "*La Devineresse* and the *Affaire des poisons.*" *Seventeenth Century French Studies* 28 (2006): 221–234.
Classen, Albrecht (ed.). *Magic and magicians in the middle ages and the early modern time.* Berlin / Boston: De Gruyter, 2017.
Coduras, María. "La presencia de la música, el baile y la seducción por la voz en *El jardín de Falerina* de Calderón de la Barca, auto y comedia." *Eclipse* 13 (2010): 19–28.
Colahan, Clark. "*El Hércules* de López de Zárate: Una posible fuente de *Los tres mayores prodigios* de Calderón." *Calderón: Actas del Congreso internacional sobre Calderón y el teatro español del Siglo de Oro.* Ed. Luciano García Lorenzo. Madrid: CSIC, 1983. Vol. 3. 1271–1276.
Compier, Abdul Haq. "Rhazes in the renaissance of Andreas Vesalius." *Medical History* 56 (2012): 3–25.
Conlon, Raymond. "Female psychosexuality in Tirso's *El vergonzoso en palacio.*" *Bulletin of the Comediantes* 37 (1985): 55–69.
Conlon, Raymond. "Sexual passion and marriage: Chaos and order in Tirso de Molina's *El vergonzoso en palacio.*" *Hispania* 71 (1988): 8–13.
Cornejo, Manuel. "La imagen burlesca de Madrid y la casa de la dama en *Los melindres de Belisa* de Lope de Vega." *Locos, figurones y quijotes en el teatro de los Siglos de Oro.* Ed. Germán Vega and González Cañal. Almagro: Universidad de Castilla-La Mancha, 2007. 81–98.
Cots Vicente, Montserrat. "Camus traductor: *La devoción de la Cruz* de Calderón." *Revista Anthropos* 199 (2003): 138–139.
Courtès, Noémie. *L'écriture de l'enchantement. Magie et magiciens dans la littérature française du XVIIe siècle.* Paris: Champion, 2004.
Courtine, Jean-Jacques. "Le corps desenchante: lectures et langages du corps dans les physiognomonies de l'âge classique." *Le corps au XVIIe siècle.* Ed. Ronald W. Tobin. Paris: Papers on French Seventeenth Century Literature, 1995. 49–52.
Coy, Jason Philip. *The Devil's Art: Divination and Discipline in Early Modern Germany.* Charlottesville / London: Virginia UP, 2020.
Cros, Edmond. *Contribution à l'étude des sources de "Guzmán de Alfarache".* Paris: s.t., 1967.
Cruz, Anne J. "Reading over men's shoulders: noblewomen's libraries and reading practice." *Women's literacy in early modern Spain and the New World.* Ed. Anne J. Cruz and Rosilie Hernández. Burlington: Ashgate, 2011. 41–58.
Curran, John E. Jr. *Character and the Individual Personality in English Renaissance Drama.* Newark, Delware UP, 2014.
Dadson, Trevor J. *Libros, lectores y lecturas. Estudios sobre bibliotecas particulares españolas del Siglo de Oro.* Madrid: Arco / Libros, 1998.
Dahan-Gaida, Laurence. *Conversations entre la littérature, les arts et les sciences*, Besançon: PU de Franche-Comté, 2006.
D'Alessandro, Alessandro. "Astrologia, religione e scienza nella cultura medica e filosofica di Galeotto Marzio." *Italia e Ungheria all'epoca dell'umanesimo corviniano.* Ed. Sante Graciotti and Cesare Vasoli. Firenze: Olschki, 1994. 132–177.
Damiani, Rolando. "Il *Liber de physionomia* di Michele Scoto e la cultura siciliana tradizionale." *Atti dell'Istituto Veneto di Scienze, Lettere ed Arti. Classe di Scienze Morali, Lettere ed Arti* 132 (1974): 437–446.

Darbord, Bernard. "La tradición del saber en la *Doncella Teodor.*" *Medioevo y literatura. Actas del V Congreso de la AHLM*. Ed. Juan Salvador Paredes. Granada: Universidad, 1995. Vol. 1. 13–30.

Darst, David H. "El discurso sobre la magia en *La cueva de Salamanca*, de Ruiz de Alarcon." *Duquesne Hispanic Review* 9 (1970): 31–44.

Dartai-Maranzana, Nathalie. "Les jeux de l'amour et du portrait dans deux *comedias* de Tirso de Molina: *El vergonzoso en palacio* et *El celoso prudente.*" *Cahiers du GRIAS* 9 (2002): 73–94.

Dasen, Véronique. "Le langage divinatoire du corps." *Langages et métaphores du corps dans le monde antique*. Ed. Véronique Dasen and Jérôme Wilgaux. Rennes: PU de Rennes, 2008. 223–242.

Dasen, Véronique, and Jérôme Wilgaux. "De la palmomantique à l'éternuement, lectures divinatoires des mouvements du corps." *Kernos* 26 (2013): 111–122.

Dasen, Véronique. "Body marks – birthmarks. Body divination in ancient literature and iconography." *Bodies in Transition Dissolving the Boundaries of Embodied Knowledge*. Ed. Dietrich Boschung, Alan Shapiro and Frank Waschek. Paderborn: Fink, 2014. 155–177.

Del Conte, Laura. "La maschera della follia: *Los locos de Valencia* di Lope de Vega." *La Maschera e l'altro*. Ed. Maria Grazia Profeti. Firenze: Alinea, 2005. 239–258.

Delgado García, Nitzaira. "El poder bajo el velo: las moras argelinas y las moriscas en Cervantes." *El universo simbólico del poder en el Siglo de Oro*. Ed. Álvaro Baraibar Etxeberria and Mariela Insúa Cereceda. Pamplona: Universidad de Navarra, 2010. 65–76.

Delgado, Manuel. "Poetry and spectacle in *La devoción de la Cruz.*" *The Calderonian stage: body and soul*. Ed. Manual Delgado. Lewisburg: Bucknell UP, 1997. 55–68.

Delgado, Manuel. "*La devoción de la Cruz*: entre la crueldad humana y la clemencia divina." *Anuario Calderoniano* 2 (2009): 97–110.

Delpech, François. "Les marques de naissance: physiognomomie, signature magique et charisme souverain." *Le corps dans la société espagnole des XVIe et XVIIe siècles*. Ed. Augustin Redondo. Paris: Publications de la Sorbonne, 1990. 27–49.

Delumeau, Jean. *Le mystère Campanella*. Paris: Fayard, 2008.

Diago, Manuel V. "Joan Timoneda: una dramaturgia burguesa." *Cuadernos de Filología. III, Literatura: análisis* 1 (1981): 45–65.

Diago, Manuel V. "La *Comedia llamada Aurelia* de Joan Timoneda: una pieza clave del teatro prelopista." *Estudis en memòria del professor Manuel Sanchis Guarner*. València: Universitat, 1984. Vol. 2. 99–104.

Diago, Manuel V. "La magia como elemento burlesco en el teatro populista del siglo XVI." *La comedia de magia y de santos*. Ed. Francisco Javier Blasco, Ricardo De La Fuente Ballesteros, Ermanno Caldera and Joaquín Álvarez Barrientos. Gijón: Ediciones Jucár, 1992. 51–70.

Díaz Balsera, Viviana. "*El jardín de Falerina* de Calderón y la escritura de Lucifer." *Revista de Estudios Hispánicos* 28 (1994): 141–162.

Díaz Migoyo, Gonzalo. "Memoria y fama de Román Ramírez." *Memoria de la palabra*. Ed. Francisco Domínguez Matito and María Luisa Lobato. Madrid / Frankfurt: Iberoamericana / Vervuert, 2004. 39–54.

Dickhaut, Kirsten. "Magische(s) Gestalten in der frühneuzeitlichen Komödie. Ariostos *Il Negromante* und Corneilles *Illusion comique.*" *Poetica* 48 (2016): 59–81.

Di Pinto, Elena. "Personajes marginales en la escena del Siglo de Oro." *Heterodoxia, marginalidad y maravilla en los siglos de oro*. Ed. José María Díez Borque, Jaime Olmedo and Laura Puerto. Madrid: Visor, 2016. 27–46.
DiPuccio, Denise M. "The enigma of enchantment in *El mayor encanto, amor*." *Hispania* 4 (1987): 731–739.
Dixon, Victor. "*El vergonzoso en Palacio* y *El perro del hortelano*: ¿comedias gemelas?." *Tirso de Molina: del siglo de oro al siglo XX*. Ed. Carmen Pinillos, Ignacio Arellano, Blanca Oteiza and Miguel Zugasti. Madrid: Revista Estudios, 1995. 73–86.
Domènech, Conxita. "El espectáculo delirante en *Los locos de Valencia*." *Céfiro* 8 (2008): 119–139.
Doménici, Mauricio. "Lealtad e identidad en *Los baños de Argel* de Cervantes." *Cervantes creador y Cervantes recreado*. Ed. Emmanuel Marigno, Carlos Mata Induráin and Hugo Hernán Ramírez Sierra. Pamplona: Universidad de Navarra, 2015. 63–72.
Domínguez Matito, Francisco. "Fama e infamia del duque de Braganza en el teatro español del Siglo de Oro." *Hipogrifo* 3 (2015): 111–124.
Dunn, Peter N. "The horoscop motif in *La vida es sueño*." *Atlante* 1 (1953): 187–201.
Duntze, Oliver. *Ein Verleger sucht sein Publikum die Straßburger Offizin des Matthias Hupfuff (1497/98–1520)*. München: Saur, 2007.
Duro Rivas, Reyes. "La fuerza de la mujer: sobre *Santa Isabel, reina de Portugal*, de Rojas Zorrilla." *"Scripta manent"*. *Actas del I Congreso Internacional Jóvenes Investigadores Siglo de Oro*. Ed. Carlos Mata Induráin and Adrián J. Sáez. Pamplona: Universidad de Navarra, 2011. 157–172.
Eamon, William. *Science and the secrets of nature*. Princeton: Princeton UP, 1994.
Edwards, Gwynne. "Calderón's *Los tres mayores prodigios* and *El pintor de su deshonra*: The modernization of ancient myth." *Bulletin of Hispanic Studies* 61 (1984): 326–334.
Egido, Aurora. *La fábrica de un auto sacramental: "Los encantos de la culpa"*. Salamanca: Universidad, 1982.
Ellis, Jonathan. "The figure of Circe and the power of knowledge: competing Philosophies in Calderon's *El mayor encanto, amor*." *Bulletin of Spanish Studies* 87 (2010): 147–162.
Enguix Barber, Ricardo. "Metateatralidad y renovación dramática cervantina. Estudio de los elementos metadramáticos de *Pedro de Urdemalas*, *El rufián dichoso* y *El retablo de las maravillas*." *Lemir* 19 (2015): 451–462.
Entwistle, William J. "Calderón's *La devoción de la Cruz*." *Bulletin Hispanique* 50 (1948): 472–482.
Ernst, Germana. "Note campanelliane. L'inedita *Chiroscopia* a Richelieu." *Bruniana & Campanelliana* 1 (1995): 83–101.
Ernst, Germana. *Tommaso Campanella. The book and the body of nature*. Dordrecht / New York: Springer, 2010.
Escobar Gómez, Santiago. *Abú Bakr Muhammad B. Zadariyyá Al Rází: Vida, pensamiento y obra*. Madrid: Universidad Complutense, 1995.
Espantoso-Foley, Augusta M. "The problem of astrology and its use in Ruiz de Alarcon's *El dueño de las estrellas*." *Hispanic Review* 32 (1964): 1–11.
Espantoso-Foley, Augusta M. "Las ciencias ocultas, la teología y la técnica dramática en algunas comedias de Juan Ruiz de Alarcón." *Actas del Segundo Congreso Internacional de Hispanistas*. Ed. Jaime Sánchez Romeralo and Norbert Poulussen. Nijmegen: Universidad, 1967. 319–326.

Espantoso-Foley, Augusta M. *Occult arts and doctrine in the theater of Juan Ruiz de Alarcón.* Genève: Droz, 1972.
Esseni, Chiara. "*Camus adattatore de La devoción de la Cruz.*" *Teatro Calderoniano sobre el tablado.* Ed. Manfred Tietz. Stuttgart: Steiner, 2002. 85–96.
Estévez Molinero, Ángel. "La (re)escritura cervantina de Pedro de Urdemalas." *Cervantes. Bulletin of the Cervantes Society of America* 15 (1995): 82–93.
Ettinghausen, Henry. *Noticias del siglo XVII: relaciones españolas de sucesos naturales y sobrenaturales.* Barcelona: Puvill, 1995.
Evans, Elizabeth Cornelia. "Physiognomics in the ancient world." *Transactions of the American Philosophical Society* 59 (1969): 5–83.
Evans, Elizabeth Cornelia. "The study of physiognomy in the second century A.D." *Transactions of the American Philosophical Society* 72 (1941): 96–108.
Exum, Frances B. "Dos comedias de Lope refundidas por Moreto: ¿*De cuándo acá nos vino?* y *El mayor imposible.*" *Lope de Vega y los orígenes del teatro español.* Ed. Manuel Criado De Val. Madrid: EDI-6, 1981. 835–842.
Exum, Frances B. "Role-reversal and parody in Moreto's *De fuera vendrá.*" *Hispanófila* 27 (1983): 1–9.
Federici Vescovini, Graziella. "Su un trattatello anonimo di fisiognomica astrologica." *Quaderni dell'Accademia delle Arti del Disegno* 3 (1991): 43–61.
Federici Vescovini, Graziella. "Profilo dottrinale del filosofo umanista scettico Galeotto Marzio da Narni. Saggio preliminare." *Presenze filosofiche in Umbria tra Medioevo e l'età contemporanea.* Ed. Antonio Pieretti. Milano: Mimesis, 2011. Vol. 2. 54–81.
Fernández, Jaime Antonio. "*Los hidalgos del aldea*: Honor, maduración amorosa y vencimiento." *Iberoromania* 27–28 (1988): 1–13.
Fernández Gómez, Carlos. *Vocabulario completo de Lope de Vega.* 3 vol. Madrid: RAE, 1971.
Fernández-Guerra y Orbe, Luis. *Juan Ruiz de Alarcon y Mendoza.* Madrid: Rivadeneyra, 1871.
Fernández Mosquera, Santiago. "El significado de las primeras fiestas cortesanas de Calderón de la Barca." *Calderón y el pensamiento ideológico y cultural de su época.* Ed. Manfred Tietz and Gero Arnscheidt. Stuttgart: Steiner, 2008a. 209–232.
Fernández Mosquera, Santiago. "Las comedias mitológicas de Calderón: Entre la fiesta y la tragedia. El caso de *Los tres mayores prodigios.*" *Hacia la tragedia áurea: Lecturas para un nuevo milenio.* Ed. Frederick A. De Armas, Luciano García Lorenzo and Enrique García Santo-Tomás. Madrid / Frankfurt: Iberoamericana / Vervuert, 2008b. 153–170.
Fernández Rodríguez, Daniel. "Las comedias bizantinas de Lope en su contexto teatral español e italiano." *Anuario de Lope de Vega* 23 (2017): 229–252.
Fernández Rodríguez, Natalia. "Influencia demoníaca y distorsión de la realidad en *Quién mal anda, mal acaba* de Juan Ruiz de Alarcón." *Locos, figurones y Quijotes en el teatro de los Siglos de Oro.* Ed. Germán Vega and Rafael González Cañal. Almagro: Universidad de Castilla-La Mancha, 2007. 139–152.
Ferrer-Lightner, María. "El dominio del espacio escénico en el *Auto de las Gitanas.*" *Argus-a* 2 (2006): without pagination.
Ferrer Valls, Teresa. *La práctica escénica cortesana de la época del emperador a la de Felipe III.* London: Tamesis, 1991.
Fiadino, Elsa Graciela. "Melindres y amor en una comedia de Lope de Vega." *Actas del XIII Congreso de la AIH.* Ed. Florencio Sevilla and Carlos Alvar. Madrid: Castalia, 2000. Vol. 1. 507–515.

Fidora, Alexander. *Die Wissenschaftstheorie des Dominicus Gundissalinus.* Berlin: Akademie-Verlag, 2003.
Fidora, Alexander. *Domingo Gundisalvo y la teoría de la ciencia arábigo-aristotélica.* Pamplona: EUNSA, 2009.
Fidora, Alexander. "Der wissenschaftliche Ort der Mantik in der 'Schule von Toledo' (12. Jahrhundert)." *Mantik, Schicksal und Freiheit im Mittelalter.* Ed. Loris Sturlese. Köln: Böhlau, 2011. 33–49.
Fidora, Alexander. "Mantische Disziplinen als aristotelische Wissenschaft. Der epistemologische Integrationsversuch des Dominicus Gundissalinus." *Die mantischen Künste und die Epistemologie prognostischer Wissenschaften im Mittelalter.* Ed. Alexander Fidora. Köln: Böhlau, 2013. 61–72.
Fidora, Alexander (ed.). *Die mantischen Künste und die Epistemologie prognostischer Wissenschaften im Mittelalter.* Köln: Böhlau, 2013.
Fischer, Susan L. "Calderón's *El mayor encanto, amor* and the mode of romance." *Studies in Honor of Everett W. Hesse.* Ed. William C. Mccrary, José A. Madrigal and John E. Keller. Lincoln: Society of Spanish and Spanish-American Studies, 1981. 99–112.
Flasche, Hans. *Die Struktur des Auto Sacramental "Los Encantos de la Culpa" von Calderón: antiker Mythos in christlicher Umprägung.* Düsseldorf: Westdeutscher Verlag, 1968.
Flores Martín, Mercedes. "Locura y cordura en *Los locos de Valencia.*" *Medicina y Literatura.* Sevilla: Padilla, 2004. 183–196.
Florit Durán, Francisco de. "Refrán y comedia palaciega: los ejemplos de *El perro del hortelano* y de *El vergonzoso en palacio.*" *RILCE* 7 (1991): 25–49.
Florit Durán, Francisco de. "*El vergonzoso en palacio*: arquetipo de un género." *Varia lección de Tirso de Molina.* Ed. Ignacio Arellano and Blanca Oteiza. Pamploa / Madrid: GRISO / Revista Estudios, 2000. 65–83.
Florit Durán, Francisco de. "Estrategias discursivas en *El vergonzoso en palacio*, de Tirso de Molina." *Criticón* 81 (2001): 89–105.
Floyd-Wilson, Mary. *Occult Knowledge, Science, and Gender on the Shakespearean Stage.* Cambridge: Cambridge UP, 2013.
Folger, Robert. "Calderón y la *mente cómica* de su tiempo: el ejemplo de *El astrólogo fingido.*" *Anuario Calderoniano* 10 (2017): 91–108.
Fothergill-Payne, Louise. "*Los tratos de Argel*, *Los cautivos de Argel* y *Los baños de Argel*: tres *trasuntos* de un asunto." *El mundo del teatro español en su siglo de oro: ensayos dedicados a John E. Varey.* Ed. José María Ruano de la Haza. Ottawa: Devehouse, 1989. 177–184.
Foucault, Michel. *Les mots et les choses.* Paris: Gallimard, 1966.
Förster, Richard (ed.). *Scriptores physiognomonici Graeci et Latini.* 2 vol. Leipzig: Teubner, 1893.
Förster, Richard. "Zur Überlieferung der Physiognomik des Adamantios." *Rheinisches Museum für Philologie* 52 (1897): 298–299.
Forster, Regula. *Das Geheimnis der Geheimnisse.* Wiesbaden: Reichert, 2006.
Franzese, Rosa. "Una traduzione napoletana del *Secretum* catalano." *La cultura catalana tra l'Umanesimo e il Barocco.* Ed. Carlos Romero-Rossend. Padova: Programma, 1994. 127–143.
Frenk Alatorre, Margit. "*El vergonzoso en Palacio*: duplicaciones y multiplicaciones." *Nueva Revista de Filología Hispánica* 42 (1994): 77–86.

Friedman, Edward H. "The other side of the metaphor: an approach to *La devoción de la Cruz.*" *Approaches to the theater of Calderón.* Ed. Michael D. McGaha. Lanham / New York / London: UP of America, 1982. 129–141.

Friedman, John Block. "Another look at Chaucer and the physiognomists." *Studies in Philology* 78 (1981): 138–152.

Friedrich, Ernst. *Die Magie im französischen Theater des XVI. und XVII. Jahrhunderts.* Leipzig: Deichert, 1908.

Fuente, Ricardo de la, and Jesús Pérez-Magallón (ed.). *El modo trágico en la cultura hispánica.* Valladolid: Universitas Castellae, 2008.

Fürbeth, Frank. "Texte der Magie – Magie der Texte. Zum Lebensraum magischer Texte in mittelalterlichen Handschriften am Beispiel der Chiromantie." *Text als Realie.* Wien: Verlag der Österreichischen Akademie der Wissenschaften, 2003. 97–113.

Funck-Brentano, Frantz. *Le drame des poisons: Études sur la société du XVIIe siècle et plus particulièrement la cour de Louis XIV d'après les archives de la Bastille.* Paris: Hachette, ^{4}1900.

Gabrieli, Giuseppe. "Giovan Battista Della Porta Linceo da documenti per gran parte inediti." *Giornale Critico della Filosofia Italiana* 8 (1927): 360–397.

Gagliardi, Donatella. "La biblioteca de Bartolomé Barrientos, maestro de artes liberales." *Studia Aurea* 1 (2007): 1–69.

Gagnon-Riopel, Julie. "*Con la lengua me ofendió, con la lengua he de matarle*: la sociedad moderna en *El duque de Viseo* y en *Saber del mal y del bien.*" *Ayer y hoy de Calderón.* Madrid: Castalia, 2002. 147–154.

Gago Saldaña, María Val. "*Il Nigromante* de Ariosto y el *Necromanticus* de Petreyo." *Actas del X Congreso Español de Estudios Clásicos.* Ed. Emilio Crespo and María José Barrios Castro. Madrid: Ediciones Clásicas, 2001. Vol. 3. 553–559.

Galeotto Marzio e l'umanesimo italiano ed europeo. Narni: Centro di Studi Storici, 1983.

Gandolfi, Giangiacomo. "Stars and theatre. From Renaissance stage astrologers to astronomy-flavored science plays." *Mediterranean Archaeology* 18 (2018): 273–280.

García-Bermejo Giner, Miguel M. *Catálogo del teatro español del siglo XVI. Índice de piezas conservadas, perdidas y representadas.* Salamanca: Universidad, 1996.

García-Bermejo Giner, Miguel M. "Burlas mágicas del primer teatro del XVI: El conjuro de personas en las églogas de Encina y Guillén de Ávila." *Esoterismo y brujería en la literatura del Siglo de Oro.* Ed. María Luisa Lobato, Javier San José and Germán Vega. Alicante: Biblioteca Virtual Miguel de Cervantes, 2016a. 141–170.

García-Bermejo Giner, Miguel M. "De juego dramático a recurso para las crisis: máscaras y cambios de identidad en los Pasos de Lope de Rueda." *Estrategias picarescas en tiempo de crisis.* Ed. Amaranta Sagura and Hannah Schlimpen. Dir. Miguel García-Bermejo Giner and Folke Gernert. Trier: Hispanistik Trier, 2016b. 29–41.

García-Bermejo Giner, Miguel M. "Profesores de secretos y medicina en el primer teatro clásico español". *Adivinos, médicos y profesores de secretos en la España áurea.* Ed. Folke Gernert. Toulouse: Les Méridiennes, 2017. 101–115.

García Fernández, Óscar. "Las fuentes clásicas en *Las mujeres sin hombres* de Lope de Vega: pervivencia y transgresión." *Campus stellae. Haciendo camino en la investigación literaria.* Ed. Dolores Fernández López, Mónica Domínguez Pérez and Fernando Rodríguez Gallego. Santiago de Compostela: Universidad, 2006. Vol. 1. 418–426.

García Lorenzo, Luciano. "Amor y locura fingida: *Los locos de Valencia*, de Lope de Vega." *El mundo del teatro español en su siglo de oro: ensayos dedicados a John E. Varey.* Ed. José María Ruano de la Haza. Ottawa: Devehouse, 1989. 213–228.

García Manzano, Agustina. "El mito clásico en *Los encantos de la culpa.*" *Homenaje a José Manuel Blecua.* Huesca: Instituto de Estudios Altoaragoneses, 1986. 141–152.

García Santo-Tomás, Enrique. *Science on Stage in Early Modern Spain.* Toronto: Toronto UP, 2019.

García-Valdés, Celsa Carmen. "*La cueva de Salamanca* en América: tradición oral y reelaboración literaria." *El teatro en la Hispanoamérica colonial.* Ed. Ignacio Arellano and José Antonio Rodríguez Garrido. Madrid: Iberoamericana, 2008. 461–474.

Gatti, Hilary. *Giordano Bruno e la scienza del Rinascimento.* Milano: Raffaello Cortina, 2001.

Gaullier-Bougassas, Catherine. "Révélation hermétique et savoir occulte de l'Orient dans le *Secretum secretorum* et les *Secrets de secrets* français." *Trajectoires européennes du "Secretum secretorum" du Pseudo-Aristote (XIIIe–XVIe siècle).* Ed. Jean-Yves Tilliette, Margaret Bridges and Catherine Gaullier-Bougassas. Turnhout: Brepols, 2015. 57–106.

Gauna, Felipe de. *Relación de las Fiestas celebradas en Valencia con motivo del Casamiento de Felipe III.* 2 vol. Ed. Salvador Carreres Zacares. Valencia: Hijo de F. Vives Mora, 1926–1927.

Gavela García, Delia. "La evolución de un género a través de sus figuras y figurones: *De fuera vendrá* de Moreto y su fuente lopesca ¿*De cuándo acá nos vino?.*" *El figurón: texto y puesta en escena.* Ed. Luciano García Lorenzo. Madrid: Fundamentos, 2007. 129–148.

Gernert, Folke. "Lecturas del cuerpo: Textualización del pensamiento fisionómico en la ficción caballeresca." *Del pensamiento al texto. Estrategias de reflexión y de textualización entre la Edad Media tardía y el Siglo de Oro.* Ed. Folke Gernert, Javier Gómez-Montero and Florence Serrano. Vigo: Editorial Academia del Hispanismo, 2013a. 123–150.

Gernert, Folke. "Relaciones de sucesos monstruosos y las *Histoires prodigieuses* de Pierre de Boaistuau." *Géneros editoriales y relaciones de sucesos en la Edad Moderna.* Ed. Pedro M. Cátedra and Mª. Eugenia Díaz Tena. Salamanca: Sociedad Internacional para el Estudios de las Relaciones de Sucesos / SEMYR, 2013b. 191–209.

Gernert, Folke. "Signos celestes y signos corporales en *La Lozana Andaluza.*" *Rumbos del hispanismo en el umbral del Cincuentenario de la AIH.* Ed. Patrizia Botta. Roma: Bagatto Libri, 2013c. Vol. 3. 41–50.

Gernert, Folke. "*La devoción de la Cruz* desde la fisiognomía. La violencia de Eusebio entre predeterminación y libre albedrío." *La violencia en Calderón.* Ed. Gero Arnscheidt and Manfred Tietz. Vigo: Academia del Hispanismo, 2014a. 229–250.

Gernert, Folke. "La legitimidad de las ciencias parcialmente ocultas: fisonomía y quiromancia ante la Inquisición." *Saberes humanísticos.* Ed. Christoph Strosetzki. Madrid / Frankfurt am Main: Vervuert / Iberoamericana, 2014b. 105–128.

Gernert, Folke. "La textualización del saber quiromántico: la lectura de la mano en Lope de Vega." *El texto infinito: Reescritura y tradición en la Edad media y el Renacimiento.* Ed. Cesc Esteve. Salamanca: SEMYR, 2014c. 559–575.

Gernert, Folke. "Cervantes y la metoposcopia: ¿Por qué (no) puede Preciosa leer las líneas de la frente?." *Esoterismo y Brujería en la Literatura del Siglo de Oro.* Ed. María Luisa Lobato, Javier San José and Germán Vega. Alicante: Biblioteca Virtual Miguel de Cervantes, 2016. 171–194.

Gernert, Folke. "Astrología y magia en escena: Calderón, Métel d'Ouville, Thomas Corneille y Donneau de Visé." *Anagnórisis* 15 (2017a): 242–269.

Gernert, Folke. "La fisiognomía en la imprenta y sus lectores." *Adivinos, médicos y profesores de secretos en la España áurea*. Ed. Folke Gernert. Toulouse: Les Méridiennes, 2017b. 21–31.

Gernert, Folke. "Los saberes de la mala mujer entre auto sacramental y comedia mitológica." *La construcción de la masculinidad y de la feminidad en el teatro calderoniano*. Ed. Gero Arnscheidt and Manfred Tietz. Vigo: Academia del Hispanismo, 2017c. 229–250.

Gernert, Folke. "La precariedad del saber oculto – el estatus problemático de la fisiognomía." *Saberes inestables: Estudios sobre expurgación y Censura en la España de los siglos XVI y XVII*. Ed. Víctor Lillo, Dámaris Montes and María José Vega. Madrid / Frankfurt am Main: Vervuert / Iberoamericana, 2018a. 75–100.

Gernert, Folke. *Lecturas del cuerpo. Fisiognomía y literatura en la España áurea*. Salamanca: Universidad, 2018b.

Gernert, Folke. "El contexto de las festivas condenas de la astrología en *El astrólogo fingido* y *Apolo y Clímene*." *El tablado, la calle, la fiesta en el Siglo de Oro*. Ed. Miguel Zugasti, Castellón: Servicio de Publicaciones de la Universidad Jaime I. (in press).

Ghersetti, Antonella. "Una tabella di fisiognomica nel *Qabs al-anwar wa-bahgat al-asrar* attribuito a Ibn-Arabi." *Quaderni di Studi Arabi* 12 (1994): 15–47.

Ghersetti, Antonella. "Fisiognomica e stereotipi femminili nella cultura araba." *Quaderni di Studi Arabi* 14 (1995): 195–206.

Ghersetti, Antonella. "Mondo classico e legittimazione del sapere nella cultura arabo-islamica: il trattato *Fifirasat al-nisa* attribuito a Polemone." *Quaderni di Studi Arabi* 3 (1999): 59–68.

Gibson, Margaret, T. A. Heslop, and Richard W. Pfaff (ed.). *The Eadwine Psalter: text, image, and monastic culture in twelfth-century Canterbury*. London: MHRA, 1992.

Gigas, Emil. "Études sur quelques *comedias* de Lope de Vega. I (*El duque de Viseo*)." *Revue Hispanique* 95 (1917): 83–111.

Gil Fernández, Juan. "El Humanismo valenciano del siglo XVI." *Humanismo y pervivencia del mundo clásico. Homenaje al profesor Antonio Fontán*. Ed. José María Maestre Maestre, Joaquín Pascual Barea and Luis Charlo Brea. Alcañiz / Madrid: Laberinto / CSIC, 2002. Vol. 1.1. 57–159.

Gilbert, Françoise. "Polimetría y estructuras dramáticas en el auto de Calderón *Los encantos de la culpa* (1645)." *El siglo de Oro en escena: homenaje a Marc Vitse*. Ed. Odette Gorsse and Frédéric Serralta. Toulouse: PU du Mirail, 2006. 363–381.

Gilbert, Françoise. "Sobre sueños y visiones en el auto de Calderón *Los encantos de la culpa* (1645)." *El mundo maravilloso de los autos de Calderón*. Ed. Ignacio Arellano and Dominique Reyre. Pamplona / Kassel: Universidad de Navarra / Reichenberger, 2007. 95–110.

Gilbert, Françoise. "Sueño y mecanismos alegóricos en el auto de Calderón *El tesoro escondido* (1679): de la revelación a la epifanía." *Compostella aurea*. Ed. Antonio Azaustre Galiana and Santiago Fernández Mosquera. Santiago de Compostela: Universidad, 2008. 191–212.

Gilbert, Françoise. "Deseo y culpabilidad: La representación onírica de un conflicto en el auto de Calderón: *Los encantos de la culpa* (1645)." *Actas del XVI Congreso de la AIH: ¿Nuevos caminos del hispanismo?*. Ed. Pierre Civil amd Françoise Crémoux. Madrid / Frankfurt: Iberoamericana / Vervuert, 2010. without pagination.

Girard, René. *La violence et le sacré*. Paris: Grasset, 1972.

Glenn, Richard F. "Disguises and masquerade in Tirso's *El vergonzoso en palacio*." *Bulletin of the Comediantes* 17 (1965): 16–22.
Gómez Mingorance, Margarita. "*Apolo y Climene. El hijo del Sol, Faetón* (análisis de dos comedias calderonianas)." *Calderón. Actas del Congreso Internacional sobre Calderón y el teatro español del Siglo de Oro*. Ed. Luciano García Lorenzo. Madrid: CSIC, 1983. Vol. 1. 461–476.
Gómez Moreno, Ángel. *España y la Italia de los humanistas. Primeros ecos*. Madrid: Gredos, 1994.
Gómez Vozmediano, Miguel Fernando. "La historiografía sobre los gitanos en el mundo ibérico (ss. XV–XXI): notas para un balance." *Revista de Historiografía* 2 (2005): 110–120.
González, Aurelio. "Técnicas dramáticas en Ruiz de Alarcón: *La cueva de Salamanca*." *Dramaturgia española y novohispana: Siglos XVI–XVII*. Ed. Lillian von der Walde Moheno and Serafín González García. México: Universidad Autónoma Metropolitana, 1993. 65–71.
González-Barrera, Julián. "La novela bizantina española y la comedia *La doncella Teodor* de Lope de Vega." *Quaderni Iberoamericani* 97 (2005): 76–93.
González-Barrera, Julián. "Lope de Vega y su lectura de la *Historia de la doncella Teodor*." *Analecta Malacitana* 30 (2007): 435–442.
González-Barrera, Julián. "Alteraciones y naufragios: una hipótesis para la fecha de *Los locos de Valencia* de Lope de Vega." *Monteagudo* 13 (2008): 107–118.
González-Barrera, Julián. "Un capitán heresiarca en la biblioteca de Lope de Vega: Henricus Cornelius Agrippa." *Revista de Filología Española* 98 (2018): 319–340.
González Cuerva, Rubén. "*El prodigioso príncipe transilvano*: la larga guerra contra los turcos (1596–1606) a través de las *relaciones de sucesos*." *Studia Historica. Historia Moderna* 28 (2006): 277–299.
Gonzalez del Valle, Luis. "Vasallaje ideal y justicia poetica en *El duque de Viseo*." *Hispanófila* 47 (1973): 27–37.
González del Valle, Luis. "Brito: Su función en *El duque de Viseo*." *Romance Notes* 20 (1979): 103–107.
González Fernández, Luis. "El festín interrumpido: Magia demoníaca y *transubstanciación* en dos comedias de Juan Ruiz de Alarcón y Mendoza." *Miscelánea filológica dedicada a Alberto Porqueras Mayo*. Ed. María Dolores González Martínez. Lleida: Milenio, 2011. 121–138.
González García, Ángel. "De cómo perdió el rabo el perro de San Roque: el morisco como médico y como enfermedad en *Quien mal anda en mal acaba*." *España: ¿laberinto de exilios*. Ed. Sandra Barriales-Bouche. Newark: Juan de la Cuesta, 2005. 49–58.
González Manjarrés, Miguel Ángel. "Poetas clásicos latinos en *De Humana Physiognomonia* de Giovan Battista della Porta." *Dvlces Camenae. Poética y Poesía Latinas*. Ed. Jesús Luque Moreno, María Dolores Rincón González and Isabel Velázquez. Jaén / Granada: Sociedad de Estudios Latinos, 2010. 1021–1032.
González Manjarrés, Miguel Ángel. "La risa en la fisiognomía latina del Renacimiento." *Studia Philologica Valentina* 17 (2015): 159–185.
González Manjarrés, Miguel Ángel. "Anotaciones críticas de Giovanni Battista Della Porta a la *Fisiognomía* de Pseudo Aristóteles." *La "mirabile" natura. Magia e scienza in Giovan Battista Della Porta (1615–2015)*. Ed. Marco Santoro. Pisa / Roma: Fabrizio Serra, 2016. 71–80.
González Ollé, Fernando. "Fisiognómica del color rojizo en la literatura española del Siglo de oro." *Revista de Literatura* 43 (1981): 153–164.

González Palencia, Ángel. "El curandero morisco del siglo XVI." *Boletín de la Real Academia* 17 (1930): 247–274 and 16 (1929): 199–222; reedition *Historias y Leyendas*. Madrid: CSIC, 1942. 215–284.
González Puche, Alejandro. *Pedro de Urdemalas, la aventura experimental del teatro cervantino*. Vigo: Academia del Hispanismo, 2012.
González Puche, Alejandro. "Berganza y Pedro de Urdemalas, dos destinos cervantinos que desfilan por la escena." *Hipogrifo* 1 (2013): 31–38.
González-Ruiz, Julio. "*En los dos uno solo*: el discurso homoerótico en *La boda entre dos maridos* (1595–1601)." *Amistades peligrosas. El discurso homoerótico en el teatro de Lope de Vega*. Ed. Julio González-Ruiz. New York: Lang, 2009. 153–164.
González, Serafín. "El tema de la nobleza en *El vergonzoso en palacio*, de Tirso de Molina." *Mira de Amescua en candelero*. Ed. Agustín De La Granja and Juan Antonio Martínez Berbel. Granada: Universidad, 1996. Vol. 2. 239–250.
Granja, Agustín de la. "Entre gitanas y astrónomos: nota para las dos primeras consultas de la *Lonja de Investigadores*." *Criticón* 47 (1989): 151–160.
Granja, Agustín de la. "Noticia de un manuscrito localizado en Coimbra: *El tesoro escondido* (auto y loa)." *Divinas y humanas letras, doctrina y poesía en los autos sacramentales de Calderón*. Ed. Ignacio Arellano, Carmen Pinillos, Blanca Oteiza and Juan Manuel Escudero. Pamplona: Universidad de Navarra, 1997. 199–215.
Greer, Margaret Rich. "Art and power in the spectacle plays of Calderón de la Barca." *PMLA* 104 (1989): 329–339.
Greer, Margaret Rich. "Los dos cuerpos del rey en Calderón: *El nuevo palacio del Retiro* y *El mayor encanto amor*." *Actas del X Congreso de la AIH*. Ed. Antonio Vilanova. Barcelona: PPU, 1992. Vol. 2. 975–984.
Grilli, Giuseppe. "*De cosario a cosario*: ritratti poetici e giochi scenici." *Otro Lope no ha de haber*. Ed. Maria Grazia Profeti. Firenze: Alinea, 2000. Vol. 2. 37–50.
Grilli, Giuseppe. "La modernización del mito: *El mayor encanto, amor*." *De Cervantes a Calderón: Estudios sobre la literatura y el teatro español del Siglo de Oro*. Ed. Karolina Kumor. Varsovia: Universidad, 2009. 75–90.
Guasch Melis, Ana Eva. "Gitanos viejos y gitanos nuevos: los grupos sociales en *La gitanilla*." *Actas del VIII Coloquio Internacional de la Asociación de Cervantistas*. El Toboso: Ayuntamiento, 1999. 327–340.
Guastavino Gallent, Guillermo. "Don Felipe de África en Valencia (1599)." *Miscelánea de estudios árabes y hebraicos. Sección Arabe-Islám* 5 (1956): 119–125.
Gutiérrez Carbajo, Francisco. "Mitología y popularismo en *Apolo y Climene*." *Calderón 2000: homenaje a Kurt Reichenberger en su 80 cumpleaños*. Ed. Ignacio Arellano. Kassel: Reichenberger, 2002. Vol. 2. 219–234.
Gutierrez-Laffond, Aurore. *Théâtre et magie dans la littérature dramatique du XVIIe siècle en France*. Villeneuve d'Ascq: PU du Septentrion, 1998.
Gutiérrez Nieto, Juan Ignacio. "Inquisición y culturas marginadas: conversos, moriscos y gitanos." *El siglo del Quijote (1580–1680)*. Madrid: Espasa Calpe, 1993. Vol. 1. 837–1015.
Halstead, Frank G. "The attitude of Lope de Vega toward astrology and astronomy." *Hispanic Review* 3 (1939): 205–219.
Halstead, Frank G. "The attitude of Tirso de Molina toward astrology." *Hispanic Review* 9 (1941): 417–439.
Hanson, Thomas Bradley, *Stylized man: the poetic use of physiognomy in Chaucer's "Canterbury Tales."* Madison: University of Wisconsin, 1970.

Henry, John. "The fragmentation of Renaissance occultism and the decline of magic." *History of science* 46 (2008): 1–48.
Herbers, Klaus. "Wissenskontakte und Wissensvermittlung in Spanien im 12. und 13. Jahrhundert: Sprache, Verbreitung und Reaktionen." *Artes im Mittelalter*. Ed. Ursula Schaefer. Berlin: Akademie-Verlag, 1999. 230–248.
Hermenegildo, Alfredo. "Parodia dramática y práctica social: la *Égloga Interlocutoria* de Diego de Ávila." *Estudios sobre Calderón y el teatro de la Edad de Oro. Homenaje a Kurt y Roswitha Reichenberger*. Ed. José Carlos De Torres Martínez, Francisco Mundi Pedret and Alberto Porqueras Mayo. Barcelona: PPU, 1989. 277–295.
Hernández Araico, Susana. "Mitos, simbolismo y estructura en *Apolo y Climene* y *El hijo del sol, Faetón*." *Bulletin of Hispanic Studies* 64 (1987): 77–85.
Hernández Araico, Susana. "Política imperial en *Los tres mayores prodigios*." *Homenaje a Hans Flasche*. Ed. Karl-Hermann Körner, Günther Zimmermann and Rafael Lapesa. Stuttgart: Steiner, 1991. 83–94.
Hernández Araico, Susana. "Génesis oficial y oposición política en *El mayor encanto, amor*." *Romanistisches Jahrbuch* 44 (1993): 307–322.
Hernández Araico, Susana. "Sensualidad musical en Calderón: *La púrpura de la rosa, Apolo y Climene* y *Las armas de la hermosura*." *Calderón 2000: homenaje a Kurt Reichenberger en su 80 cumpleaños*. Ed. Ignacio Arellano. Kassel: Reichenberger, 2002. Vol. 2. 245–258.
Hernández Araico, Susana. "La ocasionalidad de *El jardín de Falerina*." *Arkadien in den romanischen Literaturen*. Ed. Roger Friedlein, Gerhard Poppenberg and Annett Volmer. Heidelberg: Winter, 2008. 395–404.
Hernández González, Erasmo. *Estudio comparativo y edición de "La Cruz en la sepultura" y de "La devoción de la Cruz" de Calderón*. Granada: Universidad, 2002.
Herrán Alonso, Emma. "El tema de la huida a Egipto en el teatro áureo." *Cuatrocientos años del "Arte nuevo de hacer comedias" de Lope de Vega*. Ed. Germán Vega García-Luengos and Héctor Urzáiz. Valladolid: Universidad, 2010. Vol. 2. 621–634.
Herrero García, M. "Los rasgos físicos y el carácter según los textos españoles del siglo XVII." *Revista de Filología Española* 12 (1925): 157–177.
Hesse, Everett W. "El conflicto entre madre e hijos en *Los melindres de Belisa* de Lope." *Hispania* 54 (1971): 836–843.
Hesse, Everett W. "The alienation problem in Calderón's *La devoción de la Cruz*." *Revista de Estudios Hispánicos* 7 (1973): 361–381.
Hiergeist, Teresa. "Ins Gesicht geschrieben? Physiognomik (skepsis) im *Don Quijote*." *Hispanorama* 154 (2016): 24–29.
Hogrebe, Wolfram (ed.). *Mantik. Profile prognostischen Wissens in Wissenschaft und Kultur*. Würzburg: Königshausen & Neumann, 2005.
Honig, Edwin. "Calderón's strange mercy play." *Massachusetts Review* 3 (1961): 80–107.
Huerta Calvo, Javier. "Un Calderón joven y rebelde: *La devoción de la Cruz*." *Cuadernos de Teatro Clásico* 11 (1999): 178–190.
Hunt, Tony. "A New Fragment of Jofroi de Waterford's *Segré de segrez*." *Romania* 471–472 (2000): 289–314.
Hurtado Torres, Antonio. "La astrología en el teatro de Calderón de la Barca." *Calderón: actas del Congreso Internacional sobre Calderón y el teatro español del Siglo de Oro*. Ed. Luciano García Lorenzo. Madrid: CSIC, 1983. Vol. 2. 925–938.
Hurtado Torres, Antonio. *La astrología en la literatura del Siglo de Oro. Índice bibliográfico*. Alicante: Instituto de estudios alicantinos, 1984.

Hutchinson, Keith. "What happened to the occult qualities in the Scientific Revolution." *Isis* 73 (1982): 233–253.
Ibarz, Virgili. *El pensament d'Esteve Pujasol*. Fraga / Huesca: Institut d' Estudis del Baix Cinca, 1991.
Irigoyen García, Javier. "El problema morisco en *Los baños de Argel*, de Miguel de Cervantes: de renegados a mártires cristianos." *Revista Canadiense de Estudios Hispánicos* 32 (2008): 421–438.
Jacquart, Danielle. "L'influence des astres sur le corps humain chez Pietro d'Abano." *Le corps et ses énigmes au Moyen Âge*. Ed. Bernard Ribémont. Caen: Paradigme, 1993. 73–86.
Jacquart, Danielle. "La physiognomonie à l'époque de Frédéric II: le traité de Michel Scot." *Micrologus* 2 (1994): 19–37.
Jacquart, Danielle. "Autour de la *Compilatio phisionomiae* de Pietro d'Abano." *Médicine, astrologie et magie entre Moyen Âge et Renaissance autour de Pietro d'Abano*. Ed. Franck Collard, Jean-Patrice Boudet and Nicolas Weill-Parot. Firenze: Sismel. Edizioni del Galluzzo, 2013. 231–246.
Jerez-Gómez, Jesús David. "*La doncella Teodor* de Lope de Vega como modelo del *Arte Nuevo de hacer comedias*." *Romance notes* 50 (2010): 253–264.
Jiménez Rueda, Julio. *Herejías y supersticiones en la Nueva España. Los heterodoxos en México*. México: Imprenta Universitaria, 1946.
Johnson, Carroll B. "Lope de Rueda's *Comedia Eufemia*: A prelude to criticism." *Bulletin of the Comediantes* 20 (1968): 5–9.
Johnson, Carroll B. "El arte viejo de hacer teatro: Lope de Rueda, Lope de Vega y Cervantes." *Lope de Vega y los orígenes del teatro español*. Ed. Manuel Criado de Val. Madrid: EDI-6, 1981. 95–102.
Johnson, Christopher D. "Coincidence of opposites: Bruno, Calderón, and a drama of ideas." *Renaissance Drama* (2010): 319–399.
Jordan, Leo. "Physiognomische Abhandlungen." *Romanische Forschungen* 29 (1911): 680–720.
Josa, Lola. "Una concesión alarconiana al gusto: *La cueva de Salamanca*, comedia de magia." *En torno al teatro del siglo de oro*. Ed. Irene Pardo Molina and Antonio Serrano Agulló. Almería: Instituto de Estudios Almerienses, 2001. 279–287.
Junkerjürgen, Ralf. *Haarfarben: eine Kulturgeschichte in Europa seit der Antike*. Köln: Böhlau, 2009.
Kartchner, Eric J. "Subversive Supplementation: Calderón's *La Devoción de la Cruz*." *Cincinnati Romance Review* 18 (1999): 116–121.
Kodera, Sergius. "Der Philosoph als Porträtist. Malerei und antiplatonische Philosophie in Giordano Brunos Komödie *Candelaio* (1582)." *Zeitsprünge* 14 (2010): 508–531.
Kraye, Jill. "The Printing History of Aristotle in the Fifteenth Century." *Renaissance Studies* 9 (1995): 189–211.
Labarre, Françoise. "En torno a la fecha de *El vergonzoso en palacio* y de algunas otras comedias de Tirso de Molina." *Criticón* 16 (1981): 47–64.
La Charité, Raymond. "Montaigne's silenic Text *De la phisiognomie*." *Le parcours des "Essais." Montaigne 1588–1988*. Ed. Marcel Tétel and G. M. Masters. Paris: Aux Amateurs de Livres, 1989. 59–69.
Lama, Miguel Ángel. "La Biblioteca de Barcarrota. Tipología de un hallazgo." *Alborayque* 1 (2007): 159–211.

Lanuza-Navarro, Tayra M. C. "The dramatic culture of astrological medicine in early modern Spain." *Medical Cultures of the Early Modern Spanish Empire*. Ed. John Slater. Farnham: Ashgate, 2014. 189–212.
Laplana Gil, José Enrique. "Gracián y la fisiognomia." *Alazet* 9 (1997): 103–124.
Lara Alberola, Eva. *Hechiceras y brujas en la literatura española de los siglos de oro*. València: Universitat, 2010.
LaRubia-Prado, Francisco. "Calderón's *Life is a Dream*: Mapping a Culture of Contingency for the Twenty-First Century." *Bulletin of the Comediantes* 54 (2002): 373–405.
Lauer, A. Robert. "El planteamiento escénico de *El tesoro escondido*, auto sacramental historial calderoniano." *Teatro calderoniano sobre el tablado: Calderón y su puesta en escena a través de los siglos*. Ed. Manfred Tietz. Stuttgart: Steiner, 2003a. 251–260.
Lauer, A. Robert. "La estructura dramática de *El tesoro escondido*, auto musical tardío de Calderón." *Estudios de teatro áureo: texto, espacio y representación*. Ed. Aurelio González, María Teresa Miaja De La Peña and Lillian von der Walde Moheno. México: Universidad Autónoma Metropolitana, 2003b. 345–352.
Lauer, A. Robert. "Aspectos retóricos en el auto sacramental de *El tesoro escondido* de Calderón." *Anuario Calderoniano* 5 (2012): 197–214.
Lauer, A. Robert. "Actos verbales de disputa y violencia en el auto sacramental calderoniano *El tesoro escondido*." *La violencia en el teatro de Calderón*. Ed. Manfred Tietz and Gero Arnscheidt. Vigo: Academia del Hispanismo, 2014. 333–344.
Laurand, Valéry. "Les hésitations méthodologiques du Pseudo-Aristote et de l'anonyme latin." *La physiognomonie. Problèmes philosophiques d'une pseudo-science*. Ed. Christophe Bouton, Valéry Laurand and Layla Raïd. Paris: Editions Kimé, 2005. 17–44.
Lebigre, Arlette. *1679–1682, l'affaire des poisons*. Bruxelles: Éditions Complexe, 2001.
Leblon, Bernard. *Les gitans dans la littérature espagnole*. Toulouse: Institut d'Études Hispaniques et Hispano-Américaines, 1982.
Leblon, Bernard. *Les gitans d'Espagne. Le prix de la différence*. Paris: PUF, 1985.
Lee Palmer, Allison. "Lorenzo *Spirito* Gualtieri's *Libro delle Sorti* in Renaissance Perugia." *Sixteenth Century Journal* 3 (2016): 557–578.
Leland, Charles G. *Gypsy sorcery and fortune-telling illustrated by numerous incantations, specimens of medical magic, anecdotes and tales*. New York: Dover Publications, 1962.
LeVan, J. Richards. "Theme and metaphor in the *Auto historial*: Calderón's *Los encantos de la culpa*." *Approaches to the Theater of Calderón*. Ed. Michael D. Mcgaha. Washington: UP of America, 1982. 187–197.
Lewis-Smith, Paul. "Towards a new comedy: ingenio, metatheatre, and the cristicism of Lope de Vega in *La entretenida* and *Pedro de Urdemalas*." *Shakespeare, Cervantes, and Rabelais*. Ed. José Manuel González Fernández De Sevilla and Clive A. Bellis. Lewiston: Edwin Mellen, 2011. 44–59.
Lichtblau, Karin. "Maugis." *Verführer, Schurken, Magier*. Ed. Ulrich Müller. St. Gallen: UVK, 2001. 613–628.
Limami, Abdellatif. "Del referente histórico y de la realidad argelina en *Los baños de Argel* de Miguel de Cervantes." *De Cervantes y el Islam*. Ed. Nuria Martínez de Castilla Muñoz and Rodolfo Gil Benumeya. Madrid: Sociedad Estatal de Conmemoraciones Culturales, 2006. 213–222.
Linton Lomas Barrett. *The supernatural in the Spanish comedia of the Golden Age*. Chapel Hill: North Carolina UP, 1938.
Lohse, Rolf. *Renaissancedrama und humanistische Poetik in Italien*. Paderborn: Fink, 2015.

López Castro, Armando. "La música en el teatro de Gil Vicente." *Actas del VI Congreso Internacional de la AHLM*. Ed. José Manuel Lucía Megías. Alcalá de Henares: Universidad, 1997. Vol. 2. 879–894.

Lorée, Denis. "Lire le *Secret des secrets* à l'aube de la Renaissance: l'adaptation française du XVe siècle." *Trajectoires européennes du "Secretum secretorum" du Pseudo-Aristote (XIIIe–XVIe siècle)*. Ed. Jean-Yves Tilliette, Margaret Bridges and Catherine Gaullier-Bougassas. Turnhout: Brepols, 2015. 107–136.

Lorenz, Erika. "Calderón und die Astrologie." *Romanistisches Jahrbuch* 12 (1961): 265–277.

Lovarini, E. "Remarks on the *zingaresche*." *Journal of the Gypsy Lore Society* 3 (1891): 85–96.

Lozano Pascual, José Manuel. "El cuerpo como espejo del alma: Comentarios sobre la *Fisiognomía* de G.B. Della Porta (1586)." *Revista de Historia de la Psicología* 30 (2009): 207–214.

Macdonald, Katherine. "Humanistic self-representation in Giovanni Battista Della Porta's *Della Fisonomia dell'uomo*." *Sixteenth Century Journal* 2 (2005): 397–414.

Maclean, Ian. *Logic, signs and nature in the Renaissance*. Cambridge: Cambridge UP, 2002.

Madera, Nelson Ismael, *La relacion entre la fisionomia y el caracter de los personajes en "Don Quijote de la Mancha."* PhD: Florida State University, 1992.

Madroñal, Abraham. "El contador Gaspar de Barrionuevo (1562–c. 1624?), poeta y dramaturgo toledano amigo de Lope de Vega." *Voz y letra* 4 (1993): 105–128.

Madroñal Durán, Abraham. "A propósito de *La doncella Teodor*, una comedia de viaje de Lope de Vega." *Revista de Literatura* 73 (2011): 183–198.

Magnaghi, Serena. "Los conocimientos herméticos de los estudiantes salmantinos: los casos de *La serrana de Tormes* y *La boda entre dos maridos* de Lope de Vega." *De lo sobrenatural a lo fantástico: Siglos XIII–XIX*. Ed. Laura Pache Carballo and Barbara Greco. Madrid: Biblioteca Nueva, 2014. 163–174.

Mandrell, James. "Tirso and the scene of writing: *El castigo del penséque* and *Quien calla, otorga*." *Bulletin of the Comediantes* 55 (2003): 133–149.

Marcos Celestino, Mónica. "El Marqués de Villena y *La cueva de Salamanca*. Entre literatura, historia y leyenda." *Estudios humanísticos. Filología* 26 (2004): 155–186.

Mariscal, George. "Iconografía y técnica emblemática en Calderón: *La devoción de la Cruz*." *Revista Canadiense de Estudios Hispánicos* 5 (1981): 339–354.

Márquez Villanueva, Francisco. "La buenaventura de Preciosa." *Nueva Revista de Filología Hispánica* 34 (1985): 741–768.

Martinengo, Alessandro. "Huellas de la épica renacentista italiana en el tratamiento del mito de Circe, de Ruiz Alceo a Calderón." *Calderón: protagonista eminente del barroco europeo*. Ed. Theo Reichenberger and Kurt Reichenberger. Kassel: Reichenberger, 2000. Vol. 1. 203–215.

Martinengo, Alessandro. "El encanto / desencanto de la culpa: Recorrido de Valdivielso a Calderón." *Deseo, sexualidad y afectos en la obra de Calderón*. Ed. Manfred Tietz. Stuttgart: Steiner, 2001. 105–116.

Martínez, Matías. "Memorabile – Sage – Legende: einfache Formen in Zacharias Werners *Der vierundzwanzigste Februar* und Pedro Calderón de la Barcas *La devoción de la Cruz*." *Geistiger Handelsverkehr: komparatistische Aspekte der Goethezeit*. Ed. Anne Bohnenkamp and Matías Martínez. Göttingen: Wallstein, 2008. 291–314.

Martínez Torrón, Diego. "El mito de Circe y *Los encantos de la culpa*." *Calderón. Actas del Congreso Internacional sobre Calderón y el teatro español del Siglo de Oro*. Ed. Luciano García Lorenzo. Madrid: CSIC, 1983. Vol. 2. 701–712.

Mata Induráin, Carlos. "El personaje del Hombre en el auto sacramental de *El jardín de Falerina*." *La dramaturgia de Calderón: técnicas y estructuras*. Ed. Enrica Cancelliere and Ignacio Arellano. Madrid: Iberoamericana, 2006. 289–304.

Matas Caballero, Juan. "Feminismo y misoginia en *El mayor encanto, amor* de Calderón de la Barca." *Estudios sobre tradición clásica y mitología en el Siglo de Oro*. Ed. Jesús Ponce Cárdenas and Isabel Colón Calderón. Madrid: Ediciones Clásicas, 2002. 133–142.

Matsen, Herbert Stanley. *Alessandro Achillini (1463–1512) and his doctrine of "universals" and "transcendentals": a study in Renaissance Ockhamism*. Lewisburg: Bucknell UP, 1974.

Matsen, Herbert. "Alessandro Achillini (1463–1512) and 'Ockhamism' at Bologna (1490–1500)." *Journal of the History of Philosophy* 13 (1975): 437–451.

Maza, Francisco de la. *Enrico Martínez, cosmógrafo e impresor de Nueva España*. México: Ed. de la Sociedad Mexicana de Geografía y Estadística, 1943.

Mazzi, Curzio. *La Congrega dei Rozzi di Siena nel secolo XVI*. 2 vol. Firenze: Successori Le Monnier, 1882.

McCready, Warren T. "Lope de Vega's birth date and horoscope." *Hispanic Review* 4 (1960): 313–318.

McGaha, Michael D. "The sources and feminism of Lope's *Las mujeres sin hombres*." *The Perception of women in Spanish theater of the Golden Age*. Ed. Anita K. Stoll and Dawn L. Smith. Lewisburg / London: Bucknell UP, 1991. 157–169.

McKendrick, Melveena. "Los juicios de Eusebio: El joven Calderón en busca de su propio estilo." *El mundo del teatro español en su Siglo de Oro*. Ed. José M. Ruano de la Haza. Ottawa: Dovehouse, 1989. 313–326.

Megwinoff, Grace E. "G.X.8. del *Decamerón*: posible fuente de *La boda entre dos maridos*." *Lope de Vega y los orígenes del teatro español*. Madrid: EDI-6, 1981. 179–202.

Meinel, Christoph. "Okkulte und exakte Wissenschaft." *Die okkulten Wissenschaften in der Renaissance*. Ed. August Buck. Wiesbaden: Harrassowitz, 1992. 21–44.

Meixell, Amanda S. "The quest for identity at the onset of the age of reason: Calderon's H*ado y divisa de Leonido y Marfisa*." *Bulletin of the Comediantes* 60 (2008): 77–101.

Meregalli, Franco. "De *Los tratos de Argel* a *Los baños de Argel*." *Homenaje a Casalduero: crítica y poesía*. Ed. Gonzalo Sobejano and Pincus Sigele Rizel. Madrid: Gredos, 1972. 395–409.

Mesk, Josef. "Die Beispiele in Polemons Physiognomonik." *Wiener Studien* 50 (1932): 51–67.

Miggiano, Gabriella. "Marzio, Galeotto." *Dizionario Biografico degli Italiani* 71 (2008). http://www.treccani.it (visited on 9. 4.2020).

Milani, Matteo. "La tradizione italiana del *Secretum Secretorum*." *La Parola del Testo* 5 (2001): 209–253.

Milani, Matteo. "Indicazioni fisiognomiche inedite tratte dal *Secretum secretorum*." *A warm mind-shake. Scritti in onore di Paolo Bertinetti*. Torino: Trauben, 2014. 357–369.

Milani, Matteo. "Fiçonomo – Polemone (di Laodicea): sotto mentite spoglie onomastiche." *Il Nome nel testo* 17 (2015a): 319–333.

Milani, Matteo. "Un compendio italiano del *Secretum secretorum*: riflessioni e testo critico." *Trajectoires européennes du "Secretum secretorum" du Pseudo-Aristote (XIIIe–XVIe siècle)*. Ed. Jean-Yves Tilliette, Margaret Bridges and Catherine Gaullier-Bougassas. Turnhout: Brepols, 2015b. 257–316.

Millé y Giménez, Juan. "El horóscopo de Lope de Vega." *Humanidades* 15 (1927): 69–96.

Minic-Vidovic, Ranka. "La poética de la risa en los pasos de Lope de Rueda." *Bulletin of the Comediantes* 59 (2007): 11–37.

Minois, Georges. *Histoire de l'avenir. Des prophètes à la prospective.* Paris: Fayard, 1996.
Misener, Geneva. "Loxus: physician and physiognomist." *Classical Philology* 18 (1923): 1–22.
Mochón Castro, Montserrat. *El intelecto femenino en las tablas áureas. Contexto y escenificación.* Madrid / Frankfurt am Main: Iberoamericana / Vervuert, 2012.
Möller, Reinhold. *Mittelhochdeutsche Prosaübersetzung des "Secretum secretorum": Hiltgart von Hürnheim.* Berlin: Akademie-Verlag, 1963.
Mollenauer, Lynn Woo. "Justice versus secrecy. Investigating the Affair of the Poisons, 1679–1682." *Zeitsprünge: Forschungen zur Frühen Neuzeit* 6 (2002): 179–205.
Mollenauer, Lynn Wood. *Strange revelations. Magic, poison, and sacrilege in Louis XIV's France.* University Park: Pennsylvania State UP, 2007.
Monfrin, Jacques. "Sur les sources du *Secret des Secrets* de Jofroi de Waterford et Servais Copale." *Mélanges de linguistique romane et de philologie médiévale offerts à M. Maurice Delbouille.* Gembloux: Duculot, 1964. Vol. 2. 509–530.
Mongrédien, Georges. *Madame de Montespan et l'affaire des poisons.* Paris: Hachette, 1953.
Morby, Edwin S. "El *Libro de suertes* de la *Arcadia.*" *Homenaje a Rodríguez-Moñino. Estudios de erudición que le ofrecen sus amigos o discípulos hispanistas norteamericanos.* Madrid: Castalia, 1966. Vol. 2. 1–8.
Morel Fatio, Alfred. "Version napolitaine d'un texte catalan du *Secretum secretorum.*" *Romania* 26 (1897): 74–82.
Moreno Mendoza, Arsenio. "Fisiognómica, pintura y teatro." *Atrio* 12 (2006): 19–32.
Morley, S. Griswold, and Courtney Bruerton. *Cronología de las comedias de Lope de Vega.* Madrid: Gredos, 1968.
Morrow, Carolyn. "Nacionalismo y otredad en *Los baños de Argel* y *La gran sultana.*" *Estudios de teatro áureo: texto, espacio y representación.* Ed. Aurelio González, María Teresa Miaja de la Peña, Lillian von der Walde Moheno, Serrafín González García and Alma Mejía. México: UNAM / El Colegio de México, 2003. 379–386.
Mossiker, Frances. *The affair of the poisons.* New York: Knopf, 1969.
Mourad, Youssef. *La physiognomie arabe et le Kitāb Al-Firāsa de Fakhr al-Dīn Al-Razī.* Paris: Librairie Orientaliste Paul Geuthner, 1939.
Müller-Bochat, Eberhard. "Las ideas de Cervantes sobre el teatro y su síntesis en *Pedro de Urdemalas.*" *Arbor* 119 (1984): 225–236.
Mujica, Barbara. "Calderón's *La vida es sueño* and the skeptic revival." *Texto y espectáculo. Nuevas dimensiones críticas de la comedia.* Ed. Arturo Pérez-Pisonero. El Paso: University of Texas, 1990. 23–32.
Muñoz y Manzano, Cipriano. "Estudio crítico de la comedia *La devoción de la Cruz.*" *Certamen literario celebrado en Zaragoza para solemnizar el Segundo Centenario de D. Pedro Calderón de la Barca.* Zaragoza: Tipografía del Hospicio Provincial, 1881.
Mur, Maria-Christina, *The physiognomical discourse and European theatre. Theory, performance, dramatic text.* Frankfurt am Main: Lang, 2017.
Muratori, Cecilia. "From animal bodies to human souls: (Pseudo-)Aristotelian animals in Della Porta's *Physiognomics.*" *Early Science and Medicine* 22 (2017): 1–23.
Nagy, Edward. "La picaresca y la profecía dentro de la cisión estética y social cervantina en la comedia Pedro de Urdemalas." *Cervantes, su obra y su mundo.* Ed. Manuel Criado del Val. Madrid: Edi-6, 1981. 273–280.
Narinesingh, Lal. "Myth, magic and superstition in Calderon's *Apolo y Climene*: Dramatic study of the alliance between evil power and human delusion." *Myth and superstition in Spanish-Caribbean literature.* Mona: Department of Spanish, 1982. 135–178.

Nass, Lucien. *Les empoisonnements sous Louis XIV après les documents inédits de l'affaire des poisons 1679–1682*. Paris: Carré et Naud, 1898.
Navarro Durán, Rosa. "La edición de los *Libros de suertes*." *La edición de textos. Actas del I Congreso de la Asociación Internacional Siglo de Oro*. Ed. Dolores Noguera Guirao, Pablo Jauralde Pou and Alfonso Reyes. London: Tamesis, 1984. 361–367.
Nemtzov, Sarah. "El estudiante en la Comedia del Siglo de Oro." *The Modern Language Forum* 31 (1946): 60–81.
Neugaard, Edward J. "A new possible source for Calderón's *La devoción de la Cruz*." *Bulletin of the Comediantes* 25 (1973): 1–3.
Neumeister, Sebastian. "*El mayor encanto, amor*, de Calderón: aspectos lúdicos." *Bulletin of Spanish Studies* 90 (2013): 807–819.
Newels, Margarete. *Los géneros dramáticos en las poéticas del Siglo de Oro*. London: Tamesis, 1974.
Núñez Rivera, Valentín. "Metamorfosis cervantinas de la picaresca: novela y teatro." *XXIV Coloquio Cervantino Internacional*. Guanajuato / México: Fundación Cervantina de México, 2014. 95–136.
O'Connor, Thomas A. "Mito y milagros en *La devoción de a Cruz*." *Actas del VIII Congreso de la AIH*. Ed. A. David Kossoff, Ruth H. Kossoff, Geoffrey Ribbans and José Amor y Vázquez. Madrid: Istmo, 1986. Vol. 2. 365–374.
O'Connor, Thomas A. *Myth and the mythology in the theater of Pedro Calderón de la Barca*. Dublin: Trinity UP, 1988.
Oleza, Joan. "Variaciones del drama historial en Lope de Vega." *Anuario Lope de Vega* 19 (2013): 150–187.
Oliver Asín, Jaime. *Vida de Don Felipe de Africa, príncipe de Fez y Marruecos (1566–1621)*. Madrid: CSIC, 1955; reedition Granada: Universidad, 2008.
Ordine, Nuccio. "Gli inganni dell'ignoranza: Il *Candelaio* tra realtà e apparenza." *Esculape et Dionysos. Mélanges en l'honneur de Jean Céard*. Ed. Jean Dupèbe, Franco Giacone, Emmanuel Naya and Anne-Pascale Pouey-Mounou. Genève: Droz, 2008. 131–153.
Oteiza, Blanca. "Problemas textuales del teatro de Tirso: el caso de *El vergonzoso en palacio*." *El teatro del Siglo de Oro: edición e interpretación*. Ed. Luis Alberto Blecua, Ignacio Arellano and Guillermo Serés. Madrid: Iberoamericana, 2009. 351–368.
Pacheco y Costa, Alejandra. "Música, espacio escénico y estructura dramática en *El Jardín de Falerina* de Calderón de la Barca." *Teatro* 19 (2003): 79–105.
Pack, Roger A. "A Pseudo-Aristotelian Chiromancy." *Archives d'Histoire Doctrinale et Littéraire du Moyen Âge* 36 (1969): 189–241.
Pack, Roger A. "Pseudo-Aristoteles: Chiromantia." *Archives d'Histoire Doctrinale et Littéraire du Moyen Âge* 39 (1972): 289–320.
Pack, Roger A., and R. Hamilton. "Rodericus de Maioricis *Tractatus ciromancie*." *Archives d'Histoire Doctrinale et Littéraire du Moyen Âge* 38 (1971): 271–305.
Paige, Nicholas. "L'affaire des poisons et l'imaginaire de l'enquête: De Molière à Thomas Corneille." *Littératures Classiques* 40 (2000): 195–208.
Palacín, G. B. "¿En dónde oyó Cervantes recitar a Lope de Rueda?" *Hispanic Review* 20 (1952): 240–243.
Pantin, Isabelle. "The role of translations in European scientific exchanges in the sixteenth and seventeenth centuries." *Cultural translation in early modern Europe*. Ed. Peter Burke and Ronnie Po-chia Hsia. Cambridge: Cambridge UP, 2007. 163–179.

Paolella, Alfonso. "L'autore delle illustrazioni delle *Fisiognomiche* di Della Porta e la ritrattistica. Esperienze filologiche." *La "mirabile" natura. Magia e scienza in Giovan Battista Della Porta (1615–2015)*. Ed. Marco Santoro. Pisa / Roma: Fabrizio Serra, 2016. 81–94.

Paques, Viviana. *Les sciences occultes d'après les documents littéraires italiens du XVIe siècle*. Paris: Institut d'Ethnologie, 1971.

Pardo Tomás, José. *Ciencia y censura: la Inquisición española y los libros científicos en los siglos XVI y XVII*. Madrid: CSIC, 1991.

Parker, Alexander A. "Santos y bandoleros en el teatro español del Siglo de Oro." *Arbor* 43–44 (1949): 395–416.

Parker, Alexander A. "Hacia una definición de la tragedia Calderoniana." *Estudios sobre Calderón*. Ed. Javier Aparicio Maydeu. Madrid: Istmo, 2000. 327–351.

Parker, Margaret R. *The story of a story across cultures. The case of the doncella Teodor*. Woodbridge: Tamesis, 1996.

Parr, James A. "On fate, suicide, and free will in Alarcón's *El dueño de las estrellas*." *Hispanic Review* 42 (1974): 199–207.

Partridge, Christopher. *The occult world*. New York: Routledge, 2014.

Paschetto, Eugenia. *Pietro d'Abano, medico e filosofo*. Firenze: Vallecchi, 1984.

Paschetto, Eugenia. "La Fisiognomica nell'enciclopedia delle scienze di Pietro d'Abano." *Medioevo* 11 (1985): 97–112.

Pascual Barciela, Emilio. "A propósito de la *anagnórisis* en una comedia mitológica temprana de Calderón de la Barca: *El mayor encanto, amor*." *Dicenda* 30 (2012): 89–103.

Pavia, Mario N. *Drama of the Siglo de Oro. A study of magic, witchcraft, and other occult beliefs*. New York: Hispanic Institute, 1959.

Pedraza Jiménez, Felipe B. "Ecos de Alcazarquivir en Lope de Vega: *La tragedia del rey Don Sebastián* y la figura de Muley Xeque." *El siglo XVII Hispanomarroquí*. Ed. Mohammed Salhi. Rabat: Facultad de Letras y de Ciencias Humanas, 1997. 133–146.

Pedraza Jiménez, Felipe B. "*El jardín de Falerina* y la recreación escénica de la caballería." *Giornate Calderoniane Calderón 2000*. Ed. Enrica Cancelliere. Palermo: Flaccovio, 2003. 171–185.

Pedraza Jiménez, Felipe B. "Rojas Zorrilla ante la comedia de santos: *Santa Isabel, reina de Portugal*." *Homenaje a Henri Guerreiro. La hagiografía entre historia y literatura en la España de la Edad Media y del Siglo de Oro*. Ed. Marc Vitse. Madrid / Frankfurt: Iberoamericana / Vervuert, 2006. 967–983.

Pedraza Jiménez, Felipe B. "*El jardín de Falerina*: metamorfosis dramáticas." *De Cervantes a Calderón: Estudios sobre la literatura y el teatro español del Siglo de Oro*. Ed. Karolina Kumor. Varsovia: Universidad, 2009. 91–112.

Pedraza Jiménez, Felipe B. "Episodios de la historia contemporánea en Lope de Vega." *Anuario Lope de Vega* 8 (2012): 1–39.

Pedrosa, José Manuel. "Lope de Vega entre espejos, pastores y hechiceros: magia astrológica e ilusión óptica (con algunas brujas de Cervantes)." *eHumanista* 26 (2014): 328–378.

Pensado Figueiras, Jesús. "La traduction castillane de l'*Epistola Aristotelis ad Alexandrum de dieta servanda* de Jean de Séville." *Trajectoires européennes du "Secretum secretorum" du Pseudo-Aristote (XIIIe–XVIe siècle)*. Ed. Jean-Yves Tilliette, Margaret Bridges and Catherine Gaullier-Bougassas. Turnhout: Brepols, 2015. 215–242.

Peña, Margarita. "La versión española de un oráculo italiano." *Elementos* 24 (1996): 39–44.

Perrone, Giuseppina. "Il volgarizzamento del *Secretum Secretorum* di Cola de Jennaro (1479)." *Le parole della scienza. Scritture tecniche e scientifiche in volgare (secoli XIII–XV)*. Ed. Riccardo Gualdo. Galatina (Lecce): Congedo, 2001. 353–358.

Petitfils, Jean-Christian. *L'affaire des poisons. Alchimistes et sorciers sous Louis XIV*. Paris: Albin Michel, 1977.

Piccari, Paolo. *Giovan Battista della Porta: il filosofo, il retore, lo scienziato*. Milano: Angeli, 2007.

Poirson, Martial. "Les classiques ont-ils cru à leurs machines? La force du surnaturel dans *La Devineresse ou les Faux enchantements* (1679)." *Revue d'Histoire du Théâtre* 56 (2004): 181–194.

Pollin, Alice M. "Calderón's Falerina and music." *Music and Letters* 49 (1968): 317–328.

Poma, Roberto. "Les erreurs de la main. Regards croisés sur la chiromancie naturelle de Giambattista della Porta." *Die Hand: Elemente einer Medizin- und Kulturgeschichte*. Ed. Mariacarla Gadebusch Bondio. Münster: LIT Verlag, 2010. 117–134.

Porter, Martin. *Windows of the soul: physiognomy in European culture 1470–1780*, Oxford: Clarendon, 2005.

Portnoy, Antonio. *Ariosto y su influencia en la literatura española*. Buenos Aires: Editorial Estrada, 1932.

Powell, Jocelyn. "Making Faces: Character and Physiognomy in *L'École des femmes* and *L'Avare*." *Seventeenth-Century French Studies* 9 (1987): 94–112.

Preda, Alessandra. "De la commedia au livre, du manuscrit à la comédie en prose: Le parcours parisien du *Candelaio* de Giordano Bruno." *Du spectateur au lecteur: Imprimer la scène aux XVIe et XVIIe siècles*. Ed. Larry F. Norman, Philippe Desan and Richard Strier. Fasano / Paris: Schena / Presses de l'Université de Paris-Sorbonne, 2002. 157–180.

Predari, Francesco. *Origine e vicende dei Zingari*. Milano: Lampatio, 1841.

Presberg, Charles D. "Dreams of reason create monsters of culture: *La vida es sueño*." *Bulletin of the Comediantes* 53 (2001): 101–127.

Presotto, Marco. "Stampe e manoscritti nel primo Lope: il caso de *Los donaires de Matico*." *Annali di Ca'Foscari* 31 (1992): 192–212.

Prest, Julia. "Silencing the supernatural: *La Devineresse* and the Affair of the Poisons." *Forum for Modern Language Studies* 43 (2007): 397–409.

Prian Salazar, Jesús. "Notas sobre el espacio en *La cueva de Salamanca*." *Dramaturgia española y novohispana: Siglos XVI–XVII*. Ed. Lillian von der Walde Moheno and Serafín González García. México: Universidad Autónoma Metropolitana, 1993. 73–82.

Profeti, Maria Grazia. "Ambiguità e comicità: *Los donaires de Matico*." *Nell Officina di Lope*. Ed. Maria Grazia Profeti. Firenze: Alinea, 1998. 73–90.

Prosperi, Adriano. "L'Inquisizione fiorentina dopo il Concilio di Trento." *Annuario dell'Istituto Storico Italiano per l'Età Moderna e Contemporánea* 38 (1986): 97–124.

Puliafito Bleuel, Anna Laura. *Comica pazzia. Vicissitudine e destini umani nel "Candelaio" di Giordano Bruno*. Firenze: Olschki, 2007.

Quétel, Claude. *Une ombre sur le Roi-Soleil. L'affaire des poisons*. Paris: Larousse, 2007.

Rambaud Cabello, Javier. "*El prodigioso príncipe transilvano*: el ideal católico frente a otomanos y protestantes." *Repubblica e virtù: Pensiero politico e Monarchia Cattolica fra XVI e XVII secolo*. Ed. Cesare Mozzarelli and Chiara Continisio. Roma: Bulzoni, 1995. 279–296.

Rank, Otto. *Das Inzest-Motiv in Dichtung und Sage*. Darmstadt: Wissenschaftliche Buchgesellschaft, 1974.

Rapisarda, Stefano. "Appunti sulla circolazione del *Secretum secretorum* in Italia." *Le parole della scienza. Scritture tecniche e scientifiche in volgare (secoli XIII–XV)*. Ed. Riccardo Gualdo. Galatina (Lecce): Congedo, 2001. 77–97.
Rapisarda, Stefano. "Magia e divinazione." *Enciclopedia Fridericiana*. Roma: Instituto della Enciclopedia italiana, 2005. 233–239.
Ravaisson, François. *Archives de la Bastille. Documents inédits*. 19 vol. Paris: Durand & Pedone-Lauriel, 1866–1904.
Regalado, Antonio. *Calderón. Los orígenes de la modernidad en la España del Siglo de Oro*. Barcelona: Destino, 1995.
Reichenberger, Arnold G. "Fate, suicide, free will: *El dueño de las estrellas*." *After its Kind: Approaches to the Comedia*. Ed. James A. Parr, Matthew D. Stroud, Anne M. Pasero and Amy R. Williamsen. Kassel: Reichenberger, 1991. 37–47.
Reißer, Ulrich. *Physiognomik und Ausdruckstheorie der Renaissance: der Einfluß charakterologischer Lehren auf Kunst und Kunsttheorie des 15. und 16. Jahrhunderts*. München: Scaneg, 1997.
Repath, Ian. "The physiognomy of Adamantius the Sophist." *Seeing the face, seeing the soul: Polemon's physiognomy from classical antiquity to medieval Islam*. Ed. Simon Swain. Oxford: Oxford UP, 2007. 487–518.
Reske, Christoph. *Die Buchdrucker des 16. und 17. Jahrhunderts im deutschen Sprachgebiet*. Wiesbaden: Harrassowitz, 2007.
Reusch, Heinrich. *Der Index der verbotenen Bücher*. Bonn: Max Cohen & Sohn, 1883–1885.
Rey Bueno, Mar. *Inferno. Historia de una biblioteca maldita*. Madrid: Aguilar, 2007.
Rey Hazas, Antonio. "Pedro de Urdemalas: Vida y literatura." *Torre de los Lujanes* 27 (1994): 197–210.
Rey Hazas, Antonio. "La libertad de la mujer y sus límites en el teatro Calderoniano: la heroína de *La devoción de la Cruz* y otros personajes femeninos." *Toledo, entre Calderón y Rojas*. Ed. Felipe B. Pedraza, Rafael González Cañal and José Cano Navarro. Almagro: Universidad de Castilla-La Mancha, 2003. 13–42.
Rey Hazas, Antonio. "Cervantes y el teatro clásico." *Cuadernos de Teatro Clásico* 20 (2005): 21–96.
Reyes Peña, Mercedes de los. "Una nota sobre el *terminus ad quem* de *Los donaires de Matico*." *Anuario Lope de Vega* 2 (1996): 197–212.
Rheinheimer, Martin. *Pobres, mendigos y vagabundos la supervivencia en la necesidad, 1450–1850*. Madrid: Siglo XXI, 2009.
Riandière La Roche, Josette. "La physiognomomie, miroir de l'âme et du corps: à propos d'un inédit espagnol de 1591." *Le corps dans la société espagnole des XVIe et XVIIe siècles*. Ed. Augustin Redondo. Paris: Publications de la Sorbonne, 1990. 51–62.
Ricarte Bescós, José María. *Creatividad y comunicación persuasiva*. Bellaterra: Universitat Autònoma de Barcelona, 1999.
Rico, Francisco. *El pequeño mundo del hombre: varia fortuna de una idea en las letras españolas*. Madrid: Castalia, 1970.
Rico, Francisco. "La librería de Barcarrota." *Babelia*, 26.2.2000.
Roca Barea, María Elvira. "Diego Guillén de Ávila, autor y traductor del siglo XV." *Revista de Filología Española* 86 (2006): 373–394.
Rodler, Lucia. *Il corpo specchio dell'anima: teoria e storia della fisiognomica*. Milano: Mondadori, 2000.

Rodrigues Vianna Peres, Lygia. "Las obras breves en *Hado y divisa de Leonido y Marfisa*, de Calderón de la Barca. El entremés de *La Tía.*" *Teatro y poder en el Siglo de Oro.* Ed. Mariela Insúa and Felix K. E. Schmelzer. Pamplona: Universidad de Navarra, 2013. 183–198.

Rodríguez Cuadros, Evangelina, and Antonio Tordera Sáez. *Calderón y la obra corta dramática del siglo XVII.* London: Tamesis, 1983.

Rodríguez Cuadros, Evangelina, and Antonio Tordera Sáez. *La escritura como espejo de palacio: el toreador de Calderón.* Kassel: Reichenberger, 1985.

Rodríguez de Lera, Juan Ramón. "El tratamiento de los gitanos en la novela del Siglo de Oro y en las Novels of Roguery." *Estudios de literatura comparada. Norte y sur, la sátira, transferencia y recepción de géneros y formas textuales.* Ed. José Enrique Martínez Fernández. León: Universidad de León, 2002. 215–234.

Rodríguez-Gallego, Fernando. "La tentación de lo serio: a propósito de *El astrólogo fingido.*" *Anuario Calderoniano* 10 (2017): 219–236.

Rodríguez-Puértolas, Julio. "La transposición de la realidad en los *autos sacramentales* de Lope de Vega." *Bulletin Hispanique* 72 (1970): 96–112.

Rodríguez Rodríguez, Ana M. "La representación de la violencia en *El trato de Argel* y *Los baños de Argel.*" *Cervantes en el espejo del tiempo.* Ed. María Carmen Marín Pina. Zaragoza / Alcalá de Henares: Universidad, 2010. 349–366.

Rojo Vega, Anastasio. "Brujería, ocultismo y medicina en el Siglo de Oro." *Edad de Oro* 27 (2008): 267–293.

Romano, Angelo. "Michelangelo Biondo poligrafo e stampatore." *Officine del nuovo. Sodalizi fra letterati, artisti ed editori nella cultura italiana fra Riforma e Controriforma.* Ed. Harald Hendrix and Paolo Procaccioli. Manziana: Vecchiarelli, 2008. 217–241.

Romanos, Melchora. "Felipe II en la *Tragedia del rey don Sebastián y el bautismo del Príncipe de Marruecos* de Lope de Vega." *Edad de Oro* 18 (1999): 177–191.

Romanos, Melchora. "Modos de dramatizar la historia: *La tragedia del rey don Sebastiá*n en Lope de Vega y Vélez de Guevara." *Silva. Studia philologica in honorem Isaías Lerner.* Ed. Isabel Lozano Renieblas and Juan Carlos Mercado. Madrid: Castalia, 2001. 595–608.

Romo Feito, Fernando. "Verdad y engaño en el teatro cervantino: Pedro de Urdemalas." *La menzogna.* Ed. Maria Grazia Profeti. Firenze: Alinea, 2008. 101–123.

Rosado, Gabriel. "Sobre un pasaje de *El desconfiado* de Lope de Vega y probable fecha de composición de la comedia." *Bulletin of the Comediantes* 23 (1971): 6–10.

Rose, Constance H. "El arte de escribir: *Los tres mayores prodigios* de Calderón y la pintura." *Hacia Calderón.* Ed. Hans Flasche and Klaus Dirscherl. Stuttgart: Steiner, 1994. 243–252.

Rose, Constance H. "Was Calderón serious? Another look at *Los tres mayores prodigios.*" *Hispanic Essays in Honor of Frank P. Casa.* Ed. A. Robert Lauer and Henry W. Sullivan. New York: Lang, 1997. 246–252.

Rose, Valentin. *Anecdota Graeca et Graecolatina. Mitteilungen aus Handschriften zur Geschichte der griechischen Wissenschaft.* Berlin: Duemmler, 1864.

Roso Díaz, José. "*La boda entre dos maridos*: Una comedia de Lope entre la amistad y el amor." *Anuario de Estudios Filológicos* 22 (1999): 373–394.

Rössner, Michael. "Theater auf dem Theater und Bühnenpikareske bei Corneille und Cervantes. Zur *Illusion comique* und zu *Pedro de Urdemalas.*" *Romanische Forschungen* 101 (1989): 42–59.

Rudall, Diane. "The comic power of illusion-allusion: Laughter, *La Devineresse*, and the scandal of a glorious century." *Laughter in the Middle Ages and Early Modern Times:*

Epistemology of a fundamental human behavior, its meaning, and consequences. Ed. Albrecht Classen. Berlin / New York: De Gruyter, 2010. 791–801.

Ruggieri, Lorenza. "De las posibles fuentes de la comedia Eufenia de Lope de Rueda." *Tonos digital* 25 (2013): without pagination.

Rull Fernández, Enrique. "Puesta en escena y sentido en el teatro mitológico de Calderón: *Los tres mayores prodigios*." *Actas del Congreso El Siglo de Oro en el Nuevo Milenio*. Ed. Carlos Mata Induráin and Miguel Zugasti. Pamplona: EUNSA, 2005. Vol. 2. 1529–1542.

Ryan, W. F., and Charles B. Schmitt. *Pseudo-Aristotle. The "Secret of secrets": sources and influences*. London: The Warburg Institute, 1982.

Sabattini, Gino. *Bio-bibliografia chiromantica. Bibliografia di opere antiche e moderne di chiromanzia e sulla chiromanzia*. Reggio Emilia: Nironi, 1946.

Sáez, Adrián J. "Una aproximación a *La devoción de la cruz*, drama temprano de Calderón." *Contra los mitos y sofismas de las teorías literarias posmodernas: Identidad, género, Ideología, Relativismo, Americocentrismo, Minoría, Otredad*. Ed. Inger Enkvist and Jesús G. Maestro. Vigo: Academia del Hispanismo, 2010. 217–239.

Sáez, Adrián J. "Una comedia religiosa frente al auto sacramental: *La devoción de la Cruz*, de Calderón." *Ingenio, teología y drama en los autos sacramentales de Calderón*. Ed. María Carmen Pinillos Salvador. Pamplona / Kassel: Universidad de Navarra / Reichenberger, 2012. 179–196.

Sáez, Adrián J. "De Edipo y sus variantes: en torno a las fuentes de *La devoción de la Cruz*, de Calderón." *Pictavia aurea: Actas del IX Congreso de la AISO*. Ed. Alain Bègue, Emma Herrán Alonso and Asociación Internacional *Siglo de Oro*. Toulouse: PU du Mirail, 2013. 1111–1119.

Sáez, Adrián J. "Fortunas y adversidades d e Pedro de Urdemalas, un pícaro dramático." *Etiopicas* 10 (2014a): 111–127.

Sáez, Adrián J. "Violencia y poder en *La devoción de la cruz*." *La violencia en el teatro de Calderón*. Ed. Manfred Tietz and Gero Arnscheidt. Vigo: Academia del Hispanismo, 2014b. 473–488.

Saif, Liana. *The arabic influences on early modern occult philosophy*. Basingstoke: Palgrave Macmillan, 2015.

Sales, João Nuno. *Ciganas*. Lisboa: Quimera, 1988.

Sâmbrian, Oana Andreia. "El gusto del público español por las comedias de carácter histórico en la España barroca *El prodigioso príncipe transilvano* y *El príncipe prodigioso*." *Bulletin of Hispanic Studies* 89 (2012): 31–42.

Sâmbrian, Oana Andreia. "Problemas de autoridad y poder en el teatro aurisecular de argumento transilvano: *El capitán prodigioso* y *El príncipe prodigioso y defensor de la fe*." *Imagen de la autoridad y el poder en el teatro del Siglo de Oro*. Ed. Ignacio Arellano and Jesús Menéndez Peláez. New York: IDEA, 2016. 99–114.

San Miguel, Ángel. "La evolución del espacio escénico ideal en la obra en castellano de Gil Vicente." *Edad Media y Renacimiento. Continuidades y rupturas*. Ed. Jean Canavaggio and Bernard Darbord. Caen: PU de Caen, 1991. 145–159.

Sánchez, Ana Isabel. "Palabras mágicas: de medicina clásica y magia en Lope de Vega." *Anuario Lope de Vega* 11 (2005): 221–232.

Sanchez, Laurène. "Rencontres et non rencontres dans *Santa Isabel, reina de Portugal* de Francisco de Rojas Zorrilla: le religieux et le profane." *Cahiers du GRIAS* 13 (2008): 225–241.

Sánchez Escribano, Federico, and Alberto Porqueras Mayo. *Preceptiva dramática española del Renacimiento y el Barroco*. Madrid: Gredos, 1972.
Sánchez Jiménez, Antonio. "Algunos chistes astrológicos de Lope de Vega." *Criticón* 122 (2014): 41–52.
Sánchez Ramos, Valeriano. "Un saadí converso durante el reinado de Felipe IV: Don Felipe de África, príncipe de Fez y de Marruecos." *Chronica Nova* 36 (2010): 291–314.
Sánchez Salor, Eustaquio. "La quiromancia emparedada de Barcarrota (Badajoz): Los conocimientos quirománticos antiguos y medievales recogidos por Tricasso de Mantua." *Actas del II Congreso Hispánico de Latín Medieval*. Ed. Maurilio Pérez González. León: Universidad, 1999. Vol. 2. 803–824.
Sánchez Salor, Eustaquio. "La ciencia médica en la Biblioteca de Barcarrota." *Alborayque* 1 (2007): 109–135.
Santibáñez, María del Carmen Griselda. "El libre albedrío (*servio arbitrio*) en *La vida es sueño*." *Calderón 2000. Homenaje a Kurt Reichenberger en su 80 cumpleaños*. Kassel: Reichenberger, 2002. Vol. 2. 623–632.
Sarmati, Elisabetta. "Maritornes, el caballero Metabólico y Fraudador de los Ardides: Una nota al *Quijote* I, 43 (y a *Pedro de Urdemalas* II, 554)." *Amadís de Gaula: quinientos años despué. Estudios en homenaje a Juan Manuel Cacho Blecua*. Ed. José Manuel Lucía Megías, María Carmen Marín Pina and Ana Bueno Serrano. Alcalá de Hernares: Centro de Estudios Cervantinos, 2008. 755–768.
Saunal, Damien. "Autour des sources de *Pobreza no es vileza*." *Bulletin Hispanique* 48 (1946): 239–246.
Saura, Norma. "*El mayor encanto, amor* de Calderón de la Barca." *Estudios críticos de literatura española*. Ed. Edith Marta Villarino Cela and Elsa Graciela Fiadino. Mar del Plata: Universidad Nacional, 2003. Vol. 1. 169–182.
Schalk, Fritz. "Lope de Vegas *Melindres de Belisa* und *Bizarrías de Belisa*." *Studia iberica: Festschrift für Hans Flasche*. Ed. Karl-Hermann Körner and Klaus Rühl. Bern: Francke, 1973. 581–588.
Schizzano Mandel, Adrienne. "La presencia de Calderón en la loa de *Los tres mayores prodigios*." *Hacia Calderón*. Ed. Hans Flasche. Stuttgart: Steiner, 1988. 227–235.
Schizzano Mandel, Adrienne. "Della Porta: *El astrólogo NON fingido* de Calderón." *Hacia Calderón*. Ed. Hans Flasche. Stuttgart: Steiner 1990. 161–180.
Schmidt, Marie-France. "*La Dévotion à la Croix*, de Calderón à Camus: langage et dramaturgie." *Camus et le théâtre*. Ed. Jacqueline Lévi-Valensi. Paris: IMEC, 1992. 196–210.
Schmitt, Charles B. "Francesco Storella and the last printed edition of the *Secretum secretorum* (1555)." *Pseudo-Aristotle. The "Secret of secrets": sources and influences*. Ed. W. F. Ryan and Charles B. Schmitt. London: The Warburg Institute, 1982. 124–131.
Schmitt, Charles B., and Dilwyn Knox. *Pseudo-Aristoteles Latinus. A guide to Latin works falsely attributed to Aristotle before 1500*. London: Warburg Institute, 1985.
Sears, Theresa Ann. "Freedom isn't free: free will in *La vida es sueño* revisited." *Romance Quarterly* 49 (2002): 280–289.
Seidel Menchi, Silvana. *Erasmo in Italia 1520–1580*. Torino: Bollati-Boringhieri, 1987.
Serralta, Frédéric. "Sobre los orígenes de la comedia de figurón: *El ausente en el lugar*, de Lope de Vega (¿1606?)." *En torno al teatro del siglo de oro: XV Jornadas de Teatro del Siglo de Oro*. Ed. Irene Pardo and Antonio Serrano. Almería: Instituto de Estudios Almerienses, 2001. 85–94.

Serralta, Frédéric. "Sobre el pre-figurón en tres comedias de Lope: *Los melindres de Belisa, Los hidalgos del aldea* y *El ausente en el lugar*." *Criticón* 87 (2003): 827–836.
Serrano Mangas, Fernando. *El secreto de los Peñaranda. Casas, médicos y estirpes judeoconversas en La Baja de Extremadura rayana: siglos XVI y XVII*. Madrid: Hebráica Ediciones, 2004.
Serrano Mangas, Fernando. "*Eppur si muove* o *La Biblioteca de Barcarrota* y el significado de *El Secreto de los Peñaranda*." *Alborayque* 1 (2007): 11–18.
Sharratt, Peter. *Bernard Salomon*. Genève: Droz, 2005.
Shergold, Norman D. "The first performance of Calderon's *El mayor encanto amor*." *Bulletin of Hispanic Studies* 35 (1958): 24–27.
Shumaker, Wayne. *The Occult Sciences in the Renaissance*. Los Angeles: California UP, 1972.
Sileri, Manuela. "Belisa entre melindres y bizarrías: como cambia la organización dramática de la comedia urbana." *Métrica y estructura dramática en el teatro de Lope de Vega*. Ed. Fausta Antonucci. Kassel: Reichenberger, 2007. 133–168.
Silvi, Christine. "Un texte encyclopédique sous le signe de la mouvance: la diffusion des *Secretsdes secrets français dans les premiers imprimés (XVe–XVIe siècle)*." *Trajectoires européennes du "Secretum secretorum" du Pseudo-Aristote (XIIIe–XVIe siècle)*. Ed. Jean-Yves Tilliette, Margaret Bridges and Catherine Gaullier-Bougassas. Turnhout: Brepols, 2015. 157–183.
Simon, Gérard. "Porta, la physionomie et la magie: Les circularités de la similitude." *La magie et ses langages*. Ed. Margaret Jones-Davies, Patrick Rafroidi, Jean-Claude Dupas and Jean-Pierre Teissedou. Lille: PU de Lille, 1980. 95–105.
Slater, John. "La escenificación teatral de la práctica médica en el siglo de oro." *Medicina, ideología e historia en España*. Ed. Ricardo Campos. Madrid: CSIC, 2007. 601–606.
Sloane, Robert. "The *strangeness* of *La devoción de la Cruz*." *Bulletin of Hispanic Studies* 54 (1977): 297–310.
Smieja, Florian. "Julia's Reasoning in Calderón's *La devoción de la Cruz*." *Bulletin of the Comediantes* 25 (1973): 37–39.
Solms, Wilhelm. *Zigeunerbilder. Ein dunkles Kapitel der deutschen Literaturgeschichte von der frühen Neuzeit bis zur Romantik*. Würzburg: Königshausen & Neumann, 2008.
Somerset, Anne. *Die Giftaffäre. Mord, Menschenopfer und Schwarze Messen am Hof Ludwigs XIV*. Essen: Magnus-Verlag, 2006.
Sosa Antonietti, Marcela Beatriz. "Estrategias metateatrales en *Pedro de Urdemalas* (y su relación con la poética del *Quijote*)." *El Quijote en Buenos Aires: lecturas cervantinas en el cuarto centenario*. Ed. Alicia Parodi, Julia D' Onofrio and Juan Diego Vila. Buenos Aires: Universidad, 2006. 901–908.
Sosa-Velasco, Alfredo J. "La ciencia en *La vida es sueño*: una lectura experimental." *RILCE* 27 (2011): 501–533.
Stabile, Giorgio. "Biondo, Michelangelo." *Dizionario Biografico degli Italiani* 10 (1968). http://www.treccani.it (visited on 9. 4.2020).
Stackhouse, Kenneth A. "Beyond performance: Cervantes's Algerian plays, *El trato de Argel* and *Los baños de Argel*." *Bulletin of the Comediantes* 52 (2000): 7–30.
Starkie, Walter. "Cervantes and the Gypsies." *Huntington Library Quarterly* 26 (1963): 337–349.
Steinberger, Deborah. "Profiting from scandal: The case of *La Devineresse*." *Cahiers du Dix-Septième* 9 (2003): 135–141.

Stern, Charlotte. "The comic spirit in Diego de Avila's *Egloga interlocutoria.*" *Bulletin of the Comediantes* 29 (1977): 62–75.
Strosetzki, Christoph. *Calderón.* Stuttgart: Metzler, 2001.
Sturlese, Loris (ed.). *Mantik, Schicksal und Freiheit im Mittelalter.* Köln: Böhlau, 2011.
Sullivan, Henry W. "Una traducción flamenca (1665) de *La devoción de la Cruz* de Calderón que no está perdida." *Actas del Sexto Congreso Internacional de Hispanistas.* Ed. Alan M. Gordon, Evelyn Rugg and Rafael Lapesa. Toronto: UP, 1980. 731–735.
Surtz, Ronald E. "Cervantes' *Pedro de Urdemalas*: The trickster as dramatist." *Romanische Forschungen* 92 (1980): 118–125.
Swain, Simon (ed.). *Seeing the face, seeing the soul: Polemon's physiognomy from classical antiquity to medieval Islam.* Oxford: Oxford UP, 2007.
Swain, Simon. "Polemon's Physiognomy." *Seeing the face, seeing the soul: Polemon's physiognomy from classical antiquity to medieval Islam.* Ed. Simon Swain. Oxford: Oxford UP, 2007. 125–202.
Swislocki, Marsha. "De cuerpo presente: el Rey don Sebastián en el teatro áureo." *En torno al teatro del Siglo de Oro.* Ed. Irene Pardo Molina, Luz Ruiz Martínez and Antonio Serrano. Almería: Instituto de Estudios Almerienses, 1999. 43–54.
Tardón Botas, Narciso. *Reconstrucción escenográfica de la representación de "Hado y divisa de Leonido y de Marfisa", de Calderón de la Barca, dada en el Coliseo del Buen Retiro el día 3 de marzo de 1680.* Madrid: Universidad Complutense, 2001.
Taulhade, Laurent. "España fuera de España: *La devoción de la Cruz* de Calderón." *La España moderna* 242 (1909): 76–92.
Thompson, Stith. *Motif-index of folk-literature.* Helsinki: Academica Scientiarum Fennica, 1932.
Teixeira de Souza, Ana Aparecida. "Aproximaciones entre la locura y la lujuria en *Los locos de Valencia* de Lope de Vega." *Theatralia* 17 (2015): 125–136.
Teixeira de Souza, Ana Aparecida. "Violencia, traición y muerte en *El duque de Viseo* de Lope de Vega." *Theatralia* 18 (2016): 167–182.
Teuber, Bernhard. "*Santo y bandolero* – Sakralität und Profanität in den Räuberstücken des Siglo de Oro am Beispiel von Calderóns *Devoción de la Cruz.*" *Zwischen dem Heiligen und dem Profanen – Religion, Mythologie, Weltlichkeit in der spanischen Literatur und Kultur der Frühen Neuzeit.* Ed. Wolfram Nitsch and Bernhard Teuber. München: Fink, 2008. 387–411.
Teyssier, Paul. *La langue de Gil Vicente.* Paris: Klincksieck, 1959. Trans. *A língua de Gil Vicente.* Lisboa: Imprensa Nacional-Casa da Moeda, 2005.
Thacker, Jonathan. "Lope de Vega's exemplary early comedy, *Los locos de Valencia.*" *Bulletin of the Comediantes* 52 (2000): 9–29.
Thacker, Jonathan. *Role-play and the world as stage in the comedia.* Liverpool: Liverpool UP, 2002a.
Thacker, Jonathan. "*Que yo le haré de suerte que os espante, si el fingimiento a la verdad excede*: Creative use of art in Lope de Vega's *Los locos de Valencia* (and Velázquez's Fabula de *Aracne*)." *Modern Language Review* 95 (2002b): 1007–1018.
Thiengo de Moraes, Eliane María. "Astrología y emblemática en las obras de Calderón de la Barca: *La vida es sueño* y *El astrólogo fingido.*" *Estudios críticos de literatura española.* Ed. Edith Marta Villarino Cela and Elsa Graciela Fiadino. Mar del Plata: Universidad Nacional, 2003. Vol. 1. 273–276.

Thiers, Jean Baptiste. *Traité des superstitions selon l'écriture sainte, les décrets des Conciles et les sentiments des Saints Pères et des Théologiens.* Paris: Dezallier, 1679, 1697.
Thompson, Stith. *Motif-index of folk-literature.* Helsinki: Academica Scientiarum Fennica, 1932.
Thorndike, Lynn. *A history of magic and experimental science.* 8 vol. New York: Columbia UP, 1923–1958.
Thorndike, Lynn. "Chiromancy in mediaeval latin manuscripts." *Speculum* 40 (1965): 674–706.
Tobar, María Luisa. "Representación de la fiesta de *Hado y divisa de Leonido y de Marfisa*, en el Coliseo del Retiro, bajo la dirección de Calderón." *El patrimonio del teatro clásico español. Actualidad y perspectivas.* Ed. Germán Vega, Héctor Urzáiz and Pedro Conde Parrado. Olmedo / Valladolid: Ayuntamiento / Universidad, 2015. 685–694.
Tomillo, Atanasio, and Cristóbal Pérez Pastor. *Proceso de Lope de Vega por libelos contra unos cómicos.* Madrid: Fortanet, 1901.
Torres Martínez, José Carlos de. "La relación de Lope de Vega con D. Felipe de África y un relato de Miguel de Cervantes en el *Persiles* (III, VI)." *En buena compañía: estudios en honor de Luciano García Lorenzo.* Ed. Joaquín Álvarez Barrientos, Oscar Cornago Bernal, Abraham Madroñal and Carmen Menéndez Onrubia. Madrid: CSIC, 2009. 717–726.
Torrey, Michael. "*The Plain Devil and Dissembling Looks*: Ambivalent Physiognomy and Shakespeare's *Richard III.*" *English literary Renaissance* 30 (2000): 123–153.
Trabucco, Oreste. "Lo sconosciuto autografo della *Chirofisonomia* di G.B. Della Porta." *Bruniana & Campanelliana* 1 (1995): 273–275.
Trabucco, Oreste. "Riscrittura, censura, autocensura: itinerari redazionali di Giovanni Battista Della Porta." *Giornale Critico della Filosofia Italiana* 22 (2002): 41–57.
Trambaioli, Marcella. "Calderón y el mito de Medea." *Anuario de Letras* 33 (1995): 231–244.
Trambaioli, Marcella. "La figura de la Amazona en la obra de Lope de Vega." *Anuario Lope de Vega* 12 (2006): 233–262.
Trambaioli, Marcella. "El triunfo de Marfisa en *El jardín de Falerina* y *Hado y divisa de Leonido y Marfisa* de Calderón." *Calderón y el pensamiento ideológico y cultural de su época.* Ed. Manfred Tietz and Gero Arnscheidt. Stuttgart: Steiner, 2008. 551–582.
Trionfo, Aldo. "Appunti su Giordano Bruno e sulla messa in scena del *Candelaio.*" *Il teatro del Cinquecento: I luoghi, i testi e gli attori.* Ed. Siro Ferrone. Firenze: Sansoni, 1982. 99–103.
Tropé, Hélène. "La representación dramática del microcosmos del Hospital de los locos en *Los locos de Valencia.*" *Anuario Lope de Vega* 5 (1999): 167–186.
Tropé, Helena. "Teatro y locura en *Los locos de Valencia* de Lope de Vega." *Compostella aurea.* Ed. Antonio Azaustre Galiana and Santiago Fernández Mosquera. Santiago de Compostela: Universidad, 2008. 477–483.
Tuczay, Christa Agnes. *Kulturgeschichte der mittelalterlichen Wahrsagerei.* Berlin / Boston: De Gruyter, 2012.
Ulla Lorenzo, Alejandra. "Las fiestas teatrales del Buen Retiro en 1635: el estreno de *El mayor encanto, amor* de Calderón de la Barca." *RILCE* 30 (2014): 220–241.
Vaiopoulos, Katerina. "*Los melindres de Belisa*: comicità e limiti della trasgressione." *Per ridere. Il comico nei Secoli d'Oro.* Ed. Maria Grazia Profeti. Firenze: Alinea, 2001. 109–141.
Vaiopoulos, Katerina. "Neutralizzare l'altro: immagini teatrali della zingarella chiromante dal XVI al XVII secolo." *Leyendas negras e leggende auree.* Ed. Donatella Moro Pini and Maria Grazia Profeti. Firenze: Alinea, 2011. 195–209.

Valbuena-Briones, Ángel. "Mensaje y símbolo en un drama mitológico de Calderón." *Hacia Calderón. Octavo Coloquio Anglogermano*. Ed. Hans Flasche. Stuttgart: Steiner, 1988. 173–182.
Valero Cuadra, Pino. "El mito literario medieval de la mujer sabia: *La doncella Teodor*." *Las sabias mujeres: educación, saber y autoría (siglos III–XVII)*. Ed. María Del Mar Graña Cid. Madrid: Asociación Cultural Al-Mudayna, 1994. 147–154.
Valero Cuadra, Pino. *La doncella Teodor. Un cuento hispanoárabe.* Alicante: Instituto de Cultura *Juan Gil-Albert*, 1997.
Val Naval, Paula. "La tradición fisiognómica en la obra de Juan Fernández de Heredia." *Alazet* 14 (2002): 395–405.
Varey, John E. *Cosmovisión y escenografía: el teatro español en el siglo de oro*. Madrid: Castalia, 1987.
Vargas de Luna, Javier. "The colonial reinvention of magic in *La Cueva de Salamanca* by Juan Ruiz de Alarcón." *El Siglo de Oro antes y después de "El Arte Nuevo": nuevos enfoques desde una perspectiva pluridisciplinaria*. Ed. Oana Andreia Sambrian Toma. Craiova: Sitech, 2009. 169–178.
Vasoli, Cesare. "Note su Galeotto Marzio." *Acta Litteraria Academiae Scientiarum Hungaricae* 19 (1977): 51–69.
Vega Ramos, María José. "El *De Comoedia* de Donato y los Terencios con comento del siglo XVI." *La recepción de las artes clásicas en el siglo XVI*. Ed. Luis Merino Jerez, Eustaquio Sánchez Salor and Santiago López Moreda. Cáceres: Universidad de Extremadura, 1996. 533–539.
Vega Ramos, María José. "El arte de la comedia en la teoría literaria del Renacimiento." *Poética y teatro. La teoría dramática del Renacimiento a la Posmodernidad*. Ed. María José Vega. Vilagarcía de Arousa / Pontevedra: Mirabel, 2004. 47–98.
Vega Ramos, María José. "La monstruosidad y el signo: formas de la presignificación en el renacimiento y la reforma." *Signa* 4 (1995): 225–244.
Vega Rodríguez, Pilar. "Linajes de calvas, barbas y cabelleras." *Espéculo* 2 (1996): without pagination.
Vélez Sainz, Julio. "De lo científico a lo folclórico: astrólogos y astrología en el teatro renacentista." *Bulletin of the Comediantes* 66 (2014): 1–17.
Verardi, Donato. "La fisiognomica nella storia della Psicologia: Giovan Battista Della Porta." *Psychofenia* 19 (2008): 79–108.
Verardi, Donato. "L'anima e i simboli celesti nel *De Humana Physiognomonia* di G. B. Della Porta." *Sapienza* 64 (2011a): 183–191.
Verardi, Donato. "*Segni, linee e mani planetarie*. La *Chirofisionomia* di Giovan Battista Della Porta." *Esperienze Letterarie* 4 (2011b): 51–59.
Veres D'Ocón, Ernesto. "Juegos idiomáticos en las obras de Lope de Rueda." *Revista de Filología Española* 34 (1950): 195–237.
Vernet Ginés, Juan. *Lo que Europa debe al Islam de España*. Barcelona: Quaderns Crema, 1999.
Vetterling, Mary Anne Lee. "La magia en las comedias de Juan Ruiz de Alarcon." *Cuadernos Americanos* 231 (1980): 230–247.
Viaggio, Giorgio. *Storia degli zingari in Italia*. Paris: Centro di Ricerche Zingare, 1997.
Vicente García, Luis Miguel. "Lope y la polémica sobre astrología en el Seiscientos." *Anuario Lope de Vega* 15 (2009): 219–243.

Vicente García, Luis Miguel. "Lope de Vega como astrólogo: Su horóscopo de Felipe IV para las justas poéticas toledadanas de 1605 y el suyo propio en *La Dorotea*." *La dinastía de los Austria: las relaciones entre la Monarquía Católica y el Imperio*. Ed. José Martínez Millán and Rubén González Cuerva. Madrid: Polifemo, 2011. Vol. 3. 1929–1946.

Vicente García, Luis Miguel. "La violencia del Cielo: predestinación y libre albedrío en el teatro calderoniano." *La violencia en Calderón*. Ed. Gero Arnscheidt and Manfred Tietz. Vigo: Academia del Hispanismo, 2014. 555–570.

Vickers, Brian (ed.). *Occult and scientific mentalities in the Renaissance*. Cambridge: Cambridge UP, 1984.

Vickers, Brian. "Kritische Reaktionen auf die okkulten Wissenschaften in der Renaissance." *Zwischen Wahn, Glaube und Wissenschaft: Magie, Astrologie, Alchemie und Wissenschaftsgeschichte*. Ed. Jean-François Bergier. Zürich: Verlag der Fachvereine, 1988. 167–239.

Vigh, Eva. "*Il costume che appare nella faccia.*" *Fisiognomica e letteratura italiana*. Roma: Aracne, 2014.

Vigh, Eva. "Moralità e segni fisiognomici nel *Della fisonomia dell'huomo* di Giovanni Battista Della Porta." *La "mirabile" natura. Magia e scienza in Giovan Battista Della Porta (1615–2015)*. Ed. Marco Santoro. Pisa / Roma: Fabrizio Serra, 2016. 111–124.

Viguera Molins, María Jesús. *Dos cartillas de fisiognómica: Ibn ɸArab, Al-Rôaz*. Madrid: Editora Nacional, 1977.

Villarino Martínez, Beatriz. "*El jardín de Falerina*. Un auto mitológico de Calderón." *Espéculo* 31 (2005): without pagination.

Vincent, Monique. *Donneau de Visé et "Le Mercure galant"*. Paris: Aux Amateurs de Livres, 1987.

Vitse, Marc. "Burla y engaño en las tres primeras comedias de capa y espada de Calderón." *"Por discreto y por amigo". Mélanges offerts à Jean Canavaggio*. Ed. Christophe Couderc and Benoît Pellistrandi. Madrid: Casa de Velázquez, 2005. 345–356.

Vivalda, Nicolás M. "Basilio o el ocaso del monarca-astrólogo: juegos de la similitud e inconveniencias políticas en *La vida es sueño*." *Hacia la tragedia áurea: Lecturas para un nuevo milenio*. Ed. Frederick A. de Armas, Luciano García Lorenzo and Enrique García Santo-Tomás. Madrid / Frankfurt: Iberoamericana / Vervuert, 2008. 383–396.

Walde Moheno, Lillian von der. "La melindrosa de Lope de Vega." *Estudios de teatro español y novohispano*. Ed. Melchora Romanos, Florencia Calvo and Ximena González. Buenos Aires: Universidad, 2005. 205–217.

Walde Moheno, Lillian von der. "El cuerpo de Celestina: un estudio sobre fisonomía y personalidad." *eHumanista* 9 (2007): 129–142.

Watson, A. I. "Hercules and the tunic of shame: Calderon's *Los tres mayores prodigios*." *Homenaje a William L. Fichter estudios sobre el teatro antiguo hispánico y otros ensayos*. Ed. A. David Kossoff and José Amor y Vázquez. Madrid: Castalia, 1971. 773–783.

Weill-Parot, Nicolas. "Astrology, astral influences, and occult properties in the thirteenth and fourteenth centuries." *Traditio* 65 (2010): 201–230.

Weill-Parot, Nicolas. *Points aveugles de la nature. La rationalité scientifique médiévale face à l'occulte, l'attraction magnétique et l'horreur du vide, XIIIe–milieu du XVe siècle*. Paris: Les Belles Lettres, 2013.

Whicker, Jules. "Los magos neoestoicos de *La cueva de Salamanca* y *La prueba de las promesas* de Ruiz de Alarcón." *El escritor y la escena*. Ed. Ysla Campbell. Ciudad Juárez: Universidad Autónoma, 1997. 211–219.

Whitaker, Shirley B. "Calderón's *El mayor encanto, amor* on performance: eyewitness accounts by two Florentine diplomats." *The Calderonian stage: body and soul.* Ed. Manuel Delgado Morales. Lewisburg: Bucknell UP, 1997. Vol. 2. 81–104.

Williams, Steven J. "Defining the *Corpus Aristotelicum*: Scholastic awareness of Aristotelian spuria in the High Middle Ages." *Journal of the Warburg and Courtauld Institutes* 58 (1995): 29–51.

Williams, Steven J. *The "Secret of Secrets". The scholarly career of a Pseudo-Aristotelian text in the Latin Middle Ages.* Ann Arbor: Michigan UP, 2003.

Williams, Steven J. "Giving advice and taking it: The reception of the Pseudo-Aristotelian *Secretum secretorum* as a *speculum principis*." *Consilium. Teorie e pratiche del consigliare nella cultura medievale.* Ed. Carla Casagrande, Chiara Crisciani and Silvana Vecchio. Firenze: Sismel. Edizioni del Galluzzo, 2004. 139–181

Wilson, Bronwen. "The 'Confusion of faces'. The politics of physiognomy, concealed hearts and public visibility." *Making publics in early modern Europe: people, things, forms of knowledge.* Ed. Bronwen Wilson and Paul Yachnin. New York: Routledge, 2011. 177–192.

Wilson, Edward M. "The four elements in the imagery of Calderón." *Modern Language Review* 31 (1936): 34–47.

Wilson, John Delane. *Some uses of physiognomy in the plays of Shakespeare, Johnson, Marlowe and Dekker.* East Lansing: Michigan State UP, 1965.

Wörsdörfer, Anna Isabell. "Theater der Magie – Magie des Theaters: Das Beispiel der Affaire des poisons (1676–1682)." *Romanistisches Jahrbuch* 70 (2019): 218–249.

Wright, Elizabeth R. "Capital accumulation and canon formation in Lope de Vega's *De cosario a cosario*." *Bulletin of the Comediantes* 54 (2002): 33–55.

Wurtele, Douglas J. "Another look at an 'old' science: Chaucer's pilgrims and physiognomy." *From Arabye to Engelond: medieval studies in honour of Mahmoud Manzalaoui on his 75th birthday.* Ed. A. E. Christa Canitz and Gernot R. Wieland. Toronto: Ottawa UP, 1999. 93–111.

Yates, Frances Amelia. *Giordano Bruno y la tradición hermética.* Barcelona: Ariel, 1983.

Yoon, Yong-Wook, and Song-Joo Na. "Sobre la comicidad de *El vergonzoso en palacio*, de Tirso de Molina." *Hispanófila* 176 (2016): 19–38.

Zaccaria, Raffaella. "Della Rocca, Bartolomeo detto Cocles." *Dizionario biografico degli italiani* 37 (1989). http://www.treccani.it (visited on 9. 4.2020).

Zahareas, Anthony. "La función de la *picaresca* en Cervantes." *Cervantes en Italia.* Ed. Alicia Villar Lecumberri. Palma de Mallorca: Asociación de Cervantistas, 2001. 459–472.

Zambelli, Paola. "*Aut diabolus aut Achillinus*. Fisionomia, astrologia e demonologia nel metodo di un aristotelico." *Rinascimento* 18 (1978): 59–86.

Zambrana Ramírez, Alberto. "¿La astrología como ciencia?: un estudio comparativo entre el *Astrólogo fingido* de Calderón de la Barca y la versión en inglés *The Feign'd Astrologer* (1668)." *RILCE* 20 (2004): 99–116.

Zamora Calvo, María Jesús. *Artes maleficorum. Brujas, magos y demonios en el Siglo de Oro.* Barcelona: Calambur, 2016.

Zamuner, Ilaria. "La tradizione romanza del *Secretum secretorum* pseudo-aristotelico." *Studi Medievali* 46 (2005): 31–116.

Zeller, Rosmarie (ed.). *Naturmagie und Deutungskunst: Wege und Motive der Rezeption von Giovan Battista Della Porta in Europa.* Bern: Lang, 2008.

Ziegler, Joseph. "The beginning of medieval physiognomy: the case of Michael Scotus." *Kulturtransfer und Hofgesellschaft im Mittelalter*. Ed. Gundula Grebner. Berlin: Akademie-Verlag, 2008. 299–322.

Zimic, Stanislav. "El gran teatro del mundo y el gran mundo del teatro, en *Pedro de Urdemalas*, de Cervantes." *Acta Neophilologica* 10 (1977): 55–105.

Zimic, Stanislav. "Estudio sobre el teatro de Gil Vicente: obras de crítica social. I: El sentido satírico del *Auto de las gitanas*." *Acta Neophilológica* 16 (1983): 3–12.

Zinelli, Fabio. "Ancora un monumento dell'antico aretino e sulla tradizione italiana del *Secretum Secretorum*." *Per Domenico De Robertis. Studi offerti dagli allievi fiorentini*. Ed. Isabella Becherucci, Simone Giusti and Natascia Tonelli. Firenze: Le Lettere, 2000. 509–561.

Zucker, Arnaud. "La physiognomonie antique et le langage animal du corps." *Rursus* 1 (2006): without pagination.

Name index

Achillini, Alessandro 15, 22, 79
Adamantius 8, 9, 14, 16, 116
Adelard of Bath 23
Aelianus, Claudius 14
Aercke, Kristiaan Paul Guido 170
Agrimi, Jole 10–12, 24
Aguirre Felipe, Javier 28–29, 47, 50
Aguirre, José Luis 77
Akasoy, Anna 9
Albarracín Teulón, Agustín 76, 111, 117
Albert the Great 11
Alborg, Concha 118
Albrecht von Brandenburg 25
Albrecht, Johann 16
Alemán, Mateo 162
Alexander the Great 9
Alonso Acero, Beatriz 111–112
Alonso Asenjo, Julio 1, 35–36
Alonso, Amado 68
Alvar, Carlos 43
Álvarez Sellers, María Rosa 118, 144
Amezcua Gómez, José 147, 153, 156
Andrés, Christian 76, 158
Andrist, Debra D. 160
Andueza, María 163
Annus, Amar 6
Antonucci, Fausta 184–185
Aphek, Edna 6
Archpriest of Hita, see Ruiz, Juan
Arellano, Ignacio 1, 174
Arenas Cruz, Elena 126–128
Aretino, Pietro 37–39, 42
Argensola, Lupercio Leonardo de 144
Arias Careaga, Raquel 72
Ariosto, Ludovico 1, 31–32, 34–35, 73, 185
Aristotle 9, 13–14, 23, 27, 38, 116, 197
Armas, Frederick A. De 1, 77, 121, 148, 160, 163–165, 167, 170, 173
Armstrong, A. M. 8
Arnaudo, Marco 41
Arribas Hernáez, María Luisa 10
Arróniz Báez, Othón 35
Artemidorus 14, 23
Aszyk, Urszula 77, 181, 183

Aubrun, Charles V. 182
Augustine (Saint) 130, 146, 157
Autuori, Adele 9–10
Ayala, Francisco de 121
Aylward, E. T. 163

Badaloni, Nicola 18
Balbiani, Laura 18
Baltrusaitis, Jurgis 8
Balzac, Honoré de 2
Bamforth, Stephen 158
Bandera, Cesáreo 146
Baras Escolá, Alfredo 69–70, 75
Baraz, Daniel 146
Bárberi Squarotti, Giorgio 40
Barnes, Jonathan 8
Barr, Alan
Barrientos, Bartolomé 98
Barrientos, Lope de 130
Bartolomé Luises, Montserrat 41
Bartolomeo da Messina 11, 13–14
Barton, Tamsyn S. 9
Basile, Bruno 19
Báthory, Sigismund 110
Baumbach, Sybille 3
Beat Rudin, Ernst 121
Becker, Danièle 185
Belleforest, François de 158
Belloni, Benedetta 112–113
Belot, Jean 22
Benabu, Isaac 145
Benedettini, Riccardo 1
Benjamin, Walter 41, 141
Bennett, Jolynn 17
Bentivoglio, Ermete 16
Bergdolt, Klaus 6
Bermann, Anne-Katrin 1, 129–131
Bernard of Clairvaux (Saint) 146
Berruezo Sánchez, Diana 121
Berthelot, Anne 75
Bicarti, Orazio 15
Biondo, Michelangelo 17, 38–39
Biow, Douglas 39
Bizzarri, Hugo O. 10–11

Blasi, Nicola De 48
Bloch, Raymond 6
Blum, Paul Richard 7
Blumenberg, Hans 5
Boaistuau, Pierre 158–162
Boccaccio, Giovanni 62–63, 94
Boccia, Carmine 38
Boer, Harm den 18
Boiardo, Matteo Maria 73, 185
Borgia, Cesare 25
Botticelli, Sandro 167
Bouchet, Alain 19
Boudet, Jean-Patrice 6–7, 24
Boyl, Carlos 144
Boys-Stones, George 8
Boyvin du Vauroüy, Henry de 14
Branca, Vittore 63
Brasswell-Means, Laurel 2
Braunmuller, A. R. 1, 197
Brewer, Brian 163, 165–166
Briggs, E. R. 25
Brioso, Jorge 163
Brooks, William 192, 195
Bruers, Antonio 27
Bruerton, Courtney 77–78, 83, 85–86, 88, 92, 94, 98, 104, 107, 109, 111, 114, 117–118
Brunel, Magali 4
Bruno, Giordano 18, 39–42
Buck, August 7
Bujanda, Jesús Martínez de 17, 19, 25
Bunes Ibarra, Miguel Ángel de 111
Buono Hodgart, Lia 41
Burnett, Charles 6, 11–12, 23–24
Burton, Grace 146, 153, 156

Cabrero Aramburo, Ana 114
Cacho Blecua, Juan Manuel 11
Calderón de la Barca, Pedro 100, 143–186, 195
Calderón, Manuel 50–52, 118–120
Calvete de Estrella, Juan Cristóbal 35
Calvo Delcán, Carmen 8, 114
Calvo, Sonsoles 94
Camerarius, Joachim 28
Cameron, Euan K. 196
Camões, José 51–53

Campanella, Tommaso 27
Campbell, Ysla 88, 118, 132–133, 136
Campopiano, Michele 11
Camus, Albert 146
Canavaggio, Jean 71, 144
Canonica de Rochemonteix, Elvezio 105
Caputo, Cosimo 20
Cardano, Girolamo 15, 77
Cardona Castro, Ángeles 147, 181–182
Cardoner, Antonio 10, 21
Cardoso Bernardes, José Augusto 53
Caro Baroja, Julio 2, 18, 29, 77, 94, 98, 132
Carrión, Gabriela 110
Casalduero, Joaquín 69
Cascardi, Anthony J. 164
Case, Thomas E. 117
Castañega, Martín de 130
Castelli, Patrizia 23–25, 29, 50, 187–188
Castillo, Moisés R. 69
Cataldi, Paolo 18
Cavallo, Jo Ann 41
Céard, Jean 79, 158
Cecioni, Giorgio 11
Cervantes, Miguel de 2, 30, 69–70, 72–76, 151
Cesi, Federico 19, 25
Chalkomatas, Dionysios 1
Chandezon, Christophe 6
Charnon-Deutsch, Lou 69
Chaucer, Geoffrey 2
Chautant, Gisèle 188–191
Chem Sham, Jorge 163
Cherchi, Paolo 29
Cicero, Marcus Tullius 1, 23
Cirac Estopañán, Sebastián 70
Ciruelo, Pedro 130
Clarke, Jan 192, 194
Classen, Albrecht 7
Cocles (Bartolomeo della Rocca) 15–17, 21–22, 24, 27, 38, 79
Cocozza, Antonello 26–27
Coduras, María 182
Colahan, Clark 178
Collina, Beatrice 29
Compier, Abdul Haq 10
Conlon, Raymond 121
Cornarius, Janus 14

Name index — 245

Corneille, Thomas 192, 195
Cornejo, Manuel 81, 110
Cortés, Jerónimo 12, 20–21, 106–107, 113, 116, 122, 125
Cortijo Ocaña, Antonio 32, 34–35, 104
Corvo de Mirandola, Andrea 24, 26
Cotarelo y Mori, Emilio 85, 111
Cots Vicente, Montserrat 146
Courtès, Noémie 1
Courtine, Jean-Jacques 21
Coy, Jason Philip 187
Crollius, Oswaldus 149
Cros, Edmond 162
Cruz, Anne J. 107
Cuenca Muñoz, Paloma 35, 81, 92, 114
Cueva, Juan de la 144
Cuiñas Gómez, Macarena 105
Cureau de la Chambre, Marin 22
Curran, John E. Jr. 3

Dadson, Trevor J. 107
Dahan-Gaida, Laurence 1
D'Alessandro, Alessandro 25
Damiani, Rolando 12
Darbord, Bernard 117
Darst, David H. 136
Dartai-Maranzana, Nathalie 121
Dasen, Véronique 6
De Páiz Hernández, M.ª Isabel 24
Dedieu, Joseph 144
Del Conte, Laura 77
Delgado García, Nitzaira 71
Delgado, Manuel 145–146, 152, 154–155, 160
Della Porta, Giovan Battista 18–21, 25–27, 77, 106–107, 116, 143
Delpech, François 151
Delumeau, Jean 27
Descartes, René 18
Deshayes, Catherine 188, 192
Devriese, Lisa 11
Diago, Manuel V. 1, 55, 59, 69
Díaz Balsera, Viviana 181–182
Díaz Migoyo, Gonzalo 132
Dickhaut, Kirsten 1
Di Pinto, Elena 187
DiPuccio, Denise M. 173
Dixon, Victor 121

Dolce, Alessandro 17
Domènech, Conxita 77
Doménici, Mauricio 70
Domínguez Matito, Francisco 118, 139–141
Dominicus Gundissalinus 10, 24
Donatus, Aelius 1
Donneau de Visé, Jean 192
Dovizi da Bibbiena, Bernardo 34
Dryander, Johannes, see Juan Enzinas
Dunn, Peter N. 163
Duntze, Oliver 16
Duro Rivas, Reyes 126

Eamon, William 11
Edward VI of England 13
Edwards, Gwynne 178
Egenolf, Christian 16
Egido, Aurora 177
Ellis, Jonathan 173–174
Enguix Barber, Ricardo 74
Entwistle, William J. 155
Enzinas, Juan (Johannes Dryander) 25
Erasmo, Desiderio 17
Ernst, Germana 27
Escobar Gómez, Santiago 10
Escobar, Ángel 23
Escudero, Juan Manuel 175–176
Espantoso-Foley, Augusta M. 42, 129–131, 135
Esseni, Chiara 146
Estévez Molinero, Ángel 74–75
Ettinghausen, Henry 159, 161
Euclid 165
Evans, Elizabeth Cornelia 8–10
Exum, Frances B. 137

Federici Vescovini, Graziella 12, 25
Felipe de África, see Muley Xeque
Fernández, Jaime Antonio 85
Fernández de Heredia, Juan 11
Fernández de Moratín, Leandro 75–76
Fernández Gómez, Carlos 105
Fernández-Guerra y Orbe, Luis 132–133
Fernández Mosquera, Santiago 170–173, 178–179
Fernández Rodríguez, Daniel 117
Fernández Rodríguez, Natalia 130

Ferreira de Sampayo, Cristóbal 104
Ferrer Valls, Teresa 32
Ferrer-Lightner, María 51–52
Ferreras, Juan Ignacio 83
Ferrini, Maria Fernanda 8
Fiadino, Elsa Graciela 109–110
Fidora, Alexander 10
Fischer, Susan L. 170
Flasche, Hans 177
Flores Martín, Mercedes 77
Florit Durán, Francisco de 121
Floyd-Wilson, Mary 3
Folger, Robert 195
Fontaine, Charles 14–15
Forestier, Georges 3–4
Forster, Regula 9
Förster, Richard 8, 10–11, 14, 114
Forsyth, Elliott 144
Fothergill-Payne, Louise 69
Foucault, Michel 7–8, 149
Francis I of France 15
Franzese, Rosa 11
Frederick II, Holy Roman Emperor 12
Frenk Alatorre, Margit 121
Frezza, Mario 25
Friedman, Edward H. 153, 156
Friedman, John Block 2
Friedrich, Ernst 1
Fuente, Ricardo de la 144
Funck-Brentano, Frantz 188–189, 192
Fürbeth, Frank 23
Furderer von Richtenfels, Johannes 25

Gabrieli, Giuseppe 19
Gagliardi, Donatella 98
Gagnon-Riopel, Julie 118
Gago Saldaña, María Val 1
Galen of Pergamon 76
Galilei, Galileo 164
Gallo, Anna Maria 32–33
Galván, Luís 182
Gandolfi, Giangiacomo 2
Garavelli, Enrico 38
García-Bermejo Giner, Miguel M. 42–44, 46, 55, 68
García Fernández, Óscar 114–115
García Lorenzo, Luciano 77

García Manzano, Agustina 174
García Sánchez, Concepción 121
García Santo-Tomás, Enrique 1
García-Valdés, Celsa Carmen 132–136
Garcilaso de la Vega 105
Gareffi, Andrea 31–32
Garzoni, Tomaso 29
Gatti, Hilary 40
Gaullier-Bougassas, Catherine 11
Gauna, Felipe de 112
Gaurico, Luca 15
Gaurico, Pomponio 14, 17
Gavela García, Delia 137–139
Gerardo da Cremona 10
Gernert, Folke 2, 18, 24, 28, 43, 47, 69, 81, 125, 143, 149–150, 170, 192, 195
Ghersetti, Antonella 9
Giannetti, Francesco 105
Gibson, Margaret 23
Gigas, Emil 118
Gil Fernández, Juan 35
Gilbert, Françoise 168, 174
Giovio, Paolo 25
Girard, René 146, 160
Giuliani, Luigi 144
Glenn, Richard F. 121
Gómez Canseco, Luis 69
Gómez Martínez, María Dolores 77
Gómez Mingorance, Margarita 167
Gómez Moreno, Ángel 43
Gómez Vozmediano, Miguel Fernando 28
Gómez, Jesús 81, 114
González, Aurelio 132
González, Serafín 121, 132
González Cañal, Rafael 182
González Cuerva, Rubén 111
Gonzalez del Valle, Luis 118
González Fernández, Luis 129
González García, Ángel 130
González Manjarrés, Miguel Ángel 15, 19
González Ollé, Fernando 110, 121
González Palencia, Ángel 93
González Puche, Alejandro 72
González-Barrera, Julián 77
González-Ruiz, Julio 94
Gonzalo Sánchez-Molero, José Luis 35
Gracián, Baltasar 2

Granja, Agustín de la 59, 77, 81
Gratarolo, Guglielmo 17
Greer, Margaret Rich 170
Gregory XV (pope) 143, 196
Grilli, Giuseppe 83
Guasch Melis, Ana Eva 69
Guastavino Gallent, Guillermo 111–112
Guerrini Angrisani, Isa 40
Guillén de Ávila, Diego 42–44, 46–47, 62
Gundissalinus, Dominicus 10, 24
Gutiérrez Carbajo, Francisco 166
Gutiérrez Nieto, Juan Ignacio 29, 47
Gutierrez-Laffond, Aurore 1

Halstead, Frank G. 1, 76, 120
Hamilton, R. 24
Hanson, Thomas Bradley 2
Hartlieb, Johannes 29
Hartzenbusch, Juan Eugenio 104–105
Henry, John 149
Henry VIII of England 13
Herbers, Klaus 10
Hermenegildo, Alfredo 43, 62–63, 65–67, 151
Hermes Trismegistus 43
Hernández Araico, Susana 166–167, 170, 178, 181
Hernández González, Erasmo 145
Herrán Alonso, Emma 55, 58, 82
Herrand, Marcel 146
Herrero García, M. 106, 110, 125
Hesse, Everett W. 110, 121, 153
Hiergeist, Teresa 2
Hippocrates 76
Hogrebe, Wolfram 6
Hohenheim, Philippus Aureolus Theophrastus Bombastus von, see Paracelsus
Honig, Edwin 147
Horozco y Covarrubias, Juan de 29
Hoyland, Robert 8, 114
Huarte de San Juan, Juan 21, 107, 140
Huerta Calvo, Javier 147
Hugh of San Victor 10
Hunt, Tony 11
Hurtado Torres, Antonio 1, 143, 148
Hutchinson, Keith 7

Ibarz, Virgili 21
Indagine, Ioannes ab 16, 17, 21–22, 38, 191
Irigoyen García, Javier 69

Jacquart, Danielle 12
Jerez-Gómez, Jesús David 117
Jiménez Rueda, Julio 18
John of Seville 10–11, 23
Johnson, Carroll B. 62, 69
Johnson, Christopher D. 41
Jones, Philip B. 11
Jordan, Leo 2, 4
Josa, Lola 132
Juliá Martínez, Eduardo 58–59, 61
Junkerjürgen, Ralf 8

Kartchner, Eric J. 153
Kepler, Johannes 18
Knox, Dilwyn 23
Kodera, Sergius 41
Kohler, Eugen 42–44, 46–47, 62
Kraye, Jill 13

Labarre, Françoise 121
La Charité, Raymond 2
Lama, Miguel Ángel 24
Lanuza-Navarro, Tayra M. C. 4, 101, 129, 135
Laplana Gil, José Enrique 2, 77, 99–103
Lara Alberola, Eva 178, 187
LaRubia-Prado, Francisco 163, 165
Lauer, A. Robert 168–169
Laundun d'Aigaliers, Pierre de 144
Laurand, Valéry 9
Lavanha, João Baptista 77
Lavater, Johann Caspar 2,5
Lebigre, Arlette 188–189
Leblon, Bernard 28, 47
Ledo, Jorge 18
Lee Palmer, Allison 79
Leland, Charles G. 28
León, Jorge 109–110
LeVan, J. Richards 174
Lewis-Smith, Paul 74
Lichtblau, Karin 73
Lichtenberg, Georg Christoph 5
Limami, Abdellatif 69

Liñán y Verdugo, Antonio 93, 97
Linton Lomas Barrett 42
Lloret Cantero, Joana 52
Lobo Lasso de la Vega, Gabriel 93
Lohse, Rolf 48
López Castro, Armando 52
Lorée, Denis 11
Lorenz, Erika 1, 143, 148
Lovarini, E. 48, 50
Loxus 6, 8–9, 14
Lozano Pascual, José Manuel 19
Ludwig, Walther 6
Luther, Martin 5

Macdonald, Katherine 18
Maclean, Ian 149
Madera, Nelson Ismael 2
Madroñal, Abraham 75, 84, 117
Magnaghi, Serena 94–95
Malatesta, Pandolfo 25
Mandrell, James 122
Manfredi, Girolamo 21
Marcos Celestino, Mónica 134
Marino, Giambattista 104–105
Mariscal, George 161
Márquez Villanueva, Francisco 53, 63, 69
Martinengo, Alessandro 177
Martínez Blasco, Ángel 129–132
Martínez Manzano, Teresa 8, 114
Martínez Torrón, Diego 175
Martínez, Enrico 133
Martínez, Matías 159
Marzio da Narni, Galeotto 25
Mata Induráin, Carlos 181–182
Matas Caballero, Juan 173
Matsen, Herbert 15
Maza, Francisco de la 133
Mazzi, Curzio 48, 50
McCready, Warren T. 76
McGaha, Michael D. 114
McKendrick, Melveena 152–154
Megwinoff, Grace E. 94
Meinel, Christoph 7
Meixell, Amanda S. 185
Melampus 14
Melanchthon, Philip 14
Mele, Eugenio Mele 93

Meregalli, Franco 69
Mesk, Josef 9
Miggiano, Gabriella 25
Milani, Matteo 11, 14
Millares Carlo, Agustín 132, 135
Millé y Giménez, Juan 76–77
Minic-Vidovic, Ranka 68
Minois, Georges 6
Mira de Amescua, Antonio 121
Misener, Geneva 8
Mochón Castro, Montserrat 117
Moldenarius, Christian 22
Molière (Jean-Baptiste Poquelin) 3–4, 195
Molina, Julián 81
Molina, Tirso de 120–121, 123, 125
Mollenauer, Lynn Woo 188
Möller, Reinhold 10
Moncada, Sancho de 30
Monfrin, Jacques 11
Mongrédien, Georges 188
Montaigne, Michel de 2
Montecuccoli, Carlo 14
Montecuccoli, Francesco 14
Morby, Edwin S. 79, 81, 106
Morel Fatio, Alfred 11
Moreno Mendoza, Arsenio 4
Morley, S. Griswold 77–78, 83, 85–86, 88, 92, 94, 98, 104, 107, 109, 111, 114, 117–118
Morón, Ciriaco 162, 164–165
Morrow, Carolyn 71
Mossiker, Frances 188
Moulin, Antoine Du 14, 16
Mourad, Youssef 9
Mujica, Barbara 164
Muley Xeque (Felipe de África) 110, 112–113
Müller-Bochat, Eberhard 72
Muñoz Gamero, Carmen 10
Muñoz y Manzano, Cipriano 148
Muratori, Cecilia 19, 27

Na, Song-Joo 121
Nagy, Edward 73
Narinesingh, Lal 167
Nass, Lucien 188
Navarro Durán, Rosa 79
Nemtzov, Sarah 97

Nettesheim, Agrippa von 18, 77
Neugaard, Edward J. 158
Neumeister, Sebastian 167–168, 170
Nevares, Marta de 77
Newels, Margarete 144
Nicander 76
Núñez Rivera, Valentín 74–75

O'Connor, Thomas A. 146, 155
Oleza, Joan 118
Olivares, Count-Duke of, Gaspar de Guzmán y Pimentel Ribera y Velasco de Tovar 170, 178, 181
Oliver Asín, Jaime 111–112
Ordine, Nuccio 41
Ostorero, Martine 6
Osuna, Francisco de 130
Oteiza, Blanca 121

Pacheco y Costa, Alejandra 180
Pack, Roger A. 23–24
Paige, Nicholas 192
Palacín, G. B. 69
Palomo, María del Pilar 121
Pannier, Karl 53
Pantin, Isabelle 4
Paolella, Alfonso 19, 116
Paques, Viviana 31, 33, 38
Poquelin Jean-Baptiste, see Molière
Paracelsus (Philippus Aureolus Theophrastus Bombastus von Hohenheim) 25, 149
Paravicini Bagliani, Agostino 6
Pardo Tomás, José 17
Parker, Alexander A. 145, 152
Parker, Margaret R. 117
Parr, James A. 129
Partridge, Christopher 7
Paschetto, Eugenia 9, 12
Pascual Barciela, Emilio 170
Pavia, Mario N. 1
Pedraza Jiménez, Felipe B. 112, 126, 182
Pedrosa, José Manuel 76
Pellegrini, Antonio 17–18, 21
Peña, Margarita 79
Pensado Figueiras, Jesús 10
Pérez Galdós, Benito 2
Pérez Pastor, Cristóbal 81

Pérez-Magallón, Jesús 144
Pérez, Juan 32, 34–35
Perrone, Giuseppina 11
Peruchio, Sieur de 22, 191
Pescioni, Andrea 159
Peter of Abano 12, 17
Petitfils, Jean-Christian 188
Petreius, Nicholas 14
Peucer, Caspar 5
Philip IV of Spain 13
Philippus Tripolitanus 10, 13
Piccari, Paolo 19
Piccione, Rosa Maria 23–24
Pieri, Marzio 105
Pirckheimer, Willibald 28
Piro, Rosa 10
Poirson, Martial 192
Polemon, Antonius 6, 8–9, 14, 116
Pollin, Alice M. 182
Pollux 23
Poma, Roberto 22, 25–26
Pontón, Gonzalo 101, 112
Porqueras Mayo, Alberto 144
Porsia, Franco 12, 45–46, 113
Porter, Martin 12, 15–16, 22, 25
Portnoy, Antonio 34
Powell, Jocelyn 4
Preda, Alessandra 41
Predari, Francesco 29
Presberg, Charles D. 165
Presotto, Marco 78
Prest, Julia 192–194
Prian Salazar, Jesús 132
Profeti, Maria Grazia 78
Prosperi, Adriano 187
Pseudo-Aristotle 8–10, 12–13, 19, 27
Pseudo-Cocles 113
Pujasol, Esteban 21, 121
Puliafito Bleuel, Anna Laura 41

Quétel, Claude 188
Quevedo, Francisco de 2, 77
Quiñones, Juan de 30

Rabelais, François 2–3, 38–39, 127
Rabitti, Giovanna 38
Raimondo, Annibale 18

Raina, Giampiero 8, 10
Rambaud Cabello, Javier 111
Ramírez, Román 130
Rank, Otto 153
Rapisarda, Stefano 7, 11, 23–24
Ravaisson, François 189–191
Regalado, Antonio 163, 173
Reichenberger, Arnold G. 129
Reißer, Ulrich 16
Repath, Ian 9, 14, 114
Reske, Christoph 16
Restori, Antonio 82
Reusch, Heinrich 19
Rey Bueno, Mar 98
Rey Hazas, Antonio 69, 73, 75, 147
Reyes Cano, José María 144
Reyes Peña, Mercedes de los 78
Rhasis, Mohammed (Razi, Abu Bakr Muhammad b. Zakariya) 10
Rheinheimer, Martin 28
Riandière La Roche, Josette 21
Ribalta, Francisco 105
Ribas, Pedro de 20
Ricarte Bescós, José María 21
Ricci, Agostino 32, 34
Richelieu, Armand Jean du Plessis, Duc de 14, 27
Richter, Marcella 17
Rico, Francisco 24, 47, 149, 162
Río, Martín del 29, 132
Roca Barea, María Elvira 42–43
Rocca, Bartolomeo della, see Cocles
Rodler, Lucia 2, 17
Rodrigues Vianna Peres, Lygia 185
Rodríguez Cuadros, Evangelina 143
Rodríguez de Lera, Juan Ramón 47
Rodríguez Rodríguez, Ana M. 69
Rodríguez Rodríguez, José Javier 86–87
Rodríguez-Gallego, Fernando 143, 195
Rodríguez-Puértolas, Julio 82
Rojas Zorrilla, Francisco de 126–129, 182, 186
Rojas, Fernando de 27, 187
Rojo Vega, Anastasio 18
Romano, Angelo 38
Romanos, Melchora 111
Romo Feito, Fernando 73

Rosado, Gabriel 86
Rose, Constance H. 178
Rose, Valentin 10
Rosicler, Luis de 77
Roso Díaz, José 77, 94–97
Rössner, Michael 73–74
Ruano de la Haza, José María 180, 182, 185
Rudall, Diane 192
Rueda, Lope de 58, 62–63, 65–69, 151
Ruggieri, Lorenza 62–63
Ruiz, Juan (Archpriest of Hita) 2, 44
Ruiz de Alarcón y Mendoza, Juan 129, 132–136, 141
Ruiz García, Elisa 24
Rull Fernández, Enrique 121, 178
Ryan, W. F. 9

Sabattini, Gino 23
Sachs, Hans 53, 55
Sáez, Adrián J 72–75, 143, 145–147, 152–157, 160, 170
Saguar, Amaranta 20–21, 113, 116, 122, 125
Saif, Liana 7
Salem Elsheikh, Mahmoud 10
Sales, João Nuno 50–51
Salomon, Bernard 17
Sâmbrian, Oana Andreia 111
San Miguel, Ángel 52
Sánchez, Ana Isabel 76, 96
Sánchez, Francisco
Sanchez, Laurène 126
Sánchez Escribano, Federico 144
Sánchez González de Herrero, María de las Nieves 12, 45–46
Sánchez Jiménez, Antonio 76
Sánchez Jiménez, Santiago U. 68
Sánchez Laílla, Luis 99–100
Sánchez Ramos, Valeriano 111
Sánchez Salas, Francisco J. 68
Sánchez Salor, Eustaquio 24
Santibáñez, María del Carmen Griselda 163
Sanz, Omar 77
Sarmati, Elisabetta 73
Sarnelli, Pompeo 26
Saunal, Damien 88
Saura, Norma 174
Schalk, Fritz 110

Schäublin, Christoph 23
Schiller, Friedrich 147
Schizzano Mandel, Adrienne 143, 148, 178
Schmidt, Marie-France 19, 146
Schmitt, Charles B. 9, 13, 23
Schönsperger, Johann 16
Scott, Michael 11–13, 16, 20, 38, 43–46, 113, 197
Sears, Theresa Ann 163
Seidel Menchi, Silvana 17
Seneca 146
Serés, Guillermo 140
Serralta, Frédéric 83, 85, 110
Serrano Mangas, Fernando 24
Shakespeare, William 1, 3, 197
Sharratt, Peter 17
Shergold, Norman D. 170, 186
Shumaker, Wayne 7
Sileri, Manuela 110
Silvi, Christine 13
Simon, Gérard 18
Simons, Edison 94
Sixtus V (pope) 20, 184, 196
Slater, John 76
Sloane, Robert 152
Smieja, Florian 147
Solms, Wilhelm 29
Somerset, Anne 53
Sosa Antonietti, Marcela Beatriz 74
Sosa-Velasco, Alfredo J. 163
Stabile, Giorgio 38
Stackhouse, Kenneth A. 69
Starkie, Walter 69
Steinberger, Deborah 192
Stelluti, Francesco 26
Stern, Charlotte 44
Strosetzki, Christoph
Sturlese, Loris 145
Suárez de Mayorga, Pedro 18
Suidas 23
Sullivan, Henry W. 147
Surtz, Ronald E. 72
Swain, Simon 8, 14
Swislocki, Marsha 111

Taille, Jean de la 1, 144
Taisnier, Jean 18, 22, 28, 77, 165

Tardón Botas, Narciso 185
Taulhade, Laurent 146
Teixeira de Souza, Ana Aparecida 77, 118
Téoli, Carlo 34
Tesserant, Claude 158
Teuber, Bernhard 147
Teyssier, Paul 51
Thacker, Jonathan 77
Thales 165
Theophrastus 76, 149
Thiengo de Moraes, Eliane María 2, 143, 148
Thiers, Jean Baptiste 195–196
Thomas Aquinas (Saint) 146
Thomas Becket, see Thomas of Canterbury
Thomas of Canterbury (Thomas Becket) 24
Thompson, Stith 63, 147
Thorndike, Lynn 7, 11, 23
Tobar, María Luisa 185
Tobin, Yishai 6
Tomillo, Atanasio 81
Tordera Sáez, Antonio 143
Torres Martínez, José Carlos de 111
Torrey, Michael 3
Tournes, Jean de 14
Trabucco, Oreste 20, 25–27
Trambaioli, Marcella 105, 114, 178, 180, 185
Tricasso da Cerasari, Patrizio 24–25
Trionfo, Aldo 41
Tropé, Hélène 77
Tuczay, Christa Agnes 6–7, 23, 29, 53
Tudela Manuel 121
Tuetey, Alexandre 28–29

Ulla Lorenzo, Alejandra 170
Urban VIII (pope) 196

Vaiopoulos, Katerina 47
Val Naval, Paula 11
Valbuena Prat, Ángel 158
Valbuena-Briones, Ángel 166
Valero Cuadra, Pino 117
Varey, John E. 149, 155, 186
Vargas de Luna, Javier 132
Vasoli, Cesare 25
Vázquez de Benito, María de la Concepción 12, 45–46

Vega, Lope 56, 76–106, 108, 110–112, 114–115, 117–118
Vega Ramos, María José 157–158
Vega Rodríguez, Pilar 2
Velasco, Amador de 98
Vélez de Guevara, Juan 186
Vélez Sainz, Julio 1
Verardi, Donato 19–20, 25–26
Veres D'Ocón, Ernesto 68
Vernay, Philippe 73
Vernet Ginés, Juan 10
Vesalius, Andreas 10
Vetterling, Mary Anne Lee 129, 134
Viaggio, Giorgio 50
Vicente García, Luis Miguel 2, 76, 143, 148
Vicente, Gil 47, 50–53, 55, 59
Vickers, Brian 7
Vigh, Eva 2, 14, 19
Viguera Molins 9
Villarino Martínez, Beatriz 182
Villena, Enrique de 43, 134, 136
Vincent of Beauvais 11
Vincent, Monique 192
Vitoria, Francisco de 130
Vitse, Marc 143
Vivalda, Nicolás M. 164
Vogt, Sabine 8
Voskoboynikov, Oleg 12

Walde Moheno, Lillian von der 2, 110
Wall, Charles Heron 4
Watson, A. I. 178
Weber de Kurlat, Frida 77, 103
Weill-Parot, Nicolas 7
Weßner, Paul 1
Whicker, Jules 132
Whitaker, Shirley B. 170
Wilgaux, Jérôme 6
Williams, Steven J. 9, 13
Willich, Jodocus 14
Wilson, Bronwen 17, 22
Wilson, Edward M. 183
Wilson, John Delane 3
Wörsdörfer, Anna Isabell 193
Wouthers, Antoon Frans 147
Wright, Elizabeth R. 83
Wurtele, Douglas J. 2

Yarrow, Philip J. 192
Yates, Frances Amelia 40
Yoon, Yong-Wook 121

Zaccaria, Raffaella 15
Zahareas, Anthony 74
Zambelli, Paola 15
Zambrana Ramírez, Alberto 148
Zamora Calvo, María Jesús 7
Zamuner, Ilaria 11
Zeller, Rosmarie 18
Ziegler, Joseph 12
Zimic, Stanislav 53, 74
Zinelli, Fabio 11
Zucker, Arnaud 8
Zugasti, Miguel 122–123, 125